PITT THE ELDER

Man of War

EDWARD PEARCE

PIMLICO

Published by Pimlico 2011

2 4 6 8 10 9 7 5 3

Copyright © Edward Pearce 2010

First published in Great Britain in 2010 by
The Bodley Head

Pimlico
Random House, 20 Vauxhall Bridge Road,
London SW1V 2SA

www.rbooks.co.uk

Addresses for companies within The Random House Group Limited can be found at:
www.randomhouse.co.uk/offices.htm

The Random House Group Limited Reg. No. 954009

A CIP catalogue record for this book
is available from the British Library

ISBN 9781845951436

The Random House Group Limited supports The Forest Stewardship Council (FSC),
the leading international forest certification organisation. All our titles that are
printed on Greenpeace approved FSC certified paper carry the FSC logo.
Our paper procurement policy can be found at www.rbooks.co.uk/environment

Mixed Sources

Product group from well-managed
forests and other controlled sources
www.fsc.org Cert no. TT-COC-2139
© 1996 Forest Stewardship Council

FSC

Typeset in Dante MT by Palimpsest Book Production Limited,
Falkirk, Stirlingshire
Printed and bound in Great Britain by
Clays Ltd. St Ives plc

Wakefield Libraries
& Information Services

This book should be returned by the last date stamped
above. You may renew the loan personally, by post or
telephone for a further period if the book is not required by
another reader.

For Ted and Anne Nakhle
Friends and relations

Contents

Acknowledgements ix

Illustrations x

Introduction xi

Prelude: Flight and Night Fight 1

1 The Interloper and the Diamond 3

2 Eton, Oxford and Northampton
    Barracks 14

3 Meet the Grenvilles 22

4 The Peace of Sir Robert 32

5 Poor Fred and the Patriots 40

6 War with Spain: St Jingo's Eve 49

7 Carteret, Pelham and Yellow Fever 69

8 Drawing the War: Winning the
    Election 84

9 'What shall you think if he dies
    courageously?' 95

10 Two Dukes, Fox and Pitt 113

11 Hastenbeck and Rochefort: Panic
    and Recrimination 128

12 'It blew a perfect hurricane':
    Admiral Holburne's Voyage 158

13 St Malo Stands, Louisbourg Falls 171

14 Patriots Betrayed 192

15 Sturdy Yeomen and Slave Traders:
    the Militia and Goree 211

16 Hunt the Garter: Minden and Lord
    Temple 220

17 'Where ignorant Armies clash by
    night': Quiberon Bay   244
18 Deaths and Entrances: George II
    and Lord Bute   253
19 Pitt Leaves: Victories Continue   269
20 'That Devil Wilkes'   283
21 Houses and Gardens: Cider and
    America   299
22 Power Out of Mind   309
23 America and Death: The Grand
    Finale   322
    Envoi   336

    Appendix: Chatham's Mental
    Condition   341
    Notes   347
    Bibliography   359
    Index   365

Acknowledgements

No one writes a serious book without extensive debts to other people. This is especially true if you work at a desk in North Yorkshire, when not taking cheap trains to research libraries around the country, London, Oxford and Hull in this case.

Dr Perry Gauci of Lincoln College, Oxford, so helpful over my book on Robert Walpole, is himself an eighteenth-century specialist (working on a life of William Beckford). He has read the text and made excellent suggestions, all gratefully adopted. Sad thanks must go to the late Dr David Sturdy who introduced me to Hull University Library, so near and so useful, and then died suddenly soon after, very much missed.

I have thanks to offer to staff at research libraries: chiefly Bodleian, British and Hull University. The London Library, in spite of having the builders in, has been a constantly splendid resource, and has kindly favoured me with a Carlyle grant. Special thanks are offered to two of its staff, Göstia Lewwik and Amanda Corp, who have stretched points for me and gone to real trouble.

Richard Collins, now expert at making sense of, and asking questions about, my texts, has been as assiduous and indispensable as ever. Will Sulkin, commanding the Bodley Head, has been reassurance and continuity of the best, most soothing sort. Finally, my wife, Deanna, has done with a difficult text, impossible notes and wandering references the sort of job for which 'indispensable' is an understatement.

Edward Pearce
Thormanby
North Yorks
July 2009

Illustrations

The Collapse of the Earl of Chatham in the House of Lords, 7 July 1778 (*John Singleton Copley, c. 1779 © National Portrait Gallery [NPG], London*)

King George II (*Thomas Hudson © NPG, London*)

Thomas Pelham-Holles, 1st Duke of Newcastle-under-Lyne (*William Hoare © NPG, London*)

William Pitt, 1st Earl of Chatham (*studio of William Hoare © NPG, London*)

William Beckford (*John Dixon © NPG, London*)

Edward Hawke, 1st Baron Hawke (*John Hall after Francis Cotes © NPG, London*)

George Anson, 1st Baron Anson (*Charles Grignion, after and published by Arthur Pond © NPG, London*)

James Wolfe (*Elizabeth Hervey, Duchess of Devonshire, pencil and watercolour, c. 1780–1800 © NPG, London*)

John Manners, Marquis of Granby (*after Sir Joshua Reynolds, chalk, c. 1759 © NPG, London*)

Edmund Burke (*after James Barry, watercolour and bodycolour on ivory, c. 1774–1775 © NPG, London*)

John Wilkes (*Johann Sebastian Müller, line engraving, c. 1763 © NPG, London*)

John Stuart, 3rd Earl of Bute (*Sir Joshua Reynolds, oil on canvas, 1773 © NPG, London*)

Richard Rigby (*James Sayers, published by Charles Bretherton on 6 April 1782, etching © NPG, London*)

'The Times', plate one (*William Hogarth, etching and engraving, published 1762 © NPG, London*)

Introduction

This account of the Elder Pitt as 'Man of War' was not conceived as a matching bookend to *The Great Man*, the life of Robert Walpole, published in 2007. It derives from the revisionist tendency across thirty-five years which has approached Pitt/Chatham in hard detail and viewed him far more astringently than earlier rhapsodic judgements.

Paul Langford, in the bibliography to his authoritative mid-eighteenth-century volume of the Oxford History of England, *A Polite and Commercial People*, makes an important judgement. 'Pitt's Bubble has remained unpricked though it has shrunk somewhat under the meticulous inspection of Marie Peters's *Pitt and Popularity*.'

One must add that the factional aspect of Pitt, his obligations to a ferocious commercial lobby and its newspapers, the shifts, contradictions and silent climb-downs of his career have been lit as sharply by Richard Middleton's *The Bells of Victory* and by two outstanding Oxford D.Phil. theses – by E. J. S. Fraser and Michael Durban. There then followed Marie Peters's fine full-dress biography of a decade since.

The bubble, and it was a glittering one, exists in the awestruck 1827 biography by the Rev. Francis Thackeray, then flew still inflated throughout the imperial era, down to last-century works by Basil Williams and O. A. Sherrard. Within it, Pitt shimmers. Received opinion proclaims him the incomparable man, the driving vital patriot who knew that he could save this country and that nobody else could, a hero among cowardly bumblers, the visionary of empire, the director of war.

Received opinion had been received from Pitt. It took him at his word, ignored the collective nature of government action, ignored the impossibility of *any* minister, in an age of sauntering communication, telling any admiral or general how to win a war. The grandiose reputation has surely shrunk in the twenty years since Langford's quietly deadly judgement. Accordingly, this life has been written to reflect for a wider public upon the downward drift of historians' judgement of the Great Commoner and Patriot Minister.

To do this I have also returned to the major primary sources. Outstanding here are those in the secretary hand of the Duke of Newcastle's amanuensis, John Stone, and printed collections of letters like those discovered in the 1930s by Lewis Namier and Romney Sedgwick which display Pitt approaching the abhorred Lord Bute with startling reverence. I have also had the interesting experience of reading the *North Briton*, John Wilkes's astonishingly virulent, Scot-allergic journal, far rougher, if far better written, than any contemporary anthology of red-top opinion. Thanks to great finds in the 1980s, we now have the record kept by the 4th Duke of Devonshire, enlightening about Pitt – and the duke.

There was no Hansard at this time, but Cobbett's *History of Parliament*, a compendium of notes taken at the time for pamphlet, magazine and newspaper use, does the vivid service equally important in writing my life of Sir Robert Walpole. After a general pursuit of the evidence, I can see no alternative view of the first Lord Chatham *except* revision and ironically a return to the older dryer scepticism – the letters of Edmund Burke and the still penetrating *Essays* of Lord Macaulay. Pitt was an able man, an eloquent speaker and a compelling presence, but so very much the creature of personality and its attendant publicity.

However the reputation of this period for excitement, heroic and tragic conflict is *not* diminished. Wolfe is a brilliant hero yet. Admiral Hawke is the superlative sailor of record, probably the indispensable man of this war. So, since the centrepiece of Pitt's life was the Seven Years War, I have gone out of my way to write a military history in parallel with the political one. We open with a brief taste of the great naval victory of Quiberon Bay, related in full during the subsequent narrative. The misfortunes at Minorca of 'Poor Mr Byng', shot on his quarterdeck for over-caution, are here, as are James Wolfe and Quebec. But so too are the great battles in Germany involving Ferdinand of Brunswick and the genial, public house-establishing Marquess of Granby.

The defeat of Hastenbeck, the successes of Minden Bridge, Kreffeld and Minden itself, all tense and compelling, are related in some detail. Frederick the Great, as ally and key player in the war, with whom Chatham at one time sought to identify himself, also figures significantly. Politics, as we know to our cost, can lead to war and *Pitt the Elder* is about both – bloody and eternally readable topics.

Prelude: Flight and Night Fight

As for a plan, was there to be a French invasion? What were the plans? The Duke of Newcastle's reliably well-informed intelligence knew everything it needed to know. 'I who could never believe it before,' wrote the Admiralty agent John Calcraft on 8 July, 'am convinced the French will attempt something . . . There is dreadful preparation making in France.'

The French ships were excellent, bigger and better built than ours and dispassionately admired by British naval men; the French naval commander Admiral Conflans had a decent reputation, enhanced during the recent failed British assault on Rochefort. The best of his captains, men like Kersaint de Coëtnampren and Saint-André du Verger, were outstanding sailors, as was Bigot de Morogues who had been specifically detailed to escort 20,000 soldiers to the Clyde for the invasion of Scotland.

Meanwhile, the British waited. The summer of 1759 had been oppressively hot, worrying for Admiral Edward Hawke and his watching squadron, bidden by the Admiralty to keep sedulous watch upon the coast of north-western France, both Brest and the Morbihan. What now loomed was something to put the coastal raids which Mr Secretary Pitt had insisted upon during the long hiatus of early wartime into mighty perspective. They had been therapy. This would be infinitely more – more even than defence against an invasion. Navy against Navy, it would settle everything. But after the French, Hawke chiefly worried about beer. Supplied to his ships by private contractors in Plymouth, it had been turned by the heat, or so the private contractors said. Beer, for reasons of health rather than alcoholic inclination, being preferred to water, the getting, by each delivery, of foul stuff fit only to throw away was a major anxiety for a long watch on Channel approaches. Accordingly, the correspondence between Hawke, the

Admiralty and the suppliers had grown intense. A temperate man, Sir Edward talked about beer all the time! But his command, inferior ships, better sailors, superlative commander, had been furiously active and were ready for the fight, and such a fight it would be . . .

I

The Interloper and the Diamond

'This,' said the East India Company in 1682 in an urgent letter to its agent, William Hedges, is 'a desperate fellow of a haughty, huffying and daring temper . . .' Accordingly, Hedges was instructed to secure his person 'whatever it cost [in bribes] to the government'.[1]

The desperate fellow was Thomas Pitt, son of the Rector of Blandford in Dorset, and already, at twenty-nine, detestable to the rackety sub-monopoly of the East India Company. Pitt was an 'Interloper', a private trader, bribing Indian princes and their servants independently of the Company's bribes. He was doing good business and Hedges, according to the modern historian of the Company, John Keay, already identified him as the comfortable accomplice of its own chief factor in Bengal.[2]

The Pitt family had long been pleasantly respectable, with antecedents in the South West and busy about the five polite professions, army, navy, church, medicine and law. A Clerk of the Exchequer to Elizabeth I had been followed by a mayor of Dorchester, a well-regarded physician, no end of clergymen, even a poet, minor but pretty good: Christopher Pitt (1699–1748), pursuing the elevated road of Winchester and New College to become Rector of Pimperne in Dorset. Dr Johnson wrote very warmly of him in his *Lives of the Poets* and from the two pieces included in *The Penguin Book of Eighteenth Century Verse* was right to do so. There is a cool, good-tempered vigour about this Pitt, soundness, a moral worldliness:

> Well – we have reached the precipice at last;
> The present age of vice obscures the past.
> Our dull forefathers were content to stay,
> Nor sinned till Nature pointed out the way: . . .
> Their top-debauches were at best precise,
> An unimproved simplicity of vice.

Christopher was cousin to the vivid and important Thomas, as un-pastoral and un-Wykehamist as a man might very well be. Manners did not make 'Diamond' Pitt, he made himself. This is 'the desperate fellow of a haughty huffing temper', Lord Chatham's grandfather, Pitt the Eldest, country but no gentleman, controversial, uncourtly and, in the hard trading of Moghul India, effective.

The early days of the young man who set out for the subcontinent in 1673 involved subordinate alliance with Matthias Vincent, chief Company man in the Bay of Bengal, and his close ally at the Balasore* factory, Richard Edwards, either of whom could sack or enrich him. By 1678–9, and through those connections, Thomas was making serious money, notably in the Persian trade and handling 'a Cargo of Sugars from Bengal'. He was near enough to Vincent to marry his niece, but people after Vincent's blood for unauthorised private dealing were also after Pitt's.

When he returned to London with wife and baby in 1681, so did Vincent; and goods and profits outside the Company's reach seem to have come too. This, thought the Company, was a nest of interlopers to be pursued through the law. Pitt was visited with a suit in chancery and forbidden to leave England. His response was characteristic and succinct: he left England. The pursuit was virulent and directed by Sir Josiah Child personally. Child was a brazen, imperious monopolist, deviously and massively rich and more aggressive after recent support from the London courts. His prime quarry was Vincent, with Pitt, or 'Pitts', as the Company kept calling him, wanted chiefly as able and likely to abet Vincent's escape inside India.

Messages went to Company Headquarters in Madras ordering 'the first ship that goes down the Bay (of Bengal), we would have you send downe to Agent Hedges, a Corporall and 200 soldiers . . . We think it may not be amiss to have them there to prevent any insolent attempt of Pitts [sic] to rescue Vincent because Pitts being so well acquainted on the River Ganges, may carry up both the ships afore-said as far as Hughly [Hughli]. Whereas we have no ship small enough to follow up, but only the "Welfare" that is less than the others.'

The measure of Pitt's lucid self-possession appeared in later salu-tations between the *Crown* (a merchant ship captained by a Mr Dorrell,

* Otherwise Baleshwar.

on which he was travelling) and the East India Company vessel *Defence* carrying Hedges, its pursuing agent, honest man and, usefully, diarist. But the *Crown* passed the *Defence* and, as it were, blew a discreet kiss. 'They told us plainly that they were bound for Hughly. Mr Pitts [*sic*] and two or three passengers more were aboard of her. After saluting each other, we all made ye best of our way, but she, sailing best, was almost out of sight next morning.'[3]

The superior speed of Pitt's ship epitomised his style in Bengal. He moved faster and bribed better, to the satisfaction of Indian princes; here the Nawab of Bengal and his retinue also bribed. The prospect of 'securing his person' was negligible. Chancery writs did not run in India to a man served by a network of friends, the indifference of Indian rulers and ready money. When Hedges reached Balasore Roads for connections to Hughli, the *Crown* had been in port for eleven days and Pitt 'had hired a great House at Balasore, carried divers chests of money ashore and was very busy in buying of goods . . .'[4]

The outsider understood the importance of a calculated splendour. Hedges was told that Pitt had come into Balasore, literally 'with Guards and Trumpets'. Then, having created his own good impression, put about a dismal one concerning the East India Company. They were, he told the Nawab, 'in so low a condition that they could send forth but 2 shipps to fetch off their remaines with not 20 chests of treasure and that there was a new Company erected, and that hee, the said Pitts, was their Agent'.[5]

This claim, which may have been light and speculative, would in time be fulfilled. Interlopers might have their problems in England but the Company would have worse and a new company be mooted. People like Vincent and Pitt would make peace with one or other authority and do so on their own terms. Interestingly though, while the pursuer, Hedges, would become Sir William and the fugitive, Vincent, emerge from the thicket as Sir Matthias, Thomas Pitt in all his glory as MP and landowner was never knighted.

Until the early 1690s, Pitt was an Interloper, an independent trader dealing directly with local and real power and coolly indifferent to the tin-sheet thunder of London. With the Company's Directors under William and Mary clutching a tattered monopoly conferred by Stuart kings, William Pitt's grandfather would, unsurprisingly, be a lifelong Whig, fierce supporter of King William and the great shift of 1688–9.

He would, meanwhile, exploit a split among London Directors to become agent in, then Governor of, Madras.

There was, though, enough quarrelling left at the eastern end. The elaborate politics of the Company had led to frantic lobbying at court. A new company would be created while the old one survived in order, over three years, to unite them. Everywhere outside Madras agents of the unreconciled companies quarrelled and lost profits under the noses of local princes. The interloper, Pitt, in touch with the Old Company, followed his own interests. He understood hard trading to include cheerful tolerance of useful rogues. 'For my particulars I employ the cursedest villain that ever was in the world and see him cheat me before my face, but then, he is the most dextrous, indefatigable fellow in business that makes me such amends that I can afford to bear with it. 'Tis very true what I formerly wrote you, that the Old Company lost ten times as much by employing fools as they did by knaves . . .'[6]

Thomas would be called a great villain himself. He would be identified with a diamond, *the* diamond. It became the Pitt Diamond, and he would be 'Diamond Pitt'. But the jewel itself seems to have been nothing worse than the rough and ready profits of rough and ready trade. Madras, within easy reach of the mines of Golconda (a more romantic-sounding name for Hyderabad), became, says Keay, the 'Indian Hatton Gardens'.[7] Pitt, after long trading, had money to invest and decided in 1701 to head his portfolio with 'the finest jewel in the world and undoubtedly worth an immense sum'. He would talk thereafter of 'the grand affair', 'my great concern' and 'my all'. The size of an egg, it weighed 400 carats, the initial price 200,000 pagodas (the pagoda being about ten shillings 1700 English). After a great deal of souk talk, and doubtless any amount of sweet tea, the Governor quartered the price. He bought the stone for 48,000 pagodas, £24,000, at least £1.25 million of contemporary sterling. Another, smaller, diamond, estimated at a mere 6500 pagodas, went down with the East Indiaman *Bedford* in 1701.

It was all very boys' story. Governor Pitt had become 'Diamond Pitt' and the jewel apparently brought back in the heel of a shoe worn by Pitt's not otherwise very useful son, Robert. It remained on the trader's hands for fifteen years until, cut, polished and haggled over, purchased for the crown of Louis XV, it fetched £135,000, a profit of around 450 per cent. Pitt would moan that he wished he had never set eyes on it, a sentiment lacking conviction. Certainly he had accumulated ill wishers. As noted, the knighthood common with his wealth never materialised and his inheriting sons were in varying degrees all fools. Even so . . .

It says something for Thomas Pitt's nerve that his original business with Indian diamond merchants took place while he was preoccupied from early in 1702 with military defence against the siege of the Company stronghold at Madras, part of a wider intimidation strategy by Daud Khan, the Moghul Nawab of the Carnatic. This episode and Pitt's brilliant improvisation in response show his full measure: resolute and extremely capable, someone beyond business sharpness.

Pitt's garrison base was Fort St George, a perfunctory oblong structure with thin walls, 400 yards by 100. The Nawab's forces sat on the beach at San Thomé, an old Portuguese settlement three miles down the coast, and sought to bar delivery of all supplies to the Company citadel. The Nawab ordered seizure of the town, forfeiture of Company goods and detention of its officials. Nerve would be lost by lesser men in other places. In Surat the Company had paid up quickly and handsomely to the famous Captain Kidd.

Pitt recollected that his thin walls had cannon and the Nawab had not. He moved quickly and assembled trained local militias as backing for his two companies of regular soldiery. But what mattered most was his pace – quick, staccato, imperious. His recorded summary, on 29 January, opening day, is briskly eloquent of Pitt's character and worth quoting:

Nabob Dawood Khan, Dewan and Buxie arriving the night at St Thomé with considerable forces of horse and foot . . . and we being jealous [suspicious] that there are ill designs on foot against this place; to prevent their effecting which, we resolve to make ourselves as formidable as possible, for which end have taken the following resolutions, viz,

That the Trainbands of this city be immediately raised.

That tomorrow morning the Portuguese Militia be raised and posted at the outworks.

That both our Company soldiers lie at their arms night and day during the encampment next us.

That two hundred Rajpoots [otherwise Rajputs] be taken into service

to guard our out towns and the Company's cloth at the washers. That
what Lascars, not exceeding 60 or 70, be entertained to assist the
Governor.[8]

Strong actions were coupled with an emollient gesture, that 'our
Brahmin' should join up with 'our Moolah [Mullah] in the Nabob's
camp' and with a guard of soldiers, go to the leaders of the siege 'and
carry with them a small present of rosewater, Acheen oranges and
sweetmeats'.

That present (not valuable goods, normal ploy against blackmail,
but oranges and sweet stuff) was a confident gamble. Rather like the
Dauphin's tennis balls of 1415, but better thought out, it was a confident low bid, not an affront. The gift did not mock Daud Khan so
much as make clear that Fort St George, able to spare luxuries, was
set up against a siege. As Pitt pertinently put it, there was 'sufficient
for our people for two years with the open sea before us'. The Nawab
would now settle for a modest bribe and asked 30,000 rupees. Pitt sent
more oranges; the prince came down to 20,000, with half of that to
be paid only after restitution of all English goods seized. It was, all in
all, a nice combination of cool theatre, reasonable courage without
heroics and willingness to save faces. The snapped-out orders do anticipate William Pitt, the war minister. But for the high, flaunting style,
there are intimations of strength wrapped in a modest gift. Sir
Cornelius Dalton's comment is concise and hard to dispute: 'The more
narrowly the proceedings of Governor Pitt during this siege are scru-
tinised, the more difficult it becomes to find any flaw in them.'[9]

Finding no flaws was to be a concern when Pitt eventually sold
the stone. The diamond was reproduced in crystal and these models
circulated around the European thrones, notably Spain and Prussia.
George Augustus, future George II, a man of lifelong financial caution,
considered the price and did not venture. Eventually, in 1717, the
French government became a serious bidder, serious enough to have
beaten the price down heavily, though the original figure is not
known. Thomas, the Governor's second son, future MP and peer, now
made himself briefly useful. As to quality, the necessary finding of
no flaw concerned Rondet, French court jeweller. The family legend
is that the younger Thomas met Rondet for dinner at Calais. The
question of the water of the stone having arisen, Thomas met it by

suggesting that the jeweller look at it in a better light at a casement window, where a banknote of undefined value effected the French royal family's reassurance.

Governor Pitt came back to England, an early model of the Nabob, entering Parliament as a hard-line Whig, at Old Sarum (most corrupt seat in the Commons even then). He would shift to Salisbury proper, again Old Sarum between 1689 and 1716, excluding an Indian absence (1705–10). From 1717 to 1722 he sat for Thirsk before returning to Old Sarum from 1722 until his death in April 1726. After selling the diamond, he bought a large house and property, south of Reading, another, Boconnoc, in Cornwall, and estates across half a dozen English counties. His daughter Lucy's marriage in 1709 to General James Stanhope, victor of Zaragoza and future First Minister, signified arrival. Plain Thomas Pitt had reached the social and political centre. So had all the Pitts.

The family history is the environment into which William was born on 25 November 1708, third son of Robert, the diamond porter. His birth comes at the end of Robert's letter to his father discussing the Governor's latest furious dispute: 'The chief incendiary from abroad is Mr Frederick who, in a very long and ingenious manner, has made wonderful complaints of your arbitrary proceedings . . . The account of Mr Fraser's* seditious behaviour has been communicated to every manager of the Old and New Companies; but what they most resent is your threatening to whip and hang one whom they had named of their Council . . .'

William was announced to the world in that letter, a pendant sub-paragraph to his grandfather's quarrelling. These were endemic, the most virulent involving his own family. 'The misfortune which all my sons have brought on me will very speedily carry my grey hairs to my grave,' he wrote not very inventively in 1723, adding, 'and I care not how soon it is for I am surrounded with the plagues and troubles of this world'.[10]

Not that he was necessarily wrong. Robert and Thomas would conduct mutual litigation which outlived them twenty years.[11] The third son, John, called by his father 'the good-for-nothing Colonel',

---

* William Fraser, Deputy Governor of Fort St George, engaged in complex conspiracy – too complex to linger over here.

evidently pushed wildness to the clinical limit, was disinherited, picked
up the remnant of an extinct peerage and died nearly destitute.
William's father, Robert, was, by contrast, no more than ordinarily
idle, feckless and ill advised. One piece of ill advice, an apparent regard
for the Jacobites – '. . . you still adhere to your cursed Tory principles'
– would later detonate another explosion. 'I have heard that since I
came to town you are stuck in with your old hellish acquaintance,
and in all your discourse, are speaking in favour of that villainous
traitor, Ormonde.'[12] The Duke of Ormonde was James II's faithful,
capable, luckless general.

Robert was also out of favour for a bill of £500 to succeed his father
at Old Sarum. Which pocket borough, the fulminating parent
remarked, had never cost *him* more than £10! There is more, no end
of it: 'All your actions seem to be the produce of a hot and giddy
brain. You are got to the expensive end of town where money melts
like butter against the sun . . . you, who think yourself wiser than
your teachers and your father too.'[13] Robert got through money on
swagger-shows like his carriage and retinue of liveried servants in Old
Sarum, but the family itch to reproach would live on as *he*, twenty
years later, hectors the schoolboy William for an excess of shillings
in washing bills.

Mrs Pitt, the Governor's wife, Jane Innes, had also given dissatisfaction by not affording the absent Governor details of her handling
of goods and monies. (She was apparently required to trade off Indian
goods.) 'She writes me God knows what that she is about in purchases,
but not a word of what some has cost or others will cost. I have no
manner of Accompt of what I left her, what she has received or paid
since, what I have sent her or what it Sold for, but all railing against
one or other which has very much exposed my busyness and done
me a great deal of prejudice. Soe that I find great inconveniences by
trusting woman with bysiness [*sic*] which I will avoid for the future.'[14]

Thomas was a gunpowder personality, of the Indian Army (Rtd)
theatrical type. He was given to a pained extolling of his own reasonableness: 'I always esteem'd old friends as old gold,' he tells a former
Old Company colleague, Peter Godfrey, 'and in these matters I am
not given to change. Those that have known mee longest must say
that 'twas never in my temper to bee quarrelling and jangling . . .'[15]

Nevertheless, as Jane underperformed requirements, he jangled to

the length of transferring her power of attorney to a business asso-
ciate, Sir Stephen Evans, Queen Anne's court jeweller. Robert, who
brought home that disobliging instruction returning from his own
brief trading period in India, was included in the trust. When Jane
was told this by Robert, quarrel ensued – between them – at which
the Governor abused them both. His psychology was delicate: 'If what
you write about your mother be true, I think she is mad, and wish
she were well secured in Bedlam; but I charge you to let nothing she
says or does make you undutiful in any sense whatever.'[16]

In 1704 Robert wrote sneakily to Papa, 'My sisters are in Bath with
my mother and we seldom meet except in the country during summer.
I always invite them to pass the winter in London with my wife . . . but
my civility is thrown away, they being for some unknown reason, set
against me.'[17] The Governor was shocked at the mention of Bath, in his
eyes the Las Vegas of Queen Anne's England. 'Whenever I am certain
any of my children game, I will by all that is good, disinherit them.'[18]

He now spoke of his 'family who I left in a pleasant habitation . . .
removed to Bath and there are spending my estate faster than I got
it'. He also issued punctuation-defying instructions to the confiden-
tial jeweller, Stephen Evans. 'You may permitt my wife to receive the
income of my land at Old Sarum and St Mary, Blandford, in
Dorsetshire, to maintain her, her two daughters and three sons, two
of the latter I believe to have come away, if Soe, I desire you disburse
their maintenance, in which pray be thrifty, and charge them Soe too,
or I'le put 'em to short allowance when I come home, and if my Wife
draws any bills upon you, I order 'em to be returned, and not a penny
paid, for I will not allow it in my account.'[19]

Sir Cornelius Dalton, his biographer, attempts sympathy for the
old brute, arguing that 'it can hardly be contended that he had not
good reason to fear that his hardly earned wealth might be dissipated
if he allowed his wife and daughters a free hand at Bath'.[20] Mr Pitt
sounds rather like any purse-proud, imperious rich uncle of the later
Restoration stage, his letter like impotent, self-defeating rage, not a
little mad and likely to turn conflict into break-up.

As it did when, in 1706, he writes of 'a scoundrel, rascally villain'
(nowhere identified), having been 'too intimate with my family to the
prejudice of my honour and their reputation'. Not one to be detained
by the refinements of guilt and allegation, the Governor writes (crazily)

from India that 'I make no distinction between women that are reputed ill and such as are actually so'. In pursuit of which direct doctrine, 'I have discarded your mother for ever and will never see her more if I can avoid it.'[21] Not that all the rage was unprovoked. John, born in 1698, had a parliamentary seat, at Hindon, in 1714, as well as a commission in the Guards. But in the Governor's last will of 1721 he was left nothing, though £200 a year consolation was tossed to his wife.[22]

Loaned property by his father as an interim electoral qualification, he had welshed on the deal, refusing to return it. Sword in hand, he physically stole hard cash, paid as rents from one of his father's agents. The 'good-for-nothing Colonel' was promptly cut out of his will. John would then bring against its executors, his brothers, a chancery bill, described by Robert as 'vexatious and malicious . . . tending to throw odious and wicked imputations on his memory, and to blast him in his grave'. Impoverished by litigation and estrangement, John, probably mentally disturbed, would linger on alone, destitute and uncared for. Member of Parliament successively for Hindon, Old Sarum and Camelford from 1720 to 1734, he died twenty years later 'in contempt and obscurity . . . at the thatched house by the Turnpike at Hammersmith'.[23]

Thomas, born in 1688, seems to have been sane and was described by his ill-natured nephew only as a man 'of no character and of parts that were calculated only for the knavery of business in which he overreached others and at last himself'.[24] An MP for fifteen years at Wilton, then Old Sarum, this Thomas acquired the Irish Earldom of Londonderry through marriage, and lost £50,000 through the South Sea Company. His lawsuit against Robert outlived him twenty years, beyond early death in 1729 – as resident Governor of the Leeward Islands.

The Pitts were an extraordinary family, unhappy and short-lived. Robert died at forty-eight, Colonel John at fifty-six, Thomas at forty-one. They quarrelled and, with memorable eloquence, the Great Quarreller ranted at them for quarrelling. 'What hellish planet is it that influences you all and causes such unaccountable distraction that it has published your shame to the world . . . Have all of you shook hands with shame that you regard not any of the tyes of Christianity, humanity, consanguinity, duty, good morality or any thing that makes you differ from beasts, but must run aspersing one another and aiming at the ruine and distraction of each other?'[25]

Inveterate, the conflicts were bringing them (notably Thomas's quarrel with Robert) into the next generation, and keeping them indefinitely in chancery, Jarndyces of real life, the Governor's brilliant prizes rattling away in endemic discord. Pitts, immediate, remote, collateral and direct, occupied Parliament in a broad spread of mediocrity for most of the eighteenth century. Thirteen seats were occupied, from Thomas himself, entering in 1689, to the Younger (and most gifted) Pitt, William, dying in 1806.

It is claimed that our Pitt, Great Commoner, Conqueror of North America and Patriot of Patriots, future 1st Earl of Chatham, was recognised in youth by the peppery old fellow as heroic material, great prospects in store, old man's vision of grandson's superlative future, proper subject of a large, bad painting. Not to be nice about it, this is rubbish. The recorded comments of the Governor of Madras are 'he is a hopefull [*sic*] lad, and doubt not but he will answer yours and all his friends' expectation'. This is ritual aspiration, the sort of thing every grandfather with an atom of goodwill says about every grandson.

More importantly, he records seeing the sixteen-year-old boy before he goes off to school. 'I shall be glad to see Will here as he goes to Eton.' Thomas himself, second son, one of the nine children of a Dorset rector in small circumstances (£100 a year), had received very little education and all his life wrote wonderfully direct, eclectic prose in furiously non-mandarin letters. They speak a man proudly bypassing book learning for the practicalities of the sea and the counting house. His blazing success, on the back of no Greek and Latin and no old-school connections whatever with the upper political class, had opened to his grandson classical rhetoric and essential acquaintance. These, and the example of a furiously aggrandising temperament, were the materials to make 'a hopefull lad'.

2

Eton, Oxford and Northampton Barracks

The Eton to which Diamond Pitt accompanied his grandson seems in the early eighteenth century to have been a melange of vigorous things. Games of fives, 'Scrambling' and 'Shrinking' walls, cricket, the Wall Game, river boating, daily practice in composing Latin verse and the release every autumn of a ram to be pursued by boys armed with clubs and, when caught, beaten to death. This was joined with study of ancient civilisations and their literature, a private vocabulary distinguishing Etonians from non-Etonians, corporal punishment to mark for life and, despite extensive imitation, an assured difference from anything else, which quality may be appropriate to the upbringing of a ruling order.

Pitt at Eton is a topic of empty speculation, from lickerish discussion of possible ferocious floggings to yet more bad pictures of him dreaming great things beside the river. This was the foible of Lord Rosebery, Liberal imperialist, interim Prime Minister (1894–5) and owner of a Derby winner, who in campaign biography prose mistily observes that 'it will not come amiss to evoke in passing, the shadow of the lean, saturnine boy as he limped by the Thames, shaping a career or pondering on life and destiny, dreaming of greatness where so many have dreamed'.[1]

Whatever the legends and imaginings, we do know that Pitt was a good pupil. According to his doting biographer, the Reverend Thackeray, the headmaster, Dr Bland, 'highly valued the attainments of his pupil'.[2] His tutor, William Burchett, was less Olympian and clearly better informed. He sent Robert Pitt a letter in enthusiastic commendation.

Yr younger Son has made a great Progress since his coming hither, indeed I never was concern'd with a young gentleman of so good

Abilities & at the same time of so good a disposition, and there is no question to be made but he will answer all yr Hopes.

I am Sr,

Yr most Obedient & most Humble Servant,

WILL. BURCHETT[3]

Pitt was a contemporary of Henry Fielding. The novelist, born a year sooner, 1707, would make his reputation first and very early, as a playwright,* derided the warm murk of Walpolean government. This would make him an ally at one remove of Pitt the Opposition MP and, having shared the best of the Eton curriculum with him, he saw in it the wellspring of the parliamentary orator. 'Nor do I believe that all the Imagination, Fire and Judgment of Pitt could have produced those Orations that have made the senate of England in these our Times a Rival in Eloquence to Greece and Rome if he had not been so well read in the writings of DEMOSTHENES and CICERO as to have transferred their whole Spirit into his Speeches, and with their Spirit, their Knowledge too.'[4]

Eton undoubtedly had great academic strengths. The fourth form during the 1760s was studying, across a given week, Ovid's *Metamorphoses*, *Electra ex Ovidio*, Aesop, Caesar, Terence and the Greek Testament.[5] However, Fielding would say much harder things about the place. Parson Adams, Sancho Panza to the hero of *Joseph Andrews*, says to his charge: 'I have discovered the cause of all the Misfortunes which befell him. A Public School, Joseph, was the cause of all the calamities which he afterwards suffered. Public schools are the Nurseries of all Vice and Immorality.' Joseph argues back, quoting the finest Gentleman in all the Neighbourhood, to the effect that a Boy taken from a Public School and carried into the World 'will learn more in a Year there than one in a private Education will learn in five'.[6] Unfortunately, the 'finest Gentleman' is one of Fielding's most derided creations, Squire Booby. Pitt himself, according to Lord Shelburne, said that he had scarcely ever observed a boy who was not cowed for life at Eton.[7]

What Eton did give Pitt was much of the political circle of his adult political life. George Lyttleton was friend, enemy, reconciled

---

* *Love in Several Masques* was performed at Drury Lane two months after his twenty-first birthday.

friend and Chancellor of the Exchequer. Charles Pratt, Chief Justice of Common Pleas, then, as Lord Camden, made Lord Chancellor by Pitt and deviser of the case law declaring General Warrants illegal, was as close as anyone was close throughout their linked careers. Both men would essentially be political connections and William Pitt had at all times little aptitude for friendship. For Pratt it would be a following relationship; his man of law, as Philip Yorke, 1st Earl of Hardwicke, was the Duke of Newcastle's. But there would be a great difference.

The huge Newcastle Correspondence, a sizeable piece of the British Library's documentary equity, is, beneath the formality of 'Your Grace' and 'My Dear Lord', warm and personal. Newcastle is in the front line, an anxious man with, in the late 1750s, a great deal to be anxious about. Hardwicke agrees or agrees with serious reservation, advises, encourages, even consoles. Through the professional material, it is a touching relationship. Hardwicke, son of a solicitor in Dover, a risen lawyer, owed Newcastle, commander of patronage, a great deal, but the relationship outran the ties of lawyer and patron. He is indispensable, of course, but it is the indispensability of a friend. Beyond the strange and frankly negative compact with Lord Temple, Pitt followed Kipling's clipped apothegm 'He travels the fastest who travels alone'.

Eton marked the beginnings of Pitt's solitariness. He was sickly, first stricken with gout at fourteen, also asthmatic. He was unequipped either for the nice sports like cricket or the nasty ones like hunting a sheep to death. Combined with obvious very high intelligence was a pleasure in scholarship reflected in William Burchett's delight. Pitt might fairly be taken as someone withdrawn and, to a degree, calculating. Psychology apart, he lacked the cash financing the company and good times of friendship. Robert Pitt was as suspiciously uncomprehending of his son as Diamond Pitt had been of his. For that matter, for all the 'hopeful lad' flapdoodle, the old man had settled only a hundred a year of his imperial booty upon William.

Lord Rosebery, in another flight of subjectivity, sees a sign of favour. 'The shrewd old nabob had discerned the boy's possibilities should not be relaxed by wealth.'[8] What is not in doubt is the obsessional financial neurosis of Robert Pitt, which is to say his grinding meanness. The evidence of this is clearest after William has moved on and up to Trinity, Oxford, eloquent in the boy's answering letters, clearly written in the aftermath of furious displeasure.

On 20th January 1726/7
Hon'd sir,
After such delay, though not owing to any negligence on my Part, I am ashamed to send you ye following accompt, without first making great apologies for not executing ye Commands sooner.

Matriculating Fees	0	16	6
Caution Money	10	0	0
Benefaction	10	0	0
Utensils of ye Coll.	2	0	0
Common Room	2	0	0
Coll.: Servts' Fees	1	15	0
Padesway [Padusoy] Gown	8	5	0
Cap	0	7	0
Tea Table, Chinaware, bands &tc	6	5	0
Glasses	0	11	0
Thirds of Chamber & Furniture	41	7	8
Teas spoons	1	7	6
Summe total	84	14	8

I have too much reason to fear you may think some of these articles too extravagant, as they are, but all I have to say for it is humbly to beg that you will not attribute it to my extravagance but to ye custom of the Place; where we pay for most things at too high a rate . . .[9]

Most of that bill is non-optional. Almost half of it, the 'Thirds of Chamber & Furniture', is rent! Yet it comes with a near cringe, intimating fear of arousing rage in his father. Another nervous letter, much of it about a washing bill, speaks the young man's 'utmost concern' at 'ye dissatisfaction you express at my expences. To pretend to justify or defend myself in this case would be, I fear with reason, thought impertinent; 'tis sufficient to convince me of the extravagance my expences that have met with yr disapprobation but might I have leave to instance an article or two, perhaps you might not think 'em so wild and boundless, as with all imaginable uneasiness I see you do at present.'[10]

There is another aspect to this uncomfortable exchange. Educated eighteenth-century correspondence was elaborate, formal and, for us, overpolite. William Pitt generally pushed this style to excess. His letters to Lord Bute, for instance, come close enough to sycophancy to anchor there. Natural eloquence, buffed and shined up by years of construing Cicero and Quintilian, left Pitt a politician before his time. Robert Pitt was an unhappy, unsuccessful man bullied into bullying by a father as cruel-mouthed and as brilliantly successful. Robert actually needed someone craving forgiveness of *him*. Very likely, William, bright as he was, knew it.

At Oxford in 1727, Pitt wrote Latin verses lamenting the death of George I, nicely described by Rosebery as 'artificial and uncandid'.[11] He came from a family officially Whig (Old Thomas had been furiously sectarian), so it was the conventional thing to do, though on and off for thirty years he traded in bitter things about beggarly electorates and making a particular enemy of George II. Otherwise Oxford left few memorials. Washing bills are the top of it, and thoughts of lingering for academic prizes were scouted by the latest notably savage onset of gout. He was gone from Trinity after a couple of terms.

A Dutch university, Protestant and academically excellent, was a common form of further and better education for Englishmen. Given family connections there, Utrecht was chosen over the grander Leyden for a sojourn. But no more than Oxford did it hold him, and January 1730 puts him at the family's Cornish home in Boconnoc. Universities did not keep him, his health was rackety; so Pitt took the next option for young gentlemen seeking a role, the army. This would involve a commission, the famous Cornetcy of Horse dated February 1731, in the First Dragoon Guards. Marie Peters thinks it likely that the purchase price of £1000 came from Sir Robert Walpole, which is to say from the Secret Service fund, and an accommodation with young Thomas Pitt, already a government supporter with parliamentary interests to trade.[12]

The appointment meant a barracks in Northampton, not notably healthier than Oxford or Utrecht and altogether less interesting. A letter from Boconnoc to his now widowed mother in Bath and dated 17 October speaks of 'long Confinement at Quarters, at present confined here, by disagreeable, dirty weather which makes us all prisoners in this little house'.[13] He was not enjoying inert military life, and after acknowledged brilliance at Eton had been, before his twenty-third

birthday, 'a square peg in so many round holes'. There was one consolation: an officer in the days of purchased commissions had extensive
freedom, especially in peacetime, a state of affairs which the Prime
Minister, Sir Robert Walpole, hoped to maintain indefinitely. Not long
after, Walpole spiked Opposition guns by keeping Britain resolutely
out of the War of the Polish Succession.

The absence of war and a relaxed regimental discipline left Pitt free
to pursue the only remaining exercise of a footloose young man, the
Tour. It was not a full-dress Grand Tour – Venice, Florence, Rome,
and perhaps Naples. Pitt went to Paris, Geneva, then Besançon and
Marseilles, before, semi-invalid, visiting Montpellier and wintering in
Lunéville. His letters are not like the letters of Horace Walpole or
the bitingly discontented Tobias Smollett. The one to his mother from
Paris (rue St Appoline, near the Porte St Denis) is a quotidian and
ceremonial fulfilment of a son's duty to his mother: '. . . I could not
acquit myself of my Duty In not giving you this mark of my respect
and the sense I have of your goodness. I shall make my stay as short
as possible.'

That account of duty doing, elaborate in respect of 'Dear Madam'
and perfunctory toward the most interesting city in Europe, intimates
the future statesman. This may anticipate the xenophobia and drum-
roll patriotism he would preach. He would one day speak of destroying
France for ever, and a man who drank the wine and walked beside
the rivers of a country happily does not talk like that. There is an
inkling of the upper-case Patriot to come. Something else; outside
immediate practical application, when he would become vividly
engaged, Pitt was naturally incurious. He was an intelligence without
an intellectual life, not a man to read a serious book for pleasure. He
had done his classical authors at Eton and, by all accounts, done them
very well, but Cicero and Demosthenes were, for an eighteenth-century
statesman looking to oratory, more like a professional training scheme.

These letters are comparatively few, but one looks for delights at
things seen, people met, conversations. It was admittedly forty years
before Thomas Gray would hold up a quizzing glass to the Welsh
mountains and speak awe. It was not just the Romantic deficit. There
was any amount of humour in the letters of the time, notably the
political ones; and in Pitt's letters there is hardly a smile. This was a
stiff disanimated conversation of the early eighteenth century, sent to

his distant mother by 'Her Most Dutyfull affect. Son'.[14] By the turn
of the year Pitt had returned, to rejoin his regiment at Newbury.

Rosebery speaks coyly of Pitt having 'lost his heart for a time' at
Besançon, but personal relations do not feature here, apart, that is,
from a running discourse with his sister, one which for a while contra-
dicts all censure. Plain but clever, called by Lord Bolingbroke 'Divinity
Pitt', Ann was as vivaciously erratic as William was cool. She became
a lady-in-waiting to Queen Caroline who *was* curious, welcoming ideas
and controversy. Ann would also be on letter-writing terms with
Chesterfield, Mansfield and Horace Walpole, and became popular with
the cultivated Duchess of Queensberry and George II's shrewd and
influential mistress, Marianne von Walmoden, Countess of Yarmouth.

Ann and William were now close, teasing friends, and their conversation has the vivacity missing from the monotone letters to his mother.
Ann was at Bath having been ill, and William suggests his concern for
her overdoing the party round with a mocking touch. He begged, 'To
submit you to hear a little grave advice, which is not to lett your
glorious Thirst of Conquest transport You so far as to lose your health
in acquiring Hearts: I know I am a bold one to dissuade One from
dansing a great deal that danses very gracefully but once more I repeat,
beware of shining too much.'[15]

In another letter (7 January), he upbraids his garrison town while
reproaching her for a routine letter and demanding the real thing: 'To
recompense you for the dullest of Letters, what will you have me do?
I come from two hours muzzy conversation to a house full of swearing
Butchers and Drunken Butter women and in short, the blessings of
a market day: In such a situation what can the wit of man suggest to
him? Oh for the restless tongue of Dear Little Jug! She never knows
the painful state of silence in the midst of uproar.'[16]

The letters to Ann or 'Dearest Nanny' or 'Dear Little Jug' speak
the humour (and good humour) missing from those to father and
mother. They are not classics, not Lamb nor Sydney Smith, but still
a running tease of charm and gaiety, Pitt without the earnest mask,
simple larkishness, at odds with all of Pitt's life. More than most politicians he would play a part, senatorial, impassioned, a cloud of reproach
and public earnest, with stage thunder reliably flashing.

The Pitt who wrote such letters was clearly fit for company and,
advancing from his confused state of unsettled employment, would

find it in the circle of the Grenvilles. But Parliament itself, last refuge and four-square hole of this wandering peg, came in absurd form. As noted, old Thomas Pitt had, returning from India, bought a seat for himself. And Old Sarum was, even in 1700, the paradigm of corrupt seats.

Nobody lived there, but five people were entitled to vote. Site of a Salisbury antedating the present city, itself a medieval foundation, Old Sarum now belonged to William's brother, Thomas. Three years older, hard and grasping to the limits of decency, he was, as the Diamond's family went, sane and businesslike enough. He litigated with bulldog application and usually emerged in profit.

Thomas took politics seriously and at various times might bring between four and six men into Parliament. In 1727, he was elected in two seats, one each of the Old Sarum and Okehampton pairs. He took the latter and released to William the family fief, already bought, bartered and passed around. Walpole's nod was required for the nominee and Pitt expressed surprise that Thomas obtained it since the nomination now benefited a man 'declared in opposition'. He would have expected it to be reserved to someone 'more agreeable to Sir Robert'.[17] We learn from that Pitt's approximate and non-Walpolean position and the equally surprising options of Sir Robert nodding or showing tolerance.

The epitome of the Walpole system, though corrupt long before Walpole could corrupt it, Old Sarum was everything Macaulay and Lord John Russell would denounce by the column of small print in the Reform debates, but, for a young man with his way to make and fine principles to resonate, it would suffice.

3

Meet the Grenvilles

Very little is known of Pitt as MP when the parliamentary record was
thin, fugitive and technically illegal. But a tantalising reference in Lord
Egmont's diary finds a speech supporting a bill to remove placemen
'distinguished'.[1] Financed by a military salary authorised by Walpole
and representing a five-voter borough owned by his brother and vetted
by Sir Robert, Pitt *was* a placeman. The speech may or may not have
been distinguished. But for one so situated, simply to have made it
indicates wonderful assurance.

William, as his brother's nominee, would at twenty-five years old
naturally strike up with his brothers' friends, though this connection
owed at least as much to Thomas's brother-in-law, George Lyttleton,
independently Pitt's friend since Eton. Thomas had married Christian
Lyttleton, George's sister. Their uncle was Richard Temple, Viscount
Cobham, whose family and connections would colonise mid-
eighteenth-century politics. Their political opinions would, for a long
time, approximate to Pitt's political opinions.

Lord Rosebery, from 1910, deplored the link, 'a singular and baleful
influence'. Pitt 'choked in their embrace', a mortal entanglement from
which 'he emancipated himself too late'. For all his heavy Edwardian
scorn, Rosebery had a point. Thomas's friends and George's relations
were the Grenvilles, whom the American scholar Lewis Wiggins nicely
identified in the title of his study, *The Faction of Cousins*. That they were
Opposition men was not the point. Avoiding the advancement which
Walpole would thrust into any moist and outstretched hand was a
reputable way to begin a political career – and a shrewd one. But the
virtue proclaimed by the Grenvilles was the outward and visible expression of resentment by the underadvanced and dedicatedly ambitious.

Even so, opposition to Walpole's system was natural and healthy.

Sir Robert sat on the Treasury bench for hours on end, the famous box of little red Norfolk apples from Houghton behind his heels. He made the Commons his home because it *was* his home – he owned it. Walpole was the paradigm professional politician, fixing what and whom had to be fixed, but persuading gracefully where that was appropriate. He was a fine speaker and reads well yet, far pleasanter on the modern ear than Pitt in his ranting prime.

Here he is, not in Parliament but as a sort of lay counsel at the trial in 1710 of the high and florid Tory Dr Sacheverell, charged with libelling ministers. Walpole went to the central issue, the Tory and Jacobite doctrine of non-resistance to kings:

> Resistance is nowhere enacted legal . . . 'tis what is not, cannot, nor ought ever to be described or affirmed in any positive law, to be excusable. When, upon what never to be expected occasions, it may be exercised, no man can foresee; and ought never to be thought of but when an utter subversion of the realm threaten the whole frame of a constitution and not otherwise be hoped for.

Here the proper necessarily negative reasons for the benign coup removing James II are put, clear across three hundred years, lucidly, rationally and with minimum rhetoric.

Walpole's conduct of Parliament was lucid too but distinctly lower. The places and pensions which kings and ministers had casually tendered, he retailed. The Church, essentially Tory, was made Whig as, by brisk degrees, good party men were put on-bench and into-palace, what might be called unnatural selection. Places in Church, court and state, honours, ribbons, colonial posts, archdeaconries and poor pelting curacies, with all the resources of flummery, Clerkships of Stanneries or Pells, passed to men, in Parliament or owning men in Parliament, for votes: in the division and on the nail. There was a great deal to be indignant about.

However, while Walpole's iniquities rolled on oiled castors, indignation was futile. What was given could commonly be taken away, the bloodless terrorism of loss complementing the sweets of taking. The Hanoverians had needed a loyal, sympathetic minister, a requirement met with such comprehensive efficiency that Hanover had become Walpole and the Whigs. Meanwhile, since the ineptly led Tory party – loyal to the last (and High Church) Stuart, Anne – also had Jacobite tinges, opposition to Walpole could credibly be flattered and magnified as fellow travelling with treason.

None of this could have been urged against the man whose faction William Pitt now joined. Richard Temple, Lord Cobham, was rich anyway (and heavily rewarded by the ministry). Risen through the ranks of baron and viscount, he was Constable of Windsor Castle, Governor of Jersey, a 'Right Honourable' member of the Privy Council and Colonel of both the First Dragoons and the Horse Guards and a Lieutenant General. He was nevertheless a genuinely distinguished soldier. His early career had been in Marlborough's wars where Georg August, later George II, had also bravely fought. He would enjoy a further and notable campaign in the unsuccessful allied Spanish campaign. So, distinguished in wars undertaken by Whigs for the broad Whig ends, Cobham was a natural member of the winning side and new establishment.

His revolt against the Excise, and by extension against the Walpole style, was unexpected and quixotic. As a winning-side general in the war, an automatic Whig, he had sat for Buckinghamshire from 1703, then for the borough of Buckingham until, on the accession of George I, he had gone briskly to the Lords (as Baron Cobham, 1714, Viscount, 1718). Quite why legislation, sensible enough itself forty years before Adam Smith and ninety years before full-dress Free Trade, should have exploded this sweetly placed old soldier out of valetudinarian sense and ease is not clear.

However, protest was not confined to the Excise. As understandable was Walpole's refusal in May to institute a retrospective inquiry into the deceptions of the restored directors of the South Sea Company after its fall in 1720–21. Lord Hervey, loyal chronicler of Walpole's cool ways with morality, described why. The policy was to 'permit a set of annual rascals [the directors reporting every year] to cheat the Company without being punished in order to let England cheat Spain without being discovered'.[2]

Cobham's revolt followed in candid terms. He signed a Lords' motion attacking ministerial 'arts' practised 'under the protection of some all-screening minister'. Screening' (or 'skreening') meant what we call 'whitewashing'. The motion also rejected 'the influence of any man whatsoever whose safety may depend on the protection of fraud and corruption'.[3] It was the simple truth, also and again in Hervey's words, 'the sin against the Holy Ghost which was not to be forgiven'. And smartly, on 13 June, followed wholesale retribution, with Lord Cobham as chief victim. The general was removed from the command of his regiment and pointedly replaced by Walpole's son-in-law, Lord Cholmondeley. The veteran of commands against the armies of Louis XIV was overnight replaced by the Prime Minister's thirty-year-old social trophy. Such hubristic revenge could not pass without reaction.

Cobham would become in the mid-1730s a focus for all opposition. Much of it was high and principled. Cobham's friendship with Alexander Pope would trigger articulation of disgust at the perversion of government. The poet of the age had long kept his head down. A Catholic, however moderate and resistant to papal command, would necessarily go carefully. Walpole had played the Catholic card all through the 1715 Rising, the Layer and Atterbury plots, setting a cash surcharge upon all Catholics. But Pope's present revulsion had nothing to do with that. It was deep and would be eloquent. He had been fond of Cobham and a welcome guest at Stowe since 1725.

He would now elevate him into a figure of Roman nobility, an upright, honourable soldier and gentleman to set pointedly beside the cash-acquisitive and morally insensible Minister. Cobham was written into English 'A' levels. *The Epistle to Cobham* lists the response to Death of a number of vices and villainies before counter-pointing them to proclaim the virtuous man facing God:

> And You! Brave COBHAM, to the latest breath
> Shall feel your ruling passion strong in death
> Such in these moments as in all the past.
> Oh save my Country, Heav'n! Shall be your last.

Too bombastic for Pope at his open-blade best, it would be quite good enough for William Pitt into whose style 'Save my Country' would embed itself, becoming a reliable and tiring motif.

But the elevated political notions, sincere enough for Pope and Cobham, made too light a veil to hide the essential nature of Cobham's Cubs. The core of this mountaineering party was his five nephews, sons of his sister Hester (Countess Temple in her own right). Thomas, the youngest, a naval officer who, dying in 1747 at the Finisterre fight, is reported as attractive in his short life as exemplary in his sailor's death. James, two years older, and Henry, born 1717, were sleeping partners in the family corporation, gratefully collecting places and public money.

George Grenville lived to be Prime Minister from 1765 to 1767, a difficult, unclubbable man good for hard, detailed work and under-standing public finance and a forceful, effective Minister. But he shared the uncomplicated family greed. Taking up the Treasury twenty-one years after Cobham's Cubs first made such a stir about purity, he sought first the financial kingdom. He demanded and got assurance of a pension of £3000 a year on leaving office.[4] The Duke of Newcastle observed that for 'a man of Mr Grenville's rank and character' to do this on becoming 'in effect first minister, is a shameful thing; never heard of before and till the present time would not have been borne'.[5] But then, Newcastle, although he readily distributed salaried office in the maintenance of a government majority, was notoriously honest, leaving government after fifty years in one major post or another an estimated £300,000 the poorer.

Yet George Grenville worked hard and professionally at the national finances and is reckoned one of the abler occupants of the highest office. However, the eldest, Richard Grenville (1711–79), later Earl Temple, was a life-long and inveterate malcontent and *frondeur*. He would be the shabby angel of the family, greedy as of right, greedy insistently and imperiously. Against which stand a bright hour of un-calculated anger over the execution of Admiral Byng and the touch of good humour helping him understand, and stand by, John Wilkes.

This, then, was the family, less of an alliance than an infestation. According to one source, £900,000 would pass into Grenville pockets across half a century.* The Temples of Stowe would develop into battalions invading the continent of English society. They would join by marriage with other Grenvilles, making further knots with the Pitts of Boconnoc and the Lyttletons. Thomas Pitt's wife, Christian, was the daughter of Thomas Lyttleton, himself unhelpfully married to Christian Temple! Thomas's brother, our William, would much later marry Hester, younger daughter of Richard Grenville and Countess Temple (also Hester), the elder sister of Viscount Cobham. The family's

---

* William Cobbett after inspecting receipts, quoted in Rosebery, *Chatham, His Early Life and Connections*, p. 134.

base at Stowe House in Buckinghamshire would pass through the devising hands of Vanbrugh, Kent, Gibbs and Leoni, its sweeping gardens refashioned by Capability Brown. The Cobham faction owning this paradise would now use it to entertain, conspire and invest in neighbouring land and to thrive as a great factional interest. It was just after the Grenvilles went into opposition that William Pitt entered the Commons – shortly after the defeat of the Excise.

The Excise Bill had been one of those sensible pieces of legislation against which furious opposition is mounted until withdrawal is achieved. The proposal that importing merchants, evading tax on tobacco through assorted dishonest devices, should be made to pay that tax inspired horror. Their imports should be confined to bonded warehouses for release on paying the Excise. The bill was subject for much of 1733 to motions and speeches in the Commons, a welter of pamphlets and eventually street theatre. The fear among importers, powerful in the City, was that it was being merely tried out on tobacco and that an excise would spread to wine, about doing which Walpole had indeed had ideas.

However, the real scare slogan was a *General Excise*. At the thought, difficulty turned to crisis and entered parliamentary premises. Colonel Charles Howard, a loyal Walpole man, reported that 'the Court of Requests and the Lobby and the Stairs were filled with people from the City'.[6] And as the City of 1733 was a rather underbred place, the quarrel spilled on to the streets with elaborate mock funerals, staged and paid for by the tobacco trade.

The orchestrated trouble had made a great stir. Opposition apathy, contingent upon government assurance, fled to air. Marginally reliable Commons votes grew less reliable and more marginal. The situation became stickier by reason of a run of thoroughly dirty scandals. Simple larceny in the matter of the Derwentwater estates, the profitable mismanagement of the Charitable Corporation, the York Buildings *affaire*, all stank to heaven even by the worldly standards of the day. Worse, the chief men involved, Denis Bond, Sir John Eyles and Sir Robert Sutton notable among them, were not just Walpole's supporters, they represented a felonious parody of Walpole's own view of business ethics.*

---

* For a fuller account of these scandals see the author's life of Walpole, *The Great Man*, pp. 291–309.

The Prime Minister himself, accumulating sweetly, was unmoved. Very hot against Jacobites and happy to play the anti-Catholic card, Sir Robert Walpole was constitutionally incapable of indignation about money. He found the doings of Bond, Sutton and Eyles ill-advised only, and ill-advised chiefly for the carelessness of being found out. The Whig majority, in the way of any payroll, had been uncritically loyal, following Walpole like lambs to the pension scheme. But in the chemistry of politics beyond a certain point, support has a tipping point, is suddenly not to be counted upon. So it was for the Excise Bill, and Walpole, not given to prolonging illusions, was close to recognising as much.

In such circumstances, Cobham, the loyalist Whig, advanced and ennobled as loyalist Whig, had joined ardently in the revolt, throwing in his lot with distinctly low company, City tradesmen defending old Spanish practices to evade lawful imposts. It might be unfair on an old soldier to say that Cobham was doing what the Temples, Grenvilles and Pitts would generally do – grasp an opportunity and talk morality about it.

At first sight, Cobham's own motivation was hard to follow especially given his earlier non-reaction to the Salt Tax. Money levied upon a commodity chiefly bought by the poor in the form of salt meat was reasonably represented as social injustice, especially when levied to lighten the Land Tax, paid by country gentlemen. The Salt Tax had been rescinded in 1730, but, with the Treasury short of cash, had been revived in 1732. Against this legitimate target for a moral assault, Cobham had been silent. His career had been quiet, dignified and gave no trouble, but against the rational Tobacco Excise he and his clan rose in outrage to join a campaign in the lobbies, the streets and a furious pamphlet press. He and what soon became a Cobham cult were the following of an interest which would later pass for a cause.

While such opportunism was second nature to Temple, Lewis Wiggins suggests another angle. Viscount Bolingbroke, formerly Henry St John, ex-Secretary of State under Anne, ex-Jacobite and ex-candidate for treason charges, ex-Minister-in-Exile at the Court of the Old Pretender and ex-bidder for reconciliation with Walpole, was a friend of the Grenvilles. He is alleged in late gossip[7] to have advised Opposition leaders, "'So go down to the House of Commons; call John Bull's house his castle, and talk of the tyranny and oppression of the regulations of the Excise".'

Bolingbroke was a virtuoso cynic, a cynic on principle. His alleged words would have been rejected with outrage by William Pitt at almost any point in his career. Pitt was a moralist on principle. But Bolingbroke's political primer, *The Patriot King*, where the spirit of cynical opportunism took refuge, became a darling text in the circles of George III as Prince of Wales, his tutor, Lord Bute, and, with a little caution, among the admirers of William Pitt. But Martin Battestin, biographer of Henry Fielding, points to a more immediate contribution, an essay, 'The Dissertation on Partie', which Bolingbroke had published in his press vehicle, the *Craftsman*, back in 1733–4.[8]

The revolt would succeed, as revolts against Walpole's constructive and sensible measures – witness William Wood's honest copper coinage in Ireland – tended to do. Strictly speaking, the Excise legislation was withdrawn. But Walpole, speaking with his usual short clarity among friends after supper, had expressed the situation best: 'This dance, it will no farther go, and tomorrow I intend to sound a retreat . . .'[9]

However, wider revolt against Walpole failed entirely. The Excise having been withdrawn in 1733, he marched on for the next twelve months, conducting and winning the election which was due, in the usual insensitively lavish way. After which, he rolled on, distributing hard kicks and golden halfpence until February 1742. This retribution had already, pre-election, impinged bitterly upon the Grenvilles and their auxiliaries. Many of them may have taken up Bolingbroke's tin wisdom only light-heartedly, but Sir Robert was in power, a vindictive man and a good enemy, which is to say good at being an enemy. Cobham had been garlanded with honours, ribbons and emolument as good soldier in Marlborough's wars then equally good party man. An excursion into fashionable revolt would cost him everything Walpole could take away.

The effect was biblical. To be a Whig grandee in good standing under the first two Georges and Sir Robert was a variant of being in Paradise. To be stripped of all strippable lapels and trinkets was a Casting out of the Garden. It created outrage in this rather somnolent soul, whose former quiet and respectability, fifteen years of silence, gave authority to all ambitious men in Opposition looking for a creditable tent to enter. Cobham now became their figurehead.

Given the charm and hospitality of Stowe House, to which all factions against Sir Robert's faction now repaired, he became something of a society hostess. The burden outweighed the man. Pitt's own brilliant chronicler, Lord Shelburne, was not impressed. He described 'an officer, bred in the Queen's time, licentious, factious and no speaker, but who passed his time clapping young men on the back, keeping house with a good economy and saying things at his table which nobody else would say in a private room, with a good deal of shrewdness however in his conversations as well as his conduct'.[10]

For Pitt, matters were settled. He had been brought into Parliament by a brother married to Lord Cobham's niece. He was now tied into Opposition and all the penalties Sir Robert could devise for it. To make peace with Walpole, he would have estranged himself from the whole four-family tribe. He may or may not have been a natural opponent of Sir Robert's patronage system. He certainly opposed the Walpolean wisdom of not going to war. Given his talents, Pitt was always going to be different from the standard nominee member. Idly, but enjoyably, one might speculate about his brother, Thomas, marrying into the Turners of Castle Rising, the Bacons of Thetford or wedding a daughter of Sir Robert Britiffe, Walpole's man in Norwich, and William signed up to the old corps. As it is, the unkind thought lingers that a conviction may have been non-optional and the subsequent career a case of 'Assume a virtue if you have it not'.

Keeping company with Cobham's Cubs, Pitt had much of his grand public attitude rather thrust upon him. He had, too, very early in his political development watched revolt against the Excise Bill succeed. At the threshold, he had seen fervent protest defeat, however transiently, the settled and lucid condition of power. Pitt would always be indignant, always outraged. He would carry an Opposition cast of mind into executive government. The Excise revolt gave Pitt a taste of something natural to his talent and temperament, something he was meant for.

He would later make a happy marriage to a Grenville woman and become a relation of Richard Grenville twice over. And however pure and high-purposed William Pitt proclaimed, perhaps believed, himself to be, Richard Grenville* was the essence of Georgian aggrandisement.

* He would become Earl Temple through his mother (d. 1752), Countess in her own right.

The political faction of Cobham's Cubs, otherwise 'The Boy Patriots' or, as Walpole, with some nerve, called them, 'The Nepotism', may have taken full shape at Stowe in summer 1736.

There was at that time a family-and-friends gathering, involving George and Richard Grenville, William Pitt, George Lyttleton and another Cobham nephew, Gilbert West, and, finally, accompanied by his friend and muse, Martha Blount, Alexander Pope. Yet the chief emphasis of Cobhamism would be political purity. The journal *Common Sense* would serve them, at the moment when Bolingbroke's *Craftsman*, vigorous, witty, often downright distinguished, was cutting its losses and the viscount himself withdrawing to the very tolerable exile of Amboise.

The cause was argued outside professional politics. Henry Fielding, despite his links, was not a party member, but in *Pasquin* he put the Cobhamite view. An Honest Alderman says, 'I think we should stand by our Neighbours: gentlemen whose Honesty we are witnesses of, and whose estates in our own Neighbourhood, render 'em not liable to be bribed.'[11] Fielding scored a smash hit in which Walpole's *Gazetteer* recognised political purpose and the concerted promotion of the Opposition, yet commented with great candour. They 'have considered that *finished Piece* not as a Farce or a Droll but as refined Satyr of State which for excellence of Contrivance and elegance of Writing never had its Parallel'.[12]

'Satyr of State' was a natural reaction to Walpole's system of obtaining loyalty by purchase; and what Fielding articulated was an idealised and very Tory notion of politics based on land, loyal tenantry and Good Old Squire. For Cobham himself, it was an honest conviction, the anachronistic grace of unbribed yeomanry playing in the Squire's eleven with straight bats.*

However, William Pitt had been chosen for Parliament by the five voters of a closed borough sitting in a tent. It was the received pattern for Opposition as well as government. The crime of Robert Walpole was to have consolidated local practice into corporate policy. Lord Cobham had made his great challenge in the unmeritable cause of resisting the Excise. But above all other considerations, the Cobham Connection were not Boy Patriots, they were outs trying to get in.

---

* Perhaps symbolically, all cricket bats of this period were delicately curved.

4

The Peace of Sir Robert

Pitt, the new Member of 1734, served in a Parliament of which Sir Robert had become master by imposing layers of inducement all around. The Order of the Bath, revived at the Minister's suggestion, spoke George I's backing. This signal favour involved a royal glance back to a Sir Edward Walpole who had worn the almost obsolete ribbon in the previous century.

Supremely, George wanted stability and the Walpole negotiating escape from the South Sea crisis had obtained it. George wanted a Minister unambiguously Hanoverian, wholly committed to this royal family. Walpole, early member of the Kit-Cat Club, formed to promote that succession, was exactly that. He had helped prosecute the crypto-Jacobite Dr Sacheverell in 1710, and, pursuing the Jacobite plotters Bishop Atterbury and Christopher Layer, played detective very effectively. George, a calm, rational man, almost certainly simply liked Walpole, also calm, also rational.

With the King's sudden death at Osnabrück in 1727, the chance of changing ministers fell to his son, rarely calm, not always rational. As the second George found out, parliamentary power was rooted in better things than esteem. But having made himself hard to remove, Walpole worked through the Queen to bring the peppery successor on to friendly terms. Close friends with, first, a clever wife, then a clever mistress, he knew how to deal with George II. He had turned the improper use of place, public money and moneysworth to brilliant account.

By 1734 he had broken the spirit of more than one opposition. The Tories, under the young, dull Sir William Wyndham, were amateurs, country gentlemen abandoning Parliament for the hunting, given to pointlessly walking out of the Commons, a particular foible of Sir

William's, when with allies they might have injured Walpole. They were a party but they didn't do politics.

Opposition might yet have more success with a new wave of ambitious politicians, the 'young gentlemen in long neck cloths', as the inveterate Tory, Will Shippen, had derisively christened William Pulteney's followers. The Opposition Whigs were mostly uncomplicated careerists for whom there had been no satisfactory place on the Walpole carnival wagon. Men like Sir John Rushout and Samuel Sandys had fair talents and they would, in time, make good-quality trouble. Pulteney himself was a brilliant speaker, occasionally Walpole's equal. But in the years before young Pitt came into the house, the Opposition Whigs were unresolved as a political force, a pudding without a theme.

A debate maturing within the ministry would instruct the Oppositionists – failure to go to war. The idea of needing a war was, in the later 1720s, the *idée fixe* of Walpole's neighbour, brother-in-law, former friend and former political ally, Viscount Townshend. A heavily landed nobleman where Walpole was a pushy squire with a good financial head, Townshend, apart from altogether more disinterested motives, might have been Pitt's political ancestor.

In the twenties and thirties, the French government under the regencies of two dukes, Orléans then Bourbon, was run largely by tricky but hardly militaristic cardinals, Dubois then Fleury. Cynical and smart would be succeeded by more cynical and smarter yet. They would score points to get France off various hooks devised at the Treaty of Utrecht for holding her. Was Dunquerque harbour, in the clear terms of that treaty, really to be disarmed, stripped of military walls and deprived of ship-bearing depth? Their eminences did not think so. But though engaged upon well-drafted wrecking amendments to keep Dunquerque a decent military harbour, they did this essentially for pride and against humiliation. It was not for a war of revenge against perfidious Albion.

Pride was one trick of French policy, pride royal, personal, ecclesiastical; and this was, too, excellent politics, a way of winning good opinion at court. Charles Townshend was reasonably sophisticated about all this. He had been schooled by Walpole's predecessor, James Stanhope, who had done his (not always successful) fighting in Spain and was clear that France, though not to be trusted, would do rational business. It was Spain and the Empire, Madrid and Vienna, that worried Townshend.

Spain, colonially speaking, had been a loser at Utrecht in 1713 to

England's advantage. For Townshend, France had become the essential ally of mutual self-interest. Spain, minus Gibraltar and Minorca, was revanchist, wanting things back. This was not exactly nonsense. Spain was difficult and governed by Philip V, intermittently mad, and Elizabeth Farnese, an Italian woman cherishing furious and inveterate quarrels over Italian territories lost by Spain.

Then there was the *Asiento*, a by-blow of Utrecht, entitling the British to a very modest dip in Spanish South American trade – one ship a year, a detail British merchants comfortably disregarded. *Their* role was very Diamond Pitt: they were interlopers where they were not pirates. Sons of liberty and busy practitioners of the slave trade, their style had a sanctimonious truculence oddly American contemporary. Conflicts with the Spanish colonial authorities and customs would shortly give young Pitt and his City allies the chance to cry up war as sacred duty. Underneath everything, simple English greed would light long-burning fires.

In the mid-twenties, such things were simply dangerous attitudes, feelings, and, for Townshend, wild anticipations. The immediate problem was that Elizabeth Farnese, affronted about the state of play, was up for adventures. One of these involved drawing in the Empire, the grandly named non-playing captaincy of the German states plus assorted bits like modern Belgium, ruled from Vienna. In the War of the Spanish Succession, England and Empire had been allies and as nearly close as allies get. A gold-standard triumph had been shared by two authentically great generals, Marlborough and Eugène of Savoy. The Emperor Leopold (1648–1705) was a fanatical and intolerant Catholic. The English had just dumped a similar monarch, James II, into exile and were themselves fanatical and intolerant in the opposite direction. However, both were, like his Holiness the Pope, more worried about Louis XIV's armies than any point of doctrine. The two states might have been placed to remain at least on excellent terms, but for Bolingbroke's shallow opportunism and the cast of mind expressed, as shallowly, by Swift in *The Conduct of the Allies*. At Utrecht we had ratted, taking peace terms good for us, leaving the Empire too conscious of the conduct of *her* allies.

We had lost fundamental goodwill. Accordingly, when Elizabeth sent an eccentric Dutch diplomatic freelance, Jan Willem Ripperda, to Vienna in pursuit of a Spanish–Austrian entente wrapped up in an interim marriage contract between heirs, English anxiety was not irrational. But the extent and preoccupying nature of Townshend's fear were. He confided in the young Duke of Newcastle a memo[1] invoking the ghost of Charles V. *That* emperor had, in the first half of the sixteenth century, ruled Spain, most of Germany, the Low Countries and Spanish America. In Townshend's tropical mood it could all happen again.

He ran through the ill health of King Philip and his heir – 'the prince of the Asturias is in a hectical and consumptive way' – also about Philip's brother, Carlos, currently in Vienna being Austrianised and rather provisionally engaged to the imperial heiress, Maria Theresia. Townshend saw fearful possibilities: a Carlos vested with the territories of Charles V and a claim on France barred only by the unhealthy person of Louis XV. He would be placed to 'entirely overthrow the balance of power and render the liberties of Europe very precarious'.[2]

It was absurd, factually wrong and would never happen. But with Ripperda making large (and unauthorised) promises to a cash-strapped Emperor, nightmare doodlings acquired scare quality. Townshend was too historical, too retrospective, overestimating the Austrians, looking back excessively to Charles V. Producing worst-case scenarios and aided by Horatio Walpole, Sir Robert's puppyish younger brother, he drove policy toward war readiness.

Meanwhile, away from the fantasy of a sixteenth-century grand empire, Elizabeth Farnese made trouble nearer home. She instituted a siege of Gibraltar, the *Prince Frederick*, an English ship, was seized, prompting a long, noisy crisis threatening war. British consuls were withdrawn from Spanish cities; Admiral Francis Hosier was placed off the present-day Colombian coast as sort of ineffective threat plus guarantor of British merchant ships. In due course, he and most of his sailors caught the local speciality, yellow fever, and died. The French, keeping a straight face, undertook to negotiate for us in recovering the *Prince Frederick*.

Walpole, *not* a foreign affairs specialist, had allowed himself to be led by his brother-in-law into an alliance involving France, Hanover (naturally), Sweden, Denmark and a clutch of small German states. That involved buying mercenary small princes along with their soldiery deep into Walpole's surplus. The country gentlemen, more formidable than the ghost of Charles V, now paid a full-rate land tax, alien to everything Sir Robert stood for. The Tories, the peace party of 1710, the bringers of Utrecht, fell about being ironical in the Commons and print.

Will Shippen denounced raising troops. Walpole called them 'Land Forces', Shippen called them 'a standing army'. This was the language of the Whigs – and the parliamentary opposition to Charles I. Left to himself, it would have been Robert Walpole's. But it was the Tories who had fun. Lord Bolingbroke's *Craftsman* compared Carlos's chances of ruling the world with the Welsh lady who, in the event of her uncle, three brothers and two sons all dying first, might come in for a decent sum of money.[3]

It was galling for the Prime Minister. Eventually he found a way out, conciliating Austria. Charles VI's envoys were working European courts and ministers for underwriting of his daughter Maria Theresia, illegal heiress to the imperial crown under Salic Law, as his successor pragmatically sanctioned. The obvious thing for England, with her anxieties, was some sharp trading. Finally, at Soissons on 31 May 1727, the Emperor got British sanction for something that hardly concerned us: Maria Theresia's future accession. In return, the Austrians gave up the Ostend Company, a quarter-hearted imitation of the South Sea Company. It was no threat, but the British war and anxiety party had made much of it.

It had all been essentially pointless. British ships had cruised off Cadiz; in Vienna, levies were reported raised, and public money spent to distraction. Two unimportant concessions had let down a war balloon, expensively inflated. Walpole had followed Townshend passionately engaged upon diplomacy, high policy and the international stage. He now knew two things – that Townshend was no use at foreign policy and that he himself disliked adventure even more.

Walpole had accepted military spending quite beyond his natural instincts. It had set back his plans to cut the Land Tax as low as possible to keep gentlemen with land and seats voting right. Walpole had been a pro-war man once – when it mattered and had been good politics. Louis XIV, dead for ten years by 1725, had, in his lurching, incoherent way, been a serious threat. Marlborough's and Eugène's campaigns had been very necessary. Though, as Walpole, holding military finance offices during that war, also knew, they had gone on too long. Under foolish apprehensions, Townshend had dabbled in a war policy, spent money, worried his supporters, prepared for international conflict, given serious credit to the French government – for nothing. Looking back to a family compact with aggressive potential in 1700 was out of date. But the same fears, worked into a rhapsody, would be invoked by William Pitt when in 1761–2 an angry and incoherent Spain would stumble around the tail end of our war with France.

By contrast, Sir Robert saw that times had changed and that policy should adjust them. He kept up an unnecessary public panic against the Catholics, long a pious huddle threatening nobody. But it was only an ongoing dirty trick, a way to keep voters and interests loyal. War, or preparing for a war which didn't happen, was something else, something in the way of trade, business, capital accumulation and the general alrightness he was offering. When that dark horse next crossed before his threshold, Walpole would ostentatiously watch it gallop away.

The opportunity had arrived in 1733 with a factitious crisis over the Polish crown. Poland, with elected monarchs nominated by neighbouring powers, was a sad case, part client state, part standing temptation. She would eventually be partitioned – by Russia, Prussia and the Austrians – but in 1733 faced another royal election. It was a world of alternative sponsors. Vienna had earlier established Augustus of Saxony as Augustus II. They now favoured his son, a touch of heredity which might stick. France responded with a flourish of respect for Polish pride; why not a Polish king for Poland? They had the ideal candidate in Stanislaw Leszczynski, slight and suborned father-in-law to Louis XV.

At the end of a highly mixed outcome, and with England neutral, France did very well for herself. Franz of Lorraine, Maria Theresia's husband, would vacate his duchy in return for French recognition of his wife's imperial inheritance, while Stanislaw, a tool, got Lorraine, which huge iron and coal territory would revert to France on his death (in 1766)! The war was fought essentially as France and Spain against Austria. Britain had obligations to the imperial government. These had practical application in the Mediterranean, where Elizabeth hoped to regain lost Italian territory. British men-of-war along the Tyrrhenian coast could have made up for the default of Utrecht, kept Vienna friendly for when we might need it. That was the intelligent case for keeping our commitments to the Empire. There was, too, an honourable case much argued by George II, the punctilious, professional soldier doing the decent thing.

Walpole wouldn't hear either argument. Badly bitten, he was very shy indeed. The war was won by France and the Emperor was bitter. It might matter later, but Walpole contemplated money not spent and men not killed. 'Thirty thousand men dead in Europe this year', he said, 'and not one Englishman.' It was not unpopular in the country either, a quarrel between foreigners in a far-away place of which we knew nothing. Nor did the City mind: no bullion, no slaves, what was the point?

As for opposition and what might be done to challenge a dominant government, the ambitious young gentlemen in long neck cloths did not really dissent. Their concern was to find something else to disturb Sir Robert's intolerable equanimity. It stood there, of course, in the Excise proposal outlined in Chapter 3. Pitt, not yet elected, played no known part in it. Nor is he likely to have made much acquaintance among the City men organising the mock funerals, petitions and street protest, but demonstrating quite what a lobby the business world could be. The friendship, in so far as Pitt did friendships, with Alderman Beckford would come soon, but in 1733, not yet in Parliament and beyond the flimsy raptures of later admirers, Pitt left no worthwhile evidence of active engagement in events.

Meanwhile, Walpole, with his lead-weighted rubber-policeman talents, had come out of the Excise crisis intact and vengeful. Robert Walpole was better company than most national leaders, amusing, tolerant, even easy where essential power was not concerned. If you were not his enemy, you were welcome to become that profitable thing, his friend. He was not sadistic, did not break people for fun. He did ruthlessness only to utilitarian ends.

A little, politely voiced latitude might be allowed, but contradiction where it mattered, like desertion over the Excise Bill, got the parliamentary black spot. The revenge was discriminating, a teaching strike, and for the Opposition a decapitation. A pair of dukes (Bolton and Montrose), Lords Scarborough, Stair and Chesterfield were struck off every list of place or emolument they were on. The shredding of Lord Cobham's standing as a public man was simply Sir Robert's short way with whatever he defined as betrayal.

The great chance for Pitt to cut a figure did not come until late in Walpole's time amid the follies of the royal family, generation growling at a generation which snapped whelpishly back. George II, whom Lord Rosebery sensibly defends against the court malevolence of Hervey, is conceded to be a man who 'lacked finesse', and it is acknowledged that 'his foible was avarice'. But Rosebery sees rightly that hatred directed at George II for German loyalties flies in the face of human nature. George, born 1683, was as much a man of his native country as anyone living there for the first thirty-one years of his life before he left for another.

The King of England spoke good, if accented English, natural occasion for mockery in a nation which, in 1730 as now, eccentrics apart, speaks it badly and no modern foreign language at all, accented or otherwise. He was steadily unfaithful to his wife but loved her dearly. He had a furious temper, sometimes expressed by kicking people's shins. Insulting language came readily. 'You are von rascal' he had, when Prince of Wales, told the inoffensive Newcastle. His courage went beyond the battlefield into blind folly as he furiously demanded to cross from Holland on a boiling sea, from which a brave and capable admiral, Sir Charles Wager, held him back, pleading his own prudence. Lacking finesse is a nice way of putting it.

These are the commonplaces of popular history. So is the reputation of Frederick Lewis, Prince of Wales, written off by English disrespect as 'Poor Fred who was alive and now is dead' and about whom 'there is nothing more to be said'. He tried terribly hard to be Fred, a Fred whom the English would like, would applaud for passing buckets of water all night against a St James's Square fire, for charitably distributing decent quantities of the allowance his father resented paying, and, for playing cricket which, in 1751, killed him for fumbling a catch. But at home he was Fritz, as in his mother's remark from the depths of her soul, 'Fritz's popularity makes me vomit.'

Rosebery wisely observes that the Prince 'was a poor creature, no doubt, a vain and fatuous coxcomb. But human beings are constantly the parents of coxcombs without regarding them as vermin.'[4] What fought itself, and worried the neighbours in and about St James's Palace in the mid-1730s, was a problem family raging like any menage on a Liverpool sink estate. The parents openly wished the son dead; and the son, when his dying mother was finally slipping away (while refusing him a syllable of forgiveness), pushed into her room, allegedly to be sure she went. The social worker responsible here was Sir Robert Walpole who conciliated and defended mother and father while firmly identifying delinquency in the youth. Walpole was George II's man as he had been George I's. Any Opposition man looking for a focus knew where to go.

5

Poor Fred and the Patriots

The primacy of Robert Walpole in alliance with the monarch left few options to politicians excluded from government place or prime ministerial favour. Given a Minister, who with a safe majority, *and* commanding all patronage, was effectively the monarch's monarch, those options were laborious.

Politicians who were out would gather around the Prince and his new wife at Leicester House, but only unsuccessful ones or those playing very long term. The clientele could be divided between those, like George Bubb Dodington, reliably shuttling in and shuffling out, and those like Pitt, present there until something better turned up. The most unsuccessful of all eighteenth-century politicians, though he has a following with some historians, was Bolingbroke, who also had a line to Leicester House. His famous tract of 1740, *The Patriot King*, would, through the immature minds of Frederick, his wife then venomously loyal widow and the man chosen as preceptor for their son, Lord Bute, be credited much later for the acts of Frederick's slow-minded son.

The tinkling conceits of Henry St John, in the very highest office for days at the end of Anne's reign and guessing wrong through three reigns, would be blamed across 150 years for instilling absolutism into George III. They didn't, but the Patriot part of William Pitt's political doctrine can be linked to a reading of the man who planned a *coup d'état* for the Pretender, then fled to his service in exile before buying his way back to write stylishly about the politics at which he had comprehensively failed.

What all these characters had in common, Bolingbroke, Frederick and the Pitt of that moment, was the fact of being out. But Pitt, no more than Walpole, wanted to be anything of the sort. He was young, an elegant and biting speaker, interlaced with the Cobham connection, the Grenvilles, as avid seekers of office and its profits as idealists ever were. He needed, or thought he needed, those Grenvilles for a long-term career strategy. Owning a good share of seats, they exemplified Namierian practice in following the family line to serve the family interests, like a demonstration model. Prince Frederick would crudely remark that he was twenty-four years younger than his father, so Pitt, born 1708, was thirty-two years younger than Walpole. Brave and reckless defiance could be very shrewd.

So, in 1736, when George tried to brush Frederick off with minimal finance, the patriots embraced the young man, deliberately elevating him as symbol of hopeful, idealistic youth. That, in politics, is usually a mistake, familiar today, here and in the United States. The notion is of youth as embodied virtue, which, overcoming the vanity, ignorance and delusion routine in youth, will somehow purify and elevate politics. Frederick was thirty-one, facing marriage and requiring its financial adornment. George, with his customary want of marketing skills, had set out to cramp such delights. Walpole could see the injury the King was inflicting upon himself. Accordingly, though at sixty he despised the youth thing as he did the youth at issue, in the great cause of politics and muffling trouble, he extracted a reasonable settlement from the household.

The Prime Minister, thought the Opposition, should not be allowed to get away with good sense. The underdone settlement could be hymned and have drums softly rolled for it with irony, good-quality mid-eighteenth century irony. Walpole would understand and wince. George and Frederick in their separate fighters' corners would take it at face value. Professional politicians educated in classical irony, knowing their litotes and being offensive, as gentleman claimed, only on purpose, would hear a piece of elegant derision draped in the silk of deferential form. They would mark Mr Pitt sharply up.

Tindal, an early parliamentary chronicler, editorialising as the early ones do and Hansard doesn't, offers a praise readily misunderstood in our time. 'The Speech', he said, 'is unmixed with any strain but that of declamation.'[1] That, to the classically educated century, spoke only admiration. Declamation, windy and pompous to us, was what orators did. He continues with a comparison in the way of a modern opera goer. 'We have', thought Tindal, 'few models of antiquity more perfect in that kind, it being more ornamented than the declamations of Demosthenes and less diffused than those of Cicero.'

Comment would be cooler and more technical sixty years on in Archdeacon Coxe's *Life of Walpole*. 'Frederick', he says incredulously, 'is described as "a most dutiful son".' Pitt then 'descanted on his filial obedience and respectful submission to the will of his royal parents and expatiated with ostentatious eulogy on his generous love of liberty and just reverence for the British Constitution'.[2] Coxe admires rhetoric as rhetoric, but, as Walpole's biographer, he notes the context. 'The manner in which the debate was conducted, the warm panegyric bestowed on the prince, the cold praises given to the king and the acrimonious censure of the minister gave great offence and tended still further to widen the breach.'

Indeed they did, they were intended to. The modern demotic ear will find the speech thoroughly artificial, but the modern demotic ear is anachronistic. Pitt, highly literate, allusive and above all ironical, fought with the weapons of his time. He reached his audience with sham fawning as his opening, and litotes as a short knife in the guts. He was, he said, 'really affected with the prospect of the blessings to be derived by my country from this so desirable and so long desired measure . . .' In other words, 'So George is paying up. What kept him?'

There is no warmth toward his supposed hero. Frederick is the lay figure in this exercise and he very nearly breaks under the weight of a high eloquence as derisive as flattering: 'Were it not a sort of presumption to follow so great a person through his hours of retirement, we should find him in the milder light of domestic life; we should find him busied in the noble exercise of humanity, benevolence and every social virtue . . .'

Another form of rhetoric is the straight-faced statement of the untrue. Not without provocation, Frederick had spent much of his twenties as the complete rebellious teenager. To speak of 'filial duty to his royal parents' was to raise an informed giggle among parliamentarians. To roll on with his 'generous love of liberty and just reverence for the British Constitution' was to wrap poor Fred in the slogans of the Patriots in Opposition to the King's Minister, and do it with horrid politeness. 'These', he adds, of all that 'noble exercise of humanity' stuff, 'are public virtues and cannot escape the benedictions of the public.' This is a sharp poke in the eye for George: 'He's popular, you aren't.'

For all the cleverness, there is something in the performance which the refreshingly unimpressed comment of Macaulay misses. He wrote that it 'certainly deserves Tindal's compliment and deserves no other. It is just as empty and wordy as a maiden speech on such an occasion might be expected to be.'[3] This is empty and wordy with some craft.

The 'public virtues render His Royal Highness not only a noble ornament, but a firm supporter, if any could be possibly necessary of that throne so greatly filled by his royal father in the comfort of seeing the royal family (numerous as I thank God it is), still growing and rising up in a third generation, a family Sir, which I most sincerely wish may be as immortal as that constitution which it comes to maintain'.[4]

That conclusion, ironical about George, cringing about Frederick, goes rather beyond Macaulay's immediate point. However, there are so many and deadly points in the first of his two essays, one on William Pitt, the other, seeing a useful distinction, on Lord Chatham! He examines the whole matter of Pitt as speaker. He was indeed 'a great orator' yet he 'spoke without premeditation'. On the other hand, he was not a debater, 'something', he says, citing the exemplary Charles Fox, 'done by constant practice. [Pitt's] merit was almost entirely rhetorical. He therefore did not succeed in exposition or in refutation; but his speeches abounded with lively illustrations, striking apophthegm, well-told anecdotes, happy allusions, passionate appeals. His invective and sarcasm were terrific. Perhaps no English orator was ever so much feared.' But this is not depth, it is facility, and as Macaulay also noted '. . . his facility amounted to a vice. He was not the master, but the slave of his own speech.'[5]

The faces had been slapped and the boats burned. Pitt had opted for Opposition. His praise is deadly, the insult not only intended but lovingly worked upon. Clearly in the art which the political age most esteemed, the graceful giving of a performance, William Pitt was a large talent but one depending upon short-term impact rather than reflection and substance. It was theatre. Macaulay again: 'On the stage he would have been the finest Brutus or Coriolanus ever seen.'

There was, though, still calculation. Risk and the investment were being taken long in hope of great reward. Pitt had put himself outside

the interim market of ministerial reward, junior office or financial
sweets. It was a gamble but at modest odds. How long would the
sixty-year-old Walpole continue in power? The Excise Crisis had shown
him more brittle than any event in his fifteen-year tenure. Just how
vulnerable might he be? The King had been born in 1683, Frederick,
as the Prince crassly liked reminding people, in 1707. For all Pitt's flummery, when might the King oblige by dying? Such unacknowledged
but real speculation would be left looking as silly and unpleasant when
Frederick, his status dwindling in the intervening years, died in 1751,
leaving his father nine clear years of being difficult for other people.

For the moment, however, Pitt was a new, sharp talent signed up
by the Opposition. There are more legends than hard evidence about
what Walpole had been willing to do to keep this new talent in his
troupe. The talk about 'the need to muzzle this terrible cornet of
horse' smells of back formation years after. It does not remotely sound
like the cool Walpole who had kept at arm's length the brilliant
debating talent of William Pulteney. Pulteney was recurringly, across
the major business of the House, given credit for matching the Prime
Minister. Pitt had made a single, very effective speech. He had confected
some highly wrought insolence but had not begun to shake the pillars
of government. The attributed remark is no more credible than the
claim made long after by Pitt's nephew.

The second Lord Camelford would allege that, so high was Pitt's
pre-parliamentary reputation, Walpole had tried to buy off Camelford's
father, Thomas Pitt, from bringing him in for the family borough. But
Pitt's reputation before entering the Commons was *not* notably high,
known only as another Grenville follower. Even less likely is the
nephew's claim that his father, Thomas, 'preferred [William's] interests to his own and laid the foundations at his own expense for all his
brother's future fame and greatness'. Very few people behave like that,
and the coldly acquisitive Thomas was not one of them.

Walpole did not believe in good nature. The young man had income
from a Cornetcy of Horse. This was a sinecure – he had never looked
like a soldier – but on the reserve he was paid, always a useful thing.
Depriving an opponent of income was one way of making a leader's
point. The commission lay within ministerial discretion, forthwith
invoked to take it away from him. George Lyttleton, another member
of the Grenville connection, commemorated the fall in bad verse:

> The servile standard from the freeborn hand
> He took and bade him lead the patriot band.[6]

All the Grenvilles and their friends talked like this, even in prose. 'Liberty', 'freeborn', 'slavery', 'save', 'my country', as in 'Save my Country', 'accursed', 'tyranny' and the like littered their raptures. When Pitt would long after proclaim, quite wrongly, 'I know that I can save my country and that nobody else can,' he was talking Grenvillese. More usefully, he had been praised in Bolingbroke's paper, the *Craftsman*, and abused, probably by William Arnall, Walpole's prose doorman, in the *Gazetteer*. Arguably it was impolitic to sack a talented man in that it made a martyr of him.

However, power also deals in warnings. This warning was a direction to exile and both men knew where exile was situated. For a time, short or long, Pitt would become the servant of the Prince of Wales. There was nowhere else to go. But the reality was that he had flattered Frederick in terms which a man with self-knowledge would have seen as double-edged. Through all the sycophantic bombast it had been a subtle speech, one that cut throats by moonlight, and Frederick was not a subtle man. He had heard his father mocked and, being royalty, took it at face value. Cool ambiguity, like leg spin, was wasted on him.

Frederick had vacancies at his court because two men in his service judged the King's anger inadequately balanced by Frederick's employment or pay. In his base at Leicester House, Pitt would now keep company with the prideless Bubb Dodington, an intriguer so inept at intrigue as to be everywhere known as an intriguer. Everything hung upon expectation and was driven by optimism about a death. It was a little better than Bolingbroke's office for a few months during 1715–16 as Secretary of State to the Old Pretender, but had little more dignity. Dodington would, in 1744, gladly exchange another phantom secretaryship, the one held out to him in prospect by the Prince of Wales, for an authentic job. This was the Treasurership of the Navy, available, real and paying – from Henry Pelham, Walpole's long-term heir.

Twice, in 1737 and 1738, Pitt spoke on military expenditure. The former Cornet of Horse was against it. More precisely, he was against 'a Standing Army' which, in the restricted vocabulary of the Patriots, was a threat to 'liberty'. Walpole was, of all people, least disposed to war, but he favoured a base limit to keep order at home where there was growing hardship of a kind, soon in some areas to approach famine, and as a fall-back guarantee against the absurdity of a Jacobite rising.

About which Pitt was relaxed. In 1738, seven years before the '45, he derided even the possibility: 'Sir, as to the Tories and any suspected Jacobites . . . there are so few of either in the kingdom that I am sure they can give no man an occasion for being afraid of them; and therefore there is not the least shadow of reason saying they are the occasion of our being obliged to keep up such a numerous standing army.'[7] Denouncing standing armies was nothing new in Walpole's time. They had been cited earlier when the Excise Crisis was raging.

If this was a silly thing to say in the light of what happened, the whole speech looked factitious, which effective oratory shouldn't. It was altogether an inferior performance. Beginning, like the Allowance speech, with irony, irony directed at the placemen, the payroll of Walpoleans, Pitt affected surprise. This was because 'upon every question that occurs relating to public affairs they are always unanimous; and I confess it is to me a little astonishing that 200 to 300 gentlemen should, by an unaccountable sort of unanimity, always agree in opinion upon the many sorts of questions that occur yearly – and not for one, but for several years together.

'I am convinced that this surprising unanimity does not proceed from any effect of the places they have under the crown: for if it did, a man being possessed of any place in such a case I am sure would be an infallible reason for the people not to trust him with the preservation of their liberties.' This stretch, ending in classic Grenvillian style with 'liberties', has little of the quality found higher. A laboured rebuke, less irony than sarcasm, it is less Demosthenes than House Master.

He was concerned, as he shifted targets, to attack soldiers themselves. Soldiers were the object of wide citizen prejudice at this time and Pitt was not going to indulge Kipling's sympathy for 'men that guard you while you sleep'. They were instead the source of all the trouble. 'In the keeping up of such an army is the chief cause of our discontents. And these discontents are now, we find, made the chief pretence for keeping up such a standing army. Remove the army', he added, 'or a considerable part of it, and the crowd of the discontented you complain of will cease.'

He then directed himself at economy, indulging in extraordinary contempt for the soldiers and indifference to what happened to them. 'The consequences it is true, may be fatal to some of those who have been the causes of loading the nation with such an unnecessary expense, but no honest man I am sure, will think that their safety is to be put in the balance with the satisfaction of the people and the safety of the nation.'

What that meant among the abstract nouns was that soldiers could hang or starve, for all Pitt cared. It reads nasty and gets more so. 'Our half-pay is better or as good as full pay I believe in any country in Europe . . . And as for the soldiers, I believe it may be said that of at least three fourths of them, that they never underwent any fatigue except that of a review, nor were ever exposed to any danger except in apprehending smugglers or dispersing mobs . . . I should not think we were guilty of the least ingratitude if they were all turned adrift tomorrow morning.' And it goes on, expressing the same privileged civilian's dinner-table ruthlessness with a thumping false antithesis: 'Supposing they had served a campaign or two against a public enemy; is it from hence to be inferred that they should for ever after live idly and that in such a manner as to be dangerous to the liberties of their country?'

That is not just unpleasant and cruel-minded. It is astonishingly childish, ignoring every serious question at issue for the sake of vapid flashes. It was, of course, populism. Pitt had no idea any more than the government how rural rioting provoked by suffering could be alleviated. He found it convenient to call soldiers the cause. His standard cant about the 'Liberties of their country' would be answered with rough sense by Henry Pelham, a lieutenant whom Walpole increasingly valued and as Prime Minister (1746–54) someone who would retain soldiers and keep international peace.

The opponents of the regular troops, he said, 'have all alas, taken it for granted that if our Standing Army were removed, the causes of discontent would be removed likewise. Reason tells us that people who are discontented will prove rebellious as soon as the government becomes too weak to restrain their outrages; and we find Sir, by experience that no reduction was ever attended by a return of gratitude on the part of the common people . . . And it is Sir, a question whether it be most probable that His Majesty will abase his power if we shall keep up the army or that his enemies will lay aside their designs and the people return to due submission in case we reduce it.'[8]

Such exchanges were nothing new. Objections had been made to a standing army, instrument in the hands of absolutism in classic Whig theology, in the 1720s. The reality was justifiable economic discontent for which that army would be used, usually harshly, in lieu of the civilian police or substantial relief we did not have. The problems were intractable, the oratory easy. But in time the scornful enemy of a standing army would campaign furiously to establish a militia.

6

War with Spain: St Jingo's Eve

Robert Walpole, taking office in the domestic crisis of 1720–21, would stay there as long as the issues remained domestic.

The Tories, tarred by Jacobitism, were out of everything. Macaulay, describing the first levee of George II in 1727, notes 'a remarkable spectacle. Mingled with the constant supporters of the House of Brunswick, with the Russells, the Cavendishes and the Pelhams, appeared a crowd of faces utterly unknown to the pages and gentlemen-ushers: lords of rural manors, whose ale and foxhounds were renowned in the neighbourhood of the Mendip Hills or round the Wrekin, but who had never crossed the threshold of the Palace since the days when Oxford, with the white staff in his hand, stood behind Queen Anne.'[1]

They had been coming back tentatively now for a while, making common cause limply with smoother and handier men, William Pulteney's disaffected Whigs whom Walpole had denied advancement all the way into Opposition. But the Tories were no more a war party than Walpole was a war leader. The Opposition Whigs might opportunistically consider war if it played for them, but they were hardly fired up by military zeal.

As for Walpole, 'The burned child', we used cruelly to say, 'fears the fire.' He had been burned by war's costs, long and finally aborted war preparation, triggered by Townshend's grandiose terrors. Accordingly he feared all war, however charming. Sir Robert had kept Britain resolutely out of military commitments – in 1733, commitments to an ally. His outlook was more reasonable than United States isolationism in the 1930s, but there were affinities. Rather, it posed a question which modern Americans might consider. 'We are very well situated, are getting and spending. Trade admittedly is not as easy as we might wish, but what advantage comes to the country as a whole from going to war?'

He was sympathetic to trade, not to the merchants who engaged in it. They were people – the African coast slavers and West Indies planters and sugar traders – not unlike Diamond Pitt, loud, louche, self-assertive and law-contemptuous. They were the people who across 1733 had held mock funerals over the Excise, who plagued him into climbing down, then jostled him in the lobby. Beyond which, they would pursue the government to intervene on their behalf, to do something for *them*, not Walpole's way at all. The traders and their endless petitions to government sought more than diplomatic intervention. And for too many of them, war was altogether their sort of thing.

Richard Pares's defining study of the subject[2] quotes a pamphlet published during the Spanish war looming in 1738. Fearful of losing trade, notably the Spanish business, to the French, it argued with brute insouciance that '. . . it is more the true interest of these Kingdoms in general and even the merchants themselves (those who traded in Spain and the South Sea excepted), that we should continue in a state of war with them (France and Spain) so that war is carried on only at sea, than in a state of peace . . .' As long as France, Spain and the Two Sicilies were united, then '. . . our commerce, in general, will flourish more under a vigorous and well managed naval war than under any peace which should allow an open intercourse with these two nations'.[3]

Such talk was not a simple eruption, viciousness born in conflict. Back in 1727 a pamphlet had appeared with the long but still catchy title, 'Britain's Speediest Sinking Fund is a Powerful Maritime War, Rightly Managed and Especially in the West Indies'.[4] William Beckford, sugar planter and slave owner, City Alderman and habitual invoker of Liberty who would become close confidant and adviser to Pitt, would express the mentality with like ferocity. About the French and the trade they followed in his own sphere, Beckford observed that 'our trade will improve by the total extinction of theirs'.[5] This mixture of Hobbes and mercantilism spitting war potential had complex roots. They went back to the days when Robert Harley, Lord Oxford, representative of the pacific non-trading Tories, had been Queen Anne's First Minister.

Harley had won the great election victory of 1710. He wanted to end that war and take the diplomacy leading to the Peace of Utrecht (1713). Over all, the British had heavily shaded that war, but had essentially failed in Spain. The object of removing the Bourbon claimant, later Philip V, for an Austrian archduke had been abandoned. The British and Dutch, who had gone to war to keep the crowns of Spain and France on unrelated heads, negotiated trading assets as compensation. They looked for territory in South America, perhaps a little coastal town or two for illicit but unsupervised trade? The French saw sanitised smuggling as bad for their own business and the coveted bases too useful to the thieving British in any future war. Accordingly, it was the French who put pressure on Spain to make alternative concessions.

It was here that the British *Asiento* appeared. Such rights of access for specific, limited commercial purposes had been granted ten years at a time, commonly to deliver black men in chains to the Spanish Empire with perhaps access to additional merchandise. The initiative for the British trade privilege came from Bolingbroke, then Southern Secretary, offering to drop the townships for a fatter *Asiento*, admitting wider trade and worth *thirty* years. St John brought off another deal. On offer was a 15 per cent reduction in duties on goods sold in Cadiz, to be injuriously matched for our hated ally, Holland. Instead, and confined to the British, he won the entrée of a 500-ton ship every year to the Portobello fair, 'The Annual Ship'.[6]

This being a Tory deal and part of a Tory treaty, Utrecht, the successor Whigs denounced it. That didn't matter. Walpole had eloquently denounced the Peace itself, but, the case being altered, he had worked fervently ever since to keep it. But being a Tory creation, '*Asiento* and Annual Ship' involved the South Sea Company, also a Tory creation. That Company though, at this time more engaged financially than in trade, was on the worst possible terms with the merchants of Jamaica. And while South Sea had its disputes with Spain, the most virulent activists were independent traders linked to Jamaica. As for the Spanish, they had made their concessions after defeat and expected and got British merchants exceeding their rights and generally working the treaty like a wedge.

So it fell out, and very quickly. Spain faced extensive smuggling in the Americas. As Pares says, 'Some clauses in the treaty were almost useless except as a pretext for it.'[7] 'The Annual Ship' sounds very modest until one picks up the word 'refreshment' and another word, 'necessaries'. A ship's hold, once unloaded, could, by a twisting of the letter and profitable practice, become many refills: not one, but a number of cargoes unloaded. And if there were no towns to exploit, there were stretches of land, notably on the River Plate, useful, as Pares puts it, for 'refreshing their negroes'.[8] Incidentally, Pares, reflecting the sensibility of his publication date, 1936, reports the South Sea practice of bringing in 'inferior negroes'. 'The colonists', he says, 'had another grievance against the Company which was perhaps better justified. They complained that it exported all the best slaves and left them only the refuse.'[9]

There were routes overland from Peru and Chile, bringing in more business for Britain. The French had also engaged in trade well outside the terms of Utrecht. However, France and Spain being, as the British complained, on friendly terms, Spanish representations in Paris were met, if not always at once. Indeed, a Spanish expedition officered by Frenchmen finally closed this trade down. No purpose is served here by stressing the good sense of Free Trade. Every country, including the number-one interloper Great Britain, protected her own to-and-fro of goods. The British had done this in Ireland to the extent of forbidding Irish development or export otherwise than through domestic sale to England, of, among other things, wool. Truculent self-pity was the working norm of petitioning British merchants. They were trying to do things which, done by unauthorised Spaniards at Southampton or Liverpool, they would have denounced as a taking of the roast beef out of their mouths.

Ironically, the South Sea Company, having a limited legal right to enter and trade, is reckoned to have carried on a busy traffic in goods not so authorised. Following the ethical standards of Sir John Blunt and other early directors of the Company inflating the famous bubble of 1720, their accountancy was impressionistic. It was given to suggesting *minimal* corporate profits which, as trading continued merrily on, indicates interlopers' bonuses.

Cooperation over regulation denied by Britain, Spain ventured self-help, involving the *Guardas Costas*. In British newspapers and speeches, this commonly became 'Spanish Depredations'. They in turn led to freelance action by British colonial officials. Hamilton, Governor of Jamaica, 'was induced, chiefly it seems, by his private advantage to allow reprisals'.[10] Low-level violence, arrests of men and firings upon ships became the pattern. Merchants petitioned the government – very heavily – and their noisy friends in the City of London and its press made raw, patriotic noises.

Only in the late thirties did even the possibility of war over such commercial brawling emerge. Protest centred upon Spanish searches of British merchantmen. What did the treaty say? The question was 'Which treaty?' British West Indian traders wanted as little as possible to do with Utrecht, arguable as it might be in places. They liked the Treaty of 1667 and wrapped it in the union flag. In 1737, they demanded that it should govern the conduct of *Guardas*. This agreement, made in the days of Charles II, suited a civil smuggler's point of view by allowing the inspection only of the ship's papers, not the ship.

Deferring to what Walpole called 'Clamour' from the West Indian Lobby, Newcastle in 1737 took up that claim. As Sir Benjamin Keene, the long-service and expert British Ambassador in Madrid, pointed out in a private letter of 13 December of that year,[11] this was the wrong treaty. It might only confine search authority to papers, but the later, more applicable treaty, of 1670, while in principle barring British subjects from trading with the Spanish West Indies, said nothing at all about a right of search. It forbad something, but gave no authority to find out if it was being done.

It was all delightful and disputatious maritime law, but it was unreasonable to expect Madrid to accept so nuanced an authority over illegal acts without rough men coming on board and finding out for themselves. Equally unreasonably, Spain fell back on Utrecht which specifically allowed *legal* and agreed trade while asserting in a stupid, iterative way claims to all the Indies. These, they insisted, still bound everyone else, and the Treaty of Utrecht might never have been signed by King Philip. This was the Spanish end of a folly which, at the British end, said, 'We will do as we choose.' Between the two sat sensible if understandably oppressed Keene, a grown-up diplomat making the British case professionally at the Spanish court and, for his pains, known to the Patriots as 'Don Benjamin'.

The immediate situation in the late thirties was a claim/counterclaim dispute. The British claimed that legitimate cargo had been lost through the actions of the *Guardas Costas*, also that the South Sea Company had lost property during the conflicts of 1718 and 1727. The Spanish claim was for debts incurred when merchants had failed to pay Spain her legally agreed share of the Annual Ship's cargo and profits.

Pitt would get his opportunity after Keene had concluded negotiations. The Spanish court did not believe that British traders, frequently behaving like pirates and misreading the clear terms of the treaty to snatch more bites at the cherry, were entitled to anything. Keene, who knew the country well, was accused of having gone native. But if he saw the Spanish point of view, he had also learnt the impossibility when negotiating with them of achieving even the modest objectives of his own pacific ministers. Empowered to settle for £140,000, he had realised that an offer of £95,000 was the very limit of Spain's giving mood. This was embodied in the Convention of Pardo* which required ratification, meaning Parliament and an open season of indignation. With difficulty, Walpole got such sensible realism through the Privy Council. The House of Commons was different. The dispute was sordid, and more sordid on the British side, where above any imaginable legitimate claim, the interlopers' lobby demanded simple fulfilment of their expectations.

In the light of all this snarling war greed, Pitt's famous speech must be read – carefully. He started uncharacteristically with plain candour his grandfather would have applauded: 'When trade is at stake, it is your last entrenchment; you must defend it or perish.' He then moved to moral top C, and endeavoured to stay there. He was shocked at the Commons motion bearing the King's name on its letterhead. How shaming that ministers were 'cowering and taking sanctuary in the royal name'. The Speaker was told,[12] 'Sir, you have been moved to vote an humble Address of thanks to His Majesty for a measure which will appear to gentlemen's conversation as odious throughout the kingdom . . . that, low unalloyed condition abroad which is now made a plea for the Convention.' Members should

firstly try to defend on its own merits and if that is not tenable, through general terrors; the House of Bourbon is united, who knows the consequence of a war? Sir, Spain knows the consequences of a war for America: whoever gains, it must prove fatal to her. She knows it and must therefore avoid it; but she knows England does not dare to make it.

* A palace outside Madrid, venue for the negotiations.

And what is a delay . . . to produce? Can it produce such conjectures? as those you lost while you are giving kingdoms to Spain . . . But be it what it will, is this any longer a nation, or what is an English parliament, if with more ships in your harbours than in all the navies of Europe, with above two millions of people in your American colonies, you will bear to hear of the expediency of receiving from Spain an insecure, unsatisfactory and dishonourable Convention?

Sir, as to the great national objection, the searching your ships, it stands there in the Preamble as in the reproach of the whole, as the strongest evidence of the submission that follows: on the part of Spain an usurpation, an inhuman tyranny claimed and exercised over the American seas. In God and Nature declared and asserted with Resolution of parliament are referred to the discussion of plenipotentiaries upon one and the same equal foot.

The Court of Spain has plainly told you . . . you shall steer a due course, a line to and from your plantations in America if you draw near to her coasts . . . you shall be seized and confiscated . . .

I wish we could hide it from the eyes of every court in Europe; they see Spain has talked to you like your master; they see it must stand a pre-eminence of Shame as a part even of this Convention.

This Convention Sir, I think from my soul is nothing but a stipulation of national ignominy; an illusory expedient to baffle the resentment of the nation; . . . the complaints of your despairing merchants, the voice of England has condemned it; be the guilt of it upon the head of the adviser. God forbid that this committee should share the Guilt by approving it.

God is here invoked and rattled, an extension to the general intimidation. Read cold, read in any way, this is a dreadful speech, one defined by livid adjectives and equestrian abstract nouns: 'shaming', 'odious', 'inhuman', 'dishonourable', 'despairing', 'Guilt', 'shame', 'master', 'soul', 'ignominy', 'tyranny' and, indeed, 'God'.

It asks a stadium orator's questions: 'Is this any longer a nation?' It does menace: 'Spain knows the consequences to her.' It conjures images as grotesque as false: 'giving kingdoms to Spain'. Amid all the honour talk, it chiefly speaks strength and the prospect of using it, brutally, on someone else: 'more ships in your harbours than in all the navies of Europe'. This is St Jingo's Eve with that passage as a more pompous version of 'We've got the ships, we've got the men. We've got the money too.' Actually, it is worse. The central message is that conciliation and peaceful settlement are dishonourable to blood and nation when the means for waging successful aggressive war are at hand. Pitt would be praised as another Demosthenes. But this is an eloquence in which one might have clothed the mindset of Kaiser Wilhelm II.

To say that Walpole's reply makes an interesting contrast understates things. Walpole was a great Parliament man, a natural speaker. But he had no head for emotional heights, never ventured up the register and kept his soul out of debate. His response to Pitt's war music was rebuke, reasoned quietly through. But he began with a statement of his purpose in government:[13]

Sir, the greatest honour I expect in succeeding times is that it shall be mentioned that I, a Minister, endeavoured by this Convention to extricate my country out of the most disagreeable situation she perhaps ever was in, that of going to war with a nation with whom it is her greatest interest to be at peace . . .

. . . In this situation Sir, we have but a melancholy prospect of success . . . If we were indeed free of debt, if the nation were united with itself; if we had nothing to dread but from Spain, I should be very little apprehensive about the consequences of our declaring war at present . . . I can easily perceive by what arts and by whose means, all the clamour about this convention has been raised; but I am resolved while I have the honour to serve his Majesty in the Station I am in, to let no popular clamour judge the better of what I think is my country's good.

Nay, if I had nothing but my own ease and interest to consult, it would be the safest and most advantageous measure for me that could be pursued; but I shall never be for sacrificing our real interests in the pursuit of military glory . . . I shall always be against leaving it in [soldiers'] breasts to decide the questions of peace and war. This nation . . . is a trading nation and the prosperity of her trade is what ought to be first in the eye of every Gentleman in this House. Therefore Gentlemen . . . ought to consider whether our declaring war will be for the benefit of our trade . . . and whether a successful war with Spain may not involve us in a very doubtful, and a very expensive one with other powers.

These are considerations which, while gentlemen are debating on these subjects, never once seem to enter their thoughts . . . they lay it down as a maxim that we ought immediately to enter into a war. Have we no regard for these treaties? . . . They provide that the navigation to the Spanish West Indies shall be reserved to the Spanish alone excepting the case of our South Sea Company's trade. Has this stipulation no manner of meaning?

Pray what is the plain English of this? nought but that the trade to the Spanish West Indies ought to be open to every interloper of ours . . . and very likely, not only of approaching these coverts but of hovering upon them as long as we please.

This Sir, is the plain English of what the gentlemen who are for a war with Spain advance.

The eighteenth century believed in the 'Balance of Power'. The notion would become a historical cliché, but there was serious thinking behind it, thinking which underwrote the mild line of Walpole and Keene. Of course the Spanish were being unreasonable, conducting diplomacy resentfully on a basis of sclerotic contempt for give and take. Even so, going to war with them was quite as irrational and much more destructive. Pares quotes a speech by Newcastle:[14]

[The European powers] knew that while the treasures of the Indies were the property of the Spaniards or at least while they were centred in Spain, that sooner or later their subjects must have a proportionable share; because that monarchy is destitute of many of the advantages which the other nations of Europe enjoy from their manufactures and the industry of their inhabitants; and consequently, it was not in the power of the Spaniards, let them have never such an aspiring and politic prince at their head, to monopolize these treasures.

Whereas should too large a share of them come into the hands of any other nation in Europe, whose situation, power or trade render them perhaps already formidable to their neighbours, they might be employed to purposes inconsistent with the peace of Europe . . . In such a case, there is no doubt but that a formidable case would be made against the power thus aspiring; and should the differences at last come to be made up by a treaty, it would be found that the most probable best way to secure the peace is to suffer the Spaniards to

remain in the same situation, as to their American settlements as they
are now in.[15]

In other words, great wealth in militarily weak hands will come round
by way of general trade. The same wealth in strong, ambitious hands
will make a dangerous concentration of power against which other
countries will league themselves and probably go to war. And by
'strong and ambitious hands', Newcastle meant France.

There was great sense there. Adult thinking about the current Indies
navigation impasse would turn upon what parallel conflicts it might
create. By contrast, Pitt entertained no hint of a thought about the
international contingencies of a war with Spain. He had confined
himself in patriotic fashion to 'the complaints of your despairing
merchants, the voice of England', otherwise the West Indian slave and
sugar lobby.

His and the lobby's parlimentary allies would now stand the
Newcastle speech on its head. Because of the risk of general war from
a conflict with Spain, we should pre-emptively bully the dangerous
French by accelerating that war against Spain. Specifically, argued the
Duke of Argyll, now detaching himself from Walpole, Britain's naval
supremacy allowed us to beat everybody so we might dictate all terms
to every trading country.[16] If Argyll made a cool case for bullying, Pitt
worked a handy alternative, fear. If France protected Spain from us,
then the hateful Bourbons were resisting an absolute right of navigation, and war became a moral imperative as well as an obvious pleasure.

There is something deeply odious about the British war camp, a
lust for wealth, fearful contempt and hatred for the European neighbours, a brutal nationalism pre-echoing twentieth-century models.
Contrariwise, Walpole had never looked so sensible, rational and, in
the fullest sense, statesmanlike. It was not simply an earnest application of his dictum, *quieta non movere*, with dogs (or dragons)
encouraged to rest. He had a vivid anxiety about a reanimated France.
He had, admittedly, often used fear of the French as invading allies
of the Jacobites as a domestic political weapon. Which did not mean
that there was not a rational fear of this menacing conjunction
coming about.

In his excellent study of the Jacobites,[17] Frank McLynn, unlike Pitt,
identifies a formidable, latent threat. But as they acknowledged when

writing to the Pretender's court, like the conspiring Bishop Atterbury Jacobite success needed a foreign army. Walpole, guardian of the Revolution settlement and general stability, sincerely feared it. And in the midst of the hostilities now contemplated, the '45 happened. A better coordination of French military support then might perfectly well have landed men at Southampton as Charles Edward reached Derby.

The Opposition, Patriots, Pulteney Whigs, Leicester House and the West Indies lobby also rolled this drum, but as a call to fear, a war stimulant. Interestingly, the long-pacific Tories joined the crowd. Their leader, Wyndham, so readily seen as a crypto-Jacobite, now argued for a French war. French neutrality, ran the banner headline, was a sham above any imaginable legitimate claim, so it was best challenged by attacking Spain.[18] Those who were not for us were against us. The war party were exultant, the tone somewhere between Gilbert's Dick Dauntless and Mussolini.

However, as one historian of this war says, 'Much of the outcry raised against the agreement [the Convention of Pardo] and the Government in 1739, however, was at bottom little more than a struggle for office, an effort by one set of politicians to oust another.'[19] The armed aggression party would get their war, partly through a pantomime of shock and outrage, culminating in the nonsense of a merchant captain, Robert Jenkins, waving at a Commons committee a handful of cotton wool supposedly containing his ear, equally supposedly sliced off by *Guardas Costas*. Beckford, who, says Lord Shelburne, had set up the performance, 'has frequently assured me that if any member had had the fancy to have lifted up his wig, they would have found his ears as whole as their own'.[20] Such horror shows reinforced the 'democratic' element, a flotilla of petitions applauded by the Street. The war, when it came, would be mob-made.

This was a state of affairs deadly to Walpole. He understood that you couldn't conduct a war of piracy on the Spanish Fleet without stealing cargoes belonging to other people, notably the French. The greater part of what Spanish ships carried exemplified Newcastle's earlier point. Spain's wealth, given her weak home economy, went round her trading partners. *Azogues*, modest-sized but deliciously loaded ships, commonly carried silver, often bespoke as trading payment to French merchants. Even sensible Cardinal Fleury could not shrug off such assaults. Meanwhile, Walpole, dragged into a war

he did not want, could not call off predators who were also fighting.
Two pacific men found themselves contemplating conflict.

Fleury, meanwhile, was told nothing of the Pardo detail, rational
dealing after his own heart. There was, too, at this time, another piece
of royal foolishness, a proposed match between the two and already
over-related Bourbon branches, a double marriage treaty. It was done
against Fleury's wishes and beyond his authority. However, English
prejudice, anti-Catholic, anti-French and determined to be cheated, cast
the cardinal as another foreign Machiavel. The assumption, delightful
to Oppositionists, was that the cardinal had wanted war all along. We
would now be fighting France and Spain, so that would be all right.

In domestic terms, the war fever was destructive, not alone of
Walpole's policy but of Walpole. He put conflict off as long as he
could. An actual vote on the Pardo Convention, Keene's wound to
the soul of Pitt, was indeed won on 9 March 1739 by twenty-eight,
won by Walpolean methods with the payroll providing a full-strength
chorus. Of the 260 voting with the government, 234 were, in one
form or another, holders of place and remuneration. As Wiggins
shows in his cool study of the Grenvilles, families voted in family
patterns: Pelhams, Walpoles, Herberts and Claytons approving the
Convention, Bathursts, Noels and all but one of the Finches voting
against it. The Grenvilles and their extended kin, Patriots and men
out of place, also voted solidly against.[21]

As parliamentary divisions went, it could have been choreographed.
But certain parties now left the dance. Sir William Wyndham, in ballet
terms always a *balero nobilo*, statuesque, dignified but not quick on
his feet, now achieved the ultimate high-minded nonsense. He had
walked out before. Now he walked out again, proclaiming in his best
Lord Cardigan-at-the-charge manner, 'I have seen with the utmost
concern this shameful, this fatal measure, approved by a majority of
but 28, and I now rise to pay my last duty to my country as a member
of this house.' He thought the Walpole Whigs had been only 'a faction
against the liberties and properties of their fellow subjects'.[22]

This last curl of the lip outraged the normally relaxed Henry Pelham
to unPelham-like fury. But Walpole, recognising the self-destructive
impetus propelling Wyndham, pulled him back from superfluous
response. Pelham was rising in Walpole's esteem and, after the hop
and skip of the next ministry, would become his approved long-term

successor. He was receiving a master class in leaving fools to their folly. Wyndham was not just walking out, but taking the Tory member-ship with him. Further, he had intimated that he would not return, the very last way to run a political railway. He would indeed play no further part. Never much of a man for this world, Wyndham, in 1740, at fifty-two, departed for the next.

Walpole's luck was running down but he still got flashes of it. A majority of 'only 28', in Wyndham's ingenuous words, was enough for now, but not promising. Public opinion was overwhelmingly for the war. Just under two hundred years before Munich, it was that episode's perfect reverse, war at any price. There were, too, long and excessively complicated misunderstandings over the despatches of Waldegrave, Ambassador at Paris, and, like Wyndham, dying, as to fierce things said by Fleury pro forma which Waldegrave had read literally, resigning ministers to French involvement.

The 'War of Jenkins's Ear', as the early part of this long struggle, was in train. And it would be more difficult for Walpole to keep the same hand on power after the early disappointments which, in classic British style, we would soon encounter. An election was due in 1741, which in terms of a lower land tax and concern for Jacobite plots, he could realistically expect to win.

The Cobham faction was not hoping for too much. George Lyttleton, close to Pitt at this time, tried to work the Prince of Wales into supporting the war they all wanted, which meant no more railing and caballing against his father's Minister, while they did everything to confound its conduct. Young Horace Walpole wrote to a friend that 'notwithstanding the appearance of unanimity to carry on the war, the patriots and opponents are resolved to give us as much trouble as they can'.[23] As indeed some of them would try to. Chesterfield, the antithesis of Patriot feeling, but Walpole's steady, dedicated enemy, urged Lyttleton to urge Cobham to regroup the enemy's enemies in a coherent force. It was, though, mostly talk. The factions of opposi-tion were quarrellers, *grupuscules*, and they never listened to one another.

As long as policy was determined in the seven-year parliament (begun in 1734) remote from the Excise reversal, Walpole would not be defeated, not even if the Tories organised themselves competently. Within the ministry, Walpole's authority could be undermined by the combustible conduct of King Philip and the South Sea Company. Philip, in his febrile way, had talked about cancelling the *Asiento* at mere face value. The South Sea then refused to repay their charge of £68,000. Intended as a ploy, this was a detonation charge. Philip, absolute monarch and wrong in the head, withheld his first obligation to pay, then, as further and better particular, *did* suspend the *Asiento*. By international law, this act broke the Treaty of Utrecht. More important, it inflamed public opinion. The British war press now indulged in a familiar bout of 'Clamour'. In hope of getting in some quick hits, Admiral Haddock had been told by Newcastle rather airily to 'go out and commit all sorts of hostilities by sea'.[24]

Newcastle, like a good many people, was now running nervously ahead of Clamour, and had become tentatively disposed to this war, as he had to the Polish Succession affair. Relations between Britain and Spain lacked clarity. Was this straightforwardly a drawing of the sword or a rattling of the scabbard? If it were a real conflict, then, politically, this was no way to be doing things. A war with a bad beginning fought by a ministry facing an election in a few months was not a good idea.

The chance of a parliamentary explosion was supposed to have come after the early customary reverses, with a motion in February 1741 – a 'personal motion' as it was called – demanding the dismissal of Sir Robert Walpole. It was bold, defiant, all the things recommended to politicians in at the kill. The majority of 'only 28' for the Convention, the last testing vote, intimated possibilities for the next, and much steeper, one. No one, indeed, expected a majority *against* the Prime Minister or even parity with the one registered over that uniquely contentious agreement with Spain. If, however, the Opposition were to come within, say, fifty or sixty, they could call it a moral victory and go back to digging.

Even without Wyndham, the Tories couldn't get it right. Only thirty-four of them walked out in the usual high-toned, pointless way. Most of the rest voted *with* Walpole. What should have been 219 votes cast against the Minister had crumbled to 106, the majority rising from 28 to 184. Even the calling of a division at all, said an onlooker, had depended upon 'the eager warmth of Mr Lyttleton'.[25] George Lyttleton, the most disinterested of Cobham's Cubs, was also Pitt's closest friend. There is, though, no record of Pitt himself plunging into debate in 1740–41.

A fundamental cause of defeat was a disinclination among the Opposition Whigs to vote with the Tories. Bad feeling between Pulteney and Wyndham (and it was very bad feeling) had contributed. Then again the impetus from the Prince of Wales had diminished as Frederick, though still devotedly courted, cut a diminishing figure. No longer wronged by George's vengeful stinginess, he looked like an amateur politician with a grudge. Pitt's position as a uniformed courtier at Leicester House did him no good. Lord Shelburne dismissed Frederick – utterly: 'The prince's activity could only be equalled by his childishness and his falsehood. His life was such a tissue of both as could only serve to show that there is nothing which mankind will not put up with where power is lodged.'[26]

A place at Leicester House was equity for a man like Bubb Dodington to swap for minor office. William's sponsoring brother, Thomas, falling out with the Grenvilles, had grown close to Frederick, yet his campaign for a prized seat in Cornwall where Frederick was landholder and Duke would fail at ruinous cost. Indeed, if Walpole should fall, he would not be replaced by Patriots, Prince's men or Tories but by what might be called the Established Opposition. Defeated he would be in the end – by the interaction of a lagging war and a general election. Eighteenth-century elections took time, and winners did not come in wearing regimental colours. It would, though, soon be possible to discover a tilt, seats clearly lost by the ministry and taken either by plain oppositionists or men amenable to conversation with the managers. There were in any House of Commons men come to trade, to see what the Minister could give them, set beside Opposition promises. They made their final decisions on the security of those making offers.

James Oswald, commanding a majority of the eighty-eight voters of Dysart Boroughs, had run as a Walpole man. Arriving in Westminster and holding a finger to the wind, he deserted on a key vote of 21 January, meeting reproach with brazen reproach. 'You had like to have led me into a fine error. Did you not tell me that Sir R. would have the majority?' Oswald, as Sedgwick's great catalogue of MPs entering Parliament between 1715 and 1754* tells us, would hold remunerated ministerial office for nineteen of his twenty-seven years

* *The House of Commons, 1715–1754.*

in Parliament. The gap was due chiefly to a Place Act affecting his Commissionership of the Navy.

An acknowledged source puts the ministry's new immediate majority at eighteen, against forty-two in the late parliament.[27] The real test, however, came with petitions disputing election counts. In an age of panoramic corruption, there would always be plenty to complain of, impersonation, qualified voters not recognised by returning officers partisan or remunerated, and cash transactions blatant enough to be identified.

Without being too sweeping about it, the conformation or unseating of new Members petitioned against turned upon the votes of confirmed MPs cast for a single Commons office. This was not the Speakership. Arthur Onslow, in the Chair until 1760, really was unassailable. What mattered was the chairmanship of the Privileges and Elections Committee, essentially for the next proceedings, the whole House in Committee. The occupant since 1727 had been Gyles Earle, Member for and owner of Malmesbury. Also, and gratifyingly, a Lord of the Treasury and for eleven years a commissioner of Irish Revenue, he was a candid, rough-mouthed Walpolean. His wit, according to Horace Walpole, had been dealt out 'largely at the Scotch and the Patriots'.[28]

William Pulteney, leader of Opposition to Walpole for some time and running this operation, brought forward a milder candidate, milk against Earle's Madras, in Dr George Lee, a Church lawyer originally from Buckinghamshire, largely Grenville territory, but nominee in Brackley, Northants, of the Duke of Bridgwater. On 16 December, by a majority of four, Lee was chosen. The King, thoroughly disconcerted, forgot his crotchets against Walpole, allegedly offering his eldest son places in a Walpole Ministry for his Patriot friends.[29] The bid was rejected and elaborate bargaining continued across Christmas 1741 and New Year 1742.

Lee's chairmanship, though not charged with blatant favour to Opposition petitions, was not that of a man knowing his duty to pursue Walpole's interest. A government petition at Berwick was rejected on 18 January. Accordingly, on 21 January, Pulteney put down a motion, calling for a committee, to be called, without euphemism, the Committee of Accusation. Debate continued. Everyone joined in: Pulteney; Sir William Yonge, chief prime ministerial henchman; Pitt, his coming rival; Henry Fox and Walpole himself. A future major

Opposition talent (and Prime Minister), the ablest of the Grenvilles, George, made a speech which impressed.

The Prime Minister narrowly survived, but on procedural votes the game was being lost incrementally. Finally, a petition by ministerialist candidates had urged that the two successful opposition victors of Chippenham (Burgage tenure franchise, 130 voters), Edward Bayntun Rolt and Sir Edmund Thomas, had used armed men for intimidation, almost commonplace in the unreformed Parliament then, by way of a flourish, arresting the Whig sheriff! Despite probable truth, on 2 February 1742, that petition failed by sixteen votes. The instincts of all the Oswalds in the House, men mindful of the winning side, were instructed.

Walpole knew the score. His biographer, Coxe, says that he beckoned Rolt '. . . to sit near him, spoke to him and with great complacency animadverted on the great ingratitude of certain individuals who were voting against him on whom he had conferred great favours', and declared he should never again sit in that House.[30] Next day, he went to the grieving King and it was agreed to adjourn the House for a fortnight while a new ministry was formed. Walpole became Earl of Orford, and very soon attempts to impeach him, in which William Pitt played a charmless part, were begun.

Meanwhile, Lee accepted a salaried seat on the Board of Admiralty. He was told by Bridgwater that if he took it he would never represent Brackley again. Nor did he, being found a seat in Devizes to which he shortly transferred.[31]

The new government reflected George II's observation, 'I see I have two shops to deal with.' Under the formal leadership of Lord Wilmington, who as Sir Spencer Compton had fumbled things in 1727 when the new king had wanted to replace Walpole, a ministry of outs was assembled. There were some distinguished ones. William Pulteney, despite sound Whiggism, had been kept out of government on merit – too good for subordination. In Opposition, he had worked with the Grenvilles, but never trustingly. If Walpole was the first Prime Minister, Pulteney, over a decade or so, has a claim to have been the first Leader of the Opposition.

The title 'Earl Granville' was the later inheritance of John, Lord Carteret, whom long since Walpole and his brother Horatio had destroyed by tedious intrigue over a royal niece's fiancé denied a French dukedom. Like Pulteney, he had been too able. As cosmopolitan and

German-speaker, he was the most European-minded politician at Westminster, sympathetically alert to threats facing Hanover, the preoccupation of both Georges. Wilmington, according to one of Pitt's biographers, had been put into the Prime Minister's place by Walpole as personal protection – indemnity against vengeful pursuit also, irresistibly, to deny Carteret.[32]

If so, this was wisely considered. Vengeful pursuit was in a number of minds, none so vengeful as William Pitt's. A (secret) committee of enquiry should be set up though the vote to establish it was narrow, 252 to 245. Pitt hungered and thirsted to be on it. He was nearly denied: the twenty-one Committee members were chosen by the House. The first choice received 518 votes; Pitt, with 259, was the second last to scramble on. It is a point to remember against the back-formation thinking identifying a precocious hero.

Coxe speaks of him in the preliminary debate about holding an enquiry or not, indulging 'all the baneful spirit of party':[33] 'I fear not to declare', the thirty-three-year-old orator began a rolling effusion, 'that I expect in consequence of any such enquiry, to find that our treasure has been exhausted, not to humble our enemies or to obviate domestic insurrections, not to support our allies or to suppress our factions; but for purposes which no man who loves his country can think of without indignation, the purchase of votes, the bribing of boroughs, the enriching of hirelings, the multiplying of dependants and the corruption of parliaments.'[34]

It was true as far as it went, true probably further. Walpole had done very well for himself in ways quite as mysterious as those attributed to the Lord. Nobody would ever find out quite how the transformation, decoration and enrichment with Old Masters of Houghton had been achieved. Secret service money had been so extensively lavished that when Henry Pelham, Walpole's later (and Walpolean) successor, came to do the job, he managed it very satisfactorily on half as much. Walpole had been corrupt and had cheerfully corrupted men into voting for the government. He had also been immaculately sane. He was quite incapable of making such a preposterous speech as Pitt's latest. In it the abstract nouns tumble about, the clichés are proudly set up – 'hirelings' are, of course, 'enriched'. And we meet again Pitt loving his country, which turns up like a favourite dog whenever possible. And it goes to work with the leitmotif of the man's style, 'Indignation': 'purposes which no man who loves his country can think of without indignation'. This is not Demosthenes, it is cod-Latin Englished into oration.

The vengefulness was not wanting either. Pitt, fearing misplaced moderation, got his gloating in early. He insisted that 'we must enquire unless we wish to sacrifice our liberties and the liberties of Europe to the preservation of one guilty man.' He also talked about removing him to the other side of the City – to the Tower; adding the extraordinary judgement that Walpole 'deserved to be deprived not only of his office but his life'. All this, of course, as the normally sympathetic Sherrard rightly points out, came after the construction of a new government in which Pitt had not been included. The call for revenge was significantly different from Walpole's own pursuit of Robert Harley into the Tower, and in hopes of better, twenty five-years earlier. That had been in deadly earnest and highly ideological. Charles II had sent Sidney and Russell, close kin of Walpole's mentor, Edward Russell, Lord Orford (first creation), to the block. The conflict which resolved Stuart and Hanover carried overtones of the civil war which bloodless revolution had averted. Pitt's cries for blood were grand opera, a recurring indulgence.

The exaltation was too early, as it happened, for any punishment. Walpole's 'hirelings' proved very close-mouthed and uncooperative. Nicholas Paxton, bagman, which is to say Treasury Solicitor, to Walpole, observed client confidentiality to the point of going to jail. John Scrope, an elderly gentlemen over whose desk everything relating to Secret Service money passed, was offered immunity and spurned it. Which was wise as the Immunity Bill, pre-conditional to getting anything on Walpole, was thrown out in the Lords. Eventually the pursuers lost heart, and Walpole lived free to be involved rather usefully in an advisory capacity. The new government did next to nothing for the Patriots. Cobham, indeed, was restored to his honours and raised to the rank of Field Marshal. Lyttleton, who had invested the Patriot cause with a touching belief,* would later write that 'Patriotism has been made the dupe of ambition'.[35]

With the ministry itself constructed of four groupings, politics became more Namierite than ever, factions forming around not only

---

* An American wrote a biography of him called *The Good Lord Lyttleton*.

the Grenvilles, but the Bedfords and followers respectively of Argyll and Chesterfield. Ambitious politicians were milling about in loose formation. Some might be used, others put off. Yet others might go to Leicester House and court the Prince of Wales, where, to his disgust, the winner of that speech-day contest in praise of splendid Frederick remained. At Leicester House, Pitt was actually looking at applications for employment in this below-stairs quarter of politics. He might be adored by fellow Patriots, one of whom, Richard Grenville, the future Lord Temple, described him as 'speaking like ten thousand angels', but beyond such raptures he was kicking his heels.

Walpole, now Earl of Orford, had spoken to Henry Pelham, very much his horse in the longer race, against showing kindness to Grenville or the Patriots. And Pitt did nothing to gain favour from a ministry quite as close to the King and Hanover as Walpole had been. On 10 December 1742, speaking in a debate on the war relating to Hanoverian troop subsidies, Pitt made his famous remark about 'this province of a despicable electorate'. It got into the school books. But like so many of his words, it would have to be eaten.

7

Carteret, Pelham and Yellow Fever

The war into which Walpole had walked backwards would go interminably on to no very satisfactory purpose, the ministry succeeding him being made and remade. It was a dance which, unlike the Excise Bill, would, however erratically, go further. It had begun with much talk of reform which, if accomplished, would have done credit to the talk. The sum of it was to sack the uncommunicative Paxton and pass a Place Bill concerned only with *little* places whose holders were now kept out of Parliament. The Indemnity Act, as noted, was killed in the Lords. Talk of a Triennial Act, like the one which had made the parliaments of 1690–1722 so enjoyable, came to nothing.

As for the War of the Austrian Succession, it was a strange, multifaceted affair, a series of mixed doubles, many of the bouts fought on separate courts. For reasons respectively greedy and atavistic, England and Spain engaged, with much rubbish on our side about Jesuits, Inquisition and Protestant Succession. The folly of Elizabeth Farnese now matched the wind-bagging militarism of the Patriots and plantation owners. In the German-speaking world, the death of Frederick William I of Prussia, who combined military values he imposed on his small nation with an army too good, too glitteringly war-sharp actually to use, would change all that.

His heir, who had narrowly escaped the axe for attempted flight from Frederick William's brutish *Soldatenschaft* of a court, but had been made to watch his dearest friend suffer it, now succeeded as Frederick II. His court would be cultivated, musical, literary, Francophile (and Francophone), amenable to Voltairean free thought and awash with long-visiting deep thinkers. As for Frederick, he aimed, by taking the fine soldiers out of their box, to replace Austria as top nation in Germany.

His father, militarily overequipped to no clear purpose, had always treated the Habsburgs with punctilio. Accordingly, he had signed up to the Pragmatic Sanction which allowed Maria Theresia – right blood-line, wrong sex – to succeed her father, Charles VI, to the Imperial Crown despite operation in the Empire of Salic Law requiring a male line. When Charles died in the same year, Frederick hurried at in-decent speed to denounce this commitment as against moral law and invade Silesia. Maria Theresia was set back anyway by an electoral court which, under French influence, chose the Elector of Bavaria to break, for the interim, the long unbeaten run of Habsburg selection as Charles VII. The rank was titular, the war real. Maria Theresia settled for the first of a family list of residual titles as Queen of Hungary. Her army and generals (including the Irishman, Maximilian von Browne), and the family's narrowly Austrian revenues, she kept. The British, at war with her alternative enemy France, would become her allies in Europe.

Religion didn't really come into either of these conflicts but it suited the English, allied to Catholic Austria, to invoke Drake, the Armada, sacraments in two kinds only, also the role of victim favoured by so many aggressors. Frederick, deist and homosexual, went through the rhetoric of the Thirty Years War. More to the point, Catholic Spain had a mighty grievance against Austria since Utrecht where Austria, like England, a great winner, had picked up Milan and Naples.

The French had tried to sit the thing out, but Louis XV and his ministers were tied by the Family Compact, fear of which had det-onated Marlborough's wars, much as one might be tied to a fifty-six-pound weight at the margins of a river. Cardinal Fleury, tediously but rightly called 'the French Walpole', faced the same plague as Sir Robert, a war party avid for its sport. English aggression against Spain – and what else was it? – strengthened that party's hand. There was, too, a colonial element, Canadian and West Indian, in French thinking apt in a war against Spain's enemy, England. But with the English courting the Austrians, George II having accepted Maria Theresia's legitimacy, there would be pickings for France not least in Flanders/Wallonia, in an Austrian defeat. The reasons for war, none of them except Austria's creditable, were assembled.

George, concerned as to what travails British clamour and scram-bling for overseas trade might commit Hanover, was, electorally speaking, against it. And working through sympathetic ministers, especially Carteret (Granville by inheritance in 1744), the King achieved the contentious objective of Hanoverian neutrality. Frederick's father had yearned for the disputed Hanoverian territories of Julich-Berg. Young Frederick might take them. The King of England was at war with Prussia, the Elector of Hanover was not. With Austria and Prussia anxious to enlist or invade their neighbours in geographical Germany, that might be local wisdom – and it enraged more people than the Patriots. It pulled England deeper into Austrian commit-ment than she ought to go and fuelled the anti-Hanoverianism in which Pitt would swim. George, very Habsburgtreu, risked, says Paul Langford, committing England to 'No Peace without Silesia' in echo of the forty-year-earlier deadweight of 'No Peace without Spain'.[1]

Actually, the European war began better than it continued. In 1743, George famously led a successful charge at Dettingen. He was leading a medley of troops against superior forces under a serious hero, the Duc de Noailles. When an immediate address from the Commons congratulated him on escaping injury and death in the fight, Pitt's response would be crass. He met early notice of an uncontested piece of brave soldiery by suggesting the Commons withhold customary courtesy until the dangers could be checked. 'Suppose Sir', said Pitt, 'it should appear that His Majesty was exposed to few or no dangers abroad, but those to which he is daily liable at home, such as the over-turning of his coach or the stumbling of his horse, would not the address proposed, instead of being a compliment, be an affront and insult to the Sovereign?'[2] This was sour bad manners. George, with all his faults of temper, resentment and excessive Hanoverianism, was an almost absurdly brave man.

At Dettingen, the King had led a cavalry charge into French ranks and fire. Pitt talked up war, but his soldiering had amounted to knocking about a home barracks for fourteen months, something lightened by stretches of open-ended leave for foreign travel. His comments reflected not only hatred of Hanover and the King, but resentment of qualities never tested in him. This is not the knockabout invective of Opposition, like Churchill's quips against Attlee, nor sincere anger provoked by falsehood, witness Gaitskell and Denis Healey on Eden. It was perfect spite.

The King might not have exploited victory at Dettingen as fully as

strategically minded historians think he should, but it seriously affected
the course of the war – for Maria Theresia. She could now invoke the
natural anti-French and -Spanish pact with Sardinia. After France's
Bavarian nominee Emperor died in 1745 her husband, Franz, took the
imperial title, offsetting Silesian reversals. She could bow out and, at
the peace agreed at Dresden in December 1745, could call it all a draw.

The naval war stumbled on. Admiral Haddock had been sent to
blockade Cadiz, stop a Spanish army sailing from Barcelona to Italy
and stop French supplies for Spain from Toulon – far too many things
for thirteen ships to do. Thirteen warships to conduct three separate
operations against the twenty-seven of France and Spain's alliance was
flat impossible. When, in November 1741, Spanish soldiers disembarked
in Italy, Newcastle indulged his worst fault and unjustly blamed
Haddock who, unsurprisingly, had a nervous breakdown.

Meanwhile, Admiral Sir Edward Vernon, populist MP, valiant sailor,
national hero and impossible colleague, had been sent to the coast of
present-day Venezuela to blockade Puerto Bello* where he had enjoyed
a brief, brilliant but prize-free victory in 1739, and to try for Cuba
which, as he put it in his newsletter, 'will give us the key to the West
Indies'. This would show the Spaniards that 'they shall in great measure
depend upon us, the chief Maritime Power, for the very possession
of their Indies'.[3]

Vernon and the government seemed to have forgotten Admiral
Hosier, sent in 1726-7 on that earlier naval mission mentioned above
to blockade Puerto Bello, who, with eight captains and three thousand men, died of the mosquito-borne, supercharged jaundice called
yellow fever. Apart from personally surviving, Vernon simply repeated
history. He and his naval colleague Ogle and General Wentworth fell
furiously, predictably and terminally out. Sickness broke out and by
the end of the expedition in late November, only two thousand troops
were left fit for service.

The griefs of Haddock and Vernon were not the only bad news
at sea. What might have been a victory, the encounter off Toulon on
22 February 1744 of British ships and a combined French and Spanish
force, was bungled by early abandonment. Admiral Matthews is reckoned to have been badly let down by his second in command, Lestock.

* In English, Portobello.

The courts martial exonerated the junior man and cashiered the senior, though both seem to have been fairly ineffective and at spitting odds. In fairness, a modern historian of the 1740–48 war points out, the encounter marked the end of both Spanish and French ventures out of port in this war.[4] Even so, the British naval supremacy which would come down in majesty at the end of the next decade was some way off.

Ironically, the Patriots had wanted a war against Spain for an enlarged slave and sugar trade. It was going very poorly and the heroic rhetoric of Pitt and Vernon was being destroyed by repetition of last time's mistakes. Meanwhile, the war was taking its own shape. France, tied as she was to Spain, had formally come in as first observer then helpmeet, finally, 29 March 1744, full belligerent.

Pitt at this point was a backbench advocate of naval belligerence and bitter opponent of all continental involvement. He was responsible for nothing but his opinions, and his opinions were wrong. Naval activity was getting nowhere but it was bringing France into the conflict. However, by a charming irony it was a distinguished sailor who had early called out loud for a continental land war. Admiral Norris, fearing defeat against a united France and Spain, wrote,[5] 'I told Sir Robert Walpole I thought the best way to embarrass France was to endeavour to get some four score thousand men into Flanders without reckoning on the Dutch that would then be obliged to come in . . . and were I in Sir Robert Walpole's place, I would by March have an army of 80 thousand men in Flanders and the Emperor in Naples . . . the greatest hope of success is success against France.' If this sounds like geo-political doodling, it is also the sort of exponential military thinking which follows wars begun without first thinking seriously about them. Almost everything that was happening in the war made, remade and underlined Walpole's aversion.

Given an overstretched navy, we were caught up in a continental balance of power conflict with large commitments to Austria. Carteret might be building an alliance against French domination which Patriots (and patriots) might have cheered, but it looked like the prelude to all-out European war, much more than the people ringing their bells in 1740 had bargained for. They might not quite be wringing their hands, but they were thoroughly discontented and they blamed the government.

The government, having favoured war, would be judged by its

progress. Opposition, meanwhile, and very quickly, became anti-Hanoverian, anti-German and anti-George. There had been from early days subsidies to German states for troops and specifically payment for 16,000 Hanoverians. Money seems to have been resented by Patriots in eighteenth-century London rather more than blood. Hanover payments moved Pitt to the speech in November 1742 described by Richard Grenville as sounding 'like ten thousand angels'. He announced that 'this great, this formidable kingdom is considered only as a province to a despicable electorate'.[6] Pitt had either not read or not taken notice of Admiral Norris. Having got into a war which France had always been overwhelmingly likely to join against us, we actually needed the continental allies, mercenaries and hired small states who might offset French domination.

If the insult to his courage made the King loathe the sight of him, Pitt's description of Carteret was hardly more rational. Mouthing resentment from the sidelines, the Chief Patriot denounced him 'an execrable, a sole minister and a Hanover troop minister'.[7] Pitt's snarling remarks used to be quoted with admiration as the eloquence of a great man. It is also argued that of course this was just the invective of an ambitious young man. This is an indulgent treatment of the unbalanced rage with a mild charge of opportunism, of boys being boys and politics, politics.

Both the charge and the fulsome recantation when Carteret died nineteen years later are too vivid, too poster-painted for that. In 1770 the name of the dead statesman shifted in Pitt's judgement from 'Hanover troop minister', also 'execrable and sole minister practising absolutism', to something quite other. 'His abilities did Honour to this House [the Lords] and to this nation. In the upper departments of government he had not his equal. And I feel a pride in declaring that to his patronage, to his friendship and instruction, I owe whatever I am.'[8] 'Fulsome' hardly says it. Whatever the time lag and the call of convention, unreasoning rapture has followed uncontainable hatred with unconsidered facility.

The first statement is most kindly explained in terms of Pitt's physical illness and the extreme pain it inflicted. The second, though high-flown and baroque, may mark their absence. The early self-damaging talk followed wild impulses and verbalised rage out of reach. It was also terrible politics. High passion in Pitt was destructive. There was a touch here of the madness to come. The charges were also nonsense.

As Paul Langford points out, Carteret, so readily abused as the tool of Hanover, was none of the things charged. His purpose was rational and nothing any serious patriot should have complained about, the great, continuing preoccupation of British foreign policy over a couple of centuries, restraint of French continental ambitions. You fought a country as militarily superior in manpower and generally formidable as France with the allies you could get, as Marlborough did, and with the paid troops you could hire.[9] But as Langford also says, the 1740s were a time of rabid patriotism, marked by composition of the verses of both 'Rule, Britannia' and 'God Save the King'!*

The government rested upon the balance of forces in Parliament. The Pelhams, their allies and dependants, were the core but had taken in allies. The ministry formed immediately after twenty-one years of Walpole was a marriage of convenience verging upon casual liaison. It could take only limited stress. On top of which, Carteret was one of those gifted men in politics who are quite terrible politicians. Though friendly and convivial company, he did not court colleagues or stroke hair. He had a way of doing wholly justifiable things without properly justifying them.

Then again, in an aristocratic era which accommodated bourgeois talent, Carteret was absurdly aristocratic. The family was unaffectedly Norman, with pre-Conquest roots in Jersey. A Carteret had been knighted by Edward III. He was almost as absurdly educated and intelligent. According to one source,[10] he had the Greek New Testament by heart. Also, as noted and unforgivably, he spoke fluent German. Chesterfield, long in heavy conflict with him, would write in his best pithy-but-in-earnest style, 'When he dies the ablest head in England dies too.'[11] Carteret was very rich by inheritance, but, unlike many such, contemptuously indifferent to money. These are not the foundations of a successful political career.

When this war stumbled and its costs rose, and with them the volume of street abuse, colleagues wilting under fire looked for a way out and a restructuring of the ministerial carriage. In July 1743,

---

* Though one theory traces the melody of the British national anthem to a politically suspect Roman Catholic musician, disconcertingly called John Bull.

one adjustment had already been made. Spencer Compton, amiable auxiliary, risen as Lord Wilmington to the premiership to avoid unpleasantness, died. Pulteney was the logical successor, had been the logical choice when Walpole fell. But Pulteney had gone limply to the Upper House as Earl of Bath. His wife's social ambitions clogged serious politics and he now lacked the cold inveteracy essential for supreme office. Bacon famously said, 'All rising to a high place is by a winding stair.' Nearing its top, Pulteney had grown tired.

There was about him a touch of R. A. Butler, ablest member of all the 1950s Tory cabinets, of whom his colleague Iain Macleod remarked, 'We put the ball at his feet but he wouldn't kick it.' There is another parallel here. Butler was, ostensibly for his Munich sympathies but by deeper and irrational occasions, the object of Harold Macmillan's hatred. Walpole's hatreds were less neurotic. Pulteney had been his rival, had opposed him and several times worsted him in debate. Walpole was not a cricketer. No one ever accused him of being a good sport. By interesting contrast with Pitt, he did no changes of heart or strewing of rose petals. Hating Pulteney, he had set about stopping him. And now, from ostensible retreat in Norfolk, Walpole was still involved, no longer a player, rather Chairman of the Selectors.

Armed with the King's attentive interest and Pulteney's lassitude, he had an excellent candidate. Henry Pelham, leader of the Commons since the new ministry's foundation, had been in Sir Robert's latter years chief conciliator between Walpole and his own brother, Newcastle, as their positions diverged over a Spanish war. He was, too, a supporter of the Pardo Convention and Walpole's defender before and after his fall. He spoke well, too, cogent not flamboyant. Walpole's man for sure, he was so autonomously, and no sensible observer thought him a creature. Together with Newcastle, and with the family's unrelated but indispensable member, Philip Yorke, Earl of Hardwicke, Henry Pelham was 'The Pelhams', the Old Corps, the Walpole gel of sense and stability surviving Walpole. Easy, good-tempered, pacific and mindful of economy, Pelham suffered no hatreds. He had only the enemies of circumstance.

When Wilmington died, the King would naturally have preferred the like-minded Carteret but was far less resolved than Walpole, now Lord Orford. The former Prime Minister concluded a letter, 'Dear Harry, I am very personal and very free and put myself in your power,' and then gave him the best advice anywhere going about how to run a cabinet. Pelham was – and both knew it – the proper successor of that contented figurehead Wilmington. His own immediate authority did not exceed that. But for all his modesty, Pelham had capacity and instinctively sought to fulfil it. Walpole worked on him. Carteret, Pelham was told, embodied 'the great man abroad' – foreign affairs. It must be made politely clear to him to keep in his province and out of Pelham's own 'as a proof *he will endeavour to support you as much as he can* to prevent any changes or engagements to be made in the province where you now preside, detrimental or disagreeable to you and your interest'.[12] In other words, 'Draw the lines on the floor at the start and be clear where he stands and you do.' Walpole had another suggestion: 'Recruits should now be sought from the Cobham Squadron ... Pitt is thought able and formidable, try him or show him ... Whig it with all opponents that will parley but 'ware Tory.'[13] Instead, Pelham brought in a friend of his own, the lifelong alternative to Pitt, Henry Fox.

Pelham had been a middling figure, pushed, then armed. Ironically, any threat from Carteret, dubious anyway in the light of his wife's death immediately after Dettingen, would be caught up by events, the continuation of a war which, despite that flash of glory, was not being won, merely continued. Carteret might say, 'The honour of the English nation is higher now than ever it was since my Lord Marlborough's time.' But the British public had grown weary of Marlborough's honour after Ramillies. Not too many people watching the sequel nearly forty years later cared to stick around for the bloodier honour of Oudenarde and Malplaquet.

To a degree the German war was, or could be, sold as honour, a war for Maria Theresia's Silesia, snatched by the dragon, Frederick. But where *was* Silesia and, beyond chivalry, what was there in Silesia for us? British politicians knew that the British public did not have the military tradition drilled over seventy years into Prussians by three out of four Electors and the Thirty Years War. They liked *starting* wars, but in the way they liked sermons – short! Beyond which neglected truth, Carteret, dominant Minister when Henry Pelham was a steady regular, was altogether too far and too long away, also too close to the King. He was respected but remote and hence vulnerable. In Parliament the mood grew, the conspirators conspired. By

November, the ability of government to continue without extensive shuffling had come to an end.

Henry Pelham, least ruthless of politicians, was acceptable to a widening circle of factions and opinions. In this shuffle there came about the picturesquely named Broad-Bottom Cabinet, involving Bedford and Sandwich, the subtle Chesterfield and friends. Lord Gower was made Privy Seal and jobs found for the Tory leadership of Philipps and Cotton. The appointment of Sandwich was important. As Bedford's deputy, but working engine of the Admiralty, Sandwich would, across three stints, help Admiral Anson create the navy which won the next war. But while all sorts of people came in, William Pitt did not. Pelham and Newcastle both wanted him, but he had talked too much and too offensively. George could be brought to swallow many things and people he did not want, but the man who had sneered at his courage and found Hanover despicable was not among them.

Political influence would broaden out once Pelham had become something like Prime Minister. Walpole's top-dog view of magistracy and local office no longer obtained. But while Tory dislike of Hanover had been communicated to a wider group, their Jacobite *tendresse* would be finished by events. Events meant the rising in the Highlands of Scottish rebels rallying to the Young Pretender, something to put London faction and Tory sentiment into long perspective. There had been straws in the wind in 1743. Pelham wanted to raise Scottish regiments, but Secretaries of State for Scotland, territorial magnates not readily taking orders, set the tone. And Tweeddale, Scottish Secretary, saw the whole thing as panic and chimera. He continued thinking so even after the landing became public knowledge, not, in the terrifying circumstances, a good idea.

The threat was contemporary with the things suddenly going better for France. Maurice de Saxe, the ablest French soldier for decades, had achieved excellent progress in, first, Bohemia, then Dutch Flanders, all part of French designs on the Austrian Netherlands, roughly the future Belgium. The notion of activating Charles Edward Stuart against the British had charm and utility. The Pretender, like a member of a theatrical family who had lately inherited his father's business of resting, knew quite well that he was, though above a pawn, only a piece on the board. Restoring a Stuart monarchy was not a priority in French thinking. But in the opportunistic interim of war, a foolish incursion made sense. Given Tweeddale's thick-headed inertia, it began to have the capabilities of a brilliant success.

Things were not made easier for Pelham by the King being abroad with his soldier son, Cumberland, Captain-General of British forces, neither of them thinking it necessary to come home. It took time for the public to be any more alert than Tweeddale, but it would not take them long to panic. The Pelhams behaved with sense and purpose, Henry Pelham having taken it all seriously from the first intelligence in 1743. He had suggested arming Scots loyal to King and Union and forming Highland regiments, but got no response from Tweeddale whose decision it was. In his grown-up way, Pelham observed, 'I am not so much apprehensive of the strength or zeal of the enemy, as I am fearful of the inability or languidness, of our friends . . . you would scarce in common conversation, meet with one man who thinks there is danger from, scarce truth in, an invasion, at this time.'[14]

George's obduracy matched Tweeddale's. He had been told by Granville and his people that putting down the '45 was something to be done with one hand while the continental struggle was undisturbed by withdrawing men. Such thinking and resistance brought the Minister to comment that 'the conduct of a certain person is worse than ever. To speak of personal treatment is idle at this time, but we are not permitted either to give our advice or to act in consequence of any advice that is given.'[15]

Newcastle set about raising men and defences and getting ships to sea to prevent further landings. The unlucky John Byng, to be met in tragic circumstances a decade later, played a very useful part. Promoted vice-admiral, he took command of the frigate *Kinsale* bringing a flotilla from Flanders to sweep the Scottish east coast. Eventually Pelham convinced George that Cumberland should come back – with ten battalions. But it took defeat at Prestonpans, 21 September, to bring public and King to their senses. Pitt might, as professional activist, have put his eloquence behind Pelham. Instead he moved the first of a series of spoiling motions.

This one had two points, the importance of sea power and violent contempt for Pelham. The first was irrelevant in this context, the second stood in the teeth of the facts. Pitt would not have liked the thought that his own eloquent zeal had played a modest part in creating the problem. The very fact of France financing a rising against

Hanoverian government in England and raising the terror of a French invasion was a product of a sterile war originally called for and whipped on with so much talk of soul and honour by the Patriots.

Pelham's purposes in Scotland were as sensible as decent. He wanted soft hands dealing conciliation. Cumberland won the necessary victories, expectation of which had made Charles Edward's professional soldier, Lord George Murray, insist upon retreat from Derby. He then proceeded to be Cumberland, the mediocre soldier who panicked in the next war, and a man reflexively cruel. Pelham wanted conciliation, Cumberland, having done the barbarities after Culloden, wanted Scotland subjugated, a good way of winning for the crown there all the popularity it enjoyed in Ireland. Pelham did minimum retribution, buying out the dangerous autonomies of Scottish lords and an act extending royal jurisdiction throughout Scotland. This gave the Prime Minister Walpole-style influence through a new control over local appointments, sheriff-deputes and the like.

Ironically, while both Pelhams were acting with so much sense, George yearned for Granville, who shared his feelings on foreign policy, and made this clear. Pelham, who would spend so much of his life and posthumous reputation being underrated, quietly took his Cabinet with him into resignation. It was rather like Walpole's experience when dismissed by the same excitable king following George I's death in 1727. Without a majority in the Commons, George could do nothing. Pelham was quickly back and the King came to appreciate him famously, saying after his death in 1754, 'Now I shall have no more peace.'

While the matter of resisting Scottish levies and French money was taking place, Opposition politics flourished. Lord Cobham, having entered a quarrel late in life, wanted to stick to it, opposing all things Hanoverian. But Walpole, now Orford, was again urging his protégé to bring in some Cobham members, *including* the head of the clan, by pointing out the dead end they were in. 'Cobham should be put upon an explanation of his strength and dependencies,' he had written as early as August 1743.[16] Could Pelham not see that the anti-Hanoverian drone would alienate the King further and 'make measures with him and for him, impracticable'? The possibility of dispensing with Hanoverian troops was mooted as a way of drawing the Cobhamites in. A concession too far, said Orford, and no way of dealing with the King.

Where into all this did the Grenvilles and other Patriots come? The Pelhams were realists not much given to sterile hatreds. Pitt was able, in Parliament very able. Their instincts anticipated Lyndon Johnson's rough language about Robert Kennedy and the ministerial tent. Meanwhile, Pitt was swivelling into conciliation, adjusting his opinions to accommodate his improving judgement. He delivered a dramatic speech made more striking by a display of sickroom bandages and flannel, the first of many. But it was dramatic for moderation – and land forces. Indeed, he echoed the words of Norris.

When the Patriots met other Oppositionists at the Fountain Tavern in January 1744, the price in recognising war realities was acknowledged. Pitt was in agreement with a majority, including Lyttleton and Chesterfield, for sustaining the troop numbers in Flanders.[17] Cobham, sullenly consistent, wanted withdrawal, as, surprisingly, did George Grenville, who made that case in a Commons motion easily defeated. Pitt stayed silent but loyally voted with the faction. None of this hurt Carteret. The Pelhams needed allies to move against him. If the allies stuck to principles, they did him a favour.

Slowly the Patriots were learning. The Pelhams were in the market for stiffening the ministry and would not remember old grudges. But it was Carteret they were against, not George, and the King wanted the land war. In Flanders we served the Queen of Hungary, mother of future rulers of the Habsburg lands. Pitt could see this. He could also see that where Hanoverians were paid London money through Viennese hands it might, in a bad light, make them someone else's mercenaries.

Pitt, with Lyttleton, was drifting towards the ministry as Carteret was moving away. He had sensed the opportunity and sought significant adjustments to facilitate ascent. His patron, Frederick, suddenly felt the new cool of his groom of the chamber. That groom now advocated continental land war, which Frederick, as his father's enemy, could not countenance. And, on 17 March, Pitt formally resigned from his household. Considering the energy of future conflict with Newcastle, it is interesting to find Pitt strenuously agreeing with the duke over the helpful handling of a foreign, Catholic and non-naval nation, bringing Hanoverian troops nominally into the pay of subsidised Habsburgs.

Gradually the Patriots gathered around the majority opinion at the Fountain, impeded only by Cobham's resistance. Pitt feared that 'Lord Cobham could spoil it all' and wanted Newcastle to 'soften him'.[18] It was not a pretty sight: men long splendid in their virtue, seeking remunerated places, men contemptuous of the land war, promoting it. At Strawberry Hill, Horace grew drily disdainful: they were selling themselves 'for profit – power they get none . . . One has heard of the corruption of courtiers; but believe me, the impudent prostitution of patriots, going to market with their honesty, beats it to nothing.'[19] In fairness to Pitt, money was never central. He was ambitious first and last. Office, however minor and amusing to diarists, was the essential step.

In 1752 George Grenville, after a show over troops in Flanders, was in, if not happy. Probably the ablest of the group, certainly of the narrow family, he had modern numerical talents. Public money would be well managed in his hands and he would later become Prime Minister. He wanted a Treasury post. Yet not only did he not get one, but two subsequent openings passed him by, discontented, in his Admiralty job. Pelham, giving a lesser Grenville, inconsequential Henry, the Governorship of Barbados, promised the next. There was encouraging, if unfulfilled, talk of a title for Richard. This Prime Minister followed Walpole's way, but spared Sir Robert's stick. Pelham went around with incremental carrots.

The in-out-in-again episode of Carteret's second and momentary reappointment had given Pitt his chance. A small Cobham element was already inside government, brought in after Pelham had kissed hands for the first time. There were, too, Bedford's people. Pitt's antithesis in his distaste for war, Bedford was there, against the day when a rational peace treaty was wanted. The appointments were overall an accession of debating talent with clout in the press from Henry Fielding.

Pitt inside the tent must desist from what he had regularly done outside. But his was a modest place. With his militarist dreams, he yearned to be Secretary at War, which would have involved him in managing the armed forces. What he actually got, after a humbling few months as Vice-Treasurer of Ireland, was the Paymastership of the Forces, which involved seeing they were paid. This functionary's job brought one advantage, the perfect right to annexe and invest the interest from investment of any surplus. Walpole had done himself well from this pleasant custom. Fox would light up the Fleet. But Pelham had already, over several years, quietly declined profits, as had

Robert Harley forty years earlier. Pitt naturally did the decent thing, but not quietly! Keen to leave no virtue unparaded, he followed the pretty woman's dictum, 'If you've got it, flaunt it.' He was, though, no longer the scrambling man he had been. The estate of an admiring Sarah, Duchess of Marlborough (obit. 1744), brought him from that shrewd seller-out of South Sea stock a pleasant £10,000. It made honesty, virtue and the rest of it easier.

An interesting contrast is with Henry Fox. Getting the War post Pitt wanted threw Fox back into the company of Cumberland. He had been given a Treasury post in 1743; he was a friend of Pelham. But so often damned as a pure conniver, he had intense loyalty to the Old Corps and to Walpole. He had stood back from Pulteney and Carteret's attempt to effect a coup through George's authority. But he held Newcastle's imperfect loyalty to Walpole in 1741 against him. We now, thought Fox, have a deal with Walpole's enemies. It would move him back to Cumberland, emerging as the critic of Newcastle and Lord Chancellor Hardwicke. This was a stance which, over time, alienated them, while Pitt, notable Walpole enemy, settled down among Walpoleans.

Pitt himself was now set up: in office, financially comfortable, on good working terms with the Pelhams, but in an administrative post, out of the stage lighting. He was now required to observe a discretion and precluded (very much for his own good) from the tirades which had made his name and his enemies.

8

Drawing the War: Winning the Election

The King had been discreetly overruled, the government changed, William Pitt was Paymaster on £4000 a year. The war continued.

The avowed purpose, Pitt had argued, was redress against Spain for her rough treatment of British traders pushing their luck over access under the *Asiento*. It should ideally have been our share of this six-part war, a series of valiant engagements off the Spanish Main together with in-and-out dog fighting around the Caribbean islands. It was nothing of the sort. Those naval commanders and their masters, bitten in 1727, should have been warned about the ferocity of yellow fever, the tendency of sailors to die without firing a shot. But when Admiral Vernon had tried in 1741 to repeat the experiment off Cartagena, he suffered miseries enough. The Spanish Main was always linked with Francis Drake, but Drake's technique was to steal, destroy and get away very quickly. Twice burned, British authorities and admirals would, after the latest horrors, largely stay away. In the South Sea, Admiral Norris's caution prevailed.

The British navy was not at this stage the invincible thing it would become, but as the war developed there were signs. In 1747, in a battle off northern Spain, Anson's squadron, perhaps unremarkably, wiped out a much weaker French one and took much of its merchant train. Something similar would be done later in the year by a new naval name, Edward Hawke. Indeed, across 1747–8, the last two years of the war, eighty-nine French or Spanish privateers were taken. The ability of the British navy in temperate waters to reliably beat anybody else should have been evident. It filled out Pitt's rhetoric about blue water – or at any rate the grey-green stuff of the Channel and Western Atlantic. The consequences for *this* war were minor but the intimations were formidable.

Norris, belonging to an earlier generation, had been looking back to Marlborough's wars which *were* fought in Flanders, or western Germany. Current involvements, Dettingen apart, resembled that run of victories in very little. At Fontenoy on 11 May 1746 the French famously followed Queensberry Rules: '*Messieurs les Anglais, Je vous en prie, tirez les premiers.* – Tell you what, old chap, you shoot first.' But they shot better, and they won. Having won, they went on to take Tournai and Ghent from the Austrians whose cities the British had been defending.

For Frederick, fighting Britain's allies to hold his Silesian gains, this became by 1745 a war to get out of. Prussia was too small, too poor, suffered too many casulties. Frederick's own generalship was exceptional, that of his best generals even better, but he fought on the run. '*Tirez les premiers*' was no part of it. By 1746 he had done brilliantly. His ally, Leopold of Anhalt, the Old Dessauer, had crushed Saxony, at Kesseldorf in December 1745. But Frederick went in fear that numbers might finally get him. On the back of victory, he skipped the conflict without regard for his ally, France. In war and diplomacy timing was a speciality. He was too in touch with the British – on the other side but not offensively so – talking peace.

It was understood. For Pelham, this was primarily a war to be paid for. And although he had gained more power after ministerial reconstruction, he was limited by Royal Primacy. The two Secretaries of State (North and South) were directly linked to the King. Hence Carteret's contentment with the Northern Secretaryship embracing conflict in Germany. That ascendency past, Newcastle now took the post and would spend much time in Hanover with the King.

Pelham, for different reasons to Pitt, worried about the King's subsidies to German small states to fight for us. Pelham accepted the principle and necessity of preoccupying French armies this side of the Atlantic. But he was jealous to control 'every sum of money we advance'. 'The allys', he said, 'will take it and then act as suits their own conscience and security best.'[1] A careful man, financially prudent and dubious about glory, he had inherited vast national debts. Pelham and the Street (Pitt's City of London Street) had little time for one another. But what the Street wanted in this particular, Pelham also wanted. He would have been glad to get out in 1746, but Newcastle would here misread strategy.

The Dutch had been effective allies for Marlborough. As a republic they wanted the military zeal the English recalled in Stadhouder Willem III, our King William III. In 1747, the royal house was restored and Newcastle, animated by his ambassadors, drew optimistic conclusions. The British envoy to the Breda talks in 1746 was the young Earl of Sandwich. Right about many things, especially naval ones, Sandwich reported the Dutch army optimistically as offering serious strength to a late charge against the French. That came to nothing and led to serious reverses. Newcastle followed a king hoping for bargains at the conclusion, and the war dragged into those late reverses. However, Sandwich the negotiator made amends for Sandwich the military analyst, achieving more than was expected – the reputable peace available two years earlier.

The '45 Rising had dimensions beyond the march on Derby. Theoretically, it might end the war sensationally by knocking out the Hanoverian dynasty. Richelieu, admittedly a mediocre soldier, commanded invasion forces at Calais and Boulogne. Voltaire, not yet Anglophile, had written a manifesto to be distributed to the locals by French troops. George, slow to see the British priorities, was lucky in Pelham's immediate alertness. Though, as Frank McLynn points out, Louis XV himself was anxious not to alarm Protestant rulers across Germany who, detesting the Catholic Habsburgs, cooperated easily with off-Catholic, anti-Habsburg France.[2]

Much less theoretical was the effect of the Rising upon fraught markets. Their capacity to sell frightened and buy cheerful, was vividly present in 1745–6 when the basic government stock fell to seventy-four. The same impulse operated in 1748. They fell to seventy-seven with unofficial interest deals agreed at 12 per cent.[3] As credit, apart from an early shudder, had held up very well, Pelham, a finance minister by first instincts, was confirmed in opinions held two years earlier. He wanted a peace, if not glorious, then as relief. The Peace of Aix-la-Chapelle (Aachen), where negotiations had been switched, was flatly anti-climactic. To adjust Humpty Dumpty, no one had won and all should have small prizes. Frederick might feel that retaining the Silesia he had snatched was a substantial one, but neither he nor Maria Theresia thought it would stick without another fight. The Queen of Hungary, on the death of the Bavarian interloper, got the Imperial Crown back on a Habsburg head. What she didn't get was investiture of her son, Joseph, as King of the Romans, accredited heir to the Empire. Spain, now governed by the sensible Ferdinand VI, and with Piacenza and Parma acquired, was not troubled with the wasteful preoccupations of Elizabeth Farnese, but held tight to Naples.

France had done pleasantly well; victory over the British at Fontenoy had tasted good. The substantial loss had been in Canada. Louisbourg, otherwise Cape Breton, fortress above the Gulf of St Lawrence, had fallen to British/American forces under Commander Warren and Governor Shirley of Massachusetts. Getting back Louisbourg now so that one group of cod fishermen should have an edge over another was something the French felt they needed to do.

Despite Hawke's exertions, England had not emerged dominant. The victories of our Dutch ally had not materialised. The French had their places on the Ohio, the British theirs east of of it. Louisbourg might have occasioned a struggle for a continent, but America generally was simply not viewed as the struggle to the death so prominent in the City press ten years later.

There was no reason why it should. The British outnumbered the French on that continent manifold. A requirement of fighting the French to the death would need, and get, more and better war propaganda. There was, too, the naval opinion of Admiral Charles Knowles who dismissed 'this expensive, weak fortress of Louisbourg' and considered it 'the most miserable, ruinous place I ever beheld'.[4] Anyway, eighteenth-century laws of exchange or restore at peace treaties allowed France to put up her large gains in the Netherlands at the end of 1747 as something to be kept if the British clung to Louisbourg. The British doctrine about letting no potential enemy control the River Scheldt made compliance inevitable. France had, through Marshal Saxe's victories, notably damaged Austria, and she was, too, the sponsor of Prussia, a winner with Frederick and his army.

The last two years of the war were sterile on all hands. Pelham summed it all up in a letter to his brother of April 1747: 'Peace is what I want, both for the sake of my king, my country, and myself. Peace will be had. I heartily wish it may be no worse than what is represented in your paper. If so, I am sure it is to be defended, and shall be by me at least. If I have the honour to serve the king at the time of trial.'[5] In any consideration of Pitt it is a good idea to keep Henry Pelham in mind. The voice is responsible in the unpompous sense of a man taking his duties seriously. The glamour of war had no appeal for him, nor the patriotic rant. He was close to his brother Thomas (Newcastle) but distracted by none of the butterflies of hope and anxiety vitiating the duke's variable judgement.

Pelham had far less in common with Pitt. He never invoked his soul, spoke of his country only as a problem and generally made the right careful judgement. The history which used to call him a mediocrity was wrong and long seen to be wrong. As for that British triumph in the Spanish Americas of which Pitt had been chief trumpet, it didn't happen. Sending the navy with all its talents to man blockades in a tropical zone better manned by tropical diseases was no better business than in the late 1720s. As for India, the wisdom of Joseph Dupleix, French Governor of Pondicherry, who saw no point in fighting a five arms' length war there, together with the wonderfully bad communications of the subcontinent, meant that nothing remarkable happened apart from the French taking Madras with its two-hundred-man garrison and some success for Boscawen at sea.

Yet one thing had materialised in the background. Hawke's semi-privateering against merchantmen and their convoys was hardly noticed but marked latent naval strength. His late attacks were successful against French and Spanish trading ships in the Mediterranean. They echoed that faraway performance by Boscawen. The numbers were modest, but two-thirds of French Indies shipping was knocked out, unregarded at Aix-la-Chapelle, but a victory in the tropics won by ships avoiding blockade. Pitt's language about naval domination was only words. Delivering the means was something else.

Politically, Pelham was Prime Minister in fact as well as name. He had anticipated the war's end by converting late naval victories to political coin. Anson's victory off Finisterre in May 1747 made very good business. France, alert to the quiet Indian theatre, had split a fleet between the subcontinent and America as merchant convoy. Anson captured six out of nine French men-of-war and four trading ships. Like a number of English victories in the next war, the English squadron's massive outnumbering of the other side was not stressed. Pitt sent Newcastle a note: 'I most heartily wish your Grace joy of this total defeat of the naval designs of France for this year, which I conceive cannot fail to have considerable effects on their affairs in general.'[6]

The idea of calling an election before the bunting was taken down has been attributed to a shrewd bishop, Sherlock of Salisbury.[7] The story gained credit and flavour from the prompt appointment of his son to the Deanery of York and his own advance not much later to London. There is also a nice ecumenical touch as Sherlock is usually described as 'a strong Tory'.

Between the nine years of the War of the Austrian Succession and the Seven Years War fell an eight-year peace. Pelham recognised the folly of debt and the debt of war. He had wanted to be out in 1746. Given peace, he would keep it and reconstruct sound public finances. In 1749, with parliamentary backing, he set about a plan to reduce the rate of interest, not then the flighty thing of today, from 4 per cent to 3 and consolidate the National Debt. New annuities went on sale at 3 per cent, the old ones slowly reduced with the Bank of England taking up East India and South Sea debt. Pelham put up the Horse Guards building, but he hoped to have only ceremonial purposes for the soldiers. His government was as alien to the instincts of Newcastle as of Pitt, both meddlers and, in their quite different ways, drawn to conflict and optimistic about cost. Ironically, the restructured finances left at Pelham's death provided the means to fight the war beginning in 1756.

It was not an accident that Pelham did constructive, useful things. The Jewish Bill was the product of his unfanatical nature and his practical acquaintance with the Jewish financial community led by Samson Gideon, greatly helpful in creating financial channels. That bill was, as recounted, defeated by the mob. The same mob was out against conversion from the thirteen-days'-wrong Julian calendar to the spot-on Gregorian, accomplishment of an otherwise peculiarly awful Pope, Gregory XIII, but correct and the way all Europe kept the time. This mob was seen off and the date thrust forward to cries of 'Give us back our eleven days.' Meanwhile, the Gin Act of 1751 put one murderous branch of commerce under licence. It was, all in all, rather a good government. Notably for all the froth of ministry making, faction balancing and a general dance of egos, much of its best work was done by backbenchers sitting in committee. Witness the Felonies Committee whose report led to the Gin Act.

Back in the 1747 snap election, the ministry, taking the episcopal tip, substantially strengthened the current bundle of interests. Pitt was secure enough, though his credit dipped with the dedicated Oppositionists from whom he had risen. His former Old Sarum seat belonged to his brother, Thomas, who, miscalculating, had sunk his interest in the fading star of the Prince of Wales. Where William had made terms with the Pelhams he had damned, Thomas, going downhill financially, had acted as Frederick's election agent in the 1747 contest and lost four of the Prince's sixteen seats in a bad year for opposition. He got back at Okehampton with George Lyttleton, who shrewdly reverted the next year to the Pelhams.[8] But the rest of his life was a losing fight against bankruptcy. After the Prince died in 1751 and expectations with him, Thomas sold his parliamentary properties for a pension. William, no longer welcome at Old Sarum, had found a new patron, the Duke of Newcastle!

Newcastle owned much of Nottinghamshire and even more of Sussex. At Seaford in June 1747, as Lord-Lieutenant and immediate general patron, he praised the goodness the corporation had shown him, leaving unsaid the goodness he would readily strew about. Mr Pitt had well-known qualifications and would be agreeable to the corporation. His Grace proposed bringing him down with another gentleman, a Mr Hay, in hopes of their meeting the corporation's favour. It was the eighteenth-century way, a cool mix of trade and favour to which the aspirant must accommodate himself. But Pitt had made so many speeches about patriotism and political morality, supported so many place bills and generally represented himself as being above all that. The point was taken and the hostile pamphlets written. There would be a particularly bitter speech by Thomas Potter who, as a friend of John Wilkes, would champion Pitt in later Opposition. An election petition was rejected. Pitt settled back into ministerial office.

The price for joining the Pelhams, receiving public money and holding office was a larger silence than people had come to expect. Although a capable and active figure who would carry out duties commonly done by deputies, he was by reputation and choice a debater when debaters were followed like tenors. Beyond silence, Pitt had to vote for Pelhamite policies even on foreign affairs, where his pronouncements had been vivid, not to say indelible. So in April 1746 he voted and spoke in support of a motion to pay Hanoverian troops, mercenaries hired from the despicable electorate. To be sure they were not to be paid by us, but Maria Theresia's government was to be given the money to hire them.

From the Pelhams' viewpoint of wanting to differentiate themselves from Carteret's too open Hanoverianism, working through the wronged Queen took the edge off Patriot resentment. For Pitt the Europhage, it was the price of a job. A cartoon shows the shrouded ghost of Sarah, Duchess of Marlborough, appearing before a horrified Pitt with the subscription:

Ungrateful Pitt/You have me Bitt.[sic] Ten Thousand Pound/My Will you found./And did Obtain/the long sought gain/ then forct [sic] your Way/to Court for Pay/Three thousand clear*/Ten Thousand Clear/You have got a Year./Since Fear nor Shame/Can you declaim/ I Brand your Name.[9]

When he took the Paymastership, Jemmy Grenville had been found a subordinate place at the Board of Trade, something insisted upon by Cobham, anxious that nephews, cousins, sister and aunts should have something pleasant from the taxpayer. Newcastle had written to Chesterfield noting that 'Jemmy Grenville's £1,000 a year was dirtily asked and prudently granted . . .' He had also noted prophetically that 'I promise you Pitt will not rest easy until he is Secretary at War and Dick Grenville of the Treasury.'[10] Giving, like taking, was politics; and Pitt, stuck for eight years at the Paymastership, had been given at quite-modest rate, though Dick's £1000 a year and Pitt's £4000 should, to grasp their modern equivalents, be multiplied by something above seventy. Dick Grenville would in fact, as the 2nd Lord Temple, after the death in 1749 of his uncle, accompany Pitt to the command Cabinet of the Seven Years War.

Temple was an oddity. He was a character whom Vanbrugh or Etherege might have imagined, direct in a rustic, almost clownish way about becoming richer, nobler and more important than he was already rich, noble and important. Yet this crudest of aggrandisers had a deep streak of decency. Blazing outrage in the King's teeth at the miscarriage of justice against Admiral Byng after the fall of Minorca lies not far ahead. Yet soon after, he would stop government dead in its tracks at a crisis in the Seven Years War because the Garter,

---

* The Paymaster's salary was £3000 but from various allowances another thousand was added.

to which he felt a proprietory right, was being withheld by George, who could not bear the sight of him. Even so, on the greater question, Temple would set an example Pitt could not match.

The commonplaces of the Enlightenment – rejection of slavery, religious toleration and sensibility to sadistic cruelty – would come dropping slow. But Henry Pelham was the man most likely to support toleration. Comfortable in worldly business circles peopled by the new monied class, he appreciated the rational arguments for the rights of a 30,000-strong and closely confined Jewish community. So across three sessions of parliament in Pelham's time, as noted *supra*, a modest bill for giving property right to Jews and votes to their second generation was floated. In 1751 it was defeated by only thirteen votes – 129 to 116. The 1753 bill, lodged a year before a general election, began and easily passed in the Lords, then, with ministerial pressure, passed the Commons. But across the summer the newspapers, falling into a Christian rage, addressed 'The People'. 'We', to cite Thomas Hardy in a more creditable context, 'are the people of England and we have not spoken yet.' As Paul Langford puts it, 'A torrent of antisemitism flowed from the press.'[11] And as the press spoke, the Street turned out. Politicians, facing an election, fell back. The law having been made, fresh legislation was called up to repeal it.

Temple stood against this almost alone, without a hint of apology or regret. It was, he thought, a cowardly, illiberal flight before 'a clamour that has been raised among the very lowest of our people'.[12] Pitt had spoken in favour of the bill on 23 November, though, as even the friendly O.A. Sherrard concedes, he did so 'with a heavy heart and a confused tongue'.[13] It was nothing to his volte-face. 'I am fully convinced', he said. 'I believe that most gentlemen that hear are convinced that religion really has nothing to do in the dispute; but the people without doors have been made to believe it has; and upon this the old high Church persecuting spirit has begun to take hold of them. We are too wise to dispute the matter with them, as we may upon this occasion, evade it without doing any notable injury to the public. But at the same time we ought to let them know, that we think they have been misled; and that the spirit they are at present possessed with is not a true Christian spirit. If we do not do this, we do not deal honestly or candidly by them.' If he was going to cringe, Pitt would cringe piously. Uncomfortably, he drove on, avowing that the bill itself had been right 'and I shall now agree to the repeal of it merely out of complaisance [compliance] to that enthusiastic spirit that has taken hold of the people.'

Yet there are creditable things. Pitt's character contained, with the rattling egotism, an element of compassion. As Paymaster, he was responsible for the money due to military dependants like the Chelsea Pensioners. They had hitherto been paid in arrears, then, after the inevitable recourse to borrowing money at rapacious rates, they could be totally bought out. Pitt thought that they should be pulled out of this hole by payment in advance. This was not something to do by order in Council. It required specific legislation. His successful bill, introduced in November 1754 near the end of his term, required half-yearly payment of a military pension in advance, made the issuing of mortgages on pensions illegal and prevented those administering pensions from charging commission.

In 1748 came marriage. Very little is known about Pitt as male. There was no known mistress, only chatter, perhaps uttered as puffs, about all the girls who wanted to set their caps at Mr Pitt, but dared not. His ill health may have confined him, but it was at forty, with not a stain, or much fun, on his character, that he married Hester Grenville. She was sister to the five Grenville brothers and niece to Cobham. The marriage made Pitt brother-in-law to difficult Dick and combative George. The marriage was within the faction. Hester was only six years younger and, in an age which did not expend much comment on not-scandalous women, the comments are conventional but positive. Although she would bear five children, she may have intended, or been intended by Dick and George, to be a species of nurse. Pitt's gout, if the roundabout of agues and crippling pain since his teens were that, made a marriage of care sensible thinking. And care for him she did. However conventionally, Hester won and deserved the name of a very good wife, through her husband's mental and physical breakdowns and the capricious dance of moving in and out of houses and costs which she had to handle.

In 1751, Pitt took his only remotely controversial step of this period. With other Grenvilles he sought bridges to the Prince. In the view of his biographer, Marie Peters, this may have been a reaction to the increasing political role of George's other son. Cumberland was the patron of Henry Fox, Pitt's steady bugbear. When Frederick suddenly

died in 1751, Pitt broke into his customary excess. Frederick had been
'the most *patriot* prince that ever lived'.

From 1751 to 1754 he fell very seriously ill and, across that period,
avoided Commons debates. Hester was particularly needed. While
Henry Pelham held office, Pitt, too long outside, would have stayed
in. But in March 1754, it was Pelham who died. Chesterfield's valedic-
tory words, though splendid, rather understate his case. 'I regret him
as an old acquaintance, a pretty near relation . . . he meaned well to
the public; and was incorrupt in a post where corruption is commonly
contagious. If he was no shining, enterprising minister, he was a safe
one which I like better. Very shining Ministers like the sun, are apt to
scorch . . . in our constitution I prefer the milder light of a less glaring
minister.'[14] Pelham had certainly accustomed Pitt to mild sunshine.

9

'What shall you think if he dies courageously?'

Soon after Henry Pelham's death in 1754, and following the requirements of the Septennial Act, an election had been called by Newcastle,
the other Pelham and assured successor. The contest was a highly
successful affair involving the usual cheerful unpleasantness.

Bubb Dodington, shifting from Bridgwater to Weymouth and
Melcombe Regis,* described three days close to the climax of the
campaign 'spent in infamous and disagreeable compliance with
the low habits of venal wretches'.[1] As he owned enough of this rare
four-seat constituency to return three of its members to Parliament,
for which the government would present him with the highly remunerated Clerkship of the Pells, and ultimately, a peerage, this was
oversensitive.

Pitt had now a claim of merit upon promotion. He had done long
duty in the Paymaster's office, resting ministers from his furious and
frightening oratory. But promotion to Secretary at War, the post he
sought and merited, would not come from George II in normal circumstances. Newcastle and his ally, Lord Hardwicke, observed Pitt with a
mix of admiration and apprehension. The King's loathing was a
splendid alibi to be regretfully cited. And Pitt, miserably ill as so often,
had retreated to Bath. For the moment, he did not propose controversy. He wrote on 23 May to Lyttleton advising the playing of a long
hand by the family. If ministers did not at once invite the Grenville
faction into government 'our poor, depressed, betrayed, persecuted
band will have its weight if we keep our tempers and hold employments and act systematically . . . to, the great object of public good'.[2]

Newcastle was neither unaware of Pitt, nor his irreconcilable enemy.

---

* At Rochester another successful candidate was Admiral John Byng.

Once so commonly derided, he is seen more perceptively by modern
historians as a man of limited incapacity. Equipped to manage parliaments and the King, work very hard, make perfectly sensible
judgements, not least in military matters, and take good advice on
finance, he had a measure of self-knowledge. He was not a commander,
not a masterful presence. Pretty much knowing this, he sought a
colleague to do the centre-stage personality politics. He was caught
between two ambitious, able men who could make open-ended
trouble, Henry Fox and William Pitt. Very quickly, both men did
demonstration runs, attacking the duke by proxy in the person of the
low-octane, conscientious and uninteresting Sir Thomas Robinson,
made Secretary on Walpolean principles of not being dangerous.

If it came to hiring a bigger player, how much more comfortable
would be William Murray. Intellectually superior to everyone, a fine,
rational debater, easy to live with, he was timid and shy of fighting
politics. Murray, with great understanding of his own nature, would
soon insist upon the purely legal career, where, as Lord Mansfield, he
would shine very bright. Henry Fox, clever, articulate, amusing but
with a streak of self-destructive anxiety, was perfectly acceptable to
the King. A devoted Walpole man, close to Cumberland, Fox looked
right for Secretary of State but played difficult and, despite mutual
hatred, also played up to his enemy.

Pitt's flirtation with moderation no longer seemed worth the candle.
He would have, throughout his life, a single, compelling goal.
Dodington reported to Lord Hillsborough: 'From his intimacy with
[the Grenvilles] . . . he began with Mr Pitt . . . his passion was not
money; it was ambition, power; of which he had no share . . .'[3] As the
political dance proceeded, Pitt watched the detested Fox take the post
for which he hungered and thirsted. He then stepped, by calculation
or rage, probably the former, into manic mode. The opportunity would
come from those small side treaties which the Ministers of a
King/Elector had to make in any war, treaties with Hesse-Cassel or
Russia. They provided soldiers to guarantee Hanover's security. No
serious reason for the English to object to them existed. A Hanover
overrun, as it might be, even by Louis XV, would be ransomed come
the peace conference, at the expense of overseas prizes in the Caribbean
or North America cherished by the merchant lobby on whose behalf
Pitt choreographed his fury.

Lord Chesterfield, meanwhile, in a casual/prophetic comment to his friend Dayrolles, stated a central historical truth: 'The French at this time, dread a general war: their Ministry is weak, and their King weaker; the clergy and Parliament hating each other irreconcilably; they have no general in whom they have the least confidence; and for the interest they pay, it is plain that they want money . . .'[4]

For Pitt, however, such moves were the cue for his standard act. In the debate on the address he rhapsodised 'the long-injured, long-neglected, long-forgotten people of America' and argued that 'incoherent *un-British* measures are what are adopted instead of our proper force'. It would all lead to a continental war and 'within two years, his Majesty not be able to sleep in St James's for the cries of a bankrupt people'.[5] Pitt's rhetoric runs so often to apocalypse on draught. The grief is not higher taxes or serious disturbances, never mind 'little local differences'. The stress word is commonly 'slavery' although he is not recorded as saying a word against the actual, and thriving, black-skinned thing. Alternatively, it is death and dying, as in particular his 'dying country', which Pitt feels called upon to save – a verb with a high count.

That fury suddenly did its Vesuvian thing which, in the age of *opera seria*, commonly worked. It was probably helped by the gravity with which the tragedian's text was uttered. He struck the tone of a man gathering his virtue about him like a toga and defying other men to deny their baseness. It is a political art, familiar and not pleasant.

For the present, though, it had no great general effect. The treaties passed Lords and Commons and though Pitt spoke several times that autumn and next spring, he made a fierce impression but no difference to the lobby count. Hanoverian troops were to be brought over. Pitt spoke against the motion, introduced by the Duke of Cumberland's unpopular lieutenant General Lord George Sackville, and in April they arrived. But Pitt, now intensely busy in the Commons, fought on.

Chesterfield, who thought a Russian deal common sense, but had practical objections to the terms of the Hessian treaty – too long delayed with built-in inflation of costs – smiled. 'I am assured that Mr Pitt and Charles Townshend on one side, Mr Fox and Hume Campbell on the other, have distinguished themselves by the highest Billingsgate rhetoric.'[6] A favourite notion of Pitt's was a militia. English Whig dogma was clean against a standing army, but as a French invasion was thinkable, another grand old British tradition, internal contradiction, arose. Pitt kept coming back to the notion, and it would metamorphose in his son's time as a yeomanry, though for no larger purpose than to feature in *Pride and Prejudice* and *The Trumpet Major*.

It was a half useful thing to be doing and something which fitted his talents. He had energy and liked proclaiming large schemes. A vent for his general activeness, a militia also had an ideological slant. This would be a wholly British product, the manly alternative to paying a lot of ne'er-do-well foreigners to defend our liberties and hold back the tide of slavery. The motion did indeed pass the Commons. Ironically for an orator, Pitt suffered the chagrin, when the bill went to the Upper House, of Hardwicke, a considerable speaker though getting on in years, making an applauded assault and the entire undertaking being shelved.

The whole business of Pitt's war talk and anxiety contradicted not just his recent years of quiet, but the active Whiggism of the hopeful days of 1754. At that time, he had made a vehement assault on the ancient cult of Oxford Toryism. The Pitt of that month had proclaimed a purpose, 'to act upon plain Whig Principles'.[7] He had, years before, ditched Patriots and Patriot cause, come to the Old Corps for a job, taken for eight years what was offered and its £4000 a year. Now *not* advanced in the reorganisation following Pelham's death, he was again waving to the Patriots, even the Tories, and stressing equally sincere principles. If people had not been frightened of Pitt, he might well have been laughed at. A pamphlet of the day was pointedly entitled *A New System of Patriot Policy Containing the Genuine Recantation of the British Cicero*.[8]

Fox, the rival in post, was much hated, but, as Horace Walpole told his friend in Florence, 'The Tories hate both [Fox] and Pitt so much, that they sit still to see them worry one another'.[9] When Pitt orated against the infamy of Hanoverian troops, the Tories, true to the finer points of their prejudice, 'owned that they preferred Hanoverians to Hessians'. He could not at this stage even count on William Beckford. The great alderman was quiescent.

There was a good deal of Sisyphus about Pitt's career at this stage. Fox was Secretary of State, the government's system stood firm. Its settled majority of loyalists with motives Sir Robert Walpole had understood, having its price, had been paid. Pitt must look for allies,

Leicester House, the Tories, the habitual outs, the City and beyond the City, the City mob. No man more devoutly needed a disaster.

Bubb Dodington, always a handy source for movements in the futures market of gossip, notes Pitt's mood and purposes. Intermittent in his loyalty to the government and an equally optional familiar at Leicester House, centre of dynastic opposition, Dodington had been chatting widely, notably to Lord Hillsborough, who had been talking to *his* friends:

> From his intimacy with [the Grenvilles], he knew their reasons which he would tell me, and would begin with Mr Pitt . . . [he] was told by his bosom friend, Mr George Grenville who was also his that . . . [Pitt's ambition] made him very uneasy which was highly increased by the late promotions. Instead of being acquainted with and consulted about what was to be done, he was only informed what was to be done; instead of offering him his share, he received news that his most inveterate enemy was made Secretary of State . . . I said that I supposed that they did not think Mr Pitt could possibly take an office of fatigue or an office of business from the state of his health. He said that Mr Pitt replied that he himself ought to be the best judge of that . . . They should have made him well with the King who was his enemy, which they never had the least care to do . . .[10]

Pitt had left Frederick's faction in 1746 at the chance of office. In 1754, before the war changed the landscape, he had begun casting about for possibilities. Leicester House was commanded for the sixteen-year-old heir by the Dowager Princess, Frederick's widow, Augusta, whose outlook was personal and embittered. When in August 1755 Dodington '. . . passed the day at Kew. The Princess . . . inveighed most bitterly against the not pushing the French everywhere. The people would not surely bear it when the Parliament met . . . She saw the terrible consequences of it and of a patched-up peace which must break out when the French had perfected their naval plan and fell upon her son, young and inexperienced at the beginning of his reign . . . She was very solicitous to pursue the war and wished Hanover under the sea as the cause of all our misfortunes.'[11]

Augusta and the Prince were advised by the Prince's adored preceptor, a young Scottish nobleman, John Stuart, Earl of Bute. A correspondence would grow up between Bute and the former Groom of the Bedchamber to Frederick. Wiliam Pitt was out of the main establishment and trying, like any number of scrambling politicians, to get into another one. On 2 June 1755, he wrote from his country house in Hayes, Kent: 'Mr Pitt's affectionate compliments attend Lord Bute. He proposes being in Town by one o'clock today, and if it will not be inconvenient to his Lordship to call at the Privy-Garden, he will give great satisfaction to his very anxious and truely [sic] devoted friend.'[12]

The deference would deepen. On 9 August 1755, reporting on a meeting with Dr George Lee,* Pitt declared that he was 'highly satisfied with him. What shall he say he is at Lord Bute's infinite goodness to him?'[13] This is a low point in Pitt's career. Without the huge events which were about to make him, he risked becoming very like a superior Bubb Dodington, someone in whom desperation for something led him into prideless solicitation. However, where Bubb sought another high-paying place for his collection of rotten boroughs and a peerage to go with his estates, aspirational politics, par for the eighteenth-century course, Pitt wanted the Sun and the Moon and the Stars.

But in 1756 everything would change. War and all its life chances were at hand. It all began with the defeat of George Washington. The American states-to-be were governed by men who, though commonly American-born, were appointed by, and loyal to, London, *colonial* governors. At a time of uneasy coexistence with French settlements, the possibility of conflict, albeit limited, local and sporadic, was a given. The direction given to colonial governors was thus one of 'resisting force with force', with the French attitude no different. 'Force' in the shrill context of the 1750s included the building of military forts.

So when a new French development appeared on the Ohio river, Robert Dinwiddie, Governor of Virginia, 1752–8, Scot and quarreller, made an assault on settlements at the Ohio, and Colonel George Washington promptly fell over into history. Succeeding as commander of the detachment on the death of his chief, Washington was soundly defeated, driven back by the French, took refuge in a small fort and finally surrendered. It was an American failure and a British crisis. In reacting, there would be no way that the duke's government could

---

* Whose chairmanship of the Petitions Committee in 1742 had destroyed Walpole.

get it right. Discounting Forks of the Ohio as limited, local and once-off would lead to screams from the patriotic press that we were leaving God's Englishmen to French-directed perdition. Take it seriously enough to send British troops under a British commander, as we did with two regiments under General Braddock, and the French would see it as a raising of stakes and respond in kind.

Let that sequence flow and eighteenth-century wars being the hostile pair-partnerships they were, and the French–English contest could get laboriously underway. Newcastle's government was facing other developments in the same direction. The duke, who had worked hard in the past at playing close to Austria, wanted to keep this up. As recently as 1748 and Aix-la-Chapelle, we had swapped Louisbourg and its command of the St Lawrence for French withdrawal from Flanders and the sacred Scheldt. English–Austrian affinities owed a good deal on our side to the imperative of keeping the French out of decent ports on a long stretch of the Channel.

As Secretary of State, Newcastle, starting in 1749 and going several steps too far, had acted as election agent for the Archduke Joseph to become King of the Romans, pole position for next Emperor. He saw in it, as he told Pelham, the only way to keep peace and stability in Europe. To Vienna and Maria Theresia that would have been desirable, but a British alliance risked being taken as a threat to France. Austrian diplomacy played for time until, in 1753, the pleasant idea ran out of credibility.

If not Austria, then Russia: to be primed by subsidy to defend Hanover at second hand if Prussia should move against her. This had the corollary at least of sending a message to France. Fortunately or unfortunately, the move also alarmed Frederick II who set about making serious accord and alliance with Britain. The negative of this unintended and flittering activity was that Austria, fearing and hating Frederick, became a prospective British enemy, while Russia, whose Tsarina Elizabeth loathed him, might do the same. The upside was that Britain would in any imaginable war gain the dominant commander in Europe surrounded by superlative generals at the head of its best-trained, equipped and most professional army. Frederick was about to become a British national hero. There are still pubs, named in the raptures of the 1750s, serving draught Guinness under a board proclaiming 'The King of Prussia'.

A major influence behind developments belonged to a politician central to Austrian affairs long after, in Joseph II's time. Wenzel, Graf Kaunitz, wanted a French alliance: wanted it as a single-minded enemy of Frederick II, wanted it as cover and aid in the recovery of the great province lately lost to him. As Lord Acton pointed out, our Seven Years War was known in the German-speaking world as 'The Third Silesian War'.[14]

Kaunitz, engaging to deepen Austrian power to the south, needed France as ally to destroy Frederick, reducing him, went the phrase, to Margrave of Brandenburg. This was the title with which Prussia had started two centuries before. Rather than submit to that, Frederick stood ready to advance his own longer-term ambition, to swap Saxony and Bohemia and create a great north German state. Meanwhile France wasn't going to oblige Kaunitz for nothing. So he sought effective mastery of the Austrian Netherlands (Belgium since 1830). They should be shared in partition by France with the Duke of Parma – who was also Duc de Bourbon!

That measured Silesia's value to the Habsburgs. But Silesia belonged in a German empire whereas Flanders / Wallonia didn't. Moreover, the territory was a point of future conflict with France. It was a clever, well-thought-out discard. Richard Pares, great twentieth-century historian of the eighteenth century, put it succinctly: 'Austrian align-ment allowed France to play a part in Eastern Europe until 1792 and allowed Choiseul to follow an anti-British policy. Britain 1756 without continental allies. No Austria No Netherlands (United Provinces).'[15]

In immediate terms, however, a major and under-appreciated back-hand favour was done to Britain. It concentrated French efforts on the European continent, a war fought in western Germany to win Belgium. British interests in North America would be hampered by fewer troops being sent during the early stages to protect the St Lawrence forts. It meant inevitable priority for her land armies, a French strength, over her naval forces, badly needing an intense atten-tion they would not get.

In the first decade of the century Marlborough had mightily rebuffed French armies, but as the war dragged on and draws were called English victories, and as France won outright in Spain, rebuff never turned into outright conclusion. A pattern was emerging, to hold good until 1870–71, of the French dominating the continent and the British, as they liked to put it, ruling the waves. Neither the Peninsular War, a part-guerrilla struggle between limited armies, nor Waterloo, a battle of everybody against a French army which had reached Moscow, would invalidate this judgement.

For Britain, a France commanding the Scheldt was a priority anxiety, whatever might happen in Hanover. It made perfect nonsense of Pitt's overexcited speeches denouncing Hanoverian troops and the obligation to defend the King/Elector's other state. The French, dug into Ostend, would make a stake on the Ohio and large visions of empire chimerical. For all the noise in the *Monitor* and the *London Evening Chronicle*, English politicians were agreed upon a consensus: to win the key places for control of America and prevent French domination of Western Europe, both! Engagement in Germany, direct or by a subsidised second hand, was needed beyond the Hanover issue. Not letting France take Hanover was a proper concern. And first thoughts about war in Germany were turning into action. And for that, William Pitt would in due course unblushingly make the essential climbdown.

Because of America, England against France had anyway become a fixture. Pitt had talked so much and so intently about America as the prime issue and holy grail that a casual view is often taken that he had concern for these colonies to himself. Everybody serious in government, Newcastle as much as anyone, thought that America would be the place where at least the Anglo-French part of the war would be settled. But everything was complementary and very little exclusive.

Braddock's regiments sent direct to the Ohio after Washington's embarrassment demonstrated that. Unfortunately, the proper generals sent to retrieve the defeats of local militia forces did every bit as badly and on a bigger scale. On 9 June 1755 Braddock attacked Fort Duquesne and was trapped by a combined French and Indian force of nine hundred with commanding fire. Out of his 86 officers and 1373 men, respectively 63 and 914 were killed, Braddock among them. The successful retreat of the survivors was led with great skill by Colonel Washington.

It was the British way – followed in almost every conflict over centuries. And, very shortly, we lost again. The war would be fought in many places, including the pleasant island then, and for convenience here, called 'Minorca'. 'Menorca' to the Spanish and in travel brochures, it retains here the form under which it aroused so much bad feeling. The British had taken it in 1708, governed it rather well and lightly, leaving it with an inoffensively English appearance – lots of sash windows – still remarked. But the long-term grip on a place so situated and equipped for naval war at Mahon (today Catalonian Mao) reflected the wholly deserved aggressive reputation of the British in Mediterranean eyes. Any of the British Isles – Wight, Man, Lundy, Mull and a choice of Hebrides – occupied across fifty years by a Spanish garrison supported by Spanish ships, would have brought sturdy Britons into a state of paranoia.

We held it to monitor naval ports, also as booty and permanent menace. There was a touch of insouciant criminality about British pride in trespass. The reaction to losing it would be correspondingly extreme. But there were excellent sailors' reasons for the lament. Mahon was the most secure deep-water port in the western Mediterranean. Here you retreated, fitted up, repaired. It was a base, military and naval, for intercepting enemy expeditions or launching one's own. To lose it was to suffer a major reversal. In any peace treaty it would stand at the top of the British list of restitutions.

The actual losing was a commonplace muddle, marked with a certain nervousness. Naval conflict had begun with a pre-emptive strike before any declaration of war. On 10 June 1755, peacetime, Admiral Edward Boscawen, reflexively truculent, catching up with a French squadron in the fog off Newfoundland, attacked it, took two ships and made war inevitable. It was bad timing; we had struck, in one place and modestly, but as aggressors, long before we were anything like prepared in the other places. Yet it was nowhere disputed that France had two objectives for which she was making ready. First was the old bogey, but a serious one, of invading Britain itself. The other option was to take Minorca. Since this was known, it required acting upon. The man for this was the First Lord of the Admiralty, no mere bureaucrat, but a sailor, a very great sailor, Admiral Lord Anson, not very long back from circumnavigating the globe.

But he also knew that the French could not take up both options at the same time. Cabinet and King agreed with Anson's expert, wrong judgement that the Channel was the likelier place of action. Reinforcements, naval and military, which should have been sent to its garrison were not attempted until 6 April the next year 1756, when Admiral of the Red, John Byng, was despatched with a squadron to patrol the island's waters. The squadron was undersized because Anson guessed wrong, not expecting a serious French presence in the Mediterranean. Doubts rose at the Admiralty. As Minorca began to be rather more of a worry, some fusiliers were added for the garrison. It would then take six weeks to direct five more ships under Admiral Brodrick to join the expedition.

At Gibraltar, Byng, travelling in the same uncertainty as his chief, first learned from Captain Edgcumbe that the French had landed on Minorca. From this knowledge flowed the implication, spelt out in his orders, that he should round up men from the Gibraltar garrison and land himself. At the same time, he made a mistake which would recur in this war, if less fatally. He held a council of war and sought advice! This came as data about the strength of the Minorca citadel, the still British-held Fort St Philip, data supplied by General Fowke, commander of the Gibraltar garrison, data inexcusably pessimistic and wrong. Byng was led to believe that St Philip could not be defended until reinforcement came to put the whole island safely back in English hands. He could have seven hundred men from the garrison but the man offering them reckoned that attempts 'to dislodge the French or raise the siege' would 'only enable it to hold out a little longer' and that he needed much larger forces.[16] He made it clear by letter that his likely function now was the naval defence of Gibraltar, which he expected the French to attack next. What Byng did not know, and Fowke, who comes dreadfully out of this, did, was that Minorca had taken up all available French resources. If she was easily placed to take a weak citadel there, she was in no position to make any show at Gibraltar. From such information and Byng's response, political lightning would strike.

On 1 June, Richard Rigby MP, lieutenant of the Duke of Bedford, unedifying but astute politician, wrote to his patron about the report of an Irish officer, O'Hara, which had brought the Cabinet together. He described the failure of action by the council of war at Gibraltar:

> They are not to take a battalion as they are empowered by their instruc-
> tions to do, from the garrison at Gibraltar, to reinforce Fort Philip as
> well as to throw Lord Robert Bertie's regiment into the fort, but in
> every shape despairing of the relief of the Island of Minorca . . . Mr
> Byng loitering six days at Gibraltar where they said he need have staid

but 24 hours; in their resolutions declaring the relief of the place almost impracticable, and, in fine, Mr Byng writing that he is going to look after the French fleet, who he hopes to make some stand against. Their determinations are desponding into the last degree; and at this council of war were present, the Admirals, Governor Forbes, Lord Effingham, Cornwallis, Lord Robert Bertie and all the Colonels and lieutenant-Colonels at Gibraltar; so that from the drift of these letters there appears a dread even of Gibraltar, and an idea, that if that is preserved, we shall have reason to think ourselves well off . . .

Young O'Hara* who had been in Minorca, disagreed with his fainéant betters and, relates Rigby, 'says the force of the French Fleet is not above nine ships of the line, but allows their army ashore in the island to be fifteen thousand men'.[17]

In consequence of such correspondence, London was better informed than Byng. The political world had learned that the French had landed; there was now evidence before ministers that St Philip's was quite sturdy enough and could sustain a long siege. Henry Fox, Secretary of State, put it prophetically to the Duke of Devonshire. 'I doubt not our first news will be that Byng is returned to Gibraltar, and that a council of war says he did wisely. The consternation of everybody here on this is extreme.' That hardly said it. Writing to his Catholic friend, John Chute, a week later, Horace Walpole told him 'to have a thousand masses said in your divine chapel . . . I believe the occasion will disturb the founder of it and make him shudder in his shroud for the ignominy of his countrymen . . .'

Ministers had hoped, reasonably enough, that their own credit might be saved if Byng would at any rate take on the French at sea where they had none of the military advantage enjoyed on the actual island. But six days after the letter to Chute, Horace was telling Mann in Florence of the encounter (something learned through D'Abreu, Spanish Minister in London) between Byng's ships and those of the French admiral, Galissonière. He 'had sent word that the English fleet had been peeping about him, with exceeding caution, for two or three

* Described, without evidence, by Byng's furious partisan Augustus Hervey, as 'worthless'.

days; and that the 20th May, they had scuffled for about three hours, that night had separated them and that, to his great astonishment, the English fleet, of which he had not taken one vessel, had disappeared in the morning.'

If the polite world was scandalised at this history, the mood was nothing to the exasperation of the court, 'which', said Horace skittishly, 'immediately ordered Admirals Hawke and Saunders . . . to bridle and saddle the first ship at hand, and post away to Gibraltar and hang and drown Byng and West, and then send them home to be tried for their lives'.[18]

Dispassionate accounts made in our own time involve essential detail wanting in an enjoyable 1750s panic. The balance between French and English squadrons was close. Byng had thirteen ships to his opponent's twelve, but French guns were heavier. With a helpful wind change, he won the gauge, but this involved reversing course, which put him and his flagship *Ramillies* third from the rear. The battle was a difficult business for the rear to engage. The van squadron under Temple West did engage and was immediately in trouble, the foretopmast of the *Intrepid* being shot away and all control lost. For no reason ever settled, the rest of the van, which could straightforwardly have come past her, didn't. Byng's squadron backed a distance to let confusion sort itself out and then sought to engage later, while the French, pleasantly ahead of the game, turned downwind and away.

Byng's flag captain, Arthur Gardiner, had suggested turning the *Ramillies* downwind with the excellent prospect of the other ships of the rear following. Byng quoted the recent unsatisfactory case of Admirals Matthews and Lestock, where, at the court martial, Matthews, who had done just that, was censured for it. The story of Galissonière, who had moved off sharply enough, coming back and being amazed at British ships having disappeared, seems conversational.[19]

Byng would be furiously defended in print by his close friend Captain, later Admiral, Augustus Hervey. But overall, his performances over both relieving Fort St Philip and in the engagement were thin and unenterprising. The London press would have favoured a useless sacrifice, but a rational judgement says that a preliminary venture made at Minorca, finding it too securely held, *then* pulling back, would have been legitimate. But he settled without a jot of physical corroboration for the advice of a defeatist, or worse, Fowke at Gibraltar. He wrote the purpose of his voyage off without sending a reconnaissance party. His council of war stressed their weakness for action without additional garrison troops, though they were grudgingly available at Gibraltar. It was an astonishing thing to have concluded that nothing could be done by the British fleet to raise the siege 'even if there were no French fleet cruising off Minorca'.[20]

In the 'Battle of Mahon', however little the name was deserved, there was, contrary to King George's dogmatic and lethal conviction, no cowardice, but not much vigour either. Byng had failed to observe the vital rule in sailing-ship warfare of keeping his flagship *Ramillies* in the centre where it could be seen and, being seen, direct. He testified that he had expected the rest of the rear to come forward but found it retreating. That should be believed, but it was his business to give direction and he didn't. It would, too, emerge as particularly bitter news that, on 28 June, General William Blakeney, exhausted like his troops at the long siege of Fort St Philip, finally and honourably surrendered. Byng had sent his limp missive to London that there was nothing he could do or try to do on 4 May!

Pitt was alerted and wrote from Hayes on 5 June to George Grenville, 'The squadron under Mr B, after a slack & poor, distant cannonade, has retired from before M. G[alissonière]'s squadron, retired to station before Mahon. B is gone to Gib & if our account does not differ widely from French, where he ought to go next is pretty evident . . .' Musing afield, he thought that 'Asia perhaps may add its portion of ignominy & calamity to this degenerate helpless country . . . [It might be] a selfish consolation but it is a sensible one, to think that we share only in the Common ruin – next & necessary consequence of admin. without ability or virtue.'[21]

That letter to Grenville was followed by another, equally gratified, on the 16th: 'I hear however from rumour that clouds gather on every side, and Distress, infinite Distress seems to hem us in on all quarters.'

Though the son of a great victor in an earlier war, Viscount Torrington, Byng was not royalty and could not expect the caressing whitewash shown Admiral Mountbatten in 1942 after the three thousand dead of Dieppe. His career should certainly have been kept remote from major responsibility, and cashiering would not have been unjust. Though for someone only lax, limp and overcautious, honourable retirement would have been best. Being shot by firing squad on the quarterdeck of *Ramillies* nine months later was something else.

Horace Walpole's clowning was not far removed from the mob quality of public reaction. The *London Evening Post* made pre-emptive allegations of a cover-up. Across July, attacks were made without too much detail and less heavily upon Byng, never mind Anson, who had underprovided, but upon ministers, especially Newcastle. 'The public indignation', wrote John Wilkes to George Grenville, 'is rising very strong against Lord A, & Byng has everywhere some warm advocates from an Idea I hope of his innocence or at least a degree less of guilt & not from the natural inconsistency of this, and I believe every other country.' He added a little later that 'Poor Byng is the phrase in every mouth & then comes the hackneyed simile of Scapegoat'.[22]

At this time, the sentiments of mob displeasure hit Newcastle. Thomas Potter, ex-Medmenham debauchee and Patriot, one of those wild, interesting figures who should have lived rather longer, wrote '. . . his Grace being on a visit to Lady C. Pelham [Lady Catherine, widow of Henry Pelham] was somewhat alarmed at the indignation of the Greenwich mob who saluted his Grace with dust [contemporary euphemism for excrement] & humbly proposed to his coachman to drive him to the Tower'. He also recorded the declaiming of '. . . a hundred ballad singers . . . To the block with N and the yard-arm with Byng'.[23] There were the usual invocations of 'Liberty', which was 'our Birthright', and of 'Slaves,' which the British people were not to become at the hands of their ministers.

Superseded by Hawke on 3 July, Byng arrived home on the 26th. He was treated from the start as a national disgrace and held in dishonourable confinement under guard in a single room in Greenwich Hospital until court martial followed at the end of the year. This took place across a month with Blakeney, of St Philip's, one of the witnesses. Courts martial of senior officers getting things wrong were common enough and convicted officers generally went in fear of anything from reprimand to dismissal.

Sentence of death, despite the court's rightly clearing Byng of cowardice, was exceptional and not thought likely to be carried out. It provoked a furious controversy (and wonderful career opportunities). But what nobody reckoned with was the steady, convinced anger of George II. George, dangerously valiant himself without someone

to drag him back, also furious that Admiralty and ministers had passed
the moral burden to him, settled, utterly wrongly, for death. But the
matter dragged indecisively on, not a rush to judgement, more a debate
around the firing squad. Chesterfield summed things up exactly:
'Byng is reprieved for a fortnight; what will become of him at last
god [sic] knows! For the late Admiralty want to shoot him to excuse
themselves; and the present Admiralty want to save him in order to
lay the blame on their predecessors; for neither the public service
nor the life of a fellow creature, enter into consideration on either
side.'[24]

Temple, as remarked, would rage at events. The injustice of the
confirmation, combined with his natural nerve and arrogance, made
him speak to George in ways one didn't employ with reigning
monarchs. Rigby again is the reporter: 'Lord Temple pressed him some
time ago very strongly for a pardon for Mr Byng: his Majesty perse-
vered and told his lordship flatly he thought him guilty of cowardice
in the action, and therefore could not break his word they had forced
him to give to his people – to pardon no delinquents. His lordship
walked up to his nose, and sans autre cérémonie, said "What shall
you think if he dies courageously?"'[25]

But Byng did die courageously. And English readers of *Candide*,
Voltaire's critique of philosophical optimism, would see without
pleasure the heading to Chapter XXIII, 'Candide and Martin reach the
Coast of England', and what follows at Portsmouth harbour, where
they find that:

> The waterside was crowded with a host of people who were gazing
> intently at a stout man kneeling, with his eyes bandaged on the deck
> of a man of war. Four soldiers stood opposite him and fired three
> rounds each into his skull with the utmost composure, at which, the
> crowd dispersed evidently quite satisfied. Candide enquires and is
> answered.
>
> 'He was an admiral.'
>
> 'But why execute this admiral?'
>
> 'Because he has not enough dead men to his credit' was the reply;
> 'he joined battle with a French admiral, and it has been established
> that their ships were not close enough to engage.'
>
> 'But surely', exclaimed Candide, 'the French admiral must have been

just as far from the English admiral as the English admiral was from the French!'

'True enough,' was the answer, 'but in this country we find it pays to shoot an admiral from time to time to encourage the others.'

The last statement is almost universally known among educated people. Less familiar is Candide's reaction.

Candide was so taken aback at what he had seen and heard that he refused even to set foot on English soil . . .

From this particular miscarriage of both justice and good sense we have had a rough press ever since, not least from ourselves. But Byng's errors and the public response had, in slow motion, scattered the pieces and knocked the board off the table. Politics had previously followed events matter-of-factly enough. The City merchants and their two newspapers and the London mob rose and fell against Byng, but readily and with no particular logic transferred to ministers. Politicians talked anxiously to one another. Henry Fox, the strange, bright talent who would play his cards so badly and then so ignominiously, warned Newcastle that 'the City was extremely displeased with the leaving Minorca exposed'.[26]

There was a welter of pamphlets from the Tories and an address from the City to ministers proposed, one involving Beckford. Common Council was persuaded to play Pitt's tune, the Need for a Militia. Beckford was in danger of being outranted by a group wishing to block the assumed candidate for Lord Mayor, Marshe Dickinson, because he had voted for the Commons address to the King favouring Hanoverian troops.[27] In the real world, France and Austria had put their River Sheldt-threatening agreement into formal shape in May, known, ironically, as the Treaty of Versailles. Finally, in August, Frederick had invaded Saxony.

Real events now got to London politicians. Henry Fox, not a man to go into the jungle with, declared his dissatisfaction with Newcastle and on 15 October resigned. It was his job to defend the ministry. Instead, he claimed a fear of being made to carry the blame, giving no one time to do that by getting his disloyalty in first. Newcastle's next misfortune was to be denied the excellent alternative of William

Murray who, fearing the heat of the parliamentary kitchen, had swiftly
made for the Chief Justice's lodgings. The government had a Commons
majority, but had no one to lead the Commons. In an age prizing rhetoric, rhetoricians enjoyed a tropical rarity.

Only now, late in October, did the name 'Pitt' begin to be used. But
the idea of a great tide of spontaneous public will urging on their
champion is quite misplaced. The whole point of Pitt in this sort of
crisis was in his role as talented voice and vivid personality rallying
authority in the Chamber and in the places outside where trouble was
made. The duke was ready to accommodate Pitt. Newcastle might be
a poor fighter; he was also a poor hater. His long commentary in letters
to Hardwicke and others over the war and coalition years grumble and
worry (and make perfectly sensible criticisms), but there are plenty of
generous comments. And at this moment, Pitt was neither poison to
be swallowed nor Prince of Destiny, but an apt man in debate.

10

Two Dukes, Fox and Pitt

In the period preceding the war Pitt had furiously opposed all continental connections. He talked about it to fellow MPs in categorical terms.[1] Dodington would note how

> Mr Pitt returned to me, and told me that he had painted to the Duke all the ill consequences of this system of subsidies in the strongest light, that his own imagination, heightened by my suggestions could furnish him with. He had deprecated His Grace not to complete the ruin which the king had nearly brought upon himself by his journey to Hanover which all people should have prevented *even with their bodies*. – A king abroad even at this time, without one man about him, that has one English sentiment, and to bring home a whole set of subsidies! . . . few words were best – nothing in the world should induce him to agree to these subsidies . . .

Something would, something did. Meanwhile, less elevated questions of who was up and who down preoccupied him. He had raged in semi-public at Fox:

> Mr Pitt came to Lord Hillsborough's where was Mr Fox who, stepping aside and Mr Pitt thinking he was gone, the latter declared to Lord Hillsborough that all connection between them was over that the *ground was altered* that Fox was of the cabinet and Regent, and he was left exposed etc. – that he would be *second to nobody etc.* Mr Fox rejoining the company, Mr Pitt being heated, said the same and more to him, he would not accept the seals of Secretary from him, for that would be owing an obligation and superiority which he would never acknowledge; he would be nothing but to himself – with very much more in very high language and very strange discourse.[2]

But at that earlier time, before Minorca, before Fox's desertion, Pitt's great cause, the monstrous nature of subsidies, was a political non-starter. In a vote on the issue which he called six months after this outburst, on 14 November 1755, he was defeated, eloquence notwithstanding, 311–105.

However, by May 1756, as the weather changed, Fox's nerve gave out. This centrally important period cannot be understood without trying to understand Henry Fox. He was as effective a speaker as Pitt, rather on the ironic than the heroic side and the better for it. 'Fox', as Lord Waldegrave noted, 'is rather an able debator than a complete orator; his best speeches are neither long nor premeditated; quick and concise replication is his peculiar Excellence.'[3]

In other words we would have enjoyed them more than Pitt's. His enemy paid him an involuntary compliment, responding to one quick intervention with the very Pittish attitude that 'when a man has truth on his side, he is not to be overborne by quick interrogatories'. He was a long-term Walpolean, resenting Newcastle and Hardwicke's withdrawal from full support of Sir Robert in 1741–2. He had deepened this animus in 1754 with a personal attack upon Hardwicke, instigator of that year's Marriage Act, and Pelham, who backed it. A happy eloper himself – with Lady Caroline Lennox by way of a Fleet marriage – he took legislation against the device as a personal insult.

But he had made his peace and had flourished, notably after Pelham died soon after. Now, in 1756, on every calculation he was ahead of Pitt; and on 12 March, became Secretary of State. He was Newcastle's advocate in the Commons and with that essential function he would be happy and accomplished. The most convincing view of Fox's ultimate limitations sees him fearing risks and innovation. Newcastle had given him place and function but not the tokens of trust, information and seniority which his pride and insecurity needed. However, rather than go into the effective opposition of which he was capable, Fox lingered discontentedly in place. He was fearful, thinks one historian: 'For a variety of reasons, not least because success in opposition might place full responsibility for leading the government rather than just the Commons, in his hands, Fox's preference was to serve under Newcastle.'[4]

This created the worst of all imaginable worlds. 'Willing to wound but yet afraid to strike', Fox sat in office, serving indeed but not performing. When Pitt launched his portentous but very fragile assaults, Fox sat quiet, the hired guard leaning on his halberd. At the same time, he was unwilling to change sides and join with Pitt against Newcastle. The only rationale was that he expected Newcastle, stranded in the Lords and himself only a modest speaker, would eventually give him full status and authority.

A fallacy reflexively asserted by politicians is that deeds should always rank above words. Accordingly, when Minorca fell and Newcastle faced hysteria spilling into the streets, what he needed was words. Nothing else, certainly not speculative military action, would do. Words would provide an eloquent diversion of public feeling from the current rage. They would create a steady national confidence with confident assertion that Britain was poised to be the Jack who at a bound should be free: lies, in other words, but benign lies, the lies you have to do.

The Opposition should have been castigated for unpatriotic opportunism, for spreading defeatism instead of girding loins and preparing for the great struggle to assuredly guarantee yet greater victory. Churchill, facing forty German divisions with no allies at all, whistled through his teeth and talked Agincourt.* Even so, the fall of Minorca was not the fall of Dover, however much the overwrought Opposition wanted it to be. This was an eighteenth-century war like all the other eighteenth-century wars except for the likely profits. Britain, or England as we called it, was not going to be conquered. Serious men – Anson, Montague, Clevland – had done serious work at the Admiralty. We had outstanding admirals and naval captains the way Milton's God had angels. France was not going to succeed in any invasion, and all thoughts of flat-bottomed boats and employing Charles Edward Stuart were, in a word, 'diversionary'. Louis XV was not Louis XIV, still less Napoleon. The realities should have been obvious without hindsight.

Unfortunately Fox, who could have moved very credibly along the necessary upbeat line, weaselled and body-swerved. Certainly Newcastle in a crisis had a bad habit of blaming other people, but Fox defined himself by *fearing* the blame. What he might decide to do now would determine his reputation. His actual conduct damned him

---

* There is, though, a legend that after delivering the 'fight in the hills' oration, he added, 'And if that doesn't work we shall have to throw bottles at them.'

into the worst circle of narrative Hell. Instead of helping, he blamed Newcastle pre-emptively and refused his transparent duty to serve a common and urgent purpose. So when Newcastle would not excuse him from standing up to defend the government, on 10 October 1756, Fox took his resignation to the King.

Now, in November 1756, and by the hand of Fox, with Newcastle standing aside and down, Pitt would enter into the talks which made him a minister and soon, aptly, Minister of War. Neither Newcastle nor Hardwicke had set a face absolutely against his advancement. Although he made them (and so many people) uneasy, they could respond. Ironically, a factor in Pitt's sudden acceptability to the Pelhams, along with his advocacy, was precisely his involvement with Leicester House, the Dowager Princess and Bute. They were the Opposition, and in the present mood of headless outrage Opposition was dancing.

Pitt's virtue here and now was his self-certainty. So often misdirected at wild or mischievous causes, it exactly met the mood. Words mattered even when they echoed Ancient Pistol. His famous pronouncement 'I know that I can save this country and that nobody else can' should be seen in the context of the 'Oh My Dying Country . . .' blague which had featured so frequently. Not that the King shared any of the Old Corps' practical acceptance or Pitt's own rapture. George loathed Pitt for personal insult, and as someone so clearly loathing George. The King could swallow him but not keep him down.

The fall of Minorca had done the trick. Comparisons have been made with Narvik, British failure over which Norwegian town in 1940 brought in Churchill. They make poor comparisons. When Narvik fell, Czechoslovakia and Poland had been conquered, then Denmark and Norway, all this on top of Munich and six years of appeasement. With Hitler at the Arctic Circle and the Vistula, there was good cause to talk of 'saving the country'. In 1756, a very useful island had been lost by an irresolute admiral. We would have to attack enemy shipping in the Mediterranean from other bases or after longer voyages, but we still had incomparably the best-manned, led and equipped navy in all the relevant oceans. No matter: a masochistic despair was in fashion and would flourish for the best part of three years.

Chesterfield, favouring an insouciant, not quite serious despair, had

informed his friend Dayrolles on 17 June that we might soon lose
Gibraltar and also that 'The French are unquestionably masters to do
what they please in America.'[5] Chesterfield extended his despair generously to Austria. Her Versailles treaty with France (actually to a
long-term advantage) was a calamity, the product surely of Maria
Theresia's pregnancy. France would 'finally reap all the benefit of this
new and unnatural alliance'. Meanwhile, 'the effects must be dreadful
for England' because of the Hanoverian connection.[6] Horace Walpole
in August talked of cost. 'France seems to have taken the wisest way
for herself, and a sure one too, by ruining us, by sitting still and yet
keeping us on our guard at outrageous expense.'[7]

In any case, Minorca alone did not bring down the Newcastle
Ministry. Military news had been bad, notably, to certain neurotic
observers, the victories. The German war, itself so much swifter off
its tracks, had been marked late in August by Frederick's amazing
strike into Saxony. Chesterfield observed this flourishing campaign
with darker apprehensions. 'The Fields of Bohemia and Moravia will
become Golgothas, or fields of blood, this year; for probably an
hundred thousand creatures will perish there this year for the quarrel
of two individuals.'[8] That was true enough as a moral judgement and
anticipated Macaulay's famous assault. Frederick had started everything in 1740 with naked aggression to snatch Silesia, covering it with
laughing pieties about sacred Salic Law. Clear-minded, morally-wrong,
he was creating a path for history, *realpolitik* in effective action. Frederick
and his ring of superlative generals had made a bold, successful strike
into the territory of Austria's ally, an act bristling with dangerous
contingencies, but this was the measure of *our* ally. It was, too,
inevitable that Pitt, following his trade of Great Man, should unreservedly admire and exalt Frederick the Great. He was, after all, soldier
in the field, director of battles, his life at risk, the man Pitt would have
liked to be.

However, commentators saw this initiative as the last thing Britain
wanted, something she had expressly advised against. What use would
a Frederick turning into Saxony and probably, by logical progression,
Bohemia, be to the Hanover preoccupying our government when in
January they had made a convention with him? To add to Newcastle's
misfortunes, another military encounter had gone wrong: in Canada
where, as they learned in October, Oswego on Lake Ontario had earlier

fallen. It was serious enough, but, looked at in the longer view, North America was the theatre where we massively outnumbered the French, soldiers and citizenry alike. Fox's panic was a public reflection of the defeatism behind the desks of contemporary diarists. Emotionally, the country's leaders and chroniclers were creating a mood which would magnify success when it came.

The process was drawn out. Frederick invaded Saxony at the end of August. News about the fall of Oswego came at the start of October. Henry Fox left his post on 15 October. Facing necessity, Hardwicke endeavoured to bring Pitt in upon terms less exalted than he sought. They met on 19 October for three and a half hours. Pitt would share nothing in government with Newcastle, persuading Hardwicke that he was engaged upon a deal with Fox. Instead, Pitt, after talking to a little conference of Grenvilles at the home of Sir Richard Lyttleton,[9] and following advice there or his own impulse, called two days later upon Lady Yarmouth. The King's lady, astute, kindly and discreet, was the nearest approach a political outsider on manoeuvres might make. She received a list of prospective ministers. Fox's name was not on it.

On 28 October, Newcastle and Hardwicke told George that they could not go on. The departure was voluntary and in younger, more combative men need not have happened. The King did not want Pitt, certainly did not want Pitt alone, and asked Fox to speak to him. An accidental-perhaps-on-purpose meeting on the stairs of Leicester House, where both had worked the Opposition, came to nothing, neither man able to contain his dislike. It was also clear from Lady Yarmouth's list that Pitt's ministerial cabinet was a family affair jewelled with Grenvilles and Lyttletons, Cato's little Senate. This, despite his want of support in the Commons, meant a central command, unwise in a less hungry politician. The Duke of Devonshire was next asked to come into the equation to take the formal First Lordship. Such a formula meant William Pitt *in excelsis*.

But at the moment of a remarkable achievement for the leader of a sub-faction at blazing odds with the crown, Pitt talked and behaved in ways to make impossible his sustained full leadership of a ministry. Newcastle and Hardwicke, seeing the advocate government had lacked, would work with him. Pitt refused to work with them. His confidence flowed from the support, muted and *faute de mieux*, of Bute and Leicester House. He was in a delightful position but only as third choice for chief spokesman because William Murray, better mind, weaker stomach, had shrunk from conflict while Fox, juggling ambition and bad nerves, feared lonely exposure. Pitt, who could combine abject sycophancy with a readiness to fight any three of you, grew haughty and insistent. He disdained working with Fox, he would not serve with Hardwicke and Newcastle. Self-belief was not the problem. Parliamentary arithmetic and the royal veto were.

Behind such grandeur lay noisy public support in the press. *The London Magazine*'s bumper annual in December drew him as Perseus coming to the rescue of Britannia.[10] He had ditched the Patriots, embraced then ditched Frederick Lewis, and abused the Tories en route for Pelham's offer. Much of the support was wary and untrusting, however vigorously coordinated by John Wilkes's ardent and dying friend, Thomas Potter. This orgy-frequenting son of an archbishop and rackety but attractive idealist was joined by a defecting Pelham cadet, George Townshend.* These two had got together fifteen senior Tories and country gentlemen to sign a pro-Pitt letter.

They too were a war party; his enemies were their enemies. Neither the ardent sentiment of the close allies nor a few responsive Tories could sail a parliamentary majority without the Old Corps. But the Tories *might* give him a hundred votes, Leicester House, if it didn't sulk, sixty. It was a serious base but, Pitt governing all alone with the Commons majority attached under every kind of obligation to the late ministers, was not base enough. Walpole had described his faltering Excise Bill as 'a dance that will no further go'. An unadorned Pitt Ministry was a dance which would hardly get on to the floor.

However, it became more acceptable to the new outs with an emerging player. William Cavendish, 4th Duke of Devonshire, used to be casually dismissed as a decorative nonentity. Research, including discovery of papers, shows a quiet, reasonable man, calmer of disputes, builder of trust without personal ambition, of which quite enough washed around Cabinet and Parliament. Immensely rich, seeking

* Townshend was a nephew of the brothers Pelham who, as Cumberland's military ADC, had fallen out, not discreditably, with the field marshal. Horace Walpole noted one 'who with much oddness, some humour, no knowledge, great fickleness, greater want of judgment and with still more disposition to ridicule, had once or twice promised to make a good speaker' (Walpole, *Memoirs of George*, vol. III, p. 340).

nothing since he had it already, Devonshire was a sort of anti-Dodington. But then, free of malice, envy and all uncharity, he was, too, an anti-Fox. Nor was there much in common with Pitt. But as a friend of Newcastle, he could work with Pitt and play straight by both. The government forming now needed the support of factions and those factions giving support on sufferance. One must think French politics during the Third and Fourth Republics.

Pitt treated high office as something to be difficult over. He wouldn't work with Newcastle. He wouldn't work with Fox. But the practical politician slept lightly within the heroic tenor. Devonshire was a young and welcome friend of the Old Corps. At thirty-seven, with only a few months' ministerial experience (in Ireland), he would soothe the King, he would, it was supposed, be a cipher. He was acceptable. Nominated KG, then as now the real honour, and dragging his feet about the wagonload of Grenvilles, arrivistes arriving, whom Pitt was determined to place, Devonshire kissed hands as First Lord on 6 November. This was the Pitt–Devonshire Ministry, a fragile attempt to govern the country with the Opposition, to the applause of Leicester House amid the smouldering displeasure of George II.

For a start, where a ministry with no natural majority solicited support where it could and so looked to the Tories, trouble appeared at once. There were things the Tories wanted which made enemies of non-Tories. Uninstructable vengefulness flourishing there beyond any small flower of good sense, they wanted an inquisition into the conduct of former ministers. Pitt had wanted it too in his initial high-horse demands, but was thinking better of it. He must come to terms with Germany, the war being fought there and the bad news coming out. The war was up and running, and ministers followed where it went. The circumstances of war continued as obbligato to pre-occupying political manoeuvre. Pitt might please his groundlings and attempt consistency by rejecting the Hanoverian/Hessian troops due to come here, a handy piece of xenophobia to play in his wider constituency. But he couldn't divest himself of Hanover itself – or the need to defend Hanover.

So long as France and Austria stayed out of the electorate, the pressure was less. But Prussia's invasion of Saxony had brought Czarina Elizabeth, already an enemy, into the war and out of our paid-for understanding. We had a new, if remote, opponent; and Frederick's usefulness to Hanover was overwhelmed by preoccupations south and east. Pitt was in office but circumstances continued Newcastle's war policy. The Hanoverian troops Pitt wanted to be rid of were now rid no farther than Germany, defending Hanover under Cumberland. For the moment the Minister could deny British troops, but he had to request Newcastle's obliging Parliament for £200,000 to sustain the King's responsibilities as Elector. It was a long way from denouncing a beggarly electorate when the orator needed to give it large amounts of British money.

Chesterfield observed developments with prophetic scepticism:

> The Duke of Cumberland wants extremely to go with his own Regiment of Guards to be beaten at the head of the army of Observation in Lower Saxony; for that will inevitably be the case of that army as soon as Comte D'Etrées at the head of one hundred thousand men shall arrive there. Hanover is evidently the object and the only rational one of the operations of the French army; not as Hanover but as belonging to the King of England, and the Electorate is to be a replica of the present state of Saxony.[11]

In other words France would do to Hanover for its British connections what Prussia was doing to Saxony for its ties to Austria.

Actually, the precise terms of the Prussian alliance would force Pitt into a massive contradiction of a quite recent and sulphurous declaration. When Newcastle and four colleagues had signed up Prussia in the Treaty of Westminster in January 1756, Frederick had reasonably sought and reasonably obtained a call on substantial extra supplies when needed. Pitt out of office had not wondered mildly if such a commitment might not be unwise. He had told the Commons and the world that 'he would not have signed it for the five great places of those who had signed it', something unkindly remembered by Horace Walpole.[12] He now held one of those great places and, in February 1757, asked Parliament to grant extraordinary supplies to the King of Prussia. It was absolutely the right thing to do. But Pitt in office as walking contradiction of Pitt in opposition would make rather a retrospective fool of his recent self.

This episode illustrates the wider truth that differences over broad policy would prove negligible. Barrington of the War Office told the

British Ambassador in Berlin that 'These measures as declared and explained by Pitt the first day of the session differ in nothing from those of the last administration. Every effort in America consistent with our safety at home, every effort at sea, and whatever this country can do besides, given the support of our allies on the Continent.'[13]

Having benefited from fierce friends in the press, Pitt suddenly came under fire himself. On 6 November 1756, as the *Monitor* congratualted itself on having no opposition, the first issue of the *Test* came out. Almost certainly backed by Fox, it was good; 'scurrilous but well-written' is Lucy Sutherland's Oxford judgement. Such qualities are unsurprising in writings attributed to the elder Philip Francis, father of the much rougher Junius, and to Dr Johnson's Irish friend, the witty playwright Arthur Murphy.[14]

Pitt, having talked so much about it, now had to promote his Militia Bill. It got through much peppered by the friendly fire of Newcastle's associates in the Lords and passed on 25 March 1756 only after, in Marie Peters's phrase, 'important changes which modified its ideological character'. Instructively, Pitt played almost no part in promoting the bill. As for his Enquiry into the Conduct of Ministers, the counterpoised politician inside him recognised every kind of bridge burned and running quarrel he could do without. It took place only pro forma. The permanent problem for such an undertaking was that what delighted the former Patriots alienated so many people willing otherwise to support a government. The things the Pittites had clamoured for were not happening, as why, at the start of an inevitably long war, should they? On top of which the finances of the ministry had fallen into a melancholy condition.

Across six weeks of February and early March 1757, the trial, sentence and execution of Admiral Byng ran their dismaying course. As noted, the sentence had disgusted Temple who, at his uncalculating best, had stood up to George, shocking Bedford's man, Rigby, who 'had never heard of such insolence'. Pitt was also disposed, this side of heavy confrontation, to mercy. This is a good and attractive episode in the lives of both men, also of Beckford, who spoke up in the Commons for reprieve. Which did not make it good politics. John Byng passed through more than one phase of public opinion to his Calvary. The public and its newspapers had been furious for a judicial lynching. There was some shift after the sentence when death for an excess of military caution sank into men's minds. Byng, in Horace Walpole's words, had indeed become 'Poor Byng', but it had been a sentiment remote from George II, persuaded, as the court martial had not been, that Byng was a coward. Though incidentally, and surprisingly, Cumberland, near and dear, was claimed by Richard Rigby as opposing Byng's execution.

The *Test*, seeing that Pitt favoured reprieve, was strong for the firing squad. The *Con-Test*, Pitt's ally, miserably prevaricated. Meanwhile, the *London Evening Post*, another Pitt supporter, unreservedly attacked sentence and execution. In party terms, Pitt won support from Tories; and their pamphleteer, Dr John Shebbeare, wrote a blazing denunciation of the whole proceedings.* Outside the heavy political press, in two issues of the *Literary Magazine*, Samuel Johnson, voice of the conscienced Left, condemned the whole business as scapegoating by the Admiralty for its own shortcomings.

Pitt was visibly in the middle of contention, and seemed at court not the acclaimed and untouchable leader but, for a reason wholly creditable, another Minister caught in a swirl of controversy. George, deeper in resentment, was encouraged to move against him. He had a further pretext when the Duke of Cumberland, Commander-in-Chief, refused to serve abroad under this ministry. Cumberland was a political player. Fox was his man; and ironically, given his near-pacifism, John Russell, Duke of Bedford, was his ally. Back in 1751, Bedford had resigned as Secretary of State, claiming to George that he had been picked on by the Pelhams 'solely from his attachment to his son, the Duke'.[15] But quite apart from Cumberland's being the advocate of involvement in Germany, the duke must have wanted to see off the despiser of the 'despicable electorate' as simple enemy. His industrial action made sense only if there were any risk of Pitt being consistent; it heightened the pressure on Pitt–Devonshire's frail construction. On 5 April 1757, Temple, following that burst of heroic cheek to the King, was dismissed, and on the 9th, Pitt followed. It was a good way to go. His popularity slipping under the ordinary wear and tear of wartime government, he had become a victim. His decent instincts towards Byng deserved, and got, credit, but the fall healthily reflected a lopsidedness in a ministry constructed in flailing haste.

* *Fourth Letter to the People of England*, August 1756.

It was time to make a new one to fight the war for the continuing consistent ends. In the upper Grenville ranks, Temple wrote to brother George, 'My journal reads as follows:- On Tuesday, Lord Holdernesse came to me with the dreadful tidings, made offended himself at not being told a word of this matter till the day before: the enemy expected this would bring on a general resignation . . . The Duke of D[evonshire] to continue the end of the session. LM[ansfield] to hold the Exchequer . . . Offers without end to Newcastle who not only stands his ground, but I now have the utmost reason to think that his union with us is as good as done, in which case, Foxism must go to the devil . . . The freedom of the City in gold box is thought of for Pitt.'[16] What followed would be known rather charmingly as the *Interministerium*. There was a war on while Devonshire kept the shop open and made himself useful as intermediary and Lord Winchelsea looked after the Admiralty. The problem was to reconcile three groups of people between whom emotions counted above policy differences. Pitt's long campaign of deference to Lord Bute had placed him pleasantly with the Prince of Wales's adored preceptor. Young George, in the family pattern, had a vendetta against another member of the royal family. Obsessionally, Leicester House hated Cumberland who hated them back, something behind his Pitt veto. Fox was Cumberland's man in the Commons, hating and hated on similar principles. Then there was Bedford, reliant on his louche but capable Figaro, Rigby, and with views on war diametrically opposed to Pitt's. The group was completed by Lord Waldegrave, chronicler, intelligent commentator and source.

Close behind them was the King with the King's interest, authority and gift of being difficult. In a Whig world, any self-respecting monarch was a factionalist. So, George had intrigued with Fox during the Pitt–Devonshire tenure, and ministerial lists were drawn up. Although allied, Pitt and Bute had separate followings, respectively the Grenville faction, concerned for office and remuneration, and Leicester House with people in the Commons of the low stamp of Dodington and James Oswald.

The third faction was the most professional and least doctrinaire. The Old Corps, Newcastle and Hardwicke and their backbench tenants, had run or helped run Parliament and the country under Walpole and Henry Pelham. They were serious about Whig principles and loyal to George precisely as a Hanoverian king, that good, constitutional thing whose German interests weighed lightly against the historic wisdom of being a king obliged to Parliament. They did business with anyone and set their faces against no one excepting Fox, whom the mild duke uncharacteristically detested.

We were fighting a war primarily naval, but forming a government had to wait upon the findings of the enquiry into what had happened at Minorca. Not the inquisition Pitt had demanded, rather something necessary to clear the air at the Admiralty, it did this in the classic English whitewash tradition, relieving Anson of a share of blame which most historians, noting his delay and underprovision of ships, think he deserved. It was absolutely the right decision – right because Anson was a first-rate administrator engaged in getting neglected ships repaired and pushing up their number and condition – and because there was a war on. Newcastle was also and rightly disembarrassed and free to serve. With time passing, the threat from George of Newcastle starting up again on his own terms weighed enough with Pitt to help conclusions.

George had played with alternative options. Might not Waldegrave head a ministry with Fox and Bedford as chief props? It wasn't a nonsensical idea except that Fox would have lacked the day-to-day nerve for war and, anyway, George himself put no great confidence in the venture. The realities were simple. No government could last in Parliament without Newcastle's men. Pitt was the trumpet of war gathering behind him all the people and newspapers dancing in the rain of crisis. Pitt and Newcastle, Newcastle and Pitt, and their factions on terms of equality, it had to be.

For three days in the middle of June the bargaining went on. Amazingly, Pitt wanted Henry Legge, a slight, unmeritable man but loyal to him, to command the Admiralty. No post stood in greater need of technical knowledge and continuity. Legge, a lightweight in any department, had neither. Hardwicke, with a wise nepotism, stuck out for his son-in-law. As that son-in-law was Anson, victor of Finisterre in the last war, recent circumnavigator of the globe and the administrator concerned to have more ships available for war, it was an essential nepotism.

The Admiralty had been held in the recent ministry by Temple who was deemed by no one to have made a fist of it. Hardwicke, speaking to the King, talked useful pettifogs, lighting upon Legge's

becoming both First Lord and a peer. Anson was a peer, too, but it
was overlooked. Perhaps Legge might go to the Exchequer which, by
convention, kept him out of the Lords, Temple's board of Admiralty
might stay, but Anson should head it. The King was happy, Pitt able
to concede. The post most immediate to conducting a great war had
been entrusted to a sailor and administrator of the first order.

The rest of the Cabinet-making was merely political, a satisfaction
of interests. Hardwicke, with beautiful timing having done what truly
mattered, left at the top of his game. At sixty-seven, he made a wise
judgement of the strains of a War Cabinet, resigned the Great Seal
after more than twenty years but stood invited to attend Cabinet
without portfolio as essentially Newcastle's second.* Newcastle was
to be First Lord of the Treasury, Pitt Southern Secretary, concerned
with the likely regions of a naval war, while the eternally put-upon
Holdernesse took the Northern Office.

Temple, whom George would not take in a position involving audience, became Privy Seal, influence without responsibility. The new
Lord Chancellor was not Robert Henley. He would do the work, but
was given instead the diminished legal office of Lord Keeper (of the
Great Seal). Pitt failed to do anything for his young friends in the Militia
Bill struggles, the Townshend brothers. Much more reprehensibly, his
ablest relation, George Grenville, fitter than Legge for the Exchequer,
was made Treasurer of the Navy where he would seek, with the Navy
Act 1757, to accelerate the outrageously retarded payment of sailors'
wages. But Pitt's lopsided view of respective merits would be the little
rift within the family lute and, given George Grenville's talents and
capacity for resentment, bad politics.

A pendant to all this was the appointment of Henry Fox as Paymaster
General. A splendid talent, a weak stomach and a compensatory craving
for money would have the Pay Office milked – by private investment
of public surpluses. As noted, 'the right' to get rich in the job had first
been rejected by Robert Harley in Queen Anne's time, gloriously
revived by Sir Robert Walpole, quietly eschewed by Henry Pelham,
followed, to peals of self-applause, by Pitt. To Fox would come great
profits in a great war and an ignominy peculiar to their circumstance.

---

* He would be an irregular attender – to the benefit of history by way of the
Newcastle–Hardwicke correspondence.

In the long view, four years and a vast, ranging war won, this seems a splendid ministry. But hardly anyone thought so at the time. It was a government of enemies and factions following an unconscionably long interim. Ministers looked at each other's every move with an eye to its bad motive. But the logic to what had been done is caught exactly by Richard Middleton in his seminal study *The Bells of Liberty*: 'George II was anxious to secure ministers who would do their utmost to help him as Elector of Hanover. Pitt and Bute wanted men to fill the government who would check such tendencies. In the middle were Hardwicke and Newcastle who recognized the King's legitimate expectations, but were concerned that the nation's other interest did not suffer.'

A war was to be fought on land and at sea, in America and Germany, both to the grief of France. Three days had been given over to Hardwicke's consultations in creating the essentials and another two weeks to sorting out contingent details. The Newcastle–Pitt Ministry was a compromise and a very good one.

II

Hastenbeck and Rochefort:
Panic and Recrimination

The Seven Years War must be seen as a piece of cloth, spread very wide and containing a complex weave. England would make war against France largely in North America where she had made war before. The Newfoundland fisheries were part of the prize. The stations of Louisbourg and Quebec were to be disputed. Meanwhile, southward, British and colonial troops would concern themselves with French forts like Duquesne, now eloquently speaking the outcome, and a major United States city, Pittsburgh. Until the Canadian question was met, British men-of-war and detachments of marines would make tip-and-run incursions on the north-west coast of France, and France in turn would follow plans for invading Britain.

It was primarily about trade, that finite thing, out of which enemies must be driven. If Free Trade had been established as doctrine in the 1740s, there would have been no war. The author of British Free Trade, Robert Peel, an incomparably abler man than Pitt, though saddled by colonial administrators with the first Afghanistan mess, otherwise made no wars worth the name. Trade made for empire and Pitt in a loose way had that as an objective. He certainly saw America as an open space with possibilities, though we might remember Cromwell's observation, 'No man goes so far as he that knows not whither he is going.'

The conflict also contained the jealousies of an old animus. Religion had begun to be undermined by Deism in the 1690s. The moralist of this age was Voltaire, yet Pitt's war speeches were spattered with Protestant avowals. The thoroughly godless Frederick of Prussia was acclaimed as another Gustavus Adolphus, a second Protestant lion fighting another Thirty Years War. In the real world, we had lately fought Spain for merchants' plunder. Frederick, an arriviste among kings, had fought from 1740 to 1748 to take a province, and was fighting another to keep it.

A final complication was the personal interest of George II, also Kurfürst (Elector) of Hanover. That principality was too near France for its modest military capacity. George I, a man systematically underrated by the sullen British, had recognised the problem and had been ready to cede Hanover to another member of his family. It hadn't happened and *his* son, the Elector Georg August (King George II), was unreservedly devoted to Hanover. Hatred of foreigners being a habitual quality almost anywhere, hatred of Hanover could be readily worked up. The rational if burdensome defence of Hanover did not get us into the Seven Years War. It was a pendant issue, creating a handy overlap of interest with Frederick and Prussia. 'My enemy's enemy is my friend' is not a static dictum; friends change. As Austria made up to France, England's enemy, so England struck a close bargain with Austria's enemy. Frederick's defence of *territory* taken by force from Austria was a thread matching England's purpose of stealing *trade* from France. The purposes were low, the conflict preoccupying.

Pitt, as the Tories' favourite Whig, had long played the anti-German card, Hanover as 'beggarly electorate'. By contrast, 'the rogues robbing Spain', as Lord Hervey had coolly put it in the 1730s, became upright, seagoing Englishmen, heroes worth a war. That line had played on the street, played with the country gentleman and now bubbled furiously in Beckford's *Monitor*. But Pitt was not narrowly consistent. His anticipation of King George V – 'I hate abroad' – had served its purposes. We had been absorbed in the war's early days, in a familiar Mediterranean setting, hence everybody's overreaction to bad news from Minorca.

However, the necessity of involvement in continental Europe was about to be demonstrated by new military failure – two lost battles close enough in time – in Germany. Over six weeks in the summer of 1757, Prussian, then Hanoverian, forces encountered severe reversals, Kolín, 18 June, Hastenbeck, 26 July.

On the first date, six weeks after his success at the Battle of Prague, Frederick took on, with his 35,000 troops at Kolín in western Bohemia, an Austrian/Saxon force of 53,000. A mistaken tactical adjustment changed the planned flanking attack at the last minute to a frontal one. The advice of Prince Moritz of Anhalt-Dessau, a very rough and ready soldier, this was what you didn't do against a larger army. It ended when Saxon and Austrian troops, including a mass of Austrian cavalry, attacked the Prussian back ranks and settled matters.[1]

Involving as it did the loss of 13,000 men, mostly infantry, including the slaughter of his Foot Guards, then immediate abandonment of Prague, Kolín was a famous defeat. Indeed, the retreat had to be commanded by Frederick's brother, Henry, left in charge by the temporarily shattered King. His biographer, Christopher Duffy, observes: 'Kolín was for the Prussian army what the charge of the Light Brigade at Balaclava represented for the British in the nineteenth century.'[2] It was a crashing but temporary blow for morale. Frederick had lost his reputation for invincibility, not least in the excitable London press. The Duke of Bedford thought that if the news had arrived a day or two earlier, the Pitt–Newcastle Ministry could not have been formed.[3] With the new champion so diminished, we should, he implied, have sought a compromise peace.

Immediate concern echoed across Great Britain. Frederick might even be cornered and defeated altogether. For, in the words of a nineteenth-century German historian, 'All Europe was against him.'[4] There were 20,000 Swedish troops on the border of Prussian Pomerania, a Russian army could sweep into East Prussia and, what most upset gentlemen in Westminster, two French armies stood placed to cross Germany. In this war, Prussia was defending Silesian territory taken in the last war. Austria, backed by Saxony, had attacked her to get them back. If Frederick were defeated in the full, end-of-war sense, which after Kolín seemed likely, French troops would be free for America, if they could get there, for the Caribbean, even as reinforcement to Pondicherry and the French interest in India. Hanover would become part of a French zone of influence in western Germany. As for morale, French and British respectively, it didn't bear thinking about. With all this in mind, Maria Theresia celebrated Kolín by putting Nieuport and Ostend into French hands.

Newcastle was already, just before the battle, summing things up bleakly but fairly enough. 'Mr Pitt must think seriously of Foreign affairs, in a different manner from what he has done, or the King of Prussia will make his separate peace; and we shall lose the Electorate this year, and God knows <u>what</u> the next.'[5] Midsummer and after, 1757 was a shared low point for England and Prussia. Though the French ignored a British naval superiority which could deny French colonial ventures, thoughts in London were dark.

Prussia was a modest-sized country which had given enormous affront. So in one ironical respect, Newcastle had been mistaken. Frederick couldn't make a separate peace. In *this* war, he expected any ultimate defeat to be total. It was a measure of the King of Prussia's fears that he carried poison, ten measures of opium, in a little case. The recreational nature of little eighteenth-century conflicts was over. Harassed on all sides, Frederick, needing to release troops from the north, had been demanding (and not getting) a British squadron in the Baltic. The new British Cabinet, with Pitt now playing, had turned hesitation into flat refusal.

On any reading of the future, Austrian triumph at Kolín had ended all hopes of that great offensive war which should have taken Saxony by way of victory in Bohemia. The support Frederick now sought was defensive and central to British national interests. A secure Hanover and allies beyond France, what the old Corps, Newcastle, Hardwicke (and George II), had always argued as a priority, had become immediate.

Pitt's response was complex. He greatly admired Frederick, heroic kin as he saw him, a soldier adventurer driving swift and forceful action. But he was inhibited by his own stored-up rhetorical record from helping Frederick with the troops he needed or the ships to the Baltic he would settle for. Newcastle would murmur that, when we were sending Prussia £2 million cash, it seemed odd to cavil at a troop of horse. But Pitt had placed himself at the head of English xeno-phobia and could betray that constituency only by stealth. A British naval squadron policing the Baltic against Swedish or Russian moves was again something Pitt, for party reasons, could not countenance – yet. However, all thinking about the major Prussian debacle would be swamped (and augmented) by that second battle, the *British* Hanoverian disaster a little over five weeks later.

The French had been stirring westward. The Duc d'Estrées, who had been waiting for orders, got them. He was told to cross the Weser and seek the Hanover/Brunswick small state army commanded by the victor of Culloden. As peacetime administrator and forward planner, Cumberland had been rather good. This force had been largely his creation back in the forties. He had latterly been making strong and reasonable demands for more men, two further companies to each regiment, bringing the numbers up to a regimental quota of 1135 men, while ministers offered less, one extra company only to each battalion. Still significantly undermanned and himself a modest field commander, Cumberland met the French at Hastenbeck, south-east of Hamelin, on 27 July. They defeated him over three days and drove his force to the Elbe, leaving Hanover wide open.

As Newcastle told Hardwicke in a letter dated 3 August: 'The fate of Hanover is now decided: the Duke [of Cumberland]'s army was beaten on the 26th of last month and His Royal Highness is now retired to Nienburg, which leads to Bremen and Stade. The country of Hanover is open to the French, and I understand by the King that the President, Münchhausen,* was to have a conference with Marshal D'Estrées . . . the battle or rather skirmish, lasted three days; the two first we had the advantage, but Monsieur D'Estrées was reinforced (as they say) by 20,000 men and that overpowered our army.'[6] The duke had not pushed on to rendezvous with the Prussians within reach at their point of retreat, Magdeburg. Instead, without considering options, he had blundered on towards the doom of Stade. His orders had been 'to keep a retreat towards that town open and free', and he seemed incapable of thinking beyond his orders.

The effect upon George was calamitous and he told Newcastle that he would, as Elector of Hanover, apply for a separate peace. No British Minister could advise him in that capacity, but they could talk quietly and try to influence him. Parliament very quickly put up £400,000 to George as Elector and £100,000 to Hesse-Cassell. That was easy but what was needed after such a defeat at so strategic a place, when French conquest of Hanover and Austrian defeat of Prussia were likely outcomes, was men, British soldiers.

What exactly was to be done by London? Pitt was for the moment still the prisoner of his old rhetoric, his old supporters, not least Leicester House. In a letter to Bute of 6 August, he stated that though Newcastle, Hardwicke and Holdernesse had advocated sending troops to Cumberland, only his negative had stopped it. Continuing *financial* support for Hanover and Hesse was, however, 'a concession I have

---

* Gerlach von Münchhausen, 1688–1770, Hanoverian Chief Minister, also founder of the University of Göttingen.

judged it advisable to make on the grounds of a fatal necessity to the best of my understanding quite irresistible'.[7]

Limp as he was at Hastenbeck, we should not simply talk the failure of Cumberland. The numbers in that conflict are eloquent. D'Estrées had had 10,000 cavalry and 50,000 infantry and sixty-eight field guns against Cumberland's 5000 cavalry, 30,000 infantry and twenty-eight guns.[8] Pitt would need to find a new doctrine to replace the dog-in-the-manger certainties of Patriot opposition, and rather hinted at it. A day after not-yet-reported Hastenbeck, 27 July, there had been a ministerial discussion about a proposed nine thousand men to reinforce Cumberland. The tone had improved, but only the tone. 'Hardwicke and I strongly for it, Mr Pitt against but in the most decent and friendly manner possible and desires that his opinion not be followed if *we* don't think it right.' We were about to spend large sums of money to support Frederick, the Hessians and, of course, Hanover. The distinction Pitt still clung to, 'Money right, men wrong', made no kind of sense.

The pity was, as Fraser points out, that Pitt and the authority his personality exercised had stopped Newcastle from doing the necessary thing of getting troops to Cumberland before an engagement. Partly this was due to the older man's concern to keep this government together. Pitt fascinated colleagues, struck furious attitudes then made them grateful for 'a decent and friendly manner'. He had the masterly will Newcastle lacked, but Newcastle's judgement, if insisted upon, would probably have saved Hastenbeck. Yet surely he must have known why he was about to change his public mind. In Fraser's view he had been following pure domestic politics, denying what he understood to be the point of real danger so as to keep his backers happy, then gaining credit for the graceful concession. But although Pitt was highly intelligent as well as devious, he was also a febrile personality. Judgement of him must balance cold power-play against a mind and moods always erratic.

Whatever the motive, a similar response had met Frederick's call in his great need for British ships to make themselves felt at the mouths of German rivers. On the strength of a ministerial meeting in Arlington Street, Holdernesse, the other, lesser, Secretary of State, sent a message on 5 July to Frederick via Dr Adrian Mitchell, British Minister at Berlin. It affirmed Britain's support for Prussia, while also stating what did *not* need stating – that Cumberland was in deep trouble. Then, with some brassneck, it urged Frederick to try harder.

It was an *haut en bas* message not unfamiliar to struggling allies in the communications of the British Foreign Office. Did Frederick want a naval squadron to patrol the Baltic coast? We could do nothing about such a naval squadron. We had 'a merchant role to protect, . . . our Trade depends upon a proper exertion of our Marine strength'. So no ships in the Baltic, but we would create a diversion by way of a coastal raid. Some money would also be found which might 'at a critical moment enable his Prussian Majesty to supply what is wanting on our part'.[9] Holdernesse's message embodies a sort of graceful insolence which only Mandarins and Etonians quite bring off. The solicitous flummery accompanying it must have left Frederick, with Russian and Austrian armies perhaps to be joined by a French one, feeling intolerably patronised by the non-delivering British. Such austerities of helpfulness had come after Kolín but before Hastenbeck had broken on horrified Westminster ears.

But fairly soon the ministry would now move towards doing late what it should have done early. They also exercised themselves about what steps might be taken. First of all, they must steady the King. George II's favourite son had left him an occupant of his own electorate until d'Estrées should choose to take it. George was filled with despair, telling Newcastle that he meant to apply for a separate peace. 'His Majesty was calm,' wrote Newcastle, 'said he must do the best he could, he had stood it as well as he could and must get out of it as well as he could – that he had taken his park. Which I found was to make his peace, he could do nothing more for him [the King of Prussia].'[10]

Surely there were things that might be done. Frederick in his battle had lost 13,000 men, Cumberland in his, six hundred! Frederick was briefly dazed and, as noted, ceding management of the retreat from Prague to his brother. But he had rapidly pulled himself together and set about finding ways and means. The general fear was that he might make a separate peace and/or that George would live up to his early angry hints and pull Hanover out of the conflict, neutral but intact. This was a great and rolling crisis, but about one concern anxiety was mistaken. A commander like Frederick, who makes war fighting well above his strength, does not do the humiliating deal which gets him out of a war. And if he is the territory-seizing Frederick facing the wronged and vengeful Maria Theresia whose territory he took away fifteen years earlier, he has nothing to expect for doing it.

The British, reasonably enough, made immediate worst assumptions about the King of Prussia's future reliability. It was an island view. Our wars were fought at pleasing distances, with naval forces preponderating, and all we had to lose was colonial territory or trade. Frederick, from his family's corner of Brandenburg and West Pomerania, was fighting for his kingdom against France and the Holy Roman Empire. For this struggle he was always ready for the friendly means to do it with. Our anxieties that summer ensured that he (and Hanover and the Hessians) got it.

George was a different problem on which ministers must work hard. He would approve in principle, the King wrote to Cumberland on 11 August, an agreement for Hanover's neutrality. He gave the Hanover Chancellery authority to approach the Empress Maria Theresia as potential mediator with France.* Because of the British connection, the beggarly electorate would always arouse acquisitive interest in large neighbours. From the angle of a beggarly electorate, neutrality and modest cash payments made perfect local sense. British involvement there was a British interest.

Faced with an emotional collapse turned political crisis, ministers were temporarily stymied. Newcastle records in the same letter that:

> I afterwards met with my Lord President, my Lord Holdernesse and Mr Pitt . . . We all thought we could give no advice about the intended neutrality. I told them I only meant to know whether anything could be proposed by us that might induce him to stand out. I found nothing could be done. The sending troops now was thought hazardous and useless; and no great use was to be had from money, if it could be offered – Mr Pitt was very much alarmed at the Effect this would have upon the King of Prussia; and declared his Opinion that *we* should forthwith offer the most large sum of money in order to engage him to continue in his Present system and not to make peace; or at least

---

* In fact, a variant of that duty would be taken up in August by the King of Denmark.

not to give him a pretence to say that he has been abandoned by England. But when the King [of England] has made his peace as Elector (if he can do it) and has also concluded [terms with] the Landgrave of Hesse-Cassel and the Dukes of Wolfenbuttel and Gotha, it will be impossible for the King of Prussia, attacked upon all three sides, to stand out alone. The Army of Observation [Cumberland's forces] which will now be dissolved was the only barrier for the King of Prussia on that side – He will certainly endeavour to make this Peace, perhaps at the expense of the King, Both as King and Elector . . .'¹¹

Frederick wasn't going to do that and George could be worked on. His honour mattered deeply. Talk of making a private peace expressed a despair he could, with skill, be talked out of. That was Newcastle's department. Meanwhile, Pitt's cogs and wheels buzzed with drastic adjustment. His hostility toward the German connection had to become yesterday's verbiage. Hanover territory was part of the whole conflict. It had to be defended, and the money, a great measure of it, would always be found. 'I had a long and friendly talk with him [Pitt] yesterday . . .', writes Newcastle, '. . . he adhered to his principles or plan both as to time or form. But I think he would be generous as to the sum if only it could be given in his own way . . . I asked him, if the King [Frederick] would trust and determine now to get 8000 men to reinforce his Army . . . , Would he, Mr Pitt, promise to pay them another year? After a good deal of conversation I think I saw without having anything positive to ground my Opinion, that Mr Pitt would be brought to give next session 400,000£ as Elector, 300,000£ for the Hessians & 500,000£ subsidy to the King of Prussia, upwards in the whole of One million 200£.'

It was only money but this is a decisive moment, the giving big which undermines argument against ships to Frederick and troops to western Germany. Whatever lay behind Pitt's 180-point turn – Fraser's super-subtle sliding into what he had thought all along, or Mr Macmillan's 'Events dear boy, events' – it upset the Tories. John Calcraft, later close to Pitt, told Lord Loudon, 'Report of 10,000 men being raised and transports taking up . . . the Torys [sic] have all declared off with Pitt, so now we'll send troops to the Duke . . . How change-able These gentlemen are. Borough of Chester express to R. Grosvenor [Robert Grosvenor, their MP] not to give their gold box and freedom to Pitt and Legge as they begin to suspect them, and many other corps [Borough Corporations] talk of recalling theirs too.'[12] During the summer period, after Hastenbeck but before Kloster Zeven, when the situation was still, to invert the old Austrian irony, serious but not desperate, Pitt was demonstrating remarkable fluidity. But, less usefully, he had also been looking south.

Early in August, Newcastle, back from a pleasant trip to his stamping ground, Sussex, where he found 'almost all the considerable gentlemen of the County pleased with everything they should be pleased with', attended an audience which 'succeeded beyond my expectations . . . Mr Pitt talked to the King pretty much as he had talked to me [about money for Germany] & His Majesty was much pleased with it . . . said Pitt would not name how much he would give me [as Elector] . . . The present to the Landgrave (of Hesse) in his retreat and distress in Hamburg was Mr Pitt's own proposal and greatly pleased and affected the King . . .'

What followed was startling. 'After this was over, Mr Pitt rightly entered into general politics and said that since we could do nothing in the North, we must see what could be done in the South. That for that reason, we should endeavour to get Spain, not only by putting an end to our own Maritime and Commercial disputes, but also by doing something solid for Spain! And he then proposed the offering Gibraltar to Spain if they would help us to Port Mahon. For without Port Mahon, no one would *venture* to make peace and that in return for Gibraltar we might have Oran or some port in the Barbary Coast – not a new thing, Münchhausen mentioned it some time ago to the King . . .'[13]

Newcastle adds that Pitt had already floated this idea to Count Viry, the much-confided-in Minister of Sardinia. He then speaks of Pitt wanting it 'seriously considered by the King's servants; that if this did not do he was ready *to do anything* [Newcastle's italics], by which I thought he meant to make such peace as we could get'.[14] This is astonishing language coming from Pitt. As to the Spanish matter, the idea he was contemplating contradicted (and interrupted) a lifelong hostility to that declining country. Was the Secretary of State thrust into as deep a pessimism as King George, or indulging diplomatic doodling? Swapping Gibraltar, an unimportant peninsula, for Minorca, with the best harbour in the Mediterranean, served only a too obvious British interest, His Majesty's Navy recovering the perfect naval base for making war on France or Spain.

It was a non-starter. And for Pitt, invoker of treason against Walpole's Convention of Pardo and its modest commercial concessions, giving Gibraltar back would have been poison to his unsophisticated constituency. Of course, he was as ready as, or readier than, most politicians to make adjustments, but this was perhaps end-of-war talk. And a resolution by Pitt to end the war Pitt championed does not fit. It reads like a dark interval. However, what came next, early in September, would not be light at the end of the tunnel. Getting the King off his ledge could eventually be done as he worked off his rage and grief until he saw the distance below and came back through the window. The problem had never truly been a distressed George. The problem was Cumberland. William Augustus had jumped off the ledge.

By sticking to the letter of orders in a dull, subordinated way after the bad news of Hastenbeck, the worse to come materialised at Kloster Zeven. The negotiations for this Convention were opened by the arbiter, Denmark, then signed on 3 September, signed at Bremervörde by Cumberland on the 8th, and by the new French commander, Richelieu, at Kloster Zeven on the 10th. The unenterprising ghost of Admiral Byng hung clammily about the whole course of events.

Whatever orders might once have been, Cumberland had acted without consulting his Father, King and Elector. He did, however, hold something with which George had vested him. As Pitt said, unanswerably, when George tried to bluster himself out of blame, 'Full powers Sir, very full powers'.[15] Properly followed through, this signature would represent a huge French gain in the German theatre. The British creation, the Army of Observation, was to lay down its arms and go home; its Hessian and Brunswick troops were to return to their home nations, leaving the Hanover army intact but shivering and alone.

In London, this simply could not be allowed; the Elector of Hanover must denounce Kloster Zeven. The Convention ran clean against the duties of the King of England. As for Cumberland, he would soon be recalled. Never popular, he became at once an object of general contempt. The previous identification had been for brutality – chiefly Culloden. But as Horace Walpole wrote to Sir Horace Mann in

Florence, 'On such an occasion you may imagine that every old story of malice and hatred is ransacked: but you would not think that the *general* is now accused of cowardice.'[16] As for the usually irrepressible English national pride, at this moment, as Horace remarked in the same letter, 'Oh! Believe me, it is comfortable to have an island to hide one's head in.'[17]

It was essential to get out of the King's plan, and the precondition of getting out was to have the King fully in step. Ministers had no constitutional right to tell the Elector what he must do in his electorate, but there were ways. As to the Closet, Newcastle had always reinforced his excellent line to George by keeping another one open to the alternative Closet, the Countess of Yarmouth. It had been Walpole's way. Marianne von Walmoden, in modern terms George's partner, was a sensible woman who knew, almost as well as Queen Caroline, how to talk sense into him. Between them, they let the King recite his resentment at English ministers and the general neglect of Hanover. He was then gently advised as to the stark impossibility for those ministers, and the British political class, of Hanoverian neutrality.[18]

Newcastle further indicated something cheerful, also spotted by Frederick, that the terms of Kloster Zeven could not be followed on *Hanoverian* authority to disband the important Hessian contingent. Those soldiers were paid by the British, something which invited a variation on an old military saying about mercenaries. It was now *Mein Kreutzer, Mein Schweitzer*. The merely legal view of Lord Mansfield was noted and rolled about. At the very least, he said, these troops should be sent to join Prussia. Better still, the Convention having been denounced, the Hessians remained British-employed soldiers, available wherever Britain chose to send them. Specifically and urgently, Frederick said six thousand foot and horse were needed to do what had become impossible for him after Kolín – reinforce Cumberland, or whomever.

This had already come under discussion before Kloster Zeven became fact. Newcastle had thought the season too late, but was completely in favour and had found George, who had never advocated anything so drastic, ready for it.

I found the Closet [George] as much for sending troops as it has ever been against it (the measure I always thought was right) . . . It comes

<u>from the best quarter</u> and that without any suspicion of coming from
hence. Such a reinforcement might certainly enable the Duke to do
more than I am afraid we shall do by any attempt on the French Coast
... if the intended expedition to the coast of France is thought
hazardous and almost impracticable by the generals (as it certainly is
and, as I am informed by Lord Anson, do both [Admirals] Hawke and
Knowles think it is), then (as I told him) this measure [troops to reinforce Hanover] may be more formidable.[19]

The contrast between the British problems after a major defeat, problems of dual responsibility and royal will, and the Prussian response
after their reversal at Kolín, was vivid. Threatened by Austria and
Russia, Frederick had been in full retreat. His court and Treasury had
left Berlin for Magdeburg ahead of its capture, and on 16 October the
capital was entered by the Austrian general Hadik with seven thousand men. It would last only a few days while the King and his
commanders picked themselves up. And soon after, the Russians, a
key part of his misfortunes, took themselves off.

Frederick, whose regard for the written form was minimal, had
already, on the 14th, sent off Ferdinand of Brunswick with six battalions and eleven squadrons to protect the Hanoverian city of Halle.
He had followed this up by despatching Moritz of Anhalt-Dessau to
the Elbe, more strongly armed, with ten battalions and as many
squadrons, as protection for Brandenburg.[20] Prussia was still in the
deepest trouble but something was being done to cover both her own
territory and protect central Germany from the attentions of Marshal
Soubise in cooperation with the troops of German states allied to
Austria. Kloster Zeven was the low point in the entire war. But in
Britain, King and ministers had, quite understandably, overrated its
long-term significance.

The French, too, with a change of command, did something to help.
To put it simply, d'Estrées was a very competent general, having served
in the field under Berwick and Saxe and been favourably noted at
Fontenoy and Laufeld. Richelieu, who replaced him after Hastenbeck,
was not. The appointment of a duke to supersede a count who had
just won a battle looks like standard Court of Louis XV practice. In
fairness, the decision was made before the result of Hastenbeck came
to Versailles, also typical. The menace of Richelieu was distinctly slighter

than the anxiety in Whitehall. He was quite frightened himself, writing a nervous letter to Soubise, last commander but one (and a prince), complaining about the quite impossible soldiers who had just defeated Cumberland. 'The extreme misery and indiscipline have produced discontent and a spirit which makes one tremble; I have not told a tenth of this to the court, as it is useless; and having tried and examined everything, I have come to the conclusion that it is incurable for this year.'[21] Whether this was a realistic estimate of French soldiers' morale or a reflection of Richelieu's temperament hardly matters. The French army of Germany was not all the jittery British imagination had thought it. On top of all which, on 3 October, Richelieu made contact with Frederick's companion in arms, Karl Wilhelm Ferdinand,* Erb Prinz (Hereditary Prince) of Brunswick, suggesting a seasonal armistice until the spring and offering to withdraw his troops across the Weser.

Richelieu's careless diplomacy and Britain's inconsiderate refusal to recognise a surrender when it had been made for her began the process of lifting the allies up. Austria's auxiliaries, troops and officers from places like Württemberg, Protestants of both kinds, 'brave when compelled to fight', as one of Frederick's generals drily observed, otherwise unmilitary and ambitious to stay alive,[22] were not enthusiastic about the destruction of Frederick which Vienna's plans had allocated them. British anxieties after Hastenbeck and Kloster Zeven were being part calmed by events.

Meanwhile, Soubise, in concert with those undermotivated imperial troops, was advancing, but advancing slowly. Frederick, as slowly, withdrew but not to escape. In mid-September, Ferdinand of Brunswick, his little fighting party of seven thousand men outnumbered nearly six to one, successfully fought a delaying action. Then, seven weeks after Kloster Zeven, things changed with a vengeance. Frederick, the prey of forces representing so many great powers, consolidated, and, on 4/5 November, above the Saale, near Weissenfels, outnumbered two to one by French and imperial soldiers, fought and won the Battle of Rossbach, a victory close to the historic league of Blenheim and Austerlitz.

Following events, attitudes had been changing among the English chroniclers. Others remained dubious. On 15 August, Chesterfield, always a little quick on the trigger, had been winding everything down

---

* Not to be confused with his near-relation known to the British as 'Ferdinand of Brunswick'.

to certain defeat. 'The war', he told Solomon Dayrolles, 'must soon
now be at an end, for it is evident that neither we, nor our only ally,
the King of Prussia, can carry it on three months longer.' Three months
later, writing from Bath to Sir Thomas Robinson, former Ambassador
to Vienna, Chesterfield said, 'I take it for granted that the King of
Prussia's victory engrosses the spirits of all your great politicians in
town . . . he has shown his abilities in it; which I never doubted, but
noting only that there are now seven* or eight thousand fewer of the
human species than there were a month ago. France will send double
that number immediately . . .'[23] When, a month later, Frederick
followed it with the arguably greater victory of Leuthen over imperial Germans and the French under Charles of Lorraine, the salutations
were general.

The contrast between these Prussian victories and events at
Hastenbeck, Stade and Kloster Zeven had been bitter. They had,
though, demonstrated France's fragility and the winnability of the war.
Ironically, the last man now interested in getting out of the German
theatre or abandoning Hanover was William Pitt. There might have
been *Schadenfreude* in the humiliation of his political enemy and Fox's
patron, Cumberland, but events were too serious and minds too
concentrated to linger over the politics.

Happily, the Convention, a piece of characteristic overreaching by the
servants of Louis XV, had rung bells throughout the European house,
not least alerting Frederick to Britain needing him as urgently as he
needed her. Quite as important, ministers were off their constitutional
hook. On 18 September, Holdernesse formally proclaimed the Kloster
Zeven Convention to have no binding effect by reason of the illegal
dismissal of the Hessians. England and Prussia were closer than ever.

The idea of sending troops to help Frederick was indeed, as we
have seen, floated by Newcastle, responding to an account of
Frederick's wishes in a letter forwarded by our Ambassador Mitchell.
This limited and quickly forestalled scheme had not been aimed at
weakening the coastal raids, rather as a clear-cut alternative and a way
of using those Hessian troops which, with denunciation of the
Convention, returned to active service in the field.

---

* All Allied casualties, prisoners and dead were 16,000, mostly prisoners, according
to Duffy (*Frederick the Great*, p. 67).

The idea of naval involvement across the Channel had been considered for some time. The notion of a new British naval triumph, however bijou, looked well, a satisfactory playing of our strong suit. A naval action close to the French coast was highly attractive to Pitt. Though it was not thought through in any detail, he leapt at the idea and, in his usual activist way, applied himself. The staff work and intelligence he accepted were improvised, speculative and out of date, the undertaking itself a gamble. If 'Something must be done', this, he thought, was that something.

Newcastle, though making periodic civil nods toward the project, remained steadily and politely sceptical. In July he notes the preliminary moves: 'Orders lately sent Mr Titley and Colonel Yorke [Hardwicke's soldier and diplomat son, Joseph, currently emissary to Frederick] to acquaint them under the greatest secrecy with the intended expedition to the Coasts of France (as formerly proposed by the King of Prussia) wherein near 8000 land forces, marines and almost the Whole Fleet at home will be employed, and thereby a Powerful Diversion may be reasonably be expected.'[24]

Running a reliable intelligence service, the duke took its reports seriously. He had been told of French preparations: '20,000 troops of Germany assembling at Cleves for proximity to Normandy/Brittany – defence against OUR invasion BUT could go to Nieuport in October from Cleves to attempt the English coast.'[25] He sent a memorandum asking for a more open-minded option in military policy. Its message involved considering 'whether the expedition should proceed in this advanced season and stormy weather . . . ?' Might they not 'consider sending an expedition to Ostend or opening the sluices and keeping them open . . .'? He observed that 'what the French were said to dread most is Holland joining with England to prevent loss of Ostend and Nieuport'. But he noted that Pitt was opposed to a Dutch declaration and objected to a shift into Flanders.

The arguments are serious, though Holland, delightedly neutral, had shied away from military involvement in the last war. But engagement in Flanders and threatening Ostend made sense. Both were usefully closer to France's theatre of war in Germany. Pitt, however, was determined to have his raid upon northern France. The big, commanding personality played its part in Cabinet, but, according to Bubb Dodington's diary, he was also briefing against colleagues, spreading 'False rumours'.[26] Newcastle, Hardwicke and others were arguing against coastal invasions. The combination of masterful personality and that briefing drove the gamble on. 'Many people', wrote Newcastle on 10 September, 'begin to be uneasy about our expedition . . . but Pitt is deaf; and in our present circumstances especially after what has been insinuated with relation to Hanover, I don't know who dares to take it upon him to <u>stop it going</u>.'

The mechanics of what became the Rochefort plan did not lack promoters. The technical inspirer was an officer in the corps of engineers, Colonel Robert Clerk. Having seen the terrain, he thought he knew what could be done. The acting Commander-in-Chief, Sir John Ligonier, and Pitt himself were persuaded of possibilities. In July, the King was approached, expressed approval and named the officers, prerogative and enthusiastic practice of George II. The military commander was to be Sir John Mordaunt, his deputies Henry Conway and Edward Cornwallis. Mordaunt was the nephew of Lord Peterborough, a quarrelsome hero during the Spanish part of Marlborough's wars and very much Cumberland's man. Conway appears in Horace Walpole's letters as 'Dear child' and, much later, as an oddly exalted figure among the Rockingham Whigs (see *post*). And at a crucial meeting in July 1757, held at the house of Lord Holdernesse, Ligonier introduced and supported Clerk's paper. The Rochefort fortress wall, claimed Clerk, was no more than twenty-five feet high above a ditch, and not fully built, information three years old. It could be taken by escalade – troops up ladders.[27]

Pitt said very little but kept all initiative concentrated behind the Rochefort proposal. These and subsequent proceedings seem to have been very civil. At the end of the month Newcastle would write to Lord Ashburnham of 'Some little difference of opinion – 9,000 to reinforce the Duke of Cumberland upon Prince Ferdinand; Hardwicke and I strongly for it, Mr Pitt against it but in the most decent and friendly manner possible and desires that his opinion not be followed if *we* don't think it right.' Lord Chesterfield, deftly and for the record, on 4 July, a day while options still hovered, famously defined the ministry: 'I look upon his Grace and Pitt to be rather married than united, the former will be a very jealous husband, and the latter a very haughty, imperious wife. However as things are constituted, they must go on together, for it is ruin to both to part.'[28]

Pitt's private conversation bears out the fragility of the alliance but shows him making soothing noises to supporters he was effectively abandoning. The Rochefort raid having been agreed in Cabinet on 4 August, Pitt wrote to Bute on the 6th saying that, though Newcastle, Hardwicke and Holdernesse had advocated the sending of troops to Cumberland, only his negative had prevented it. Bute's response encapsulates the Leicester House thinking Pitt would once have endorsed. Proclaiming himself 'not quite such a friend of Newcastle as you seem to be . . . he knows the deed of sending troops abroad is totally inconsistent with the being of this administration . . . One improper concession would be fatal to us all.'[29]

Bute deluded himself. Pitt had seen for some time the urgent relevance of fighting France in Germany. He made play of reluctant concessions to Newcastle and the others when he fully agreed with their conclusions. Despatch of troops to the German theatre had been postponed for a year by his politicking, but they were becoming an avowed fixture in his thinking. Meanwhile, Rochefort was something British and alone, good Patriot and Leicester House politics. But even if it and its successors had been relatively successful, winning skirmishes and briefly holding a few towns before orderly retreat with a clutch of loot, they would still have been strategically trivial.

The presentation, as modern business would call it, was good. Joseph Thierry, source of topographical information on the target area, was a pilot with twenty years' service in the French navy before his flight as a Protestant from the triumphalist clerical strain currently asserting itself in France.*

Thierry was confident that for commencement, landing and first stage, an assault on the fort of Fouras, near Aix, was the one good option. Failing which, nearby Chataillon, two miles north, would do as well, both objectives being within reach of Rochefort by way of a decent road. Ligonier followed up this information by estimating how many troops the French could turn to for defence. Despite initial increases putting the total at perhaps 200,000, they were, after commitments to Germany, reckoned at a mere 40,000. Meanwhile, on her north-western

---

* This would climax in 1762 with the breaking on the wheel of Jean Calas, innocent Toulouse merchant and Protestant, about which Voltaire breathed fire.

coast, Ligonier expected no more than 10,000. On paper it could be done. Newcastle, though still inherently sceptical, gave it a friendly hearing. As for the German conflict, it seemed, after so much British talk, to have drifted beyond our ability to influence it.

The seaborne raid had a natural appeal to the Street, Tory backbenches and Beckford's newspaper. It followed a great native tradition. Had not Drake, in 1587, singed the King of Spain's beard by a swoop-and-burn raid upon Cadiz? Besides, the navy was English, its excursions directed to attempt the French coast. It fitted that exalted selfishness so often called patriotism. The army was the German King's private delight and diluted, anyway, with foreigners. William Cobbett, who had similar clenched instincts, went to jail long after for denouncing the flogging of English troops by German mercenaries. (English sailors, by contrast, were flogged exclusively by other English sailors.) Orwell's observation that the English do naval patriotism, but fail to get a catch in the throat at the sight of red or khaki, had been a broad truth over the centuries before he made it.

Even so, Pitt instinctively played very rough, not least by conflating early and legitimate thoughts about how to use Hessian troops with what might be preferred to the naval raid. Dodington's and Newcastle's comments about such 'insinuations' and 'false rumours' are accepted by E.M.S. Fraser. Neither Newcastle nor Hardwicke suggested the expedition's resources should be diverted to Germany. But given Pitt's claim that before Hastenbeck only he had prevented troops being sent to Cumberland, it is hard to believe he did not float the rumours. They served him well with supporters assuaging anxieties that, in joining with Newcastle, he had agreed to support 'common measures' militarily.

Fraser's judgement on all this is that Pitt was engaged in the politics of backward advance. Newcastle would have liked to send troops to Cumberland but did not wish to shatter his fragile marriage with Pitt. He had left strategic decisions in Pitt's hands and, had they been sent before 26 July, the date of Hastenbeck, and had either averted defeat or won a victory, they would have shifted the balance of the continental war. It is hard to disagree with Fraser's contention that 'Resistance to reinforcements was surely the sacrifice of obviously sound strategy to the delays of a purely political manoeuvre.'

Ironically, the least enthusiastic voices over a naval raid on Rochefort were those of admirals. Edward Hawke had dragged his feet and made disobliging objections from the very start and Admiral Knowles concurred. Newcastle recorded an authoritative naval conversation: '. . . the intended expedition to the coast of France is thought hazardous and almost impracticable by the generals (as it certainly is, and as I am informed by Lord Anson do both Hawke and Knowles . . .)'[30] When the meeting to decide things was called on 4 August, the plan no longer had any apparent utility to the German campaign and argument rested more upon doing something.

There were intelligent doubters. The Duke of Devonshire worried out loud that sending away the navy to raid the French coast might encourage France to raid ours. And Devonshire, Pitt's temperamental opposite, noted the style of the Secretary of State's leading contribution to the meeting. It was, he noted, 'a curious performance, being instead of plain orders, a long and most laborious piece of oratory'.[31] The raid was intended, said the preamble to the report, rather making Devonshire's point, to add 'Life and Strength to the Common Cause'.[32]

So Rochefort it was to be. But it would be undertaken for reasons of *faute de mieux*, because, having started, it was embarrassing to stop, a quick snatch at a spot of mid-price glory. It was, after so much bad news, something of a headline strategy. Unease was reflected in the limitations imposed on the invaders. A long siege was out because it would give French forces time to get there and besiege the besiegers. Faith was put in getting up and over the walls on ladders and not stopping after that.

Ligonier was strong for this, citing previous success at Bergen op Zoom and our own calamity, the too vividly recollected fall by escalade of Mahon citadel in Minorca. However, both successes had come after prolonged sieges expressly forbidden to Mordaunt. Ligonier was thinking speed and departure, hit and run. Mordaunt was authorised to rove from the Basque Roads at the river mouth down the banks of the Charente to find something glorious to do. But on the premise of necessary speed, he was denied an artillery train. Anyway, a less happy rover than the flair-free and laborious Mordaunt would be hard to come by. From its outset and at several hands, the expedition was rather overnannied.

All this time, the situation in Germany was deteriorating. The key instruction-giving meeting ahead of the Rochefort raid had been held on 8 August. The actual expedition sailed from Chatham on 6 September. Cumberland had been beaten at Hastenbeck on 16 July. The subsequent humiliating surrender and convention had been signed, at Bremervörde, by Cumberland on 8 September, then at Kloster Zeven by Richelieu, on 10 September. There would be on average, in the happy days before twenty-four-hour news, a full seven days' delay before London learnt the outcome. Decisions were therefore being made before, during and after receipt of late and momentous news. The caution unnecessarily urged upon Mordaunt might make for incoherence, but it was perfectly natural. There was a case for sending troops to Germany. But the argument which Pitt had put predicated the raid as the unique course to follow, and the raid was about to fail fairly comprehensively.

The requirement was that soldiers and sailors should be back at the end of September. The struggle to stop the King's implosion into declaring Hanoverian neutrality was the discordant background music to ministerial meetings over naval planning. The season declined into expectation of heavier seas and bigger storms. Anson quoted to Newcastle two lords of Admiralty, Hay and Elliot, saying after a visit, 'that both land and sea officers *talked down* the Expedition'.[33] As Newcastle had said *supra*, 'But Pitt is deaf . . . I don't know who dares take upon him *to stop its going.*'[34]

The actual operation showed itself as serious war-making on 10 September when sixteen ships of the line, nine frigates and fifty transports set out. The naval command was as distinguished as any assembled in the century. Hawke commanded and as his biographer R. F. Mackay observes, eleven of his captains would rise to at least vice-admiral rank. There were present for this undertaking Howe, Keppel, Denis, Rodney, Byron, Brodrick and Knowles. Facing contrary winds, the force reached the Basque Roads on the 20th. At which point Hawke, who did not normally make mistakes at all, made an interesting one. Spotting a French warship, he signalled Howe on the *Magnanime* to chase it. Unfortunately *Magnanime* carried an important supercargo, M. Thierry. Consequently the pilot, with direct personal knowledge of reading of the waters of coast, roads and river, was left stationary at sea as his ship concentrated its fire on the little island of Aix and its fortress.

Howe set about this task to the satisfaction of everyone except the French garrison. As Robert Clerk wrote years later, when Howe was an admiral and a lord, 'In the island of Aix there were five or six twelve-inch mortars with proper parapets . . .' But Howe anchored only forty yards out and 'kept an incessant fire for about thirty five minutes'.[35] The Governor of Aix had no use for a valiant death . . . With two dead on the *Magnanime* against one within the fortress, a civilised surrender was negotiated.

But could that small victory be followed by a landing on the mainland opposite? Unfortunately the briefings of Clerk and Thierry had ignored the shallow water on the other side. Hawke was not deterred, having already had soundings taken by Brodrick before the conclusion of the Aix operation was signalled. The water, he judged, was low but not too low, a landing could be effected with the transport vessels running aground at low tide, a mile and half short of the beaches, whenever Mordaunt asked for it. But Mordaunt, to quote Hawke's out letters, was 'peevish', demanding, before anything was actually done, a council of war. Hawke had been as opposed as Anson to the mere idea of an expedition. But he favoured it now. Mordaunt could say fairly enough that troops, splashing through a mile and half of water, might, under any competent concentration of fire, be steadily picked off. This was a Red against Blue conflict. The distinction was that the sceptical navy wanted to make a fight of a scheme they had always doubted, while the never very enthusiastic soldiers stuck to their original hesitation.

In a military crisis a council of war is the equivalent of asking a Lord of Appeal to resolve a strike. But Mordaunt's instructions, approved by Pitt, gave him in Article Four 'full authority to summon a Council of War'. He had received, and would use, a right of peremptory pause. Hawke found 'the debates of the Council on the 25th ulto [which continued for three days] so various, tedious and uncorrected that it was impossible to take minutes.' Having lost time, the generals reckoned that the lengthy fight involved in taking Rochefort by ladders would go on too long. They looked askance at Clerk's assurances about defences and sluice gates and questioned him hard.

After so much French marching time had been spun out, Mordaunt wrote Rochefort off and instead gave thought to Fouras. This fort stood at the base of a little peninsula, well away from the river mouth

and to its north. Might not this (mentioned as an option at the ministerial meetings) do instead? General Cornwallis, who had argued
that Rochefort itself was vulnerable, but the landing before the
assault impracticable, now opposed the Fouras idea. It was too
speculative and they didn't know enough about it. But Mordaunt and
Conway, perhaps as fearful of the fury of George, Pitt and the press
as of French fire, let the sailors persuade them. The attempt would
be made.

Hawke favoured a daytime raid 'to prevent mistakes and surprise
while, at the same time, it would strike more terror'.[36] The generals,
whose soldiers, denied artillery, were likely to be fired on, favoured a
night raid. But an overwhelming discretion prevailed. The generals
then discovered a welcome problem. An offshore breeze would make
disembarkation slower, six hours to land men, another six on the ebb
tide getting them off: too long, too risky. (In fact, there were no cannon
at Fouras. The only threat to men embarking or disembarking had
been at Aix, and the Aix Fort had been knocked out – by the navy.)
Hawke, civil but smouldering, quoted *his* orders, which were to take
his ships back to England 'as soon as operations permitted'. And there
were no operations now, were there? It was his intention 'to proceed
to England without loss of time'.

A few weeks later, Hawke would enjoy great good fortune, not
apparent at the time. Improviser and working opportunist, he had
hoped to offset Rochefort with a freelance naval action. A group of
French fighting ships, under Dubois de la Motte, was making its way
from Brest to Basque Roads. In the second week of November, winds
were boiling up. Hawke had planned to rendezvous with *Unicorn*
and *Hussar* to search west of Finisterre for the French squadron
returning from Louisbourg, key objective in North America. The
weather proved too much for him. Between 17 and 23 November
there was nor flying hence nor tarrying here. And on the 23rd Dubois
got his ships into Brest.

It had been Hawke's luck *not* to catch him. On arrival in Brest, the
thousand cases of virulent typhus they carried were quickly communicated to the local population. 'The stench', wrote a French surgeon,
'was intolerable. No person could enter the hospitals without being
immediately seized with headaches; and every kind of indisposition
quickly turned to fatal fever as in the old days of the plague.'[37]

Thousands died in Brittany from the contagion and, if the weather had held and Hawke had returned to Torbay after a great victory, thousands would have died in Devon.

But England was unaware of this splendid negative. Preoccupied with Rochefort, it was in recriminatory mode. In fact, despite press scuttle, there was no cowardice during the Rochefort expedition, only a wonderful excess of caution. Clerk would leave a memorandum justifying what he had proposed and arguing rather impressively that, given the will, a way had existed. Among the army command, though apparently unwell and not much involved, was a certain James Wolfe. However, his comment that 'in particular circumstances and times, the loss of 1,000 men is rather an advantage to a nation than other-wise, seeing that gallant attempts raise its reputation and make it respectable' is a disquieting insight into the heroic mind. Wolfe would soon die following his own stark precepts on the Heights of Abraham, but his words put Sir John's caution in a more sympathetic light.

The response at home fluctuated between derision and rage. Horace Walpole, writing to Sir Horace Mann, delightfully settled as British Resident in Florence, begins skittishly: 'We have often behaved extrav-agantly and often shamefully – this time we have united both. I think I will not read a newspaper this month till the French have vented all their mirth.' But he proceeds to make a shrewd point:

> If I had told you two months ago that this magnificent expedition was designed against Rochefort, would you have believed me? Yet we are strangely angry that we have not taken it! The clamour against Sir John Mordaunt is at high-water mark: but as I was the dupe of clamour last year against one of the bravest of men [Admiral Byng], I shall suspend my belief until all is explained. Explained it will be somehow or other: it seems to me that we do nothing but expose ourselves in summer, in order to furnish enquiries for the winter; and then those inquiries expose us again.[38]

One must allow for General Conway being Walpole's close friend. But, overall, few comments were so reflective. Garments that season were worn rent, and self-pity general. Mitchell, at Berlin, thought that 'The English 'til now were envied and hated upon the Continent. At present, they are despised.'[39] Chesterfield thought in his cheery way, that 'This winter, I take for granted must produce a peace, of some kind or another, a bad one for us, no doubt, and yet better than we should get the year after.'[40]

The brilliant but unstable Charles Townshend who, a decade later, would add his own mite to national misfortune by putting duties upon the American colonists, added orchestral colour to the gloom by observing (absurdly) that '. . . this year under the direction of genius and public spirit, has turned out very like its predecessors and every month in it has been distinguished by some new defeat and some additional misfortune . . . language cannot describe to you the resentment and the dismay which is visible among all orders of men . . . sober and thinking men admit that this country has run its race; that as in other past monarchys [sic], the genius of our people has undergone a change, and we are longer capable of being successful through our own councils or arms.'[41]

There was another factor – public discontent at rising prices, especially of grain. In October, wagons carrying flour were hijacked in Northamptonshire and riots took place in Bakewell, Derbyshire.[42] Pitt knew very well that those other public disturbances had been unrelated to the making of a nice naval judgement off Minorca. Nevertheless, fired by a dreadful harvest and soaring grain prices, they had lately brought him to office. Mills at that time were destroyed across Warwickshire, Derbyshire, Staffordshire and Northants, and there had been urban disturbances involving miners in Nottingham and Coventry.[43] The price of grain was still high and the militia, Pitt's own unpopular innovation, had sparked the riots in Bakewell. The idea of Rochefort as another Minorca ran very readily in the minds of melancholy observers like Chesterfield.

Pitt was combustible and minded, at first instinct, to send the expedition back to take the Île de Ré. This island had provided an unhappy precedent when ships were sent in 1629 by a reluctant Charles I to relieve the besieged Protestants of La Rochelle, producing a similar but longer-drawn-out fiasco than Rochefort. This distinctly wild notion was put up by the Secretary of State at a meeting of 7 October. Holdernesse and Ligonier, presumably feeling that the army needed to retrieve credit, supported him. Newcastle, Granville, Mansfield and, significantly, Anson, First Lord of the Admiralty, killed it off.

Pitt's horrified reaction at the fiasco is worth quoting against commentators who argue the effectiveness of such raids. French troops had been detached and, more important, as N.A.M. Rodgers points out, Aix Roads was no longer a French secret after Hawke entered. Accordingly, future French invasion plans were discouraged from using that haven, probably the most convenient, moving instead into Brest. All this is true long term. Good effects would operate, but they formed no part of Pitt's thinking, immediate or contingent. Talk of 'Pitt's System' is a back formation. If there ever was a Pitt System beyond thinking big and taking chances, Rochefort was no part of it. Henry Fox's quip about 'breaking windows with golden guineas' was fair comment. The strategic detail of Aix Roads was a chance and happy finding, perfect serendipity.

Rochefort having failed conclusively, Pitt was concerned to escape blame, not least from his admirers. As Fraser puts it, 'Whenever something with which he was identified went wrong, he invariably threw out accusations of secret attempts at "subversion" and claimed that "the People had been inflamed by art and management".' With colleagues he flew into wild charges and lost control. Fraser cites Newcastle talking about Pitt: He '. . . puts it to a prevailing opinion that neither the king nor the Duke wished success to the expedition thinking of it as a chimera of Mr Pitt's which must miscarry; in order to show that the only practical thing to do was to employ our whole force in a German war and this he is with Lord Loudon's conduct in North America. He talked high and passionately with us. He did not see how he could go on . . .'[44] Paranoia follows the heart. Pitt accused the land officers of not protesting against the plans if they thought they were wrong. Pitt had been told precisely by soldiers and sailors, notably Hawke, that the raids were a poor business. They *had* proved a poor business so the soldiers and sailors were to blame.

His loyalists rallied to the call. For Thomas Potter, failure at Rochefort was clearly due to some scoundrel deal by which the English force did not push its advantage in order, after Hastenbeck, to get better terms for hateful Hanover. 'It is to no purpose to talk of misconduct of the officers concerned', he wrote from Bristol. 'The people carry their resentments higher.'[45]

This nonsense was not confined to tavern chatter. It came quite naturally from Pitt's friends, likewise perfectly certain that somebody was betraying them all the time. Beckford's *Monitor* across four issues in October and November, demanding severe inquisition into events, murmured the deadly name 'Byng', and suggested that Hanoverian influence was at work.[46] Such hysteria, 'enemies within', 'treason', 'Hanover as enemy' was not confined to the multitude, nor to loud-mouthed arrivistes like Beckford. Chesterfield, for all his urbanity, picked up the hysteria and transmitted it in a sophisticated way. In a letter to his eternally patronised bastard son, Philip, he laid a knowing finger to the side of his nose.

There must, he thought, 'have been some secret in the whole affair, which has not yet transpired; and I cannot help thinking it came from Stade (Cumberland's Headquarters). We [he meant the King] had not been successful there; perhaps we were not desirous, that an exped-ition, in which we had been neither concerned nor consulted, should prove so: Mordaunt was our creature; and a word to the wise will sometime go a long way. Mordaunt is to have a public trial, from which the public expects great discoveries – not I.'[47]

It is important to appreciate the minds of people without the full details set out before them. The country had lately heard nothing but bad news. Pitt, so recently cheered on by the view-halloos of patri-otic Englishmen making his sort of noise, now heard it again, but he was acquiring stag potential. He played quite seriously for about a week with the idea of joining the mob and publicly blaming Hanover for Rochefort. It would involve saying that Hanover and its friends, including his colleagues, had somehow organised defeat, had pulled punches to throw the fight to demonstrate the need to concentrate resources in Germany. The idea, involving a splendid tableau, William Pitt against the Enemies of England, George II and most of the Cabinet, was crazed.

It would also have been suicidal. Chesterfield's point about Newcastle and Pitt being mutually dependent was plain truth. George II, told that he, the King, had conspired to humiliate the British navy by sabotaging victory, would have dismissed him out of hand. But the successor ministry might have faced mob riots on a grand London scale, a logical climax in bleak economic times, for the Patriot movement. Accordingly, Pitt shifted his position to simply printing his instructions to the expedition and making them the basis of his defence. With all the cod theatre of which he was capable, he talked of a trial to resolve all, a trial perhaps of Sir John Mordaunt, perhaps of William Pitt.

There is no reason to excuse the essential Pitt flaws of character here. He was still being tricky, still a little mad and making for his natural element, the limelight. But as the common light broke in, the next move could only be what it always was going to be, an ineffective enquiry, 'We do nothing but expose ourselves in summer in order to have enquiries in Winter expose us again.' Horace Walpole had been right. Pitt would defend the planners, Clerk and Thierry, and blame the military officers.

The Rochefort failure was attended by a long shudder of recrimination which didn't end with the enquiry. The publicity had been bad and the private comments of Horace Walpole reflect 'the great grumbling among the coffee house, tavern and punch house politicians' he had recorded at the end of October. Horace with his friendship ties to Conway derided the implicit doctrine on Pitt's side that 'Nothing could be well till the army was subjected to the civil power. They were to obey, not to reason. Those sent in the late expedition had laughed at it even at table – nay so had some of the Cabinet.'[48] The implication of this is that officers given unachievable objectives should proceed blind. Either the waters were or were not too shallow too soon for ships to make the approach near enough for a surprise landing, something of which military men on the spot might be thought the best judges.

The Minister had sent instructions on information gathered from specialists like Thierry and Clerk. Mordaunt and his colleagues might or might not have succeeded on that guidance, but at the battle scene, they had to have a power of deciding. Newcastle, who smelled motives, told Hardwicke in a letter of 23 October that 'the enquiry was to vindicate and establish the practicality and great advantage of the project and in order thereto to lay before the officers, the ground on which it went'.[49] Hardwicke himself pointed out that the commanders had been barred by their oath from voicing their opinion of the wisdom of Rochefort.

They could not, however, speak out afterwards when the enquiry had pronounced. Pitt, for what it was worth, could fall back on a pamphlet published by an unidentified well-wisher: *A Vindication of Mr Pitt wherein all the Aspersions . . . related to the affair at Rochefort are unanswerably confuted* (London, 1758), which proclaimed, on page 47, that 'The people of Britain see that the purpose was of the true patriot stamp.' The problem, of course, lay with the outcome.

It was reasonable for Pitt to defend his own judgement; and Newcastle's first instinct, too, was one of anger at the circle of soldiers who had held the interminable council of war. Writing to Hardwicke as the news was breaking, he refers to 'the most extraordinary unintelligible and absurd proceeding of the land officers upon our expedition'. But all the old bones of contention within the ministry rattled as he reports that 'Mr Pitt is outrageous, is not angry with the officers, but puts it to a prevailing opinion that neither the King nor the Duke wished success to the expedition but think of it as a chimera of Mr Pitt's which must miscarry; in order to show that the only practical thing to do was employ our whole force in a <u>German war</u> ...? He talked high and passionately with us. He did not see how he could go on, and that in those circumstances he did not know whether he should enter at all into the affairs of Germany as he should otherwise have done; ...'

High words and the working out of a tantrum understandable in disappointment, but, as the same letter scrupulously reports, it did not continue. The last sentence broken off above continues: '... but your Lordship will see that he altered his mind as to that. He behaved very properly and well last night.'[50] But Pitt's moods had a shuttlecock quality.[51] In another letter Newcastle quotes him, anticipating Humpty Dumpty: 'All equally guilty. All should be punished. A court martial for all. Some secret reason. Some connection with the nationality ... These gentlemen about. Behind the King's chair at the opera. See everything look ill. Suspicious.'[52] The mood would pass, the mood would be recognised by Pitt as doing nobody any favours. Didn't we know there was a war on? But then Pitt had good reason. He was under fire from his own people. The *Monitor*, normally sedulous in loyalty, was raging late in the year. They had trusted Pitt but they did not trust Pitt in a ministry. Anyone familiar with the Labour Party in the 1970s will recognise the tone.

The trial itself was anti-climactic. Hawke told the court that he had never seen much utility in attacking either Aix or Fouras. The job to be done was at Rochefort, and the best land approach, as reconnoitred by Brodrick, was at Chataillon which, in turn, could not be covered by French fire from Fouras. For himself, he had come as close to the shore as possible on the great day, 28 September, and had personally directed the transport officers, something unusual for him. Hawke, with perfect truthfulness, kept himself where he had been all the time: in the clear.

As for Sir John, the court, conscious of the firing party so very recently shooting Admiral Byng for holding a council of war, declined renewal. The army had no more need now than the navy then of such encouragement. Sir John Mordaunt was adjudged on 11 January 1758 not guilty of any precise charge and left the court as Byng should have done, discredited but not disgraced, and not to be shot. King George read the court's report, looked at its signatories and swore about men he thought no better than Mordaunt. But against a smooth wall of official sense, before going mechanically on the record as accepting the conclusions, he raged in vain.

12

'It blew a perfect hurricane': Admiral Holburne's Voyage

In the meantime more bad news was on its way. Pitt's concern for Canada moved him to early action. Actually that had already been in 1756, before his access to office, the ministry's chief priority. He had no difficulty with colleagues in setting up the first venture directed at the North American theatre. It should involve, like past excursions, the taking of Louisbourg as first concern.

Pitt's own theme, conquest to the west, looking beyond the Ohio river, reflected his own large-minded (or grandiose) outlook. Louisbourg was the Queen Gate of the St Lawrence. Taking it was important to campaign and war as French coastal towns never could be. And taking it would be the accomplishment of a great enterprise. However, argument about Canada had been plagued by the supposed underperformance of Lord Loudon. It was due neither to fear nor idleness on his harassed part. The idea of making for the St Lawrence and its key fortress had been Loudon's at a time, 1754, when Pitt had been arguing that this was a conflict better handled by British settler volunteers who knew their way about. Loudon had set his plan out for Cumberland back in the autumn of 1756, and had his full proposals brought across the Atlantic by an envoy, Thomas Pownall.

Loudon understood that a successful campaign meant lots of men and a deal of money. He wanted 10,000 backed by a proper fleet. There was otherwise no point in doing anything in Canada. Loudon's thinking back in 1756 fitted the grand Pitt view of Blue Water and Outremere. But at that time, such necessary expansiveness could not be done. Fears of an invasion of Britain were up and buzzing, discouraging largesse with men. For although Anson at the Admiralty had achieved great things, having available 93 ships of the line, 125 other craft commissioned and a payroll of 54,000 sailors,[1] soldiers were something else. Pitt, trying to be cooperative, offered Loudon eight thousand, probably too few, without really knowing where he would find them.

The first undertaking would be made in 1757. Vice-Admiral Francis Holburne was now directed to convey troops to Canada and allocated fifteen ships of the line. This meant going to Halifax, the Nova Scotia township with a harbour from which to ferry men on to the St Lawrence and Louisbourg. Hit from the start and much of the way by terrible weather, Holburne did not get away from his moorings until the last week of April and then, finding that the troops he should carry were concentrated somewhere else, picked them up at Cork which he finally left on 8 May. Loudon, by contrast, was on time if not ahead of it, waiting in Halifax with men lately trained in siege warfare.

What would happen next on the home stations of England and France reversed the pattern of the war: the French for once got the naval essentials right! Hawke, keeping watch on the Channel, was clogged by quick and frequent runs for repair and reprovision. The French Brest squadron under de la Motte would get and take its chance of getting out during one such absence. With similar agility, Kersaint de Coetnampren, a Breton sailor respected by his opponents, had got away to the Guinea coast before the arrival of Admiral West, sent to *stop* him getting away. Kersaint was now making for Canada as a useful place to be. Bauffremont in the West Indies had similar ideas and when the British watch returned home, he followed. Three separate but converging French squadrons came together at Louisbourg.

Meanwhile, the Marquis de Montcalm, French overall land commander in North America, had moved into the space which Loudon's move to Halifax had vacated. The back-up forces for Fort William Henry, upon which Loudon's deputy, Colonel Monroe, was relying, did not materialise. Too much time had been spent gathering dawdling provincial troops. Accordingly, Montcalm took the fort. The correspondence is eloquent:

Loudon to Pitt New York 3 May 1757
I am extremely happy to find that the preparations I have made, and the plan I had prepared for, in a great Measure coincides with the Orders I have now received . . . there are so many Difficulties to remove

in this country, in order to set things in Motion, that being on the
Spot is necessary at present; how that may be hereafter, I cannot say,
but I hope things may go smoother . . . The Militia are the real inhabitants; Stout, able Men, and for a brush, much better than their
Provincial troops . . . but then, the Militia cannot be detained any time
in the field, but will return home [and] whilst they stay in that back
Country, they insist on being maintained at the King's Expense . . .
but this is much Cheaper than the maintaining a much smaller number
of Provincials the whole Campaign . . . Under the articles of Artillery
they [the Provincial troops] have included Tents, Drums, Colours, All
Camp Necessaries, Platters, Pans, Keggs and a number of other things
. . . And I think it more necessary to be on my guard in all claims of
this Sort because when once settled, there is no bringing it back again;
and it is the constant Study of every province here to throw every
expence upon the Crown, and bear no part in the Expence of this
war themselves.[2]

Holburne, on the *Newark*, thought (wrongly) that he would soon
be making progress:

Holburne to Pitt, Newark, *in Cork Harbour 7th May 1757*
I have the Honour to acquaint you that the Troops are all embarked,
the Transports come down the Harbour. And Everything is ready for
sailing, which nothing but the Wind coming more southerly prevented
our getting out this Afternoon . . .

For Loudon it was a time for trouble in the ranks, to be followed
shortly by one damn French ship after another, then waiting for
Holburne and balancing the risks of any move he might make.

London to Pitt New York May 30th 1757
On 11th (May) I had the honour to receive by the Packet the duplicate of your Letter of February 19th . . . [Admiral Sir Charles Hardy],
having complained that sailors, both from the men of war and transports, had deserted, in order to get on board the Privateers from the
great profit they make there of this port alone, having brought in
prizes to the value of about two hundred thousand Pounds Sterling
. . . and that these sailors were harbour'd in Town. I immediately

surrounded the town with three Battalions to prevent their making their escape, whilst he [Hardy] Employed the sailors in taking up the Deserters ... without going into this Measure, we could not have Sailed for want of Seamen ...

We have received intelligence, by three Privateers, just arrived with five French Merchant Ships whom they took, that on the 4th of May, Mo.ʳ De Bauffremont with the French Fleet consisting of one Ship of 80 guns, two of 74, two of 64 and a frigate of 26 guns; that he took the Trade [wind] with him: from Cape St Francois ... [an] informant further told us that his brother is Master of the *Tonnant* that he had told him that fleet was bound for Canada; (in which they include Louisbourg) and that the fleet at Martinico [Martinique] was to follow them, consisting of one Ship of 70 Guns, two of 60 and two frigates, and that they expected at Louisbourg, five ships from France ... Our Situation here, is the Troops are all Embarked; and the last of the Ships will probably get to the Hook to-morrow or next day; for convoy we have one 50 Gun Ship, the *Sutherland*; we have two of 20 guns, the *Nightengale* [sic] and *Kennington*, two sloops, the *Ferret* and the *Vulture*.

I have had a meeting with Sir Charles Hardy & Major General Abercromby to consult what is proper to be done ... The French [sic] Fleet is probably gone on to Louisbourg; but if they have any Notice of Us ... they may hover on the Coast for us; If they meet us, there is an end of the Troops that go from hence; if they are gone to Louisbourg, and Admiral Holburne is not arrived as from all the Accounts the Merchant ships bring ... Mo.ʳ de Bauffremont has nothing to keep him in Port, and my risk is up by Halifax. But on the other hand, if we remain here Idle till we can hear from Halifax which may be a month, the Campaign is lost; therefore I have never hesitated a Moment in my own Mind, and Sir Charles Hardy and Major General Abercromby agree with me, that it is proper to run that risk and sail ... We have this day four men arrived who made their escape from Montreal. One of them was sergeant in the 50th Regiment ... [who acquaints me] ... that two regiments are Marched toward their Forts of Crown Point and Tienderoga [sic] ... [and that] he left Montreal May 7th; and the Language there was, if we attacked Cape Breton, that would not stop their attacking our Forts; if we went to Quebeck they must apply their whole Force to defend it; as if that were taken, they could not live, but must all submit and become Prisoners of War.

The Admiral's weather report was consistent with all the other bad news.

Admiral Holburne to Pitt, Newark, *at Sea June 6th 1757*
As I have met a Vessel bound to England I think it incumbent on me to endeavour to acquaint you of my being so far only on my way, having met Contrary Winds and bad weather these fifteen days past; I am endeavouring all in my power to pursue my Voyage: A Squadron of French Men of War, consisting of eight sail of the Line and Two Frigates, are gone before us and a great way . . . they must have been from Brest as they were seen a great way to the Northward of the Western Islands.

Events and French forces crowd upon Loudon, making his mind up to move.

Loudon to Pitt, HM Ship Sutherland *at Sandy Hook 17th June 1757*
On the 8th I received a letter by Express, from Mr Hancock at Boston enclosing a letter . . . containing an account, of Mr Lane in a Fishing Vessel, having seen on the [fishing] Banks on the 5th of May, Six Sail of large Ships which he judged to be men of War, 20 Leagues from Halifax.

And after that, Captain Patten, from Cadix [*sic*], saw likewise in the morning of the 28th of May, eight large Ships; that he saw nothing of them in the evening which makes it probable they came from the Southward . . . I have had a Meeting with Sir Charles Hardy, and Major General Abercromby – I was clearly of opinion that we ought to sail next Morning, as I do not doubt Mr Holburne, if he is to come this year, must be on the coast of Nova Scotia to protect Us there. And we have taken every Precaution by sending him two expresses, to acquaint him with our informations and motions . . . Sir Charles Hardy as well as I, sees there may be danger of accidents happening with the Enemy . . . and that if we do not now sail, the Season will be so Far advanced, nothing can be done, therefore I think it a risk we ought to run; . . . [Having now seen] letters from Governor Lawrence of June 1st . . . reporting large Ships being seen off [New York] on May 29th; and Letters from Captain Rouse . . . from whence it appears to me, that if they are the French Squadron, they were in their Passage to Louisbourg; as none of the three Ships stationed to look for Mr Holburne's Fleet, seems to have seen them; therefore I made no Change in my Opinion. The 19th, the Wind was Foul, and the 20th we sailed.

By way of a swift sloop or any ship going the right way, Downing Street passes on good intelligence, bad news and not very good instructions to the admiral and adds anxious encouragement:

Pitt to Admiral Holburne Whiteball July 7th 1757
Intelligence having been received which gives room to think it probable that the Several French Squadrons which have sailed this Year from Europe under the Command of Mo.ʳ Bois de la Mothe, Mo.ʳ De Baufremont and Mo.ʳ du Revest, may all be directed to proceed to North America and to form one fleet there; His Majesty has been pleased to order the *Somerset* and the *Devonshire* of 70 guns each, the *Prince Frederick* of 64 Guns and the *Eagle* of 60 Guns to sail forthwith to reinforce the squadron under your Command; and it is the King's pleasure that upon the Arrival of the Four Ships above mentioned, you do immediately despatch a sloop to England with an Account of the Conditions of Your Ships and with the best Intelligence you have been able to procure as well as those of the Enemy, as of their operations and future Destination ... I must [not] omit most strongly recommending you to act with the greatest Vigour against the Enemy, and doubt not but that you will so apply the powerful force, now under your command as will effectually answer the great View of His Majesty and the general expectations of the Nation: ... And in case you shall receive Advice of the French fleet sailing Homewards, it is the King's pleasure that you should follow them as close as may be, and with the Utmost Expedition in order if possible to fall in with them either before they reach Europe or on the Coasts of France; where by means of a number of English Ships, properly stationed, the Enemy may happen to fall into a Position between Two of the King's Squadrons.

That message was the measure of ministerial helplessness in an age of glacier communication. Pitt was a keen minister watching everything he could get a glimpse of. He could send extra ships. He could ask for full information (which he would be many weeks in getting) and he could invoke George II in a football manager's morale-boosting lecture despatched perhaps nine or ten weeks from its object, a ship moving away. He finished by advising Holburne what to do in a contingency likely to have arisen before the Minister's message reached him. Direction went round and round like powerful wheels in mud. The actual instruction is, anyway, dubious.

Nothing, however, stopped Pitt trying to be useful.

Pitt to Lord Loudon Whitehall July 18th 1757
. . . I have the Satisfaction to inform your Lordship that the two new Highland Battalions, commanded by Lieutenant Col. Fraser sailed from Cork on the thirteenth of last month . . . I am further to acquaint Your Lordship that in order to reinforce the Troops under your orders, His Majesty has been pleased to direct a Draught of 1000 Men to be made from the Several Battalions in Great Britain and Ireland. And also that Nine additional Companies of Highlanders, consisting each of 100 men be forthwith . . . – these Draughts and Additional companies are all to be embarked so as to arrive in America by the Months of October when the Ports will still be open [ice-free] . . . The King is persuaded that His Most Gracious and Timely Attention to supply the Body of Troops employed in the important Service off North America cannot fail to animate the Zeal of all his subjects there . . .

Discounting the last sentence of florid man-management, Pitt was tacitly accepting the complaints of every informed British voice on the unreliability, rapacity and doubtful utility of so many Americans. But as to the option of forcing a fight at sea, he is obliged in the next letter, written on the same day as he addresses Loudon, to tell Holburne why the extra ships promised on 7 July have gone off in the wrong direction before adding a breathless addition to say that they have been caught up with and redirected.

Pitt to Admiral Holburne July 18th 1757
Sir, The Eagle Man of War will probably have brought you my Letter of the 7th Instant (see supra).

I am now to inform you by what Accident the four Ships mentioned in the enclosed, did not sail together, according to the notice therein given to you; the *Devonshire & Prince Frederick* passed by Plymouth with a fair Wind (to put themselves under the Command of

Commander Moore) the Day before the orders had reached Admiral Harrison there for their proceeding to North America, and tho' the *Sheernesse* was immediately despatched to recall them, there was so little hopes of her coming up with them that it was thought proper the *Eagle & Somerset* should sail . . . but I this Moment learn that the *Sheernesse* has, most fortunately, overtaken those Ships which are to proceed to put themselves under your command . . .

This good news of retrieval was followed in the same letter by a clear reversal of the letter of 7 July (sent again in duplicate). Holburne was now told, 18 July:

Pitt–Holburne 18th July 1757
With regard to what is contained in the latter part of the Enclosed Letter concerning your following with the utmost Expedition the French Fleet on their return to Europe . . . I am to signify to you that it is His Majesty's Pleasure that you are to consider the conjunct Operations of His Majesty's Fleet and Land Forces in North America as the first and preferable service and that consequently you will not leave these Parts with the Fleet under your Command so long as any of the great objects of those Operations, so strongly recommended and enforced in the King's Instructions & Orders to the Earl of Loudon and yourself, may with any Reasonable Prospect of Success be still pursued; . . .

The first problem, the *Devonshire* and *Prince Frederick* getting away one wind too soon, was nobody's fault, not their captains' nor Pitt's. Everyone was trying to move at the first, rare, weather opportunity, and in 1757 urgent messages did not move urgently. The second correction is neither fortuitous nor blame-free. We can forget about 'His Majesty's Pleasure'. George was told most things and grumbled about most of them. But not remotely will this volte-face have been at royal insistence. Between the lines of an embarrassed letter surely lie either the opinions of colleagues or Pitt's own recovery of common sense.

He had earlier advised the man seeking a vital rendezvous for the Canadian campaign to chase French ships returning to France, the instinct of a young, flustered lieutenant. At Quiberon Bay, the great and terminal sea fight of this war, the French commander made the same elementary error. On that day in November 1759, Admiral Conflans, with the clear duty to bring his fleet to Quiberon Bay as immediate refuge, would waste his lead over the pursuing Hawke by pointlessly engaging a clutch of modest English ships.

Pitt at three thousand miles' distance was proposing the same muddle. Having thought that the troops could be raised locally, he had rightly been persuaded by Loudon that the essential object was an investment of Canada with British ships and troops. Loudon was already in Canada, hopefully in Halifax. Holburne's fleet was his essential support. To tell the sailor that if he saw any promising French ships he should chase them was dreadful distraction from the agreed central purpose. Making his own mind up, Loudon would take the sensible course of retreat anyway. He could not chance Holburne's ferocious weather leaving him and his troops on an island outnumbered and without means of getting off it. The anxieties of the British authorities in North America continued:

Governor Pownall of New York to Pitt, Boston August 16th 1757
I landed at this place August 3rd; on Saturday August 6th a letter directed to the President of the Council from Genl. Webb (dated Fort Edward distant 260 miles, July 31) came to my hands acquainting me that he expected to be attacked by a large body of the Enemy. I immediately ordered the three most western regiments of the Government to March to the extreme western Frontiers of the Province ... Upon receiving August 7th a letter from Capt. Christie ... That Fort William Henry was invested, I sent Sir William Pepperell ... up to the frontiers to collect a Body of Troops and send forward any Reinforcements the case should require ... I have constantly from time to time by Dispatch Vessells, acquainted the Earl of Loudon with every particular I have receiv'd, what the particulars of the Surrender of the William Henry are ...

Governor Pownall to Pitt, Boston Sept. 4th 1757
Sir,
... I had the Honour of writing to you on the 16th and 18th of August. Copies of which letters I sent three several Ways Acquainting you sir, that the French after destroying all the Works, and blowing up the Fort William Henry, Had returned to Canada with their Booty ... I wish I could say that my Orders have been or will be obeyed to

the effect I mean. The Militia of this Province is utterly ruined and lost . . . His Lordship applied to me for quarters for the Highland Battalion commanded by Lt. Col Fraser . . . I have, contrary to the Opinion of the Governments Best friends here, succeeded in persuading the Legislature to find them Barracks Beds Utensils Firewood and Light . . .

From the Peculiar State the Government is in, and from the Peculiar temper of the People in these Countries, I was forced to use a peculiar Method of Application and to acquiesce in their peculiar Method of doing it . . . Thro a dispute into which the two Houses of Legislature got engaged with each other, I have failed in my Application to them for Recruits to be sent to Admiral Holbourn . . . I have returned received a letter from Admiral Holbourn who is returned to Halifax, he went and looked into Louisborough Harbour within less than a League, he counted two and twenty Sail of Ships of War, seventeen of the Line.

The experience of the first attempt to advance Britain's power in Canada had ended disastrously. Buried in Pownall's grieving and frustrated despatch were the sullen antipathies to be expected given 'the Peculiar temper of the People in these Countries'.

With a larger French fleet sitting waiting in Louisbourg, the British command faced a likely requirement of fighting with heroic indifference against superior numbers. Doing what, despite the demands of heroic newspapers, sensible military men usually do, they stopped and thought about it. Like the generals and admirals of the coastal raids, Loudon held a council of war which, in the way of councils of war, decided to stop the operation. They were almost certainly right. Troops landed on an island to fight a battle require ships to get them off. Given the superior French naval and military numbers, the possibility loomed of being defeated and left without a retreat, something military textbooks discourage. The critics, Chesterfield for one, shaking their heads, were in mourning for a gamble coming off. The gamble failing is rarely present in such distant reflections.

Soldiers and sailors now had to make the best of things. On 20 August, Holburne had written to Holdernesse, junior and resentful Secretary of State, and a month later, not very tactfully, enclosed a duplicate of the message in his own letter to Pitt of 17 September. He had made first for Louisbourg. Advised not to cruise off that station 'exposed to the risque of Separation in the Fogs so frequent off this coast',[3] he made for Tor Bay on the southern coast of Nova Scotia, only to be set back by thick fog on a barely explored bay full of lethal rocks. Finding his way about, Holburne had turned towards Halifax and, placing himself at the edge of the harbour, agreed with his senior officers, Holmes and Fowke, to anchor, keep together and send out light, swift ships for intelligence.

Letters of this sort, despatches from commanders to the government, were served by the small ship which could be spared. Accordingly, they were usually kept open over a number of days to include later news. So Holburne could announce the slow, serial arrival of the ships sent to him by Pitt: 'Four Transports with part of the Highland Battalion arrived here on the 24th past, but the *Enterprise* with the rest of the Transports not before the 28th.'

Having obligations beyond the Louisbourg venture, he had sent them straight on down the coast to protect Annapolis. On the 5th, *Somerset* and *Eagle* turned up and, two days later, so did the message that he would be getting 'four Line of Battle Ships'.[4] Moving safely away from Halifax against the advice of his pilots, he was shortly afterwards delighted to see the long-awaited *Devonshire* and *Prince Frederick*. His reconnaissance officers, Mantell and Laforey, reported that they had been 'baffled by winds which prevented them getting close enough to look into Louisbourg'.

On the 16th, Holburne, 'Having received intelligence of a Man of War making signals', abandoned the practice of floating provocatively just outside in hope of drawing the whole or some part of them out after Cruisers. Getting intelligence, he tells Pitt, was now the most useful thing he could do and took his own ship into the bay. He observed the Vice- and Rear-Admirals and 'the Same Number of Line of Battle Ships & Frigates we had formerly seen'.[5] His estimate for Pitt was that 'the Enemy' would get away by the end of that month, September, probably making for the regular French citadel of Brest. He would follow, steering via Ushant, setting rendezvous for every ship concerned, fifteen leagues west of it. Pitt, with this information, would be able to direct further ships there.

Military commanders and ministers tried to keep in sync. Sailors hoped to anticipate where a Minister would want them to go next. The weather helped; war was a seasonal thing, naval warfare especially so. So Pitt's letter to Holburne of 4 September pretty much tells Holburne to do what, in the letter of 17 September, Holburne has told Pitt he has just started doing it. With decent winds they will read these two letters in November.

Pitt's says that 'you are directed when the Season of the Year shall render it unsafe for the Ships to keep the Seas to return to England with such part of your Squadron as you shall think proper under the command of a flag officer . . . and, that in Case of the French Fleet sailing Homewards, you should follow them with your whole force gathered in one Body'.[6]

Whatever the efforts of pen and ink and sloop to convey them, what was bidden and already intended did not happen. The weather of the journey back was signally worse than the weather of the journey out. Holburne's letter of 29 September, twelve days out, quotes that of the 17th when 'I was then cruizing off Louisbourg in hopes of falling in with the Enemy's Fleet near that Port, or in their Passage to Europe, whither I intended to follow them close should they escape me here.'[7] His ships had managed to cope with the wind of the 24th but 'towards the Evening of that Day it began to blow very hard at East'.

When that wind veered south, 'it blew a perfect Hurricane and drove us right onshore, the Wind continued Violent till near eleven next day when providentially . . . it came round to the Westwards of the South, we had but just room to wear the ship clear of the Breakers and saw several ships at anchor with their Masts gone without having it in our power to give them the least assistance in this great Distress, and had the wind continued to blow onshore but one hours longer every Ship of the Squadron must unavoidably have been lost.

'I stood off seven Leagues and brought to in order to pick up and assist as many Ships as I could, the next day, the 26th in the Morning we saw sixteen Sail, six of them dismasted and two of these being a great way to Leeward I sent the *Bedford* & *Defiance* to take them in Tow & bring them to Halifax . . .'

With one ship lost and having seen twelve dismasted, from an original fifteen, there was nothing for it but return to immediate haven and refit. For the only consolation was that Halifax, to which he was now returning and had sent the *Lightning*, spare cruisers and two transports, was clearly secure anyway. He had seen enough observing the hurricane to be sure that 'for some part of the Time, it blew right into the Harbour'. Also by the time he had a refitted squadron fit to leave Halifax 'the Season will be so advanced that there can be no danger of the Enemy's making any Attempt on Halifax . . .'

Pitt's reaction in a letter to his wife announced that 'most calamitous news demands me this night and many' adding, 'May a degenerate people profit in the school of misfortune.'[8] Whatever that might mean, the full picture was much better. Dubois de la Motte passed up the chance of taking or destroying a dismasted fleet and then ran into his own calamities, a desperate shortage of food, an outbreak of scurvy and, on his return to Brest, that savage plague of typhus which we have seen Hawke avoid by failing to catch de la Motte.

The expedition was now off and minds concentrated on refitting, largely at Halifax. Loudon, unable to risk being left without the intended reinforcements, had, of course, returned to New York while Pitt spoke of his 'Treachery'. Put sanely, he meant a complicated debate about priorities which had been going on since early days. Loudon was an advocate of numbers. He was too much obliged to the (not very good) best efforts of the governors of American provinces whose men did not readily stream to the flag and a fight with the French. He preferred the hard men of the frontier and looked around for local militias if the governors would create them, but needed too what England could supply – ships carrying British soldiers. Anson, thinking in naval terms and rationally, wanted Holburne to bring the battered ships back to England for a fuller refitting; Loudon wanted ships and men on the spot. Pitt would compromise by setting about creating proper resources in Canada, a naval base on Loring Island in Halifax bay. That undertaken, but not of course accomplished, he required Holburne pretty superfluously to take eight ships of the line back to Halifax harbour for the refit.

For Loudon, the politics were bad. He had been in post during defeats, most recently Fort William Henry. He was, after all, Cumberland's man and, while Loudon had been frustrated and Holburne had gone through a hurricane, events had, as remarked, turned out far worse for Cumberland.

13

St Malo Stands, Louisbourg Falls

Rochefort having failed, Mordaunt's court martial having been a howling embarrassment and Pitt shifting blame by leaks all round, it was time to do something useful. However painfully for George, whose affection for William Augustus came welling up after the first anger, Cumberland had to go and, in October, went.

As for a replacement, one need not look long. Achieving distinction at Rossbach had been Prince Ferdinand of Brunswick. Of the blood royal, an advantage at selection boards, also Frederick's brother-in-law, he was, oddly, on pure merit, an outstanding commander. Frederick, though sometimes badgering him to move faster when it was impossible to move at all, understood him as one outstanding soldier knows another. His mind, quick where Cumberland's had trudged, made him a born getter-out-of-trouble where William Augustus had met reverse by lurching into defeatism. How much George II knew is uncertain, but he had clearly seen reports. And, like his ministers, preoccupied with undoing Kloster Zeven, George had also been corresponding with Frederick. He wanted a proper Prussian soldier.

He got one. Ferdinand put up pay, got in regular meat supplies and a daily shot of schnapps. Leaving a garrison in Stade, scene of humiliation, he marched them toward Celle and Gifhorne beyond the Aller. But given the baggage, march-unfitness and sodden weather, progress was slow. Brutality by French troops, destroying much of Celle and burning children to death in an orphanage, genuinely outraging the troops, drove up morale. The Weser, its bridges destroyed, was impassable. At New Year, Ferdinand waited for English pontoons and guns. He had described privations to King George on 5 January 1758: 'The rough weather and particularly the bad state of the men's boots and the shortage of supplies have forced me to suspend operations and cantoon my troops.'[1]

Ferdinand's campaign as Hanover commander was taking shape. He received ten squadrons of dragoons and hussars from Prussia, commanded by the Duke of Holstein-Gottorp, someone 'you can trust with any task you are unable to undertake in person'.* The Hanover army now accumulated men as Hastenbeck casualties straggled back. The possibilities would be signalled, not by the departure of Richelieu, no great loss, but what it intimated. Richelieu had written to Paris asking to be allowed to give up his command. Abruptly, on 7 February, he left without waiting for his replacement Clermont's arrival on 14 February. The recurring professional *déshabille* among French commanders was not a feature with Prussian soldiers or English sailors.

Rossbach was the circumstance behind positive developments. Before it, Frederick could not have spared an officer of such quality. He now had elbow room, yet after Hastenbeck needed to have the British come up to scratch. He had had the French and imperial troops, as the leading authority puts it, 'on the run'.[2] Frederick knew about Richelieu's groggy troops, at once victorious and demoralised, but his right flank was open. A proficient Hanoverian army would be invaluable. He wanted Ferdinand to work for him through George and Hanover. Ferdinand was persuaded, but he had conditions. He would work only to the Elector himself, King George / Kurfürst Georg. Taking direction from Hanoverian politicians (or generals) was not on.

Ferdinand next persuaded the Erb Prinz of Brunswick, Karl Wilhelm Ferdinand, to come in and take an independent command. He found the army of Hastenbeck angry but also convinced that it had not been defeated *as an army*. Ferdinand was a natural leader beyond the dashing and heroic, though, as we shall see, at the Aller bridge he could do the full, rattling yarn thing, sword in hand. More important, he understood how to make squabbling people march, creating personal trust in an army with first loyalties elsewhere. Reasoning and encouraging, he brought doubting Brunswick officers, headed by Zastrow, Cumberland's deputy, along. Resuming the campaign in February, Ferdinand took delivery of his English pontoons and crossed the Aller in two groups, to Verden and Rethem. It was all done in the slush and

---

* He was, though, a footballer on loan, wanted back in July.

miasma of north Germany in mid-February, but the force coped well
– unlike the French. Ferdinand, despising direction from the rear, personally led the taking of the bridge over the Weser at Hoya.

'The Weser was covered in floating ice; the night was rough; no
fisherman could be found who had the courage to put us across. I
found gold and the men found a supply of courage . . .' He captured
a French soldier. 'He looked at me and tried to escape. But I seized
hold of him myself and grasped him by the throat. "You are a lost
man," I said, "if you speak a word", and I pointed my sword at his
breast. "Where are your comrades?" . . .' And, for the loss of thirteen
men killed, 'We were the masters of the bridge.'[3]

Having secured Hoya, they moved on to Nienberg and Neustadt, fair
points for an assault on Bremen. Meanwhile, the British naval squadron
came up the Weser for Ems, held by the Comte de Saint-Germain.
Clermont, inheritor of Richelieu's raggedy troops, was now cut off
from communication with Bremen and feared a British landing. None
happened but pressure mounted. Clermont sought retreat to Hamelin
and the Weser, as 'broad and wide' then as for the Pied Piper. Other
factors were emerging. Doubting his troops' strength for the full
journey, Clermont settled for a garrisoned town with further troops.
They would encamp at Minden.

Ferdinand had independently acknowledged Minden as potential
block between Clermont and the Weser. His artillery under
Schaumberg-Lippe struck. On 15 March, after a two-day siege, Minden
fell. Greater things would happen around Minden in seventeen months'
time, 1 August 1759. But this March encounter was important enough.

The campaign in defence of Hanover now had a British following.
Its ups would be cheered, its downs matters of concern. We were, as
the saying goes, 'in Europe'. So, hope having seen off experience,
another naval excursion loomed. The first casualty of this one, a shy
at St Malo, was harmony among the naval command. Hawke had
been the success of Rochefort. His ships had demolished the fort at
Aix. The navy, ready to attempt anything asked, grieved at not being
asked. Admittedly a sorrowing Anson had spoken sadly to his father-
in-law, Hardwicke, about the council of war: 'The Fleet, having done
well and all in their power gives me satisfaction; but why Hawke put
his name to any council of war when I warned him so strongly against
it, astonishes and hurts me.'[4]

Hawke was the greatest sailor of the day and not a seriously arrogant man. But he was touchy and offendable. He had his own reservations about coastal raids generally, but if there were to be one, he expected the naval command. Pitt and Ligonier, working through Anson, were assembling the craft for an undertaking, details of which were kept close. It was not to be pinched in resources: 'as many as possible' seems to have been the core of Pitt's drift to the First Lord. It emerged that the intention was to split the force. Half would take up the watch at Brest where anything France might throw at England would be assembled. The other flotilla would support. The original (very private) plan was to give Hawke the major command, with Howe, destroyer of Aix Fort, running the transports.

No problems flowed from that disposition. Unfortunately, Hawke knew nothing. He had been cruising in the Basque Roads, taking soundings for any future purposes. Hawke had also been perfecting a potent new approach to naval war. He had issued the order to Pratten of the *Intrepid*: 'You are to curb and annoy the enemy . . . keeping the frigates and cutters close in with these ports, that you may have constant intelligence of the motions and proceedings of the enemy.'[5] By such close fighting, backed by optimally informed vigilance, would Hawke win the great battle of Quiberon Bay. Such directions required unleisured conduct of surveillance and conflict. Passed on by Hawke's disciple, William Locker, they would, long after, guide Nelson.

But the Commander-in-Chief's position had not been allocated and Hawke at Portsmouth had been told nothing. On 10 May Howe emerged at 4.00 p.m. and showed him his own orders as commander of the support group. Hawke somehow took these as orders for another attack on Rochefort with Howe commanding.

He took this misperception as a slapping down by authority and proof that, for all he had done, he no longer had official confidence. Already while Pitt looked for someone to blame during the post-mortem on that first failure, Hawke had concluded that the Secretary did not much like him. He was right. Pitt was not good at other people, he had no expertise in naval matters, nor military, despite his few months in barracks. He had wanted a triumph; Rochefort had not been that triumph. Pitt had no competent opinion of Hawke but, squirming under failure, took against him. He did, however, have the sense to form decisions from people who knew his worth.

Hawke's response could have been fatal '. . . Last cruise I went out on a particular service almost without the least means of performing it. Now, every means to success is assured, another is to reap the credit; while it is probable that I with the capital ships might be ordered to cruise in such a manner as to prevent his failing in the attempt . . .'

At the next sentence, one hears the outraged voice rising. 'To fit out his ships for this service I have been kept here, and even now have their Lordships' directions, at least in terms, to obey him. He is to judge of what he wants for his expedition, he is to make his demands and I am to comply with them. I have therefore directed my flag immediately to be struck and left their Lordships' orders with Vice-Admiral Holbourne [sic]. For no consequence that can attend my striking it without orders shall ever outbalance with me wearing it one moment with discredit.'[6] For a naval officer to strike his flag invites court martial, dismissal from the service and every horror attending defiance of naval authority. When he learnt that the premises of his action were not correct, Hawke descended into an ocean of his own misery. He would have been as much in the wrong if they had been true. The new object would actually be St Malo, and Howe was down to run the transports.

Hawke had muddled the information, had acted with affronted pride – not vanity, an important distinction – and could have ended his career there and then. But the navy was, to a degree, self-contained. It did not like politicians. And unlike Pitt, happily remote from decisions about Hawke's future, the Navy Board knew a great deal about sailors, knew what a sailor Edward Hawke was. Anson, First Lord and Admiral of the Fleet, was not comfortable with him and horribly embarrassed by the episode, but he knew Hawke's quality. Oddly, or perhaps not oddly, King George, with his instinct for courage, had an idea of it too, and large sympathies. The original mistake meant that he could never now take the command of the St Malo enterprise. But he was needed for his abilities and no other officer, however talented, could take it over his head.

It was Anson who squared the circle and managed to retain an out-of-order alpha talent. George Anson, sixty-one, a little dry from dedicated administrative employment, happily undertook command of this moderately interesting little raid. Hawke, vastly grateful, took second place under him. Lord Hardwicke, honorary naval person as Anson's father-in-law, having feared 'the public losing the benefit of Hawke's service', remarked that, 'Surely this will be very right and the only way to retrieve, as far as may be, the rash step he so strangely took.'[7] The navy knew how to keep a secret. The episode was kept out of the newspapers and the struck flag hoisted on HMS *Ramillies*. Ironically, a fortnight out of Portsmouth, Hawke went down with bronchitis and feverish pain. The expedition to St Malo had triggered a crisis in the command. It could now get on with invading St Malo.

What actually happened next took its time. Its object resolved and its *équipe*, assembled across winter and spring, provoked forlorn expectations of better planning than at Rochefort. Inspiration for what should be done originated with Ligonier, now joined by the 3rd Duke of Marlborough and Lord George Sackville. Marlborough was a name, Charles Spencer an unexceptionable professional soldier. Sackville was Leicester House's man, and involving that faction concerned Pitt above military organisation. George II, at seventy-five, was quietly diminished as source of expectations. Making appointments among regular favourites of the Dowager Princess, her elder son, Prince George, and his tutor, Lord Bute, was serious business.

Sackville would have several reputations, all bad, not all fair. Transferred to Germany, in 1759, he would, through an allegedly deliberate delay before battle, become in the eyes of not only German officers 'the Coward of Minden', bitterly denounced by Ferdinand for when bidden, not coming.*

The coastal plan had a touch of brutality, bombardment of a town and citizens. St Malo, being set upon an island, could not be invested in the usual way. But with mortars and red-hot shot, the generals thought it might be 'reduced',[8] treating the civilian population in uninhibited fashion, a touch of *Schrecklichkeit*. The generals also fancied holding St Malo for a while to upset and, improbably, distract the French.

The hopes were of sustained investment of St Malo itself, hopefully bringing French troops scurrying from the Rhine. The dream was that by 'making feints or really landing in different parts, to oblige the Enemy to keep a great Force' at the coastal perimeter. Pitt's

---

* For a defence of Sackville's conduct, see Mackesy, *The Coward of Minden*.

instructions, rich in 'the Liberties of the Empire' and threats to the 'Independency of Europe', left Marlborough the final military decisions. After Rochefort and several cooks progressing round the broth, this was sensible. But it didn't work any better.

Horace Walpole, writing on 11 June, was frivolous. 'Last Thursday se'ennight our great expedition departed from Portsmouth – and soon separated. Lord Anson with the great ships to lie before Brest, and Commodore Howe, the naval hero, with the transports and a million of small fry on the secret enterprise.'[9] Five days later, Walpole wrote to General Conway, joint-underperformer at Rochefort, with cheerful news of nothing very much: 'Well my Dear Harry, you are not the only man in England who have [sic] not conquered France. Even Dukes of Marlborough have been there without doing the business. I don't doubt that your good heart has ever been hoping in spite of your understanding that our heroes have not only taken St Maloes, but taken a trip across the country to burn Rochefort only to show how easy it was. We have waited with astonishment at not hearing that the French Court was removed in panic to Lyons . . .'[10]

The facts had been sparse and the achievement disappointing. But let the 3rd Duke of Marlborough describe things. The punctuation is intermittent but the drift clear:[11]

[Marlborough to Pitt]   June 6th 1758 Cancalle Bay
We were very unlucky in our Passage by contrary winds which kept us in sight of the French Coast for several days; however we have been fortunate enough to make good our landing with part of our force last night, without anything that can be called opposition. A small battery or two opposed our landing which Mr Howe soon silenced with his Ships; and the resistance the grenadiers soon found from the Peasants is too trifling to trouble you with. The first landing consisted of as many His Majesty's Footguards as could be disembarked with Major-General Drury; the Grenadiers of the Army with Major Genl. Mostyn; the whole commanded by Lord George Sackville . . . We are now disembarking the remainder as fast as possible and I will march forward to St Malo's as soon as I see a retreat made practicable. the [sic] intelligence we get is that [French] Troops are collecting but as yet we hear of no considerable body being assembled. I have the Honour . . .
    Marlborough

[Marlborough to Pitt]   11th June 1758 Cancalle

I ordered the country to be reconnoitred . . . and I was soon convinced that the Enemy either through Panick or Weakness, would not oppose our March: for only some few Regulars were mixed among the Garde de Cotes, armed peasants &c; and they behave so little like men, that they did us no mischief; not withstanding the country was seemingly impractical for an army to pass thro', the Roads bad, and very narrow, the enclosures small and the Hedges very thick with Ravines interspersed and in short, entirely different from what I had it represented. But however it was necessary to lose no time lest they should recover from their first fright and prevent our Proceeding . . . marching in two columns I had not gone much above a league when I perceived by the Situation in the Country, that any Succours sent from or towards Cherburgh [sic] might without difficulty cut in between our Main Body and Intrenchments. [Leaving a guard] to preserve our Communications, I proceeded with the remainder to Paramé near St Malo's. The Quarter Master General had reconnoitred towards St Servant and found that country still more impracticable than what we had hoped, being filled with numerous Houses and high Stone Walls and yet unless we could possess ourselves of that Town and its Country as well as of Paramé, it would have been impossible to obey His Majesty's instructions . . . the bringing Mortars of Heavy Cannon even as far as Paramé . . . would have been most difficult, thro' such roads and with so few Horses: but when I found I must still go a League [c. three miles] further to St Servant thro' Roads not used by Carriages, I despaired of having any use from our Artillery; the Common Communications between Paramé and St Servant being under the Cannon of St Malo's.

However I made the experiment, moved some of the mortars and stores several miles, attempted making the Roads, but to so little effect that I found it could not answer especially as the investing of St Malo's was not practicable, as I could not prevent supplies being flung into the Town by the River from Dinant, and a bombardment would have an effect whilst the Burghers were not awed by a numerous garrison; and as reinforcements are hours gathering in, all Expectation of that sort was at an end, especially as no Communication could be preserved between our Camp and St Servant; so that our little army by being so dispersed with the different services, we were under the necessity of providing for, would have been liable to have been incircled [sic] by very small numbers. In this situation I found it necessary to execute my orders with all possible Dispatch. I accordingly ordered Mr Elliott with the Light Dragoons to push into St Servant the very night I got to Paramé, but I was soon obliged to reinforce that Post with a Brigade [under Waldegrave]. Before the Brigade arrived, the Volunteers, pickets and Light Dragoons had set fire to several of the enemy's ships at low water, and burnt many of the naval stores and next morning . . . burnt all the Privateers some of thirty, several of twenty and eighteen guns, and in the whole destroyed upward of 100 ships.

St Malo's is better and more regularly fortified than imagined, but most conveniently situated for a Bombardment and if our Expectations had been answered in being landed near the Place, I do believe we might in the first Hurry, have succeeded but the Pilot did not think any place except the Bay at Cancalle sufficiently secure for the shipping . . . to judge from the consternation and Distress of the Country that I doubt not but the Intelligence we have had of troops being upon their march from all sides is true and in that case, a powerful Diversion of the Enemy's Forces will be made, but as I was unwilling [meaning 'unwilling as I was'] to leave Paramé I could stay there no longer with safety. I ordered the Dragoons to take Post . . . toward Avranches, sustained by a Brigade of Guards knowing that by that precaution, I could neither be surprised or interrupted . . . and on the 10th, fell in with the Head of the Enemy's column and by taking some Prisoners we learnt that the body might consist of about 10,000 Regular Troops . . . I thought it necessary to march to Cancalle which I did without Hurry and in great security, as it was no longer safe to keep Troops uncollected, I should have been pleased to have marched towards this Body, could I have done it without risking the being put between two Fires as I could not learn what fires what numbers had been sent from Britany [sic] to St Malo's.

I am now re-embarking in order to continue our operations on some other Part of the Coast . . .

John M

Marlborough did re-embark after Howe's ships had driven back a French attack on them, but his next letter begins anti-climactically:

Cancalle Bay June 19th 1758

I am sorry to date this letter from the same place as my last but the wind has been so contrary and at the same time so fresh that our attempt at getting out of this Bay has been ineffectual. that [sic] we might if possible do something even in this unpleasant situation, I went with Lord Geo. Sackville and the Engineers in a small Frigate, to reconnoitre Grandville and found it . . . too well guarded by Batteries and two different Encampments between our place of landing and the Town to attempt it without any probability of Success.

The moment the wind changes we shall sail for the Coast of Normandy . . . I shall propose to Mr Howe the attempting to bombard Granville to draw their attention that way which he will do if practicable. I am

Marlborough

At sea June 24th 1758

. . . we have been most unfortunate in our Weather: wind bound many days in Cancalle Bay, we are at last got into the channel, by Tiding it against a Northern wind; now we are clear of the French coast the wind is at East, which I fear will not only make our getting to the Coast of Normandy, but occasion such a swell as may prevent our attempting to land . . . these unfortunate Delays, not only consume our Provisions but enervate the Troops by being too long closely confined in the Transports.

The ships you mention have joined us and as soon as the weather permits, we shall distribute a proportion of the Men among them . . . Our sickness does not increase to any great degree, but as the Beer is now out, the Seamen tell us we must expect the bad effects from the Water and spirits allowed instead of it . . . I shall only beg leave to observe to you that with the force I have, it is not reasonable to hope that the French can be long, without assembling a superior number of Troops in any place where we can land; and if they do, it will not be easy to re-embark in the face of them, without risking more than I imagined My Instruments entitled me to do; for which reason I had resolved to venture any Engagement in which numbers would give me a prospect of Success; but in case of a Superiority on their part, to have re-imbarked [sic] with as little loss as possible. But if His Majesty by directing me to be reminded of that part of my Instructions, means

The Collapse of the Earl of Chatham in the House of Lords, 7 July 1778.
American-heroic work of J. P. Copley – with a hint of *Iolanthe.*

King George II (*left*), peppery, valiant, unreasonable and gently managed by the Duke of Newcastle (*below*), a disinterested public servant who scorned reward.

William Pitt (*right*), was against Britons becoming 'slaves' to the Spanish and French, his closest ally and publicist, William Beckford (*below*), owned 30,000 slaves on his Jamaican plantations.

Edward Hawke (*right*), the greatest British sailor before Nelson and destroyer of the French navy, was politically protected by George Anson (*below*), circumnavigator and First Lord of the Admiralty. Essential man.

The [underwritten lines were found in his] pocket after he was killed Septr 13th 1759

*the words are missing —

But since ignoble age must come,
disease y death's inevitable doom,
That life which others pay let us bestow
and give to fame what we to nature owe.
Brave let us fall, or honored if we live,
or let us glory gain, or glory give —
.... such shall our lives a Sovereign State
.... to those who dare not imitate

James Wolfe (*right*): national hero, coldly ambitious, improvised superbly, died even better. John Manners (*below*), as Marquis of Granby (built all those pubs!) a warm-hearted, brave man who was loved by his soldiers. A good European, served under Ferdinand of Brunswick during the Seven Years War.

Edmund Burke (*right*),
Lord Rockingham's grand shadow,
cast Pitt into a long, cool perspective
and described his orations as 'fustian'.
An outsider . . . but not as far outside
as John Wilkes (*below*) – blind to
Scottish splendours. He was
'That Devil, Wilkes' to George III,
but 'Jack' and delightful company
to a charmed Dr Johnson.

John Stuart, 3rd Earl of Bute and
British prime minister from
1762 to1763 (*right*), was a Scottish
nobleman and therefore a prime
target for Wilkes's bubbling rage.
Richard Rigby (*below*), an Essex
boy, landed but low. He was
the Duke of Bedford's fixer.

Hogarth's xenophobic, puritanical view of the age entitled *The Times* – a menagerie of the age's dramatis personae, including Pitt, Frederick the Great and Wilkes's collaborator, the cheerfully disgraceful parson-poet, Charles Churchill.

that I am to pay less regard to the safety of the Troops than I have done, I shall be ready when properly authorized, to act implicitly according to any orders that may be sent to me, without the least Regard to what I might think, rashly risking such a Body of His Majesty's Forces. I have the honour to be . . .

Marlborough

Marlborough himself comes well out of that account. He is not a great soldier – and not a glory hunter either. The last eighty words of the final letter, 24 June, are a blazing pre-emption of the Whitehall requirement that he should run soldiers and sailors into a losing and pointless fight. He secures his exit, follows the book and will not do stupid risks. It would have been a comfort to have served under a general who thought like that.

The failures are of planning: no discreet reconnaissance ahead of the raid to find narrow roads where carriages, and so also artillery, do not go, plus thick woods and high walls suiting defence. Worst of all, there is no knowledge that St Malo was linked by water with Dinant and thus impossible to invest. The higher command, military and political, has to be faulted here. Marlborough's mild surprise that various things were not as he had supposed suggest that he and his men had been sent into *terra incognita* and bidden to make the best of it.

In the circumstances he did well enough in destroying so many small ships. But these would be support ships for convoys. Destroying them set back French trade and helped English predation, but, at eighteen to thirty guns, they were not part of the naval war where one went with fifty to eighty. Above all, the raid failed in its objective, a successful assault on St Malo, the near impossibility of which a London strategist would have discovered by proper intelligence.

Meanwhile, business with Frederick also concluded, the full War Cabinet had formally approved the major North American venture of Louisbourg. A long information hiatus would lie between overwrought salutations at departure and the tribulation and success of the actual campaign. However, Beckford's *Monitor* took some of the North American celebration on account. On 23 April, when the force was still being knocked about and rained on in the west Atlantic, it announced that 'British liberties were no longer to be trusted to the guardianship of Hessian and Hanoverian hirelings. America became

the chief object of our armaments and France the pole to which all
our councils and operations pointed . . .' It ended on a high point of
rhetoric: 'Will not every honest man revere that public spirit which a
degenerate age cannot bear?' The members of the Cabinet supporting
the American action they had never actually opposed had, higher up
the page, been treated to columns of the *Daily Beast*. 'Self-conviction
wrought at the same time upon their dastard souls; perceiving that
this was no expedition suppressing the cries of the people . . . they
were glad to slink into retirement.'[12]

The actual expedition had set out on 23 February, the military
command with Amherst, naval leadership with Boscawen. Amherst
was appointed by Pitt, but at the urging of Ligonier. Politically, he
belonged to Cumberland's faction. In the last war he had fought at
Dettingen, Fontenoy and Rocoux, had worked on Cumberland's staff
gathering military intelligence (1746). At Hastenbeck in 1757 he had
somehow survived his patron's disgrace, continuing as commissary to
the Hessians, Hanoverians and Buckeburgers.

Politically, the general was spattered, quite innocently, with black,
admittedly provoked, marks. The real ones are for posterity. Amherst
had a hatred of the Indian tribes and his response pre-echoed the
American soldier of eighty years later, 'Mad Anthony Wayne'. They
were not to be taken prisoner, and he adopted the proposal of a
Colonel Bouquet that blankets infected with smallpox should be
presented to them – precisely Wayne's technique. The ring of his
words is not pleasant. 'You will do well to try to inoculate the Indians
by means of Blanketts, as well as to try Every other method that can
serve to Extirpate this Execrable race.'[13] Domestic politics and civilisation apart, he had the good opinion of Ligonier which Pitt accepted.
Steady and competent, his great qualities lay in patient and efficient
administration, soon evident at Louisbourg.

The journey took over eleven weeks of reliably dreadful weather
to reach Halifax. The undertaking would though, between February
and July, have inevitable tribulations. At Louisbourg the French had
six thousand men and five ships of the line. So, on 11 June, Amherst
reminds Pitt: 'The last opportunity I had of writing to you was on
the 17th May by a Virginia Man bound to England, I then acquainted
you with my Expectation of seeing Halifax in a day or two . . .'[14] A
day or two had been lengthened by winds and fog to eleven before

he met Boscawen coming out of Halifax to set down a force under Monckton. For days the message had been Wind, Fog and Impossibility. But on 6th June, the weather lightened and Amherst got his men into the boats only for his admiral to veto a landing. Like the French coast raiders, he was kept waiting and cruising.

He had looked anxiously for a landing place, but the French were protected from ships by a number of 'posts', Martello-type firing stations. On the 8th before daybreak, his ships, splitting into three divisions, began a bombardment. Amherst commended the enemy's conduct. They 'did not throw away a Shot till the Boats were near in Shore and then directed the fire of their Cannon and Musketry upon them. The surf was so great that a place could hardly be found to get a boat on shore.' A certain James Wolfe begins here the short blaze of his late career when 'notwithstanding the fire of the Enemy and the violence of the Surf, Brigadier Wolfe pursued his point, and landed just at their left on the Coast, took post, attacked the enemy and forced them to retreat, many Boats overset, several broke to Pieces, and all the men jumped into the water to get on shore'.

That was absolutely not the heroic conclusion. Amherst reported 'the roughest and Worst Ground I ever saw'. They got through and began an investment, but 'the wind increased and we could not get any thing on shore'. And as night fell, the general reckoned three officers, five NCOs and thirty-eight troopers dead 'of which eight were shot the rest drowned in trying to get on shore'. During the next three days 'the weather continued extremely bad' until after high surf had prevented them getting all their tents on shore, and his light six-pounder guns and other artillery were landed. Amherst's letter to Pitt was written in the aspirational style of all transatlantic military communication at this date: 'in Case Admiral Boscawen should despatch a ship to England, in my next I hope to give a good account of our progress'.[15]

On 23 June Amherst informed Pitt of another action, begun the day his last letter had been finished. Unsurprisingly, it involved Brigadier Wolfe who, with an assortment of grenadiers, rangers and light infantry, was sent 'round the North east harbour to the Light house point, with an Intention to Silence the island battery and . . . attempt to destroy the Ships in the Harbour'.[16] It was done, most of it (though the ships to be destroyed, a major ambition at this stage, are not mentioned), on the day of Amherst's current letter, lighthouse point taken and abandoned posts with them. But there had been setbacks. A supporting fleet under Admiral Hardy was blown out to sea and though, finally on the 16th, the soldiers landed twelve days' worth of provisions, getting the artillery off proved impossible. However, by degrees, during brief runs of fine weather, Amherst's men reliably brought more artillery on shore. And on the 17th they destroyed the ships in the harbour.

Essentially Amherst was now conducting a siege while being served with a thin trickle of provisions and having got underhand only a fraction of the artillery without which sieges fail. Almost a fortnight after establishing the force, he heard from the blown-about Admiral Hardy that, during the prolonged landing, over a hundred boats had been lost. Boats provided escape in shipwreck but more immediately would transport anything, including troops. Good weather turned up on the 16th, lasting until the 21st. During that interlude Amherst and two of his officers, Williamson and McKellar, did a fair reconnaissance and heard Colonel Bastide propose Green Hill as route pointer. They took two mortars and three 'royals', smaller guns for the batteries at the now captured lighthouse.

On the next day they captured a French ship but it brought intelligence of another escape. Which, wrote Amherst, 'shews how very difficult it is to block up the Entrance of the Harbour, it appears to me to be impossible'. On the 21st the weather was 'very bad'; on the 22nd it continued. And on the 23rd he described to Pitt what had been happening.[17]

Amherst did not send another letter until 6 July, when he reported enemy fire on the lighthouse and its batteries and 'the temporary building they called the Advance Redoubt'. On the 26th (June) three hundred pioneers were sent to Green Hill. Admiral Boscawen managed to land two hundred marines. Wolfe was asked to bring his artillery round the harbour to attack the shipping again. On the 27th, cannon were landed. On the 28th, troops, behind a temporary embankment called an epaulement, amid cannonading, began establishing themselves up 'the Road over the Bogs', and recorded the death of Messervy, much-admired shipbuilder, and an outbreak of smallpox among the skilled workforce he commanded, affecting all but sixteen of his 108 men.

The 29th brought heavy fire on the epaulement; the work on the road was proving harder and taking longer than expected, and 'the Enemy',[18] as Amherst levelly called them, sank four of their ships into the harbour mouth. The 2 July saw epaulement and road still making very slow progress 'from the extreme badness of the ground', there was yet more cannonading and 'we skirmished all day with parties out of the Town'. The 3rd saw Wolfe as military engineer working on an earthworks at the front closest to the enemy's position, 'at 650 yards from the covered way with an intention of erecting a battery to destroy the Defences of the Place, it being pretty well on the Capital of the Citadel Bastion'. The 4th was marked with 'a great Fog'. On the 5th, men working on the epaulement died when 'the Frigate cannonaded on it without ceasing'.

The 6th, on which Amherst dated his letter, was marked by a peaceful moment when, under a flag of truce, a French sloop sailed to Sir Charles Hardy's ships 'to carry some things to their wounded Officers and Prisoners'. Amherst's conclusion, before making the humble and obedient servant forms, was to list 'the many difficulties of landing every thing in almost continual Surf, the making of Roads, draining and passing of Bogs and putting ourselves under Cover'. It was all taking much longer than he could wish, but 'I beg to assure you Sir, that no time shall be lost in advancing and I doubt not but, the necessary Precautions being taken, our Success will be very certain'.[19] It is a touching document, dogged struggle doggedly recorded, very far from the heroic words in London.

Seventeen days later, reporting on events of the 7th, the general is recording a visit from Drucour, the Governor defending Louisbourg, letters accompanied by a drummer to himself and Admiral Boscawen, a request that fire should not be directed at the French hospital. Amherst had accommodated this with the suggestion of shifting the hospital to a ship or a harbour in the island. But the fire and counter-fire, what Amherst calls 'cannonading', continued on the 8th. The next day broke the monotony of firing when '. . . in the night, the Enemy made a sortie where Brigadier Lawrence commanded, every thing had been so quiet it was expected by some, others I fear, were not so vigilant and suffered for it, the enemy came from Camp Noir and tho' drunk, I am afraid rather surprised a Company of Grenadiers of Forbes's commanded by Lord Dundonald . . . Major Murray who commanded three companies of Grenadiers immediately detached one and drove the Enemy back very easily, Whitmore and Bragg's Grenadiers behaved very well on this occasion.'

The consequences were melancholy and in the patient Laconian way of a professional soldier familiar to such things, Amherst recorded: 'Lord Dundonald was killed, Lt. Tew wounded and taken prisoner, 1 corporal 3 Men killed 1 Sergeant 11 men missing 17 Men wounded. the Sortie was of five Picquets supported by 600 Men . . . Beside what wounded they caryed [sic] into the town, one of which, a Captain, died immediately. The Enemy sent out a Flag of truce to bury their dead, which when over the cannonading began again . . .'[20]

So it continued across July: some progress on the epaulement, 'the Enemy throwing many shells', all night rains such that 'not a man in detachment could have a dry thread on', 'a great many shells', 'the Citadel bastion firing very smartly', the Enemy working hard at Cape Noir / Breton, an assault on the French defences by 'a Battary [sic] of seven Mortars with some twelve Pounders to ricochet the Works and the Town'. 'Shells into camp supposed to be intended against our powder magazine, Br. Wolfe taking possession of some hills where we made a lodgement, the enemy fired very briskly from the Town and shipping.'

The struggle was now turning. On 21 July, British troops would see three French ships, *Entreprenant*, *Capricieux* and *Superbe*, burning out in the harbour after a massive explosion of powder. 'They kept burning very fast', wrote Amherst coolly; 'and we kept firing on them the whole time to try to hinder the Boats and People from the Town to get to their assistance.' Then, on the 22nd, after further bombardment, came the conclusive strike: 'Our Shells put the Citadel in Flames . . . The siege', Amherst hoped, 'will not now last many days . . .'

Capitulation fell to the premature veteran, known, at barely forty-seven, as Old Dreadnought, Admiral Edward Boscawen, who, back in 1756, may have given the fuse of war its final spark by a precipitate assault. He gave Pitt in a letter of 28 July carried by Captain Edgcumbe, an 'Account of the Reduction of Louisbourg, the Isle of St John's and its Dependencies . . .' which informed him that 'the Garrison are Prisoners of War and consist of twenty-four companies of Marines and the four following Battalions, Cambise, 2nd Battalion; Volontaire Etrangere, 2nd Battalion; Artois, 2nd Battalion; Burgoyne, 2nd

Battalion.' He added a list of ships taken, sunk, burnt or blown up. There were two of 74 guns, three of 64, one each of 50, 36 and 26 guns.[21]

Amherst and Wolfe both wanted to accelerate the ultimate British conquest, of Quebec. Upon this, Boscawen set a firm foot; his ships were underprovisioned, he was carrying five thousand prisoners and autumn was descending. Boscawen, game for most hazards, contemplating a winter in Canada after a summer of mounting seas and descending rain, felt, reasonably enough, that conquering Louisbourg would do for 1758.

British forces *ought* to have taken Louisbourg. In soldiery they outnumbered the French more than two to one, 14,000 to 6000. But Amherst's despatches demonstrate how little of a casual conquest it had been. Amherst's patient professionalism, with Wolfe bubbling but contained at his side, did the business. The implications for Pitt's dreams, pitched wider still and wider, were very large. Quebec had been sensibly postponed, but the base for that assault had been secured and the first Frenchmen turned out of their unquestioned territory. But that victory was almost immediately offset. News now reached Pitt of defeat further south at Ticonderoga where Abercromby, faced by a serious French soldier, Montcalm, had moved too soon.

When the appointments were being made, the Hardwickes were all sceptical. Joseph Yorke, soldier, later diplomat, who rated Wolfe and Amherst, went on: 'There are good and spirited men amongst the officers there, but I must tell you beforehand that Abercrombie [*sic*] is a man of no genius and must therefore be assisted.'[22] Hardwicke was no more impressed: '. . . I was present last winter at the meeting where he was proposed to be appointed, and from the character then given of him, expressed my disapprobation . . .'[23]

Character had nothing to do with it. Amherst had plenty of regulars; Abercromby, starting from New York, depended on local volunteers and levies whose slow arrival delayed him. Pitt in Whitehall had laid down a time for their arrival – early May; they turned up in early June. Boscawen, bent on Louisbourg, had been delayed – longer – by weather, and it hadn't mattered. Louisbourg already had good troops there and five ships of the line.

Ticonderoga would be protected by the main French army under the Marquis de Montcalm, an anxiety. What one did not do outside

Ticonderoga was what Amherst had doggedly done at Louisbourg – wait. On top of all which, Abercromby in early July was still missing his artillery, exactly as Amherst had been. He now received faulty intelligence that 30,000 French reinforcements were expected. Already under pressure of time, he put himself under more. Campaigns, for all Pitt's talk about system and a coordinated strategy, were individual enterprises. No help came from Louisbourg, but Montcalm had heard the bad news and, accordingly, made straight for Ticonderoga.

Desperate for time, wanting guns, given wrong intelligence and on his own, Abercromby unwisely attacked the fort. He argued that if he had succeeded in this rushed assault and taken it, then, 'even at the expense of some good officers and men, we should have forced the Marquis of Montcalm to have retired to his boats, leaving the garrison to be besieged'.[24] The action is best described in his own words.

'Lord Howe at the head of the right Center column supported by the Light Infantry, being advanced, fell in with a French Party, supposed to consist of about 400 Regulars and a few Indians . . . our Flankers killed a great Many and took 148 prisoners . . . But this small Success cost us very dear, not as to the Loss of Numbers for we had only two Officers killed but as to Consequences. His Lordship being the first Man that fell in this Skirmish . . .' There followed much talk about how 'universally beloved' the deceased lordship was, also 'respected throughout the whole Army'. Abercromby concludes that 'it is easy to conceive the Grief and Consternation his untimely fall occasioned'. He then adds far more melancholy words: 'The Army as I observed before, being dispersed & night coming on fast, I collected such Part of it as were within my Reach & posted them under the Trees, where they remained all night under Arms.' He reported to Pitt a few dispositions, one of which, Colonel Bradstreet's spoiling assault on stores and shipping for Fort Frontenac, proved, within limits, a success. But it was only a useful fallback operation and in letting go 3600 men for it, Abercromby was demonstrating that, for 1758 at least, Ticonderoga was no longer an objective.

His expedition had been rather worse than the coastal raids, but had better excuses. It was something altogether bigger, dependent on unorganisable local auxiliaries and, most important of all, up against almost the whole French Army of Canada. It would not anyway, like a half-cock coastal raid, be left at that. Amherst was on the same continent and placed to renew the assault. 'Next year' had a hopeful ring in Canada. In Brittany the phrase guaranteed another expensive irrelevance, Henry Fox's golden guineas, followed by a flurry of public relations. Failure at Ticonderoga might have diluted victory at Louisbourg, as the later game of two halves on the French coast at Cherbourg would have done in a dispassionate light. But Ticonderoga *without* Louisbourg would have been perfect calamity.

But the *Monitor* didn't need an actual victory to start its tribal dance. Four days after Amherst in Louisbourg was *writing* his victory despatch, the voice of the City enquired menacingly, 'When did Britain appear more terrible to her foes, more respectable to all nations than in the Year of 1758?' Rightly anticipating victory, also anticipating St Jingo, the paper praised 'Our men, money and ships' which 'under faithfull and wise counsellors are a match for the whole World . . .' The Bismarckian tone was sustained after a routine dismissal of the foreign allies we no longer needed. For '. . . we are in a condition to carry fire and sword to the enemy's country . . .'[25]

The mood which the *Monitor* expressed with such crude verve only reflected Pitt's own new access of assurance. He would now spend public money with a new confidence that expenditure bringing assets and triumphs was something to boast about; meanwhile, the *Monitor* and the other Patriot papers would hold up the sum to the light and express delight. 'Ten million four hundred thousand pounds – cheerfully and expeditiously raised – such is the spirit of this nation when they are satisfied with a minister and approve of the measures pursued by the Cabinet.'[26] The passage appears just below the copy about Britain never having appeared 'more terrible to her foes', an interesting combination of opulence and bullying.

When, of course, victory proper was registered, the raptures were loud. 'The loss of Cape Breton will be severely felt by the French; its conquest is big with the greatest advantage to the British Crown.' They were, too, interspersed with shrewd assessments of the good business to be done on seized banks and shoals. 'This will secure and extend our fish trade and improve our navigation in the provinces hitherto served with *bacalao* [dried fish] by French bankers.' Reconciled to such triumphs, the *Monitor* sketched in the future role of a Greater Britain. It was for us '. . . to maintain the dignity of the British flag and the dominion of the seas: to secure a free navigation and to extend our Commerce'. Ministers maintaining this satisfactory state of affairs would be 'the darlings of the people and under them, the Royal Diadem will shine with proper lustre'.[27]

The style might be counting-house bathetic, but the eye for 'great advantage' was sharp enough. It was understood that chivalry had no future. We had won, we had the means of control and the French must knuckle under, said the *Monitor*, pointing out that we could force 'the French Ministry to accept of such terms as may prevent effusions of blood and treasure'. We now had the 'strength and method of making war from the sea'. If, for the moment, City of London publicists responded most keenly 'to securing and extending our fish trade', there was a wider appetite in the editorial's swelling hubris: England, 'big with Great Advantage'.

Marching in parallel a couple of months and three thousand miles apart, came anti-climax. The serious business had been and would be in Canada and Germany, but, bad habits being endemic, it was resolved to make yet another coastal raid on northern France. This time the objective was Caen with a fallback option at Cherbourg. After early rebuffs, this episode ended in August with the temporary taking of Cherbourg, largely an occasion for drunken riot and the irrelevant capture of a quantity of brass cannon. It would be a through-paced and completely mismanaged affair, leaving Marlborough's landing looking like Hastings. There was a political twist to this expedition. It was tactfully decorated with General Bligh, formerly Marlborough's deputy, highly acceptable to Bute and generally served by officers close to Leicester House. HRH Midshipman Prince Edward, an adolescent of no ascertained talent, was brought along as public relations. The Dowager Princess Augusta and her court might have been dropped by Pitt as he found prospects with the Old Corps, but George II himself was probably no more aware of his mortality than his Secretary of State. Pitt's letters to Lord Bute in the last two years of the reign breathe abjection.

The essential idea was to find a spot; might it be Morlaix or perhaps Le Havre or somewhere between them? Morlaix was too close to Brest where the invasion-boat building was carried out and hence strongly protected, though a wrecking incursion there might have had some point. A second attack on St Malo had the charm of lightning striking twice and so being unexpected. It was also, in the circumstances of Pitt's networking, the preferred option of Leicester House. It was astonishing levity on Pitt's part. Bligh and Howe were decent professionals best left to judge for themselves, but they operated according to the wisdom of Bute and Augusta and their court soldiery. Then, as with the unhappy Holburne, the weather – in July – turned horrible, separating Bligh, military commander on land, from Howe, naval commander at sea. Bligh had therefore to turn and march away from St Malo, the objective and – so as to keep in signal distance of Howe – toward Matignon, not the objective.

Trying to get out of the awful hole in which he was placed, Bligh tried his hand at retreat to St Cast and its suitable beach, losing by casualty and prisoners in the course of a wretchedly managed march upward of seven hundred men. Poor Bligh came home to be cut dead as only George II knew how to cut a man dead. As for Pitt's chances with Bute, they stumbled before the virtuoso incomprehension of the Earl himself. He blamed Newcastle, who had nothing to do with the raid, and was pretty cool to Pitt. Addressing his 'worthy friend', he designates Bligh, 'the conqueror of Cherbourgh', 'the only man that has been victorious in France'. And as for the treatment of their man, it was something 'a greater person than me never will forgive'. A greater person than me: the Dowager Princess or the future George III?

The full three-part conflict itself, finishing dismally at St Cast, took place across the summer months into early September. Louisbourg was won at the end of July and communication of the victory reached London in September, just in time to stifle the public blame which St Cast deserved. The real achievement of Amherst – and of Ligonier, who had selected him – now served to divert indignation from the intended diversion.

14

Patriots Betrayed

Louisbourg, having been taken, was excellent news but it would not be London news until September. Meanwhile, St Malo was miserable news postponed only three days. Delayed two weeks by Pitt's gout, then agreed on 19 May, landing on 7 June, limping back at the end of that month, it was another clear failure and a fringe failure at that. The *Monitor* treated the general policy of coastal actions to a catalogue of self-congratulation. 'Though not crowned with the utmost advantages as might have been expected from their force and commission', the long weekends on the Norman and Breton coast had scotched 'all hopes . . . of an invasion upon our dominions; protected our trade and navigation; ruined their commerce from the four winds, and cut off their last efforts, for continuing the war, and favouring their usurpations on our settlements in America'.[1]

Beckford's office poet cannot disguise total untruth. The ships and soldiers had been sent for political reasons to register some sort of victory, an excuse for bonfires and a parliamentary vote of thanks. Naturally, episodes which actually were creditable, like the encounter off Cartagena in February and the successful blockade of the Basque Roads, did not escape gilding. They were fit to take a place 'prior to the emblazoned trophies of Blenheim and Ramillies'.[2]

Horace Walpole is sometimes wrongheaded, but his comments about the latest expedition, when writing to Conway on 16 June, says it all about the first St Malo raid of the first half of June: 'Well in half a dozen wars we shall know something of the coast of France.' And as he relayed later military news to Horace Mann in Florence: 'I was awakened with an account of our Army having re-embarked after burning some vessels at St Maloes. This is the history, neither more nor less, of this mighty expedition. They found the causeway broken-up, stayed from Tuesday night till Monday morning within sight of the town; agreed it was impregnable, learned that ten thousand French (which the next day were erected to thirty thousand) were coming against them, took their transport and were gone . . . to play at hide and seek somewhere else. The campaign being rather naked, is coloured over with the great damage we have done and with the fine disposition and despatch made for getting away.'[3]

The events leading to the Battle of Krefeld on 23 June were only a modest time lapse behind the glories of St Malo. But for the purpose of underwriting Pitt's great shift of policy by Pitt, their timing was immaculate. He had spoken to Dodington only two years before of every Englishman resisting 'with his body' the sending of any British troops to Germany. It had been a major theme of his Patriot days. However, having accepted the King's initiative in commissioning Ferdinand to command Hanoverian and Hessian troops resisting French attacks on the Electorate, Pitt had agreed in February to heavy subsidy. In late June, he had swallowed his eloquence and offered Parliament a proposal to send four regiments of cavalry and six thousand British soldiers to Germany. He now, with perfect timing, rejoiced at news from Germany of an uncontested and significant victory. The success of Ferdinand employing those Hanoverian and Hessian troops had been achieving against the French deserves some account.

Back in March, Count Clermont* had wanted to cross the Weser, which French troops had been commanding. He sought the defensive move of getting behind a river. He could make a battle for it, anticipating next summer's event, but his letter describes troops unfit to fight. Getting nicely over a river made more sense. The Duc de Broglie would take his soldiers through Kassel, Warburg, Unna, Düsseldorf and Cologne. Saint-Germain would go through Münster to Wesel. Meanwhile, the men garrisoning Emden would travel through Emmerich. These moves ended that campaign. They were all going to the same destination, across the Rhine. It was, for the interim, a comprehensive retreat.

The effects were serious. The French had suffered 16,000 casualties, including 10,000 sick, prisoners of the Hanoverians. Ferdinand's losses by the same test were not trivial, with six thousand sick, but their

---

* Also L'Abbé Clermont.

forces had now come together, and Ferdinand would now display his wider qualities as a commander, qualities of recovery, recruiting, care, practising war in small encounters with lingering French parties. He would have 40,000 men passably ready for May. Meanwhile, across the North Sea, the penny was very quietly dropping. With spring and a fit army, Ferdinand had a choice of mentors about what to do next.

In England, Pitt would for some time be sending naval raid upon naval raid, taking troops for long weekend incursions on to French soil. George II, who, deeply grateful to Ferdinand, had awarded him a sword of honour, was pushing for that military coordination in Germany with the Channel raids second choice, all he could so far get from Pitt. Now the British Minister asked, could not the Prince make a raid – on land – into France to increase the naval incursions' impact?

Ironically, Frederick, whose (casual) suggestion those naval actions had been, was distinctly cool. But Ferdinand, who had dashing tendencies, made his own mind up. He would help the British with just such an adventure. On the evening of 1 June, literally corner-cutting with a bridge of boats starting just inside Dutch territory, he passed the Rhine. 'I cut a bit into the territory of the Republic of Holland . . .' he recorded. Meeting no immediate French response, he sent a detachment ahead from Cleve, taken that first day, to Goch, near where an encounter with the French sent them backwards to Xanten. Ferdinand pressed on toward Lobith, taking more men across the Rhine at Rees, a modest advance earning Clermont bitter words from Versailles, a letter from the *Maîtresse en titre* herself. '*Quelle humiliation, Monseigneur*', tutted Madame de Pompadour, '*laisser débarquer 6000 hommes et établir un pont sur le Rhin!*'[4] It was just what an outmanoeuvred commander wanted to hear from a judgemental harlot. Humiliated or not, the French were withdrawn to Rheinberg where the depending Clermont settled on high ground and sought a defensive action.

Which he did not get. Ferdinand made a night attack, Holstein-Gottorp right, Spoerken left, he himself leading. Both wings failed, Holstein-Gottorp getting lost, so Ferdinand put the assault off by a day. The alerted French had retreated to Neuss, leaving 12,000 men holding Krefeld. On the 18th he sent ten squadrons and eleven guns to cut communications behind Neuss. Before this could start under the Erb Prinz's command, the French were spotted returning to

Krefeld. Hanoverian forces stopped where they were in concentrated ranks, fifty-eight groupings of cavalry, thirty-five of infantry. After which prudential exertion, the French attack didn't happen!

A separate French force had been going back under Marshal Soubise to the Austrian theatre when he was told by the Minister of War, Belleisle, to join Clermont and, specifically at Krefeld, to attack Ferdinand. The French outnumbered the Hanoverians two to one in horse, slightly more in infantry. Ferdinand frequently sent an observer (or went himself) up the church tower of St Toenis, the best lookout post at hand. He would hold his final command meetings there. Spoerken was to take a light force north of Krefeld to harass the French right. Under the Prince's command, the main forces were to move in groups south-east and south-west of Clermont to opposite ends of a great ditch and rough palisade, or *Landwehr*.

By a happy accident, despatches from Versailles had reached Soubise, senior but separate commander here, with new directions from Belleisle telling him now to carry on as intended towards Bohemia where he was urgently needed. This pantomime of contradictions happened because the Minister, informed that Clermont was retreating, expected no clash. Meanwhile, Clermont, misunderstanding his orders to attack, on 20 June settled for holding tight near Krefeld where Ferdinand settled for attacking him.

The French cavalry was placed behind the *Landwehr*. With nearly two to one superiority, they were strongly placed, with marshland and the Rhine to their right. Leftward, scrubby and cluttered with farm buildings, despite another useful ditch at Holtehoefe, was more problematic for defenders. Ferdinand, down from his church tower, opted to march from St Toenis. Leading it in person, he swung eight miles behind the enemy's left through Vorst and Anrath. Meanwhile, mixed cavalry and infantry, under Lieutenant General Oberg, seized two crossings of the *Landwehr* at Am Stock and Mai, respectively centre-left and centre-right. Spoerken took his forces, twenty-three squadrons of cavalry and thirteen infantry, with a group of light troops to his left, north of an empty Krefeld. In a war fought according to so many rigid and misunderstood directions, everything must now be done by eye and ear, the immediate officer's judgement.

Clermont began with a mistake easily made. Between 6.00 p.m. and 1.00 a.m. he mistook the sound of an enemy advancing for those

of parties reconnoitring. Finally, alerted, his first response – so late
– was to send troops to his own right flank to face the heavy fire of
the Erb Prinz's men, clashing with his left near Holtehoefe. This was
a serious fight for the crossing. It lasted four hours, with the French
retreating until succoured by Clermont's reinforcements. Holstein-
Gottorp, meanwhile, had wandered along the *Landwehr*, seeking and
not finding a crossing (there were five in all). Mistaken or not,
Clermont was doing well and the Erb Prinz was in trouble from that
nicely timed reinforcement. At the same time, recognising military
climax, Clermont sent cavalry to one of the crossings Holstein-
Gottorp hadn't been able to find, at Engerhof.

There had been good generalship on both sides. Ferdinand, also
alerted to the Engerhof crossing, sent a messenger to Holstein-Gottorp,
directing him there. The Erb Prinz's troops were isolated and putting
Ferdinand, hurrying undermanned to the rescue, in great danger. They
had charged and been driven back, but that conflict now drew in every
senior officer on a broad field within reach of the information. Oberg,
deciding to be useful where he could hear most noise, crossed the
Landwehr at the two central places, Am Stock and Mai, and joined
Holstein-Gottorp, making a crucial change. At the epicentre, the battle
proper, the Hanoverians had the numbers. Fighting continued; there
was nothing like a French rout, but after the best efforts of a group
of Grenadiers had been driven back, it made proper sense for Clermont
to make an orderly retreat.

But if this was the centre of the battle, the radial parts were still
busy. Spoerken might have made victory conclusive by going south
to attack the retreat, but the natural defences of boggy ground next
the Rhine stopped him. Also, with liaison between that group of light
troops and the main body almost non-existent, he was relying upon
casual and inaccurate information, mostly pessimistic. The French
retreat could not, in failing light, be pursued and caught. Clermont
had withdrawn to Neuss; Ferdinand held the field of Krefeld. Though
not a rout, this was clear and undisputable victory: 5200 French dead
or wounded against 1800 Hanoverians, with 3000 Frenchmen prisoners.

It contrasted with Hastenbeck and the stumbling incomprehension of both commanders, with Cumberland losing, largely by his
own inert literal-mindedness, against a commander in no better
shape. Clermont by contrast, though not quite a first-rate soldier,

thought on his feet and knew the difference between prudence and defeatism. Ferdinand was established as a man of permanent buzzing initiative doing things for himself, his own reconnaissance officer on that tower. He was, too, the sort of general who leads attacks against weak points personally.

Krefeld was a middle-weight battle. It scored a valuable point without changing the balance of things decisively, but in England it resonated. Pitt, disregarding prejudices, recognised a winning for a winning, a splendid soldier for a splendid soldier. Perhaps most important, the derided Hanoverians, those feeble troops devouring wasted money, were clearly men of mettle. And Pitt did see the picture as it changed. He had acquired troops to preoccupy the French and keep them out of Hanover or any other mischief. Linking Ferdinand to Prince Eugène, British darling in Queen Anne's time, was very much less fanciful than the *Monitor*'s comparisons.

Was Ferdinand lucky? Did he owe rather a lot to Holstein-Gottorp and indeed to Oberg, who had turned up exactly where and when wanted? Well, they too were splendid soldiers, and they were beating the French. The contrast with Sir John Mordaunt and the current rather underpowered Duke of Marlborough was sadly instructive. The shift in Pitt's attitude was conclusive. The man who had talked of not sending money was sending it. The Minister, horrified at Englishmen fighting a continental war, was up for the fight. Parliament was asked for fourteen squadrons of cavalry, and five battalions of foot soldiers to go to Germany, and they went. The 23 June 1758 had made everything very clear.

After the battle, came *news* of the fall-out. This was a victory, victory over a French general and army, three thousand French prisoners, more than five thousand French dead, the French driven back across the Rhine – and the *Monitor* didn't care for it. Success had come three weeks after St Malo which the paper had forlornly puffed. All true believers in all parties are quick to believe that they are about to be double-crossed. So they usually are, so they usually should be. The rational case against continental involvement was that it hadn't worked last time. The irrational reason was that it was a change of policy and as such unpatriotic and unEnglish. Pitt was a very good politician. Good politicians take an extreme position either out of office or bargaining for advantage. Moderately radical men affect to be very left-wing men, then by small steps, often upon points, attenuate.

Back in 1754–7, Pitt had wanted the Patriots and Tories as augmented parliamentary brass. He also wanted the City as faction, crowd-shifter and newspaper proprietor. Success was the objective, winning the war the means to winning success; a strong showing in Germany was producing the good news demonstrating success. 'A foolish consistency is the hobgoblin of little minds.' And the rest of Emerson's epigram would have delighted Pitt. It is, he added, 'adored by little statesman and philosophers and divines. With consistency, a great soul has simply nothing to do.' The greatness of Pitt's self-absorbed and scheming soul is problematic, but consistency is no more useful to a sharp politician.

The Tories, Patriots and City had to be handled very carefully, likewise Leicester House and Lord Bute. In his overtures, Pitt had talked only of cavalry, which Bute (and Beckford) could live with. He now slipped in the full fighting battalions under cover of the Rhine crossing:

> My Dear Lord,　　Friday 23 June 1758
> As nothing can be of greater consequence than that the War should continue, on our part, on the offensive, and that Prince Ferdinand shou'd be enabled to maintain and push his operations this side of the Rhine, I have ventur'd to suggest the sending some squadrons of English cavalry to reinforce the King's army there . . . As we have had more conversations than one on the subjects of *some troops* joining for *an offensive operation, on the Rhine*, I have the satisfaction to understand your Lordship's ideas favour mine on this important question . . .[5]

Bute who, despite family hatreds at Leicester House, was fairly rational, had seemingly given such a nod and his reply accedes, hoping only to have Pitt 'make it clear that a small body shall not lead to a great one'. By contrast, Prince George, the future George III, distrusted Pitt. On 2 July, he is suspicious all round, telling his 'Dearest Friend' quite shrewdly that: 'I had but little hopes that these cautious g[eneral]s chuse to think any part of the F[renc]h coast fit for them to land, when once they had left off attempting something on the coast of Brittany; I suppose they will have orders to go on some other expedition, or else I am certain the K[in]g will make a push to have them

sent to G[erman]y; and I can't help feeling that your wavering friend
would not be against it; if this unhappy measure should be taken we
shall be drawn deeper in a Continent war than ever; and when I mount
the thr[on]e I shall not be able to form a M[inistr]y who can have the
opinion of the people.'⁶ George wasn't quite up to date with developments, but he had Pitt's plans and actual conduct nicely worked
out; and 'Your wavering friend' would have produced a wince. Not
that Pitt was wavering, simply making a 180-degree turn.

Circumstances were making Germany an essential part of the route
plan; and if the Patriots and Leicester House winced, Pitt grew
cheerful. His response when writing to commanders demonstrated
hearty optimism. His letter to Amherst in North America of 10 June
announces rather prematurely 'an Account that on the 5th and 6th
Instant His Majesty's Troops had been so fortunate as to make good
a Landing, with little or no Opposition in Cancalle Bay, about seven
miles from St Malo'. He then states that 'His Majesty's Forces under
the Command of Prince Ferdinand of Brunswick, had by the best
concerted Plan, executed with the greatest ability, happily passed the
Rhine on the 2nd Inst. There is the greatest reason to hope that this
fortunate coincidence of Events will not fail to have the best effects
in Discounting and Distracting the Views of the Enemy and Distressing
the French in such distant Parts.'

Having given Ferdinand's early advance decent credit, Pitt now set
about bucking Amherst up. He was 'persuaded that . . . this agreeable
News will not only give you the greatest Pleasure but may also have
its Use in adding fresh Spirit and Vigour to the Operations of the
Troops under your Command.'⁷ This was honest optimism, legiti-
mately keeping remote commanders cheerful. In the same spirit and
in the teeth of the evidence, the government was now handling reversals with more sophistication (and duplicity). The first one, Rochefort,
had been a failure; it was announced as a failure . . . and Pitt had set
about blaming everybody else. About St Malo he was marketing its
modest start as a triumph. The style was catching. Before the four days
of invasion were up, Captain Smith, ADC to Lord George Sackville,
headed a despatch 'from His Majesty's Dominions in France'. But an
adjutant's windbagging had now been paralleled by something substantial, a strategic victory for the despised Hanoverians. Pitt could now
report the victory at Krefeld with the French nudged back across the

Rhine. One should make the most of an allied victory. The humiliation of midsummer 1757 had been comprehensively extinguished. Pitt,
never given to understatement, promptly linked the two clashes, strategic
and marginal, to proclaim victory all round.

Frederick's biographer, Duffy, reflecting on Ferdinand's long-term
role, describes 'a near genius for independent command that was to
keep the French penned up in Western Germany for the rest of the
war'.[8] He left Frederick free in the east. For England, it was valuable
as the French, undistracted, might perfectly well have cramped the
Prussian west flank, leaving Austria a feasible task and Britain without
Hanover. Ferdinand, by confining so many Frenchmen around the
Weser and the Ems, reinforced the British navy in denying the possibility of a dash at Canada. When first and vital blood was drawn
there, at Louisbourg, the undermanning of French forces would be
doubly stressed. Frederick, primarily fighting the Austrians, valued
any distraction of the concentrated French. Anything on their coast
would be trivial compared with his own fights at Rossbach and
Leuthen and the Anglo-Hanoverian Minden to come, or indeed that
coalition's constant manoeuvring. The coastal excursions were stage
fire, which might, we hoped, be overvalued by the French military
politics!

Pitt now had a scenario which accommodated Frederick a little
without gravely troubling *Monitor*, City or Tories. The *Monitor* had a
busy obsession about French trade. It had hated Rochefort as something done to help the Germans, but it now began to see coastal
activities as separate parts of a potential blockade. They were nothing
of the sort, but the thought of it excused St Malo and its successors
to Beckford.

The current successes in Germany provided the uplift and military
enthusiasm in which the xenophobic press rejoiced generally, but
hoped to see done by British forces under the Union flag. There was
no denying the thrill which any victory on 'our side' imparted. Lord
Egmont might try to play down Krefeld in the July pamphlet attributed to him, *Things As They Are*. That major battle, he insisted, was
merely something promoted and oversold to make the new German
involvement of British troops acceptable. The purpose, he continued,
was 'to make it go down more glib with soldiers and people under
all the smoke and flash of that recent success'.[9]

Back in May, Lord Chesterfield had expressed from the sidelines Pitt's revised thinking – of war in America *and* Germany? Both were conducted against France – why not engage in both? He had said so, however, with a champagne elation which missed the long, murderous grind of the German war. 'The King of Prussia is probably by this time at the gates of Vienna making the Queen of Hungary . . . sign a peace on the ramparts of her capital.'[10]

Early June in St Malo having been declared a great victory, it was possible to argue with less controversy for another bite of the French coast. Chesterfield in his ubiquitous way recorded the half-kept secret of the next venture, the preliminary activity but not the intended objective: 'We have a great exhibition preparing, and which will soon be ready to sail from the Isle of Wight: fifteen thousand good troops, eighty battering cannons, besides mortars and every other thing in abundance fit for either battle or siege. Lord Anson desired and is appointed to command the fleet employed upon this expedition; a proof that it is not a trifling one.'[11]

In fact, the new undertaking had created almost as much contention among the military as the preliminaries to St Malo. The Westminster politics had been easy. Newcastle had never believed in coastal raids, and the miracle to dent his agnosticism had not occurred. But the duke was a well-mannered unbeliever. 'We must play a little with expeditions', he wrote to Anson. Germany was the key theatre, but 'the Enemy should at the same time be entertained with Expeditions, if a diversion could be procured'.[12] Such good humour could be afforded, for Pitt's thinking was changing out of sight. He had told the Commons in December 1757 that he 'would not send a drop of our blood to the Elbe to be lost in that ocean of Gore'.[13] On 19 April 1758 he thought, 'Circumstances might arise for sending troops to Prince Ferdinand providing they could be recalled at any moment and not sent for the purpose of protecting petty states but for the Common Interest and decision of the War as a whole.'[14]

It was cant, but necessary cant. Pitt was driven by his record. The calculated rhetoric against a German campaign had the backing of people honestly sharing such prejudices. But there was a formidable distinction. Many Tories, still faintly haunted by the ghost of Jacobitism, were simple, believing extremists, upon whom Pitt's pulsing music had played. However much distrusted, he was the only considerable politician speaking their language. Other supporters, representing South American and Caribbean trade, defined themselves, in the sense of Richard Cumberland's later play, as 'West Indians'. Their money was in sugar and/or slaves; Pitt was an unreserved champion of colonial interests. Fighting France to prevent her taking preponderant power in North America was thought essential by the Old Corps. But Newcastle and Hardwicke, like Fox and Cumberland, did not owe political prominence to City men. They did not confuse an acknowledged national interest with the main prop of their careers. Pitt, builder of a personal following, precisely did.

However, if the Prussians won battles and Ferdinand led Hanoverians and Hessians to victory against French marshals, the case was altered. It was a winning side which sensible politicians wanted to join. In practical terms, the German theatre had now turned from expensive speculation to weapon against France. In political terms – that is, publicity terms – the German option should no longer fill the principal backers of the Patriot and Great Commoner with quite such disgust. So Pitt approved ventures to German river mouths. Again, while still fancying another coastal excursion, he was now actually ready *to send men to Germany*. Across spring and summer, Pitt is explaining the decision in terms of a non-existent straight line in his thinking.

To Lord Bute, conduit to the next reign and its favour, so anti-Hanover, so long courted, Pitt's approach is studiously downbeat. Before Krefeld, he responds carefully to Bute's sullen negativism: 'A thousand real thanks for my noble friend's salutary caution. Be assured, I will not be drawn further than my own conviction authorised by your concurrence, shall suggest.'[15]

That is nearly as subtle, if not so witty, as de Gaulle's response to the French settlers of Algiers: *'Je vous ai compris.'* Pitt's convictions were limitlessly elastic and he would work hard getting that concurrence by flattering Bute and offering him pre-emptive agreement. But the royal tutor was an easy mark for oil. 'It was my father's foible . . .', wrote his daughter, 'to be too open to flattery, especially of the kind which consists in professions of devoted attachment, and my mother constantly said that Pitt and Temple poured it upon him with a profusion which sometime excited in her doubts of their sincerity – on his part indignantly repelled.'[16] The campaign was long, the tone high. 'May my noble friend's earnest labours in planting the seed of moral virtues never be frustrated and may the reviving country reap the happy fruits of a prince trained to love his people and to wish generously to reform them.'[17] Pitt knew his man. This mimic style led Bute very gracefully; Pitt knew the steps of the dance.

Confidence is flattery at its most effective. The War Minister briefed the Palace dominie with busy details. Relentlessly, says Fraser, 'a flurry of notes couched in extravagant and effusive language, kept [Bute] informed about the progress of the war'.[18] It worked, possibly by volume: 'You have already been most explicit in your declarations that a small body shall not lead to a large one, which would be ruin.'[19] Even Newcastle contemplated inviting Bute to his house in Surrey, but drily remarked that 'the Claremont peaches are not yet ripe enough'.[20]

William Beckford struggled with his conscience. The decision to reinforce Ferdinand, he said, contradicted past promises in the Commons. But he made a distinction fine to the point of metaphysics, between cavalry, to be sent with Patriot approval, and infantry, occasioning them deep unease.[21] After that French retreat, impressive, however temporary, Pitt had a line the Patriots would buy. The Tories of 1721–42, who, with their splits and principles, had made so little progress against Walpole, would now, when allied with Patriot Whigs, accommodate events. The money for Hanoverian army supplies would go sweetly through Parliament in January. What Ferdinand particularly wanted was to fill the space of that temporary French withdrawal with British troops – under him! Even the *Monitor* made encouraging noises. Conflating profit with virtue, they trumpeted a just war against filthy France and for destroying anything French. The raids had disappointed the enemy 'of an invasion upon our dominions; protected our trade and navigation'.[22]

The *Monitor*, West Indian-owned voice of the narrowly focused mid-eighteenth-century City of London, was as mercantilist as xenophobic. There was a finite volume of trade in the world and the point of 'a just war' was to take as much of it as possible from France. The paper's mood shifts under the reader's eyes. On 19 March, there is a trumpet blast of righteous warning to tricky politicians not keeping the island race's interest upmost in steady-beating hearts. Pitt gets a shot across the bows: 'No Minister ever was or will be popular but

from real or apparent virtues. If he wears the mask for his own sake
only, it will be short lived whatever may become of his power, whether
it sink with his reputation or by vile corruption and the art of lying
to the king and people, he may establish it for a while.' On the other
hand, 'if he feels the force of his own eloquence; if his heart glows
with the honest zeal to save and serve his country . . .' The eye of the
Monitor is upon him.

But having got that sweating exordium out of the way, the paper
lightens its style and, with a spattering of underlinings for the slow-
minded, talks practical self-interest: 'It was wished that <u>foreign
connections</u> which had been a <u>millstone</u> on the neck of our <u>old</u>
Ministers might become a <u>garland</u> on the <u>new</u>. It is said that subsidies are subsidies still to whomever they are paid, Peter or Paul; and
that it is all one to us who leads the dance in Germany, if we are still
to pay the piper . . . I think there is a wide difference whether I pay
money to Peter or Paul if Paul be more able and willing to assist me
than Peter, if we can make good bargains, then at a certain expense
such as we can afford secures to ourselves so great and natural an ally
as the King of Prussia.'[23]

And the paper grew exultant at the notion of blockading French
ports. In this glow of quiet national satisfaction, on 19 April the subsidy
for the King of Prussia was renewed, and additional funding for the
armies of Ferdinand of Brunswick passed the Commons painlessly.
By July, Andrew Mitchell in Berlin was being told of the troop plans
for Ferdinand: 'The more sensible [City men] are now come to be of
opinion that it had been a right measure to have sent them last spring.'[24]

The situation, changed for some time now, would be acknowledged to Cabinet council colleagues at a meeting on 20 June. Even
so, coastal outings were a comfortable habit pleasing the Pitt
constituency. Did they not, asked the *Monitor*, 'ruin French commerce
from the four winds and cut off their last efforts for continuing
the war?' They were nugatory and badly planned but impossible to
write off.

So the next, highly secret, coastal episode should have priority,
but then in parallel, with the destination veiled, as 'where they could
be most useful', six thousand men should go to Hanover, the number
being later craftily converted to nine thousand. This was all very
well and promising for the future, but the Rhine/Weser station

immediacy demanded something else. The French might have retreated across in some disorder, but they had only retreated to sort themselves out.

Ferdinand, for all the trumpets, had been under no illusions. Everything pointed to a new French assault aimed at catching him between the lower Rhine and Hesse. Meanwhile on 26 August, Frederick, with 37,000 men, would confront the Russians at Zornberg in one of those murderous victories which feel like defeats: 12,800 of his men and 18,000 Russians would be dead by evening. A few weeks after, he would engage on 12/13 October at Hochkirch, another losing draw. For Prussia, the smallest of the three continental contenders, nine thousand dead *was* a defeat.

Meanwhile, if Ferdinand was to help England, he needed support at the western end of the continental conflict from which Prussia proper was divorced. Facing a new French force under Marshal Contades, he asked for further ships to trouble the enemy at the mouths of the Weser and Elbe, also two regiments to garrison Stade where Cumberland had retreated after Hastenbeck. On 1 August, at Lord Holdernesse's town house, a thin party of ministers approved the ships. Garrison troops were something else. They came on top of troops already directed to Hanover. Ferdinand might be looking out for Contades, Pitt could see the Patriots. They had been brought on side over the Elbe and Weser, but would see in this provision an escalator to continental excess. The request was reasonable, the risk to a garrison less than that to fighting troops, but Patriot politics wouldn't stretch to it.

The King wanted the regiments sent and saw them as *his* regiments; Newcastle saw a reasonable request actually affecting remoter conflicts. To Holdernesse, he used a Pittish, grand horizon expression. 'Ministers in this country where every part of the world affects us, in some way or other, should consider the whole Globe.'[25] 'France', he said, 'will revenge itself on Hanover.'[26] He thought in terms of ha'porths of tar being denied where the prize and loss at issue were too great for nice economy: 'I fear everything from the march of Prince Soubise if it gets into the King's country, the King will insist that Prince Ferdinand return to it with his army to protect his country. Pitt will grumble if not oppose and [have] English troops recalled – all the dangerous allegations about Hanover arms and measures.'[27] Newcastle and Prince

George wanted and feared opposite things, but both started from the sound premise of not trusting Pitt.

Pleasantly at this point, in early August 1758, one of the coastal raids went right. Cherbourg castle was taken. Earlier spotted by Marlborough as undefended to landward, it was reached after a landing at Urville. The local militia next proving the nature of all militias, town and castle were wisely surrendered. Horace Walpole spoke of the first serious British landing in France since the Hundred Years War, and quantities of brass cannon were paraded in London and brought to the Tower. It was small beer compared with the fights to the east but it could be drunk.

Turning to that conflict, George II, with an appointment to make for the new command in Germany, now exercised his prerogative and, over the heads of Marlborough and Lord George Sackville, chose Lieutenant General William Bligh with James Whiteford, Lord Granby and William Kingsley as his staff.

In fact, the effect of county militias against professional troops has always been negligible whatever incidental gallantry might emerge. Pitt's militia was strictly for show but not to the French. There was to be no invasion of England now because France was not ready for one. Before the legitimate celebrations of meeting the actual destruction of French naval invasion forces, London opinion at least and much of its press had already celebrated a non-event.

As the year advanced, thoughts of invasion declined temporarily but overseas news was mixed. Horace Walpole made the notes in another letter (24 August 1758) to Mann in Florence. He began by lamenting what everyone was cheering. 'Our expedition has taken Cherbourg shamefully – I mean the French lost it shamefully, and then stood looking on while we destroyed all their works . . . it proved to be an open place that we might have taken when we were before it a month ago.'[28]

The immediate news from Canada, familiar here, seemed sad. Walpole called it 'a chapter of cypresses', informing Horace Mann that 'The attempt on Crown Point has failed; Lord Howe was killed in a skirmish; and two days afterward by blunders, rashness and bad intelligence, we received a great blow at Ticonderoga.' In which circumstances, he declared his hope that 'Cape Breton may buy us Minorca and a peace'.[29]

Horace was following best eighteenth-century military thinking.

You went on campaigns, lost an island, took a fortress and allowing a small prize for whoever edged the contest, you swapped back the best things taken. This was not Pitt's way. He dreamed of smashing France, of ever-rolling glory and command of trade. To which end, Hawke now, with a bombardment of Le Havre where invasion work was being done on carrier boats, intimated the frightening things he would do. As news filtered through across late 1758 and almost all 1759, Pitt's grand presumption would come true. England, as we usually called ourselves, was on the edge of its Year of Victories.

But there were costs behind even upper-case Victories. Somebody has to raise extraordinary, not readily repeatable, sums. They were all the harder to raise because back in the days of the Pitt–Devonshire administration, Pitt had made an extraordinary appointment. He knew nothing about finance, neither did Devonshire. Appropriately, the Chancellor of the Exchequer,* with brief intervals from April 1754 to March 1761, had been the Hon. Henry Legge who thought he knew something and was wrong.

Legge, inexcusably in a Finance Minister, behaved politically. The term 'Pitt's Sancho Panza' was put about. Worse, he had an inexperienced and untrustworthy Secretary, Samuel Martin, who gravitated to Pitt's friends in the City. Now there were several Cities, the 'monied men' gathered around the likes of Sir Joshua Vanneck and Richard Linwood, and a noisy, political City, undermonied and essentially trade rather than finance, then came the adventurers, planters, rich in sugar and slaves, often, ironically, radicals in English terms, loosely the Beckford element. Ironically, the man whose thinking most pleased this faction was monied all the way through.

Sir John Barnard, 'occasional conformist', i.e. covert dissenter, persecutor of theatres – he had been moving for censorship ahead of Walpole – was also a kind of fiscal democrat. He resented the comfortable ways in which the rich accommodated a ministry as large and ready subscribers within a closed ring of invitees. Barnard was convinced that if the doors were opened, the many little-monied would outperform the few serious-monied. He was also keen to experiment with lottery finance. Beckford's sort of people also

---

* An eighteenth-century Chancellor was a lesser figure than today's fiscal master, subordinate to any First Lord of the Treasury taking his title seriously.

detested a privilege they didn't share with the conspiratorial world of the stockjobbers. Legge was keen to try his hand at this financial equivalent of Pitt's politics, money-market populism, a pitch to the Little Men.

As Lucy Sutherland, specialist authority, puts it, 'The Seven Years War was far the most expensive that had ever been fought and imposed heavy strains on the immature fiscal system of the country.'[30] It consequently preoccupied Newcastle with a financial crisis. After the fall of Pitt–Devonshire, when the seas of expenditure rose higher, Newcastle had endeavoured against his personal grain to wrestle with intolerable numbers. He acknowledged having no talent for an art which Pitt candidly fled. However, after initially asking too much, too diverse advice, he came increasingly to rely upon Samson Gideon.

Gideon, a Christianised Jew, orthodox only in finance, had been a close contact, friend even, of Henry Pelham, a prime minister who did understand finance. He was by far the best man Newcastle could talk to when glorious war raised Treasury debt from £3 million for 1757 to £6.6 million for 1759, beyond all question crisis debt.*[31] The latest subscriptions for loan paper had been conducted as an open auction, admitting brittle participants operating on credit beyond the terms of subscription. Foreign war expenditure spilt the gold reserve to the point where the Bank feared failure to 'pay the bearer on demand'. The management, falling back, refused to discount bills and threatened a 'call on circulation'.

Gideon wrote to the Governor and deputy Governor defining the two functions as 'the very vitals of credit'. The letter was known in the market when fear of the call had been setting things downward 'till after the receipt of my letter; perhaps that might apprize and give them an opportunity to declare that there was no foundation for such report, which indeed has had an extreme [sic] good effect . . .'[32] One part of which was a 3 per cent rise of the funds. Newcastle also took Gideon's advice never to meet a subscription strike with a higher price. He never did, and the calmed pool of monied men duly subscribed for the year. The April 1758 crisis passed. Early in the Year of Victories, this was the preconditional one. The wise orthodoxy of not experimenting in the middle of a war had been learnt. In 1759, Victorious

* By 1761 it would be £12 million.

and Glorious but desperate for cash, the Treasury would successfully follow it. To the life-and-death question of money for a great war, the duke did not know the answer, but he knew a man who did.

The initial problem back in 1757 had been Legge's lottery. A lottery, not in itself an unworkable financial device, was disastrous as Legge ran it. The idea was to seek £1,050,000 at a guinea a ticket, backed up nine weeks later by launching a bundle of annuities to bring in £2.5 million. The ticket buyers would be entitled to an annuity (at a lower rate of interest). It was too complicated for the market courted, and Legge and his adviser, Henriques, made it even more complicated: fixed term or not fixed term? With transferability? What grades of reward? But those not winning a prize would have subscribed to government debt for nothing.

The advantages to the government were apparent, those to the public not. As John Calcraft observed, 'Legge's silly lottery fills . . . so slowly that there are not 40,000 tickets yet subscribed for, though all placemen have been harassed into the subscription.'[33] Overall Legge's scheme raised about 12 per cent of the requirement. Newcastle was told at the start, 'You may depend on it that the money will not be raised, and the season advances.'[34] And the substantial men, Sir Joshua Vanneck and John Gore MP, advised by Gideon, came up with a boring and workable orthodoxy, a closed subscription to raise £3 million at 3 per cent.

The serious rich were exactly that. They would subscribe to something they understood for a return they wanted. Legge had done populism, had called up the People in an offer which big finance *and* the People humiliatingly rejected.[35] Gideon stirred himself for the duke. He had oracular authority in the City. His nod was negotiable exchange. He also had social ambitions: to get out of the ghetto as, in 1753, Henry Pelham had tried to help London Jews to do. They lived apart under restriction and Pelham's bill had been withdrawn following riots. Being a Christian, Gideon could move physically out; as an old man, he wanted full English entitlement for his descendants. Accordingly he added urgency to the buying advice given to those able to buy.

A letter discovered in the Chatsworth Papers illustrates his cool method of giving approving government paper as good business. It has 'Mr G–' (Gideon) alluding to 'Mr D– (the Duke of Devonshire) advising sundry people to buy as bidden. One example concerns the banker, Francis Gosling: 'Mr G– has desired Alderman Gossling [*sic*] to make his payment upon £100,000 the first day, upon any terms that Mr D– shall fix upon; and does not confine his contributions to the terms of the proposal.'[36]

Samson Gideon would achieve with this the social breakthrough he had rather touchingly yearned for. He could not be raised personally on the ziggurat of the British class system. But his son, Sampson with a 'p', thirteen and at Eton, was shortly after raised to the baronetage as Sir Sampson. However absurd, it was a marker, the beginning of something, a post-dated decent return on good sense.

15

Sturdy Yeomen and Slave Traders: the Militia and Goree

Jeffrey Amherst was the dull, slightly aggrieved one. He was the senior commander overall in Canada. But Quebec, the Castle Despond of North American campaigning, which demanded panache and an original mind, was deputed, in a brilliant move, to the erratic, unpopular and creative James Wolfe of whom more, much more. Wolfe would win 250 years of full-colour national fame, soldiering as theatre with climax and perfect, fatal curtain. Amherst only conquered Canada, for which he is remembered in the names of four small towns in New England and a women's college of some distinction.

However, Ticonderoga came first and mattered because forces from the still narrow southern territory of British America could only enter French Canada through passes here or at Crown Point. Gaining it would open the door to what the French inexplicably called British aggression. Ticonderoga had, as related, battled Abercromby in July/August 1758, Montcalm having arrived first with the main French forces to dig entrenchments before the citadel. Abercromby, already delayed by his dawdling local levies, had responded in a nervous rush without waiting for his artillery. The result, 1600 losses of regulars, had made conquering Canada look harder than it was.

Abercromby had fought the wrong battle too soon. James Wolfe, notoriously uncharitable, had talked of a lost golden opportunity but, as Middleton remarks, in wanting to fight the entire French army he was alone. The famous coordination of Pitt's remote strategic planning simply did not happen. Amherst a year later had certain advantages. Montcalm wasn't there, and his successor, with a much reduced force, thought a bloody siege not worth the candle, the news reaching England in the second week of September

Even so, the journey, if laborious, was thorough. Amherst lacked money to hire the locals he despised. 'The Americans, if left to them-selves, would eat fryed Pork and lay in their tents all day long.' Weather slowed down his transport. Beyond which, he had expected Wolfe's presence on the St Lawrence to effect an evacuation of the French and hung back till it did. He made elaborate precautions, like raft-building, for the siege which never happened. So, when Wolfe, bemused by the complex defence of Quebec, would need him, Amherst was behind schedule and beyond communication. Nevertheless, following his own belt-and-braces procedure, Amherst picked up Crown Point, abandoned by the French on 1 August, taking command of the other roadblock to successful British occupation. In 1760, Amherst would effect the full conquest of Canada. However, trudging in his reliable way toward Montreal a year *after* the Year of Victories, he was doomed to immediate and historical second billing in modest type. Wolfe, twelve years younger and usefully dead, would command front of stage as an immortal.

The year 1758 had been fretful, full of bad or no news, the charade of a militia, the running futility of coastal raids and long waiting for glory and possession in remote, coveted Canada. In the days of toiling communications, great things go on in one place while people fret about what might be going on in another. Lacking hard news, they are a ready market for speculation – not all of it wrong; and for an island, invasion rates high as risk and possibility. Sometimes the concern is paranoid, sometimes, witness Napoleon who never came, the best accounts are fictional, like Hardy's *The Trumpet Major*, showing the Squire's nephew, Festus Derriman, commanding the unhandy men of the county militia and running for cover after reports that Boney had been seen at Budmouth (Weymouth). Sometimes, as with Philip II and Hitler, the concern lacks a funny side.

Even before Minorca fell, the idea of doing something across the Channel had appealed to the French First Minister and Commander in-Chief. Aimed at offsetting England's alliance with Prussia, it assumed difficulty in taking Hanover as peace treaty ransom, and sought an improved repeat of 1745 for a sensational stand-off. The plan might speak of marching on London, but Glasgow and Edinburgh in French hands would rate above Hanover. The thinking imagined diversion, not conquest, a notion of how one got the intolerable British navy briefly out of the way.

Fear that France might again be sending flat-bottomed boats bringing popery, wooden shoes and grenadiers to conquer the glorious nation in her redoubt gave a frisson to people who liked that sort of thing. Surprisingly, Pitt, normally thriving amid fearful alert, reacted at first with near indifference. The Militia Bill had been his thing, dragged through a cool Commons and past cooler colleagues. The British navy had made French reinforcements to Canada very nigh impossible. If it could be congregated on defensive alert in the Channel and up the east coast, men and matériel might be rushed across the Atlantic. Alternatively, a foothold in Scotland? Then there had been that stroll to midland Derby eleven years before. Accordingly, poor Charles Edward, thirty-seven, no longer beau, the long fraying of his life begun, but someone who had fought with credit at Dettingen, as at Prestonpans, was sought out wherever in Italy the French had last exiled him. He was made up to and generally cajoled. Charles Edward believed nothing, but played along with the '59 Rising which never was as an alternative form of boredom.

But a proper cause for invasion was Britain's success abroad. North American victories and want of progress in Germany after Hastenbeck had done two things. They had taken soldiers and sailors away from this country and had pushed frustrated French thinking in the directions, not wholly rational, which follow successive defeats. French naval thinking, commonly platonic, was for a fleet in the Atlantic and another in the western Mediterranean, neither adequate, which might come together at the north-west corner of France to create a time corridor when getting men to Dorset or Lanarkshire might be accomplished.

France was the soldiering country, England the naval one. It was natural to seek work in one's natural element. The chances might be remote, but the English had some occasion to be careful. Our not quite acknowledged imperial mission had taken ships a long way off – fifty-nine out of the round hundred available. French commitment in remote areas was significantly less. Accordingly, she could, in our common waters, put up forty-three ships to our forty-one. In fact, rather a lot had been done – by Ligonier and others with the direct encouragement of the duke as First Minister. A commitment had been made in 1756 to create ten new regiments, raise the men to make up eleven regiments of light dragoons and the recreation under Admiralty control of a force of Marines.[1]

One of these creations then was the charmingly named Royal American which would serve with effect at Quebec. Anxiety about invasion had played its part in the underresponse to Minorca and its dangers. Anson in particular had been so seized with an invasion threat that, in the words of one Pitt biographer, Stanley Ayling, he 'thought it proper to take a calculated risk there, maintaining unquestionable supremacy in the Channel where the maximum danger lay'.[2] It was a risk which ought, at his court martial, to have saved Admiral Byng from serving as terminal encouragement. And Henry Fox had argued at that time for sending full weight of ships and had been outvoted. Newcastle would defend the decision later after Minorca, with English priority: 'What was said when this question was before us was that the *heart* must be secured in the first place.'

When, towards the end of 1758, the notion of invasion rose again, Kraken-like, from the sea which should be crossed, a plan existed to be activated. Belleisle, Minister of War, wanted all the French ships which could be found concentrated at Brest. They were, under Admiral Conflans, to escort 20,000 soldiers under the Duc d'Aiguillon for Glasgow then the Western Highlands, leaving enough men to take Edinburgh. A small diversionary force under François Thurot, a privateer in rather British style, would make for Ireland and all its possibilities. The largest body, 26,000 troops, would be drawn from those currently in Flanders and Brittany. Conflans, returning from his successful delivery round, would bring the flat-bottomed barges now building along the north-western French coastline out for the short-haul southern landing on the northern shore of the Thames estuary, something Newcastle's intelligence well knew.

All this would come to the grievous naval conclusion of Quiberon Bay with which this narrative began. What matters here is the British reaction – to what they knew and what they feared. A great deal had been done – over the long and short terms – by Sandwich and the dominant influence since 1746, Anson,* and also by John Clevland, long-standing Admiralty Secretary. One way to get ships home was to recall

---

* Whom Pitt had described as 'unfit to command a cockboat on the Thames', quoted Ayling, *The Elder Pitt*, p. 192.

them. Our mere forty-one ships of the line at home would all, by late May, reckoned Anson, be battleworthy. These did not include (like the French total of forty-three) ships in the Mediterranean station. Ten new ones had been built, a number of French vessels had been taken and put to service, witness the *Magnanime*. Nine new vessels had been ordered at the end of 1756, among them the readily manoeuvred two-deck 74-gunner built to stay at sea in the worst weather. By the middle of 1757 there were six of these, with ten more being constructed.

Bitten at Minorca, Anson in 1759 was shy of underproviding anything. Still less would he let instructions be vague. Boscawen, the most uncompromising naval officer in sight, was given plain directions. He was not to let the French Mediterranean squadron get into the Atlantic, but if they did, he was to chase them. As to the detail, Boscawen was experienced and capable enough to decide that for himself.

While this was afoot, Ligonier, facing wide dispersals of serving soldiers, set about pulling together an army specifically for national defence. Given disposals to Germany, we had 20,000 regulars in the country. Numbers for immediate defence of likely French landing points were well below what he wanted. Immediately, there were 10,000 men with a further 5000 in Scotland where they might be urgently needed, plus 4000 engaged on shipboard.

There were in fact good reasons why the alarm which Newcastle had communicated from the start should be taken up. One of them was the progress of the war in Germany. Ferdinand had been thrown on to the defensive. Defeated at Bergen, north-west of Frankfurt, on 13 April 1759, he had been forced into a retreat north towards Alsfeld. Austrian troops, sighted at Vacha, threatened his communications.[3] He would be lucky that Saint-Germain, placed to march east against him, did not. As an expert observes, that 'might well have turned a tactical reverse into a very serious defeat indeed'.[4]

He would get very little help from a preoccupied Frederick apart from the customary advice and scolding. Anyway, at Kolín on 18 June, Frederick's own defeat took place by the careful Austrian follower of Fabian tactics, Field Marshal Daun. The King two days later evacuated his great prize of Prague, retreating into serious thinking in the Bishop's Palace of Leitmeritz,[5] followed not long after by a general Prussian retreat out of Bohemia.

So fully were German operations now accepted by Pitt that these

reverses shifted him out of his earlier cavalier attitude to invasion. A
France whose ally, Austria, had shattered the triumphant condition of
one enemy might well have new initiatives of its own, especially when
details of Belleisle's thinking were coming through. British ministers
fidgeted. A meeting followed, on 8 May, at Lord Holdernesse's house
in Arlington Street. The Duke of Bedford's correspondence positively
jumps with intense anxieties and baroque syntax about the security
of Ireland. He attended Arlington Street, stressing 'the state I laid
before them of his majesty's government in Ireland, . . . the smallness
of the force I must (on account of the garrisons, leave in the great
towns for the security of the Protestants), [and] put myself at the
head of, should the enemy land in any of the south-west parts of
Ireland . . . that too great precaution could not be had to prevent an
attempt of this sort; and should it [the invasion] be attempted with
success, to preserve at least Leinster and Ulster from the calamity of
becoming the seat of war.'[6]

It was a fair point. Creating panic or enthusiasm by reports that
'the French are on the sea' had a future. But there wasn't actually
anything that could be done. Brutally, the available British army wasn't
big enough. All efforts were directed at Torbay, the best point from
which to monitor and/or engage the French. Bedford had to content
himself with stating that 'Upon any certain notice of the enemy's
intention to land any where in Ireland, I hold myself in readiness to
depart at an hour's notice, and to put myself at the head of the few
troops we have . . .'[7] Such fervour from the pacific head of the Russells
is significant, though the Cabinet's feeling that the duke should not
move until it was absolutely necessary suggests that his histrionic fretting was not yet contagious.

Ten days later they agreed that a squadron should cruise off the
French coast near Brest to watch what Anson identified as the 'enemy's
force in Brest'. Pitt, presumably given some idea of Belleisle's three-
prong plan, proposed transports accompanying this force with a view
to getting the men we didn't currently have to the Scottish and Irish
destinations of a French fleet not yet assembled.

Anxiety about invasion was useful to Pitt. It was also gratifying to
have a possible function, however brittle, for his militia, conceived as
politics and therapy. At the end of May, Pitt brought a royal message
to the Commons acknowledging an invasion threat. Then, across late

June, he began calling out the militias, county by county. Horace Walpole was wryly impressed. 'All the country squires are in regimentals . . .' though 'How knights of the shire who have never shot anything but woodcocks, like this warfare, I don't know; but the towns through which they pass adore them in their scarlet faced with black, buff waistcoats, and gold buttons.' For Pitt, affairs were paradoxical. He had initially been scornful of invasion, but was coming round to genuine concern.

The militia, though, was a political object from the early days of office and marching well with the political Englishry, the Gallant Yeoman thing which, like Leicester House – German Princess and Scottish Confidante – he delighted to stress. It had, too, been something to please Tory country gentlemen in the House. A show of it all pleased them now, a headline, something seen to be done. Edward Gibbon had a happy time leading a troop of the Hampshire Militia. Even so, everyone was clear that invasion could be met only by the ships of Clevland, Bedford and Montague and by sailors far less fetchingly dressed.

Pitt's friends in the press, harmonious with the Secretary, but some way behind the beat, had scorned invasion threats across late May and June. The *Monitor* shrugged them off but grew rapturous about the militia, as did the *London Evening Post*.[8] This contradiction of the feelings at Holdernesse's was underlined by Beckford, who spoke of the militia having made it possible to 'laugh at invasion'.[9]

'That never-to-be-tested scratch force was perfect public relations.' Doing 'nothing in particular and doing it very well', it achieved easy insubstantial wonders for Pitt's reputation. Pitt's ostentatiously defiant manner and high-profile activity raised general confidence for no clear reason.

Another cheering event would follow on 31 December. Fort Louis on the Senegal river was captured. The expedition had a history going back to the Pitt–Devonshire Ministry. Pitt had been approached by Cumming, a Quaker, not that one would have noticed. On the coast of Senegal and the island of Goree he had traded in slaves, gum, gold dust and ivory against the settled and resentful French interest. Having been rebuffed by the ungrateful French, he had lobbied in 1756–7 for a military attack upon them, a small-scale trade war to deprive them of a major commodity and make Englishmen, including Mr Cumming, rich.

It was Pitt's sort of thing, daring and aggrandising: the outline of a plan of attack involving Cumming's contacts with a local chief to whom a letter, to be signed by King George, proposed a naval incursion. On 9 February 1757, while still in office with Devonshire, Pitt had written to the slaver a letter promising 'my best assistance in obtaining an exclusive charter in your favour for a limited term of years . . .' So the idea itself had been well received and adopted, not so a warning about the terrain, important to troop safety. For when another merchant, Samuel Touchett, made four attempts to warn Pitt about the local rainy season and consequent ground and health conditions for troops, he never gained a hearing. The scheme, lapsing with Pitt's dismissal in April 1757, was revived in February 1759. Success would 'consolidate British control of the African slave trade'.[10]

Small excursions were typical of a country with an undermanned army and an agile, adaptive navy. They also fitted sweetly with Patriot and slave-trader thinking, something appealing to mercantilist sentiment and tradition. For the British had been in Goree in the mid-seventeenth century, when the Company of Royal Adventurers into Africa had traded on a stretch of the west coast in slaves, elephants' teeth, hides, redwood (for dyes) and malagueta pepper. But the Second Dutch War and Admiral De Ruyter had, as one historian of slavery, Nigel Tattersfield, puts it, 'destroyed their main basis of operations at Goree Island on the Gambia'.[11]

Taking Fort Louis, which yielded an immediate quarter of a million, captivated Pitt, making him very urgent for more. Anson concurred. This entire territory was valuable to the French; they would do their best to get it back. On the day of the news, he ordered a naval flotilla, intended for Jamaica, to be diverted to the Slave Coast and specifically Goree. A squadron and a battalion were to be sent under Captain Augustus Keppel. Ordering was one thing, making the journey another.

Keppel explained from Cork in September the difficulties of going by Pitt's imperious timetable and was told to take a chance on the risk. Leaving in November, he lost two ships in a storm, but on 31 December 1758, with his Marine commander, Colonel Richard Worge, he captured the forts on Goree. The completed and reinforced conquest of both territories deprived the French of Senegal of up to eight thousand tons of gum for their silk and linen trade. Mastery here would also bring in the proceeds of 1200 slaves to be sold to our other territories in the West Indies.

Capturing the French islands in the West Indies was a more urgent concern. And urged on by Beckford, scenting a British near-monopoly, Pitt had launched an expedition to take Martinique from the French. But British plans to blow up the citadel were interrupted, to general surprise and French satisfaction, when a local militia of a few hundred men drove them off.[12] But Pitt had thoughfully offered an option, attacking Guadeloupe.

Actually, the force under Thomas Hopson, another Ligonier nomination, had originally been directed to the richer island. Hopson tried something easier, a siege at Guadeloupe which turned sticky and in the middle of which, in February, he incontinently died with three thousand men, half their force. His successor, Barrington, tried going round the island until, on 1 May, he found himself taking the French surrender.

The impressive inadequacy of some French commanders makes a showing here. Barrington's astonishing despatch relates that he had just signed the surrender agreement when he was told, 'Monsieur Beauharnois, the General of these islands had landed . . .; with a reinforcement [2600-strong] from Martinco . . . as soon as he heard the capitulation was signed, he re-embarked again.'[13] Victories are, of course, glorious and in this case had been ingeniously obtained, but it was delightful to be opposed by a combination of bureaucracy and blue funk. In places like Arlington Street, minds were upon the English Channel, when, six weeks later, a pleasant piece of real news was put before them. On 14 June, Newcastle would tell Devonshire that Guadeloupe had fallen.[14]

16

Hunt the Garter:
Minden and Lord Temple

The Death of Wolfe, the Soviet-style celebration of James Wolfe by an American painter, Benjamin West, captures the stage-heroic image of a great soldier, not only conquering but creditably dead. Wolfe deserves better. Despite that bloodthirsty remark about a thousand deaths being worth it, Wolfe was vividly human. In Dublin he had an affair with a widow described as 'the Irish Venus'. When depressed, and he was often whelmed in private despair, he got very drunk. Possibly to please anxious parents, Wolfe, just before departing to death *and* glory, had become engaged. The choice reflected his tactical opportunism – Catherine Lowther, sister of James Lowther, future 1st Earl of Lonsdale, a man wholly barbarous but superabundantly rich. Then, not long before the golden climax of his life, Wolfe suffered a major breakdown.

Wolfe was aggressively but creatively ambitious, bubbling ideas; and he attracted appreciative patrons like Cumberland, Richmond and Ligonier. But despite the romantic legend of his preferring to have written Gray's *Elegy** to conquering Quebec, James Wolfe was not Prince Hamlet; he was a very observant technician. His new ideas reflected a technical grasp to fascinate military historians. His biggest notion, borrowed after alert observation of Prussian practice, sounds modest but was central to infantry's impact. The hip-level hold on a rifle with bayonet turned a defensive weapon offensive, and in one expert view would make a key difference to battlefield success in such places as Waterloo.[1] Wolfe's other technical innovation parallels Hawke's insistence upon restraining a ship's guns outside pistol shot. Wolfe wanted fire held for maximum accuracy, a simple proposition not then much practised.

---

* Published in 1759, one of that year's gentler victories.

Wolfe's insistence upon the rightness of his thinking irritated his first (and generous) patron. Cumberland, controlling men performing inadequately in one sort of drill, the shoulder-held rifle-bayonet, had hopes that at least they would do it together. Coming up with a better drill confused things. Insisting on its superiority looked like insubordination, and this young officer was the perfect model of the difficult junior. No one valuing the good team player would have hired Wolfe. He was a first-rate man thinking and talking critically among unexceptional superiors. Yet somehow the talent was discerned and tolerated.

Wolfe was present at Culloden, to which various legends of chivalry, flimsy but not necessarily untrue, would attach themselves. One was that he had refused Cumberland's order to shoot a wounded Jacobite officer; all we know for certain is that the son of the man named, Charles Fraser of Inverallochie, later served under him. Not disputed, though, was jumping the gun on his superior, Amherst, during the Louisbourg expedition by sailing clean out of the base, Halifax, without waiting, after explaining where they should land, advice Amherst ignored.

Wolfe had earlier been lucky in the good opinion of Ligonier, something achieved in the shambles of Rochefort. Wolfe tried out his theories on Sir John Mordaunt's staff, and, despite the expedition's muddle, he found keen takers while the drill and early firing showed strongly. Sir John Ligonier was good at spotting talent and within a week of succeeding Cumberland as Commander-in-Chief, on 21 October 1757, he raised Wolfe, at thirty, to brevet colonel and command of the 2nd battalion of the 20th Foot. When, in April 1758, this body became a regiment, the 67th Foot, Wolfe became full colonel. Having, after anxious fretting, got thus far, Wolfe progressed quickly. Making a decent personal reputation at Rochefort, he was selected for Louisbourg, upon which undertaking the sun would shine. There, as detailed earlier, initiatives like bombarding from the lighthouse point underlined the flair and originality. After landing at Freshwater Cove came a successful bayonet charge in the improved Wolfe style. At Louisbourg, whether by Amherst's wise discretion or because he simply took it, Wolfe enjoyed something close to an independent command.

Success there, concluding with French surrender on 27 July, might have brought Amherst, the steady, competent victor, the command for Quebec. However, the failure of Abercromby at Ticonderoga,

combined with Louisbourg six weeks after midsummer, gave everyone
pause in what was still a war of seasons. Ministers awaited fuller information about Ticonderoga, Quebec and French dispositions. There
would, though, be rather more humility in Westminster directives.
The outline was broad: a siege or assault on Quebec from Louisbourg,
approach Montreal from the south, take Niagara, attack Fort
Duquesne. At Louisbourg, the two major commands would go their
separate ways, trusted to find the destinations for themselves.

Wolfe had originally wanted what most professional soldiers wanted,
a place in the German wars. John Mostyn's instincts that this was the
real military thing were Wolfe's, but Ligonier declined to gratify them.
Next best would be an independent command for Quebec. Having
won a name at Rochefort and a bar to it at Louisbourg, he was well
placed to lobby. Ligonier, possibly having ideas of his own about a
posting, took him, 22 November 1758, to Pitt. Wolfe played the innocent. He knew nothing about a plan for Quebec (actually called 'River
Command') but, with crafted naivety, spoke of readiness 'to serve in
America and particularly in the river St Lawrence if any operations
are to be carried on there'.[2] The son of a professional soldier, Wolfe
had to rise by nicely balanced merit and brass neck. Here, he combined
extremely good information about the expedition with a light application of innocence.

It worked. By Christmas, he was circulating friends and colleagues
with offers under his independent command, Quebec Independence
would, though, be modified by politics. A valued colleague, with
serious North American experience, Ralph Burton, was substituted
by Pitt and Ligonier for the grandson of Walpole's old ally, Townshend.
George Townshend lacked relevant experience but, brother of a
marquess, he had lines to both Newcastle and Pitt. Wolfe, least courtly
man in the service, sent him a letter of biting non-welcome.

He was no more responsive to the officer commanding the squadron
for vital employment exploring the St Lawrence. He had a poor opinion
of Philip Durrell. It was possibly mistaken, for Durrell had serious
experience of North America. But Wolfe at once complained (unsuccessfully) to the very top that Durrell was not good enough. This
officer, he told Pitt, he knew to be 'vastly unequal to the weight of
business: and it is of the first importance to the country that it does
not fall into his hands'. He was, as they say today, judgemental.[3]

Such griping apart, preparations proceeded efficiently. Wolfe would also be fortunate in the commander of the accompanying naval force, Charles Saunders, one of the best of a fine selection of admirals and Anson's man. For despite some interference, the idea of Pitt fostered by admirers, one doing him too little credit, is of a dervish-like Minister exacting speed and efficiency where they did not exist. That is also injustice to Anson's Admiralty and extensive orthodox consultation.

When Saunders and Pitt agreed the need for more supporting frigates, Pitt asked Clevland 'what difficulties there may be in the way of this proposal?' It was Admiralty business and Pitt had the sense to know it was. The Admiralty through Clevland had, on New Year's Day 1759, asked the Port Admiral at Portsmouth, Holburne, victim of the 1757 weather, for fitted-up ships 'with all the expedition that is possible'.[4] By the end of January, the squadron was essentially ready. Meanwhile, Wolfe had found time for a swift trip to Bath, romance and that engagement to Catherine Lowther who (as Duchess of Bolton) would outlive him by forty years.

The expedition, leaving Spithead on 14 February 1759 and enjoying tolerable weather, reached Halifax, Nova Scotia, on 30 April, then Louisbourg in mid-May. The immediate problem concerned numbers. No army delights in starting as the underdog and Wolfe, anticipating 12,000 men, would pleasantly find that an expedition to the French sugar island of Martinique had siphoned off three thousand, a move risking another dismal reversal. As the original 12,000 were already stationed in North America waiting for ships, the ministry had probably counted them as a single force, before disregarding its own double use when informing Wolfe.

There now began a round of characteristically active staff work on particulars for the Quebec assault. Advice for the field had been taken back in London from a local topographical specialist, the engineer Major Patrick MacKellar. From his prisoner of war's discreet survey of 1756–7, the command learnt that frontal attack up vertical cliffs into narrow, easily defended streets would be a mistake. They also hoped, on his tentative assessment, that the back fortifications were incomplete, making rear attack attractive.

Having struck base on Orleans Island, four miles downstream from Quebec, Wolfe contemplated navigating the rocks of the St Lawrence and seeking, upriver, a landing point for climbing to the high ground

dominating Quebec from the west. He was also learning that preliminary theories require secondary testing. He planned to use the lesser
river, the St Charles, passing before the Quebec promontory, likely
stretch for a smart action with the defenders. He had talked of stealing
'a detachment up the River St Lawrence . . . three, four, five miles or
more above the town'. This would put them on the Beauport Shore
on the left/north bank. Montcalm, gallant image of a hero, more
importantly sound tactician, thought he might, and had covered the
Beauport Shore with soldiers and fortifications. Wolfe also discovered,
just below the water and out of immediate sight, that the river
narrowed by a rock shelf. Big ships carrying heavy gunnery could not
cover a landing. Quebec was a natural fortress defended by an alert
commander: end of first theory.

Wolfe was an outstanding talent dancing on the edge of failure
through excessive self-reliance and distrust of colleagues. He made a
plan, then reconsidered it alone, before unnerving everyone with last-
minute amendment. Monckton would take his men to the North
Shore. Land batteries at Pont Lévis would fire at Quebec. The resented
Townshend, trying, like the despised Durrell, to help, was on 9 July
put down east of the Beauport Shore to be joined by men from
Murray's brigade. They were to create a jangling diversion separating
Montcalm's defenders from Wolfe's grenadiers assaulting St Michel.
If the defenders turned to fight Monckton and Townshend, they would
open the way for his own troops. If not, then the others should have
a clear run. It was a good example of how having three thousand men
bespoke for the French Antilles stretched resources for a multiple operation.

Wolfe then changed his mind, almost certainly rightly, also unnerv-
ingly. The St Michel assault would be the only thing. Monckton's men
would go straight in behind him while the other brigades would, hopefully, come in by boat, as hopefully catching the tide. This was Plan
B, and at brisk, immediate notice, it was cancelled. Montcalm, already
holding an intercepted letter from Amherst about strategic objects,
had made his own judgement of tactics. No kind of fool, he asked
himself what he might do commanding an English force breaking
into French property.

Guessing an assault on St Michel, he set up gun batteries at St
Michel. Wolfe, guessing in turn, judged that, where there were guns,

there would be troops taken from somewhere else. He and Montcalm were engaged on a perpetual telepathic dance, so where might they be shifting from? Reconnaissance up the Montmorency river beyond the Beauport defences found no point where troops could cross. Plan C proving impracticable, Wolfe doubled the commitment. The next attack (upstream from Montmorency village) would no longer be a foray, but full-dress assault. This meant involving all hands who now waited for the order to advance at *low* tide, when it came. This was Plan D; repulsed on 31 July by steady defence, it failed.

The effect on Wolfe was brutally personal. He was a taut string and close to snapping. The nervous breakdown* which followed took him out of all experiment, apart from destroying French settlements and sending a forlorn plea to Amherst; and on 19 August he retreated to his bed. Wolfe embodied all the qualities: original, vital, a spring of ideas and ardent in purpose. But, unlike Pitt in Cabinet, he commonly clutched every option to himself, not trusting, not expounding. If the century's communications had reached the electric telegraph, Arlington Street would have known about the unstable, manic commander who had run four plans of attack, ditched three, doubled his commitment on the fourth and found the enemy waiting. He would have been relieved of his post and recalled. As for history, it would, in Auden's phrase, have said 'Alas'.

However, on 28 August, he crawled out of bed, half shrugged off his condition, and at least consulted his brigadiers over new attacks on the secure Beauport lines. Civilly, the brigadiers shook their heads, proposing a more cautious and roundabout plan of their own, a landing twenty miles away at Pointe-aux-Trembles. Wolfe assented and, astonishingly, let detailed planning fall to George Townshend. He would be saved from a destiny on the sidelines by the weather which, on 8 September, justified postponement of Townshend's version, Plan E. Feeling part recovered, Wolfe went on the river and made history.

On that trip, he spotted the Anse-au-Foulon, a handy cove, from which a narrow, rough path ran from the bottom to the top. This placed them beyond and above Quebec, what would be known as the Heights of Abraham. The brigadiers having seen it too, the Anse and its path became the final plan. The boats which on 12–13 September

---

* Middleton argues that Wolfe had contracted fever.

went upriver would find themselves beyond the Anse. But Wolfe trusted in their skill and courage for infantrymen to make a cliff-face climb and, after the French-speaking Captain McDonald had bluffed a sentry, to hold the road. The climb done, all ten battalions of British troops stood in full battle line. Montcalm, anticipating so much, had not reckoned on the semi-vertical approach. French troops arrived at the end of a sprinting rush.

Taking nothing from Wolfe's achievement in finding and at great pains passing the only chink in an impregnable defence, the French forces were not equivalent to those fighting in Germany. Militia men and Indians were fighting regulars.[5] What chiefly mattered was that the British had the initiative and made the most of it. As Richard Holmes says, 'Montcalm's men came on in three columns, and were met by an opening volley at a mere 40 yards, one of the most destructive in military history which stopped them in their tracks. The British fired one more volley and charged . . .'[6]

The personal narrative would be dismally simple. Wolfe wanted a place from which to see. He had scrambled up a knoll, from which he was seen, and a French musketeer shot him. He did not die at once and was carried to the rear with the knowledge that the battle would be won and Quebec would fall. Emily Dickinson's perfect words about a battle lost apply here to a battle won and its victor:

> On whose forbidden ear
> The distant strains of triumph
> Break, agonised and clear.

As it was, he had filed anguished copy to London. Holdernesse had been told, 'My constitution is entirely ruined without the consolations of having done any considerable service to the state; or without any prospect of it.'[7]

The Quebec victory was many things: notably recovery of a prize surrendered in 1746 after the last war with France. It implied further steps which matter-of-fact, non-star-material Amherst would steadily achieve. Above all, it was perfect theatre: the young and gallant captain dying as his opponent died – Montcalm would not survive the Heights of Abraham either. It was theatre with the Green Room sulks and backbiting left discreetly out. Wolfe had secured immortality by dying.

Field Marshal Montgomery would live thirty and more years after El Alamein, years of snappish memoirs, his own and colleagues', his insensible vanity and staccato style delighting unsympathetic caricature. Wolfe enjoyed all the consolations of death.

However, for the government all this was mid-September news with a sailing ship's news expected in late November. Wolfe's last message was dated Halifax, 6 June! They were worried about money, the costs of another year's war, recent evasion of the British Channel watch by François Thurot, privateer. He would menace the Irish coast, where the fretting Lord-Lieutenant, Bedford, hoped 'the nobility and gentry of this kingdom . . . might be brought to prevail on their tenants and dependants to enter the army and thereby bring into it a better class and rank of people than would otherwise enlist'.[8]

They were lucky not to have more to worry about in Canada. British forces had during postal silence suffered defeat at French hands there, with Wolfe's victory close to being cancelled. For there had been a second battle on the Heights of Abraham, a French victory. With Wolfe dead and the citadel taken, most of the command, Admiral Saunders and Brigadiers Monckton and Townshend, had returned home. Brigadier James Murray commanded an exhausted, underprovisioned, freezing cold, scurvy-bitten garrison. French despair not being universal, Lévis, commanding at Montreal, in April 1760 took serious numbers downriver. Murray, who might have done better in a siege, marched valiantly out and was promptly defeated.

Murray now got his siege, without his guns or a third of the 60/70 per cent of men *initially* fit for battle. What happened next is perfect boys' story, a damn close-run thing to end damn close-run things; it would make a decent film. A single sloop was despatched down the St Lawrence, still partly iced, carrying to Halifax and the Governor, Charles Lawrence, sealed despatches actually addressed to Amherst, busy elsewhere. Lawrence, assuming urgency, opened them. Fortunately Anson's naval wisdom had earlier convinced Pitt that leaving frigates at Halifax under Admiral Colville was a good idea, such a good idea that in March they had sent more. And it was one of these, the *Lowestoffe*, which now led the charge up the St Lawrence.

The importance of local decision-making and contingency provision is shown by the dates. Murray had written in April that he could not hold out beyond 11 May. Pitt received that despatch on 17 June.

But the *Lowestoffe*, London's March afterthought, arrived below Quebec just ahead of the Halifax frigates on 9 May! They proceeded, almost routinely, to destroy the French ships, also a provisioning flotilla unhappily just arrived. Lévis's brilliant episode was terminated though not without giving the British government, two months' mail away, a summer's anxiety at a prize dropped and feared lost. Pitt wrote to his wife giving thanks 'to Almighty God'.

Meanwhile, local, indeed immediate, concerns began to assert themselves. Invasion crept into ministerial minds as a serious prospect. Witness the concern about Thurot. Then again, by the high summer of 1759, the campaign in western Germany had taken a strong turn in favour of the French. After a signal victory at Bergen, the town of Minden, lost to the Allies shortly before Krefeld, was noticed by the French general, J.C. Fischer, as too lightly garrisoned. So, on 9–10 July, it was attacked and won back by Broglie, pleasantly surprising his superior, the Marquis de Contades.

Prince Ferdinand now balanced shock at a sudden, humiliating shift in the campaign and an unhelpful wigging from Frederick. The Prussian king had anticipated defeat by three days in a letter, latest of a small procession, telling the Brunswicker to smarten up and pull himself together. 'Remember Rossbach,' he said, citing his great victory where the younger man had been valiantly involved. '. . . Remember your battle of last year and how you chased them around . . . [one should] give battle to the enemy even at the risk of defeat . . .' Any retreat might cause you 'to lose your supply depots . . . thus spreading panic among your troops, which is ten times worse than the risk of battle . . .'[9]

The Seven Years War is littered with advice from remote persons in authority to men sweating in the field. Only Ferdinand, as the immediate fighting man, could judge whether action would be decisive or precipitate. He was lucky to have as unofficial (civilian) ADC and future biographer, Christian von Westphalen, whose note of 9 July tacitly advises not taking too much advice from anyone. A sentence sums up the whole case against the most eminent second-guessing: 'Your Serene Highness will never achieve half of what He could as long as He continues to act according to His own lights.' This was a truth fully understood by Hawke, Wolfe and the best British commanders. It had been very far from the minds of Sir John Mordaunt and the Duke of Cumberland.

Ignoring Frederick and, in this instance, also George,* King and Elector (who had sent a worried letter), was a first duty. Ferdinand was fully up to it and, preparing for action, settled for the defensive engagement which current French success and sure advance had made the only option. It would be an unequal affair. The Anglo-German forces were 41,000 strong against 51,000 French. But beyond numbers the battle's deciding action was a matter, in Richard Holmes's words, of 'an attack on a vastly superior force of French cavalry by six British regiments'.

Initially placed south of Osnabrück, where George I had died, he secured Bremen with a garrison of four battalions, and sent General Estorff to do the same service at Nienberg. He had next placed men on either side of the Weser. The expectation was a French attack, readiness for it was everything. The unhappily named Todtenhausen (sepulchre), north of Minden and on the west bank of the Weser, was one marker. A line of defence was chosen running from a point a mile south of that village, through Kutenhausen to Stemmer. It was marked with another *Landwehr*, and the river would cover the right flank defending it. With the hills of the Wiehen Gebirge zigzagging south, the Weser at the east and a line bordering the marshland to the north, there was effectively a Minden defile, something unwelcome to troops going down it. The battle of Minden outside the town would involve French endeavours to prevent allied forces taking back a French prize.

The term 'Allies' is in order, signifying German small-state contingents, also the British forces which Pitt had been persuaded to send. Present since the previous August, the troops had not yet faced a significant engagement. At Minden, notable regiments were the Inniskillings under Colonel Harvey, the First Grenadiers under Sir John Maxwell, the 23rd of Foot, and the Royal Welsh† Fusiliers, who would distinguish themselves by charging faster than the flank commander, General Spoerken, thought wise. Other British regiments and senior officers would be heavily involved with great credit. The matter of

---

* Frederick had described George's charge at Dettingen sixteen years before, heroic and at risk at the very head of his troops, but doubtfully useful: 'He gave signs of courage but no order relative to the battle.' Quoted Holmes, *Redcoat*, p. 81.
† As Savory spells it – more usually 'Welch'!

Lord George Sackville commanding cavalry on the right would be something else. But overall, British and Hanoverian soldiers fought together quite well enough for Marshal Contades.

The French commander had been wrong-footed. His forces were dispersed. To advance he needed specifically the detachments of Armentières and Chevreuse. Their thirty-six squadrons of cavalry and twenty-two battalions of infantry would seriously strengthen him. But, busy elsewhere, they could do nothing before late July. Ferdinand needed an early fight, Contades a postponement. In a small skirmish the Erb Prinz drove French hussars out of Luebbecke.* Two of Ferdinand's commanders, Dreves and Schlieffen, brought him up to almost 10,000 men. The commander of a large advance French group recognised enough troops to isolate him.

Uncertainty about the Erb Prinz's strength would provoke Contades to early action when he needed to delay. The unwelcome, faraway wrong advice came from Belleisle, Commander-in-Chief from Versailles. His notes urging Contades to fight soon rather than trust his informed judgement did more harm than Frederick's hectoring did Ferdinand. For Ferdinand had been watching everything. Through 29–31 July he had received clear reports on French movements. He knew Saint-Germain was coming from Rinteln, that nothing was happening at Hartum, or Todtenhausen, that an infantry road was being driven through the hills toward Gohfeld, that the French, leaving Gehlenbeck and Luebbecke, were probably bound for Minden. He knew they were two hours out of Luebbecke, having established Hussars near a mill at Quernheim, that enemy cavalry had left Rinteln at 4.00 a.m. on the 30th, apparently for Vlotho, and that on 31 July at 9.00 a.m., a cloud of dust was appearing between Minden and Herford. Finally, he knew that from Todtenhausen at 5.00 p.m. on 31 July, Broglie's marching trumpet had sounded.

The British would get their first battle order when three hundred of Colonel Harvey's Inniskillings marched to Luebbecke to reinforce Major General von Gilsa. Lord George's cavalry was placed to the right with three Hanoverian forces, perfectly placed for crucial intervention. At 6.00 p.m. on 31 July, Contades authorised a dawn assault. Broglie's immediate force, having traversed French-occupied Minden, should join artillery and grenadiers, make for Todtenhausen and savage

* A village at the far west of the defile, *not* the Baltic port.

Ferdinand's left support. Seven columns, after discreetly bridging the ditch, would await dawn. Broglie would lie behind the right wing under Nicolai, whose eight battalions would face Wangenheim's Hanoverian left flank diagonally.* Nicolai would support Broglie if needed. Otherwise Contades, plagued by his remote betters, took care not to badger his subordinates. They had broad instructions and must react to events. However, plans being unknowable, Ferdinand was planning a night attack to strike at dawn as, in symmetrical fashion, was Contades.

The French began with luck. A rainstorm kept Broglie's advance secret, an advantage he wasted after outlying Hanoverian picquets had initially retreated, by staying unenterprisingly put. While he waited for Nicolai, an alerted Wangenheim used artillery against the French grenadiers with harsh effect. British troops now entered the war. The British infantry, officially Spoerken's but with a velocity of its own, pushed past Schelle's (perhaps grateful) forces, excepting a single battalion. Following German example, they knelt, avoiding all but the first artillery fire. By six the Hanoverian left wing at Kutenhausen, using its artillery well, was getting the advantage.

Nicolai's French rescue was halted by a confusion common between capable soldiers. Broglie, out scouting the land, saw two infantry columns going full tilt beside a column of cavalry. These were largely British, infantry commanded by Earl Waldegrave.† His papers and comments reflect an intelligent, eccentric British figure who might have flourished under the pencil of Osbert Lancaster. Just then, he was going too fast, outracing Spoerken, of whose wing his troops formed a part. Ferdinand, admiring but concerned, sent the Duke of Richmond to tell him that they might wish to stay together with the other cavalry and shouldn't exhaust themselves. They drew breath in a clump of trees, then charged again clean into the French cavalry's left. Spoerken's artillery now came up under the British captains MacBean and Phillips for a battle of artillery and artillery.

Advancing British and Hanoverians, both in red, including Waldegrave's post-haste troopers, having passed Scheele's columns went

---

* Georg August von Wangenheim, a Hanoverian, christened surely for George II, had excellent English connections, having lived there and collaborated closely with Lord Granby.

† Waldegrave's full complement at the start of 1759 consisted of the 12th and 37th Foot and the Welsh Fusiliers.

deep into battle and acquitted themselves outstandingly. Despite notable
losses, they were saved by that artillery fire from the full effects of the
French guns. When the first line of eleven squadrons of French cavalry
under the Duc de Saint-James charged, they paid a dreadful price from
accurate infantry rifle fire. The suicidal quality to French courage in
this savage fight caught the cavalier insouciance of Allied response.

Lieutenant Montgomery of 12th of Foot described '. . . a most
furious fire from a most infernal Battery of 18 18-pounders . . . It might
be imagined that this cannonade would render the Regt incapable of
bearing the shock of unhurt troops long before on ground of their
own choosing, but firmness and resolution will surmount any difficulty. When we got within about a hundred yards of the enemy, a
large body of French cavalry galloping boldly down upon us; these
our Men by reserving their fire, immediately ruined . . . These visi-
tants being thus dismissed . . . down came upon us like lightning, the
glory of France in the Persons of the Gens d'Armes. These were
almost immediately dispersed . . . We now discovered a large body of
infantry . . . moving directly on our flank in Column . . . We engaged
this Corps for about 10 minutes, killed them a good many, and as the
Song says, the rest then ran away.'[10]

Saint-James personally went back to bring out his second line to be
selectively shot dead by foot soldiers fast-loading single-shot muskets.
Lieutenant Montgomery again: 'The next who made their appearance
were some Regt's of the Grenadiers of France and as fine and terrible
looking fellows as I ever saw. They stood us a tug, notwithstanding
we beat them to a distance . . . we advanced, they took the hint and
run away.'[11]

The French advance now became an allied advance upon two thousand men from the elite cavalry, the Gendarmerie de France and the
Carabineers under a rare commoner, Lieutenant-General Poyanne. As
Savory, historian of this English army, observes, Sackville's cavalry,
placed for just such a flank intervention, would have been welcome
but did not come. Instead Welsh Fusiliers, Hanoverian guards and
troops under Hardenburg took losses, but in sword-to-throat fighting
did not give way. The beginnings of victory materialised as Imhoff's
column, accompanied by artillery, arrived rather late but with perfect
timing. Against the guns, the doomed men commanded by Saint-
James charged for the last time, died or were driven out.

The French centre was shot away following another and hopeless charge by the remains of the French inner right under Beaupréau. They were caught by Hessians charging with bayonets as Holstein-Gottorp's cavalry hit them again from behind. Apart from Beaupréau's six-battalion core, the French position had now become a melée with Allied victory almost achieved. All forces converged on the central fight. Broglie's left flank yielded ten battalions. Wangenheim, a regular of the campaign, sent in sixteen squadrons of cavalry. Nicolai's troops in flight from them went clean into Broglie's cavalry ranks.

This encounter was finished. But on the Allied right, Spoerken, with many British troops fighting, was under serious pressure from the Saxons under Lusace. Having taken much of the heat, they badly needed reinforcement. The Hanoverians Scheele and Wutginau sent seven battalions combined. Even so the British troops under most pressure from Lusace's Saxons had to give ground. But Scheele's men and gunfire halted the attack in this last, true action of the battle. The French made a full retreat and, in Savory's judgement, pursuit by a certain twenty-four squadrons of cavalry would have achieved a rout.

However, the commander holding back those twenty-four squadrons, fresh troops handily placed in Hartum at an easy angle to Lusace's Saxons and able to intervene decisively, was Lord George Sackville. Lord George, remote and ineffectual if hardly angel, did not appear, as he had not appeared earlier in the fight, when a cavalry charge would also have been valuable. Fortunately, that part of the fighting would be resolved by Scheele's men and the guns. The French retreat, ordered almost superfluously, was, thanks to Sackville, fairly orderly. Bitterly, it involved retreat through Minden itself, the prize once lost to Ferdinand, then won back and now surrendered again. The French continued beyond the Weser and away to Kassel, seventy or so miles south. There were great struggles to come, also reverses, but when the Allies encamped at Marsberg, Hanover had been made safe, and a serious threat to Frederick and the Prussians (seriously defeated at Kunersdorf) greatly eased. Our war in Germany went well and, Sackville apart, British soldiers had given a distinguished performance in arms with the Hanoverians. In Southey's words about a battle fifty years earlier, it was a famous victory.

The rights and wrongs of Sackville have been debated. He was already an unpopular figure, a horrid contrast to the good-natured, jolly and very brave Granby, adored by his men. Controversy is not fully resolved, Piers Mackesy writing a well-argued defence, *The Coward of Minden*. Almost certainly, Sackville was not a *coward*, just touchy, neglectful, arrogant and late. Non-appearance was not for want of a summons. Ferdinand had several times sent orders to come. And they were orders. He was the Commander-in-Chief. All officers, however, free to make judgements in the field, had to obey his direct injunctions.

Reginald Savory, himself a soldier, is clear. 'Seldom if ever has there been in battle such disgraceful disobedience.'[12] The case compares badly with that of poor Byng. In respect of Minorca, Byng was under-strength and given bad, local counsel. Persuaded by an officer with supposed local knowledge that Minorca citadel could not be relieved, he held back. Sackville was within sound and foul smell of a great battle fought *à l'outrance*. Under C-in-C's orders to relieve men under fire and bombardment, he did nothing. An act of pique best explains it, with Sackville not so much coward as paradigm of the intolerable English milord proud beyond his duty. At one point, while Sackville was receiving instructions, Granby, conscious that they would be needed, brought the cavalry squadrons forward, only for the returning Sackville to stop them.

Ferdinand was, unsurprisingly, outraged. On 13 August, he wrote to the King/Elector a letter which opens: 'Sire, I find myself obliged to represent to Your Majesty, that if He wishes me to continue in the very honourable appointment of Commander-in-Chief of His allied Army in Germany, He should be graciously pleased to make a notable change in this army by recalling Lord George Sackville commanding British troops. His behaviour on the day of 1st, was not such as to help either the Cause in general or me in particular, and that at the very point at which affairs might have been within an ace of being lost; on the other hand . . .'

The tone is quiet but implacable: '. . . As the matter is so very grave, I dare to insist on the recall of the said Lord George Sackville . . . and without this prompt change, I will be of no more use to this army . . .'

Even Serene Highness does not lightly address Majesty in such cool terms. They said that if Sackville were not dismissed on the instant, Ferdinand would throw up the glittering command in which he was making such a name. He had no need to insist. George's hatred for cowardice recurs, a political constant. He had been unjust to Byng because of it. Sackville would be court-martialled, dismissed, declared unfit to serve in any capacity and the court sentence read before the assembled army to demonstrate that 'neither high birth nor great employments can shelter offences of such a nature'.

Despite this embarrassment, Minden had been something splendid, a battle with something of Marlborough's wars about it. If the indispensible general was a Brunswicker, Granby was the nicest possible version of an English nobleman, bumbling, brave and kind. If Sackville had been late to the point of never coming, Waldegrave had been too fast in the most creditable and effective way. British soldiering, with a large Scottish and Welsh admixture, had performed with very great credit unbroken by a council of war.

As 1759 advanced, victory would not be universal. The German scene had darkened seriously with, so very soon after Minden, that defeat of Frederick on 12 August at Kunersdorf near the Oder (and not so very far from Berlin). The 7 October would see Berlin fall to the Austrians and Russians. As the Prussian courtier, von Lehndorff, put it, 'The fall of Berlin signifies a frightful loss. All the resources to sustain the war are gone at a single stroke. The enemy have possession of our machines, our factories, our powder mills and countless other stores.'[13] Saxon troops, whose country Frederick had invaded and would invade again, had cut up particularly rough, smashing his best china (Nymphenberg) at Charlottenberg Palace. Meanwhile, the Russians stood at the Oder. It would take Torgau, fifteen months later, 3 November 1760, and an uncovenanted Russian withdrawal, to get the capital back.

Later, as the Prussians righted themselves and fought on, the King would happily recall that an attempt to drag away his favourite and now retired charger, Grau Molwitz, was foiled by the horse himself digging in his heels and refusing to be dragged.[14] But for now, as Frederick told his Foreign Minister, 'My coat is riddled with musket balls, and I have had two horses killed beneath me. It is my misfortune to be still alive.' Frederick's biographer, Duffy, observes, 'More than 6000 of the Prussians had been killed outright, total casualties amounted to about 19,000 men or nearly two fifths of the army.'[15] Next year's battle would be for Berlin. Meanwhile, in England King, Court and Secretary of State were preoccupied by something rather different.

What had happened to the Prussians at Kunersdorf and in the temporary occupation of Berlin might have been a defeat to change the whole outcome of the war. The Battle of Minden had at the end of July 1759 been a serious chapter in this serious war. The sea fight at Quiberon Bay, so very close to it in time, was its naval equivalent, but more immediately conclusive. The Lilliputian court tantrum which would follow the German battles and, in late autumn, overlap with Quiberon Bay, then drag well into the New Year, remains absurd across 250 years. The contrast is humiliating.

A Garter in Edward VII's time meant one sort of thing. In George II's day it meant the exalted honour of a knighthood, leaving other knighthoods to country gentry and late arrivistes, meant its charming blue riband and make-way precedence throughout Society. Richard Grenville, Earl Temple, had been in the government throughout, but after his valiant quarrel with the King over poor Byng had dropped out of the narrative. That brave insolence did him credit; with George, it had done him no good. He was in the ministry but not active there, not something this slightly odd man ever minded. Temple recalls Belloc's Godolphin Horne – 'But Oh, the lad was deathly proud.' In token of who he was, what he owned and to whom he was related he wanted a Companionship of the Most Noble Order of the Garter. He wanted it very particular, and nothing else would do.

In September 1758, on the death of one Companion, Lord Carlisle, Temple had applied to Newcastle. The duke, knowing the explosive potential, mentioned the claims of Ferdinand, lately winning at Krefeld, or Holdernesse, a Secretary of State, and generally played for time. 'There would', he said carefully, 'be difficulties.' Temple was good at difficulties. It was a very nice government they had here, they wouldn't want anything happening to it. He only sought the Garter lest his 'real reluctance' to bring it up should become reason for passing him over, and wasn't it proof of his 'solidarity with the Ministry'? He would be thought 'wanting to myself and to my own situation if I did not lay these wishes before the King'.[16] George II's hatred for Temple being

HUNT THE GARTER: MINDEN AND LORD TEMPLE

in the same league as Temple's finished insolence, Pitt's failure to discourage his brother-in-law guaranteed a crisis.

The French invasion of this island was being put together and the Bank of England had declined to help the Exchequer with a vote of credit. It was an incredible day for a superfluous politician to be arguing about a mark of social precedence.

But Temple did not think so. On 14 November he resigned the Privy Seal. The question was not war nor peace nor continuation of government: it was the fetching blue riband of the Garter and for that the resignation of both men was threatened.

Pitt had praised Temple's motives and nowhere advised restraint.[17] Time passed and the people about the courts of King and heir, Buckingham House and Leicester House, people like Count Viry, Sardinian Minister, noted a growing edge between Leicester House and the Pitt/Grenville faction. The Prince of Wales and Lord Bute were angry that Temple had kept them ignorant of his moves. But into the most noble nonsense of decorations came Pitt's calculation. George had passed the mid-seventies. It was not wisdom to snub Prince George as he had lightly snubbed Prince Frederick. Relations with Bute, tutor, mentor and confidant (see *post* Chapter 18) were anxious; his letters to Bute have a beseeching quality. Temple, despite irritating Leicester House, was their man, token of Pitt's acceptability on the great day of George II's death. For all the heroic talk, Pitt wanted life after that death.

Newcastle, putting the business of the ministry sticking together above everything, tried to buy Temple off with a bauble. The Lieutenancy and Custos rotulorum of Buckinghamshire was proposed. That gained three months of Temple sulking *quietly*, refusing, for example, to attend Newcastle's dinner for George II's birthday. But in March 1759 Count Viry, postman to Quality Street, told Newcastle that Temple meant to resign and that Pitt would follow him.

The summer passed with George's contempt for Temple unamended, Temple's appetite ever more raw and the duke caught in the middle. Newcastle's qualities were disinterest, hard work and decent good sense. What he lacked was any sort of proud anger. Hardwicke, whom the historian of Grenvilles, Lewis Wiggins, thought 'alone retained any sense of reality',[18] wanted to tell Pitt to urge Temple to give up *immediate* prospects. The war was tilting in the right direction.

We held profitable French colonies, Minden was won and Hanover secured, the Canadian expedition, business now of the sailors and redcoats fighting it, was at the end of a laborious postal chain.

If Pitt had been told that his resignation would be sincerely regretted, he would have retreated. But Newcastle was never going to do that. He had no head for operatic quarrels and wanted George to buy peace with a riband. The departure of Pitt would make no difference to a war which soldiers and sailors had got the hang of. The House of Commons was another matter. Pitt was the trumpet there. His faction with the Tories, puffed by the élan of victories, would make government difficult; who knew how difficult? As Newcastle told the King, 'No man Sir, will in the present conjuncture set his face against Mr Pitt in the House.'

For George, the Garter which, as professional royalty, he cherished would be 'disgraced'. So it would, but the ministry, *a* ministry, had to be kept together. Pitt, as so often, mixed calculation with unreason. He had always dismissed patronage but now complained that 'He is so treated he can't make a tidewaiter* . . . He will not open the session . . . He can't see himself and his relatives slighted . . . He is not owned by the King . . .'[19] As so often with Pitt exalted, there is no telling the line between strategic paranoia and the real thing.

It rattled on. On 17 October, four days after Wolfe had ascended from the Anse-au-Foulon, won the battle for Quebec, been shot and died, Pitt proclaimed that 'His point was and ever should be the Garter.' On 26 October Devonshire says briskly, 'Mr Pitt Disposed to quit unless Lord Temple has the Garter.'

The Secretary blew hot and cold. Newcastle was always ready to welcome, gratefully, 'the civility of Mr Pitt'. But for Pitt a quarrel was something to play upon.[20] Joseph Yorke, Hardwicke's son, had passed on an interesting tip, not, as strictly he should have done, to Holdernesse, Northern Secretary of State, but to Newcastle. (One cannot say too often that this was a very departmental government. British governments were generally so then, but, given the spare flammable materials left around, the practice was reinforced.) But Yorke was Hardwicke's son and the King had authorised the contact. The

---

* A minor customs post usually carrying a vote to be used for the government candidate, very much ministerial small change.

information itself related to *La Dame inconnue* who was supposed to have information relating to possible peace contacts. This had a pleasant ring of later spy fiction, Ladies on Trains and the like. Whatever she might have known was lost in the crackling office quarrel innocently provoked.

For, unfortunately, Holdernesse heard about it and took heavy umbrage, seeking to exclude Yorke from the exploratory talks at The Hague. Pitt joined in, welcoming a more respectable excuse for threatening resignation. Newcastle spelt out the realities to George: 'It is not Yorke's correspondence that is the point; it is Sir, another object which has been refused and thus it will be now, and then one thing, then another, if his great object is not achieved.'[21]

In the early autumn of 1759 we are let into the notes of an onlooker. William Cavendish, 4th Duke of Devonshire, was a friend of Newcastle, but an objective presence at Cabinet Council because everyone trusted him, for once a political figure present as a public duty. Cavendish took notes of meetings and corridor conversations, from September 1759 to early October 1762. His 'Memoranda', discovered and transcribed by P. D. Brown and K. W. Schweizer,* come from the mouth of a thoughtful horse in regular attendance upon events. On 11 November, Devonshire told Lady Yarmouth that he 'had good reason to think [Pitt] would resign his employment . . . [and] would either quit or would show his ill humour by obstructing the measures and distressing the King's affairs'.[22]

On 14 November, with the great sea battle days away, Temple sees Devonshire. 'Met Temple in the outward room' (at the Palace) 'who told me he was going to resign.' Devonshire tried to raise Pitt in the King's eyes by quoting the shift in his thinking. [Pitt had] 'said he had formerly notions that this country could stand by itself and ought not to meddle with the Continent; he saw his errors it was a narrow and erroneous way of thinking; . . .'

Next Devonshire against his practice talked to Pitt 'Very civil, very cool, and decent, pleased with the King's condescension.† I told him that after the service he had done the public and the justice they did

---

* Published in the Royal Historical Society's Camden series 27 in 1982.
† In 1760 and long after 'Condescension' meant, not a patronising manner, but friendliness.

him [that] ought to induce him to finish the work he had begun and secure the country a good peace that it must be the work of all the ministry and not a part of it . . . upon the whole I think he does not intend to quit. At least not at present.' Devonshire also floated the idea of the Garter firmly promised until the end of the session. Pitt 'after much talk owned that he wished it and was of opinion for it, but that the subject was of so delicate a nature considering the part he had in it that he could not speak to Lord Temple' but agreed to pass on Devonshire's suggestion of a meeting.

Having lowered the temperature, on 15 November he called on Lady Yarmouth where he 'found that the King was alarmed and ready to do anything . . . the levée was over, Lord Temple much pleased with his reception. Gave the King an account of my conversation with Mr Pitt, and told him that I was to see Lord Temple in the evening and desired to know what powers:

'"You may tell him I desire he will take the Privy Seal again."

'"That will not do alone: you must Sir, allow me to give him hopes of Garter at the end of the Session."

'"When I make a promotion."

'"But, Sir, that must be at the end of the Session."

'"Well, I will, provided Mr Pitt stays in to make the peace and they will support my affairs."[23]

'Saw Lord Temple in the evening, he agreed to take the Privy Seal, would not accept the garter on terms but would be proud of it as a mark of the king's favour.'[24]

Everything now seemed gracefully settled, which it wasn't. The delay was good for ten weeks across Christmas/New Year. On 30 January, Temple, resenting delay, decided to start again and 'expressed great wrath at the Duke of Newcastle's having meddled about the Garter', something which the King raised with Devonshire who 'hoped H.M. would give the Garters away immediately'.

'He said "You know I promised to do it at the end of the session, I will keep my word; why am I to be plagued? I don't care to do it sooner."

'"Good God Sir, what can it signify to your Majesty, whether you do it now or three months hence; is it worth while to risque putting your affairs into confusion for such a trifle?" . . . I could not get a promise but we parted in very good humour.'[25]

'[Still] Jan 30. Went downstairs, related what had passed with the King and desired her [Lady Yarmouth] to enforce it; said it would be confusion if not done . . .'

'Jan 31: Went to Lady Yarmouth who told me that the king would do as I desired and that I should notify it to Lord Temple and Lord Rockingham.'*

It wasn't quite over even now. Devonshire continues immediately: 'From thence went to attend the King in the Drawing Room, a letter sent in to me from Lord Temple saying that after what had passed, he must decline accepting the Garter; put it in my pocket and went from Court to Mr Pitt, told what was done and complained of Lord Temple's manner, and that I thought I had reason to expect to be consulted before such a step was taken. He endeavoured to justify Lord Temple and was greatly pleased. I desired him to communicate it to his Lordship who sent me a letter assuring me that all difficulties were removed and that he accepted most thankfully.'[26]

The account of Pitt's resignation given by Sherrard, writing in the early 1950s, reflects the boys' story image of the High Victorians. 'The King gave a blunt refusal, whereupon Pitt, like another Achilles, stalked to his tent and began to unbuckle his armour. His action left the political world aghast. Nothing had ever shown them more clearly how completely Pitt dominated the political scene, what pygmies they all were compared with him, and how essential it was his hand should remain on the Helm if America was to be won and Hanover saved.'[27] The reality is of events becoming too serious for such grandstanding and attitude-striking. Pitt and Temple had behaved outrageously, but got their pointless way because that reality made giving way the sensible way out of a silly game.

As to saving Hanover, Pitt had wasted a year, and had denied Cumberland reinforcements to keep quiet his personal faction (whose principles he no longer accepted), until he should be better placed to abandon them. Canada, by the consent of the entire Cabinet, was getting all the naval and military support its commanders wanted with the exception of three thousand men removed for the aggrandisement of trade in the slave-raised sugar of Guadeloupe. Pitt was

---

* The future Prime Minister, a Lord of the Bedchamber, was to receive the Garter at the same time, an altogether more congenial candidate.

offering resignation as they neared the climax of a major war to obtain
social cachet for a long-term crony. Temple's links with an increasingly disabused Opposition, doubling as the hereditary succession,
repaired Pitt's own connection there. His original ties had been diminished by accelerating abandonment of commitments once shared and
which he had once shouted in the street. No soldier, Pitt was never
Achilles, but he was a very fly politician.

Eventually there would be a return to sobriety. We did remember
that there was a war on. So much so that the ministry began to be
exercised by the possibilities of Peace. Despite the 'Save my Country'
routine making up Pitt's high 'C's, the war concerned winning or
losing tracts of colonial territory and trade. There would be mood
swings, of course, especially in so febrile a man. And as the autumn
wore on, the earlier time-lapsed miseries of dead, victorious Wolfe,
enclosed in that last despatch, would come in, just before the news
of his triumph. 'There is such a choice of difficulties', the young
general had written in his last despatch, 'that I own myself at a loss
to determine.'

Meanwhile, for the King of Prussia the business in hand really was
a matter of saving his country (and crown). That autumn, he was
placed to get a peace to secure what he held. Given war with Austria
and his new enemy, Saxony, the actual victories had needed to be
miraculous, but there had also been serious defeats. Getting out ahead
of the game had more than charm. Minden had indicated an occasion for peace on excellent terms, excellent for Prussia and probably
Britain, which last point would harden when the good, slow news
finally came in the autumn from Quebec.

When that arrived in mid-October, the response was heartfelt.
Newcastle had written to Hardwicke on 15 October saying that Wolfe's
despairing letter would be published in the *Gazette*, but with omissions.
'Mr Pitt', he wrote, 'with reason gives it all over and declares so publicly.
I think I see that he is not quite satisfied with Wolfe in his heart . . .'[28]
Yet, as Newcastle mentions in the same letter, both Anson and the
King had belonged to the party which had expected a victory.

Hardwicke's reply comes next day and, quoting his daughter, Anson's
wife, is dramatic: 'I was never more surprised in my life than after
reading your Grace's letter and poring over the extraordinary Gazette
from beginning to end and finding some black atoms arise as to the

event, to open a letter from my daughter, Anson, dated from the Admiralty at half an hour past ten at night and read that Quebec was taken on the 18th of September and that this came by an express arrived that instant in 25 days from that place . . . In the midst of my joy I am filled with grief at the death of General Wolfe, which I look upon a very great public loss.'[29]

Meanwhile the counterpoise to Frederick's shrewd instinct for collecting winnings was British belief in, and French hope of, a cross-Channel invasion. The frisson of 1757 had died away with very little added to the scatter of earthworks from that date thrown up around Chatham, Portsmouth and Plymouth. Kent and Sussex, already the cricketing counties, were sportingly sustained by a handful of artillery batteries, each one sustained by a master gunner and his apprentice, all for £6000.[30] Meanwhile, should the French be on the sea, the Duke of Bedford was preparing Ireland with that scratch defence he argued could 'only be effected by giving the Nobility and Gentry the like encouragements which have been given in Great Britain'.

More relevantly, Sir Edward Hawke drew the logical conclusion from the logistical problems of Channel raiders by setting accurately to map that coast. It was a useful thing to be doing anyway. It kept the watch on the Channel and kept it very visibly.

17

'Where ignorant Armies clash by night': Quiberon Bay

That a major French effort was coming was not doubted, though, like a second marriage, it would always be a triumph of hope over experience. The latest defeat came in an attempt to unite ships from the Mediterranean together with those in the Atlantic ports. Lord Bristol, Ambassador in Madrid, reported that 'twelve ships of the line and three Frigates from Toulon under the Command of M-de La Clue passed through the straits of Gibraltar in the night between the 16th and 17th of this Month, August, that five ships of the line as well as three frigates have put into the Bay of Cadiz, and it is not known what course the other seven large ships have steered'.[1]

Letting these ships reach Rochefort would reinforce the fleet, one wing of the planned invasion. Ideal for France would be a union of *three* forces. For 16–17 August, Bompart, squadron chief to Conflans, now returning from the Antilles, should bring into Brest seven ships of the line with seasoned crews. Expected by friends, Bompart was urgently looked out for by his enemies, Hawke's captains superfluously bidden by the Admiralty 'to keep a proper strength down the Bay to intercept them'. More usefully, their Lordships directed *Sandwich*, *Belliqueux* and *Torbay* out of Plymouth and into the coastal cruise.[2] If all three sets of French ships could snatch up the waiting land troops when weather had driven Hawke away, then the game would be afoot.

Events and superior seamanship would put hopes into retrospection. On 17 August, seven French ships were spotted by a lookout in the squadron of Boscawen, least particular of attacking British sailors. They belonged to La Clue, pushing uneasily north from Cadiz. Observation was mutual, not recognition. Playing Admiral Clouseau, La Clue took Boscawen's squadron for friendly ships and waited!

Courage not wanting, a three-hour battle followed. *Centaure*, her captain killed, and effectively wrecked, after a valiant three-hour fight, struck colours. The French were brave enough but did not win naval encounters, big or little.

Out of a squadron of seven, two ships only, *Souverain* and *Guerrier*, sensibly shifting course, had escaped. Boscawen had concentrated his pursuit upon the rest, pursued it all night and into Lagos Bay where, characteristically disregarding Portuguese neutrality, he burned *Océan* and *Redoutable*. As prizes, he took *Modeste* and *Téméraire*. This last lived on nearly a hundred years until painted by Turner, *The Fighting Téméraire* en route for the breakers, it became immortal. Out of seven French ships, only the fugitive two, one badly damaged, remained.

Hawke learned this on 12 September when Speke, captain of *Resolution*, handed him a letter from Boscawen dated 20 August. Returning a reply, Hawke conveyed anxiety at a reinforced French fleet then relief: 'I was in great pain lest the enemy should have escaped you.' The victory was 'as fortunate an event as could have happened for our Country, as it has entirely overset the schemes of the French'.[3] So it had. As militias exercised and paraded, the schemes of the French would never match the reality of encountering Hawke's ships.

So what *were* the schemes of the French? The folly of the French authorities had been outstanding. Having, in the 1750s, left their North American territories underdefended and seen Wolfe take Quebec in a dying victory with English conquest assured, France had fallen back upon desperate measures. No measure could have been more desperate than invading England – strategic regression, antiquarian thinking. For France, despite conversations with the Young Pretender, was no longer seriously in the business of a Stuart restoration. Invasion, flat-bottomed boats and a Scottish campaign made a last diversionary throw in a long, losing war. As has been spelt out, tradable occupation of territory not conquest was the object. Invasion *after* defeat in Canada and frustration against Hanover was a last scrambling at a vertical wall.

They were not winding down a drawn war. Cross-Channel occupation was a wild venture, undertaken because this war had got out of hand. England's Year of Victories had been France's year of defeats. Invasion was desperation in heroic form. Even so, properly planned, it might, just imaginably, have been a late and saving long shot.

D'Aiguillon, landing near Glasgow, might march 20,000 soldiers upon Edinburgh, buttressed by Thurot's assault on Ulster that might pre-occupy British defences north and west. The return voyage, east to Ostend, might then ferry waiting troops (ghosts of Alba's men never landed by Armada galleons) to Essex. Serving at the least as wonderful theatre, it would leave a British government unspeakably embarrassed, foundation for negotiations about bits of Canada. Merely dropping D'Aiguillon's soldiers in Scotland would, in dark times for France, have been diverting in every sense. It would still have been wisest to cut the losses of the war France was losing and shift to serious diplomacy. *Not* doing so served the London trade lobby in London and would shift Pitt himself into larger aspirations.

Bompart's West Indies squadron had actually reached Brest on 7 November and their crews were immediately transferred to Conflans's ships. It was an achievement turning upon Hawke's being away, also an accession of ships colouring ministerial delusions that its baroque scheme could work. If Bompart had also been intercepted, the inva-sion would likely have been dropped. The Admiralty man, Calcraft, had described the invasion plan as 'dreadful'. So it was. Getting troops out and ahead on a winter sea requires swift embarkation as much as hard sailing. It means the troops, transports and convoy together at the start! Awful Channel weather in November was a short odds' horse assuring retreat to haven (usually Torbay) of the watching squadron of inferior British ships under a superior commander. Efficient French management would have had troops waiting in a harbour town for embarkation on to waiting boats (plus convoy), then, at the first wind shift, running at the target fast! But efficient French management had to wait for Napoleon. In 1759, Conflans, vice-admiral, was left to start his Scottish voyage with impossible logistics.

Not having French sailors and soldiers, ships and transports settled together gave the British navy busy supervision and probable early engagement. At Port Louis were twenty-four French transports and seven frigates. At Nantes, six thousand troops awaited their convoy. The bulk of the army was in the Morbihan, a recessed stretch down the coast, with the ships and their admiral at Brest! The 'unfortunate idea', as the distinguished French historian, Lacour-Gayet, in *La Marine Militaire Sous Louis XV* describes it, 'of putting a squadron to sea from Brest to embark an army from the Morbihan when it was as easy to assemble that army at Brest itself', created every opportunity for Hawke. Conflans in his flagship *Soleil Royal*, together with *Tonnant, Eveillé, Formidable, Héros, Glorieux, Superbe* and *Bizarre*, twenty-one ships of the line, stood in Brest Roads. Hawke and his captains stood in their place, waiting.

Instructively, Hawke had been trying to persuade his thick-headed London broker to buy government stock for him *now*, what you do if you expect to win a war or, like the Rothschilds, you *know* it has been won. The fidgets of distant investors had driven it down, but it would rise ferociously after any major victory. Of this, the admiral, alert to relative strengths and in the middle of things, was serenely certain.[4] By contrast, a contemporary British naval historian, Frederick Hervey, describes French captains fighting rather 'to preserve their honour than in hopes of obtaining victory'.[5]

Meanwhile, the obvious English course was urged redundantly by Hawke's superiors: to watch the Morbihan, the coast around the obvious area for French assembly. However, on 9 October, their Lordships demanded a concentration off Brest, out of which the French had been disinclined to move. Following instructions of 21 September, to 'keep a proper strength down at the Bay' to meet Bompart, this was a complete shift-about. The Admiralty, lately urgent for the Morbihan, would settle for 'small cruisers' there, and Hawke had to shift to the Brest coast Vice-Admiral Geary (just directed to Rochefort).

It might have been a worrying jumble. But the French naval commander was under advice worse than anything Hawke received. If Conflans stayed put, direct British attack on his ships would only be sporadic. If they had been in the Morbihan, specifically Quiberon Bay, security was guaranteed. For the British had learnt about the enormous difficulties with which it was spiked. Quiberon Bay was a recessed haven behind a rampart of ugly rocks known as 'The Cardinals'. The problem lay in getting from one place to the other.

Pilots helping the English *Achilles* through the Teignouze Passage on 10 October had run it on to the rocks. But the courtiers and politicians instructing Conflans had always inclined to the beautiful nonsense of Montrose, despising the man 'That puts it not unto the touch/To win or lose it all'. Conflans had grimly undertaken, in late season, to get from Brest to Quiberon Bay, not as haven but prelude to collecting troops and making past HM Navy for the Irish Sea and Scotland.

When, in November, a furious storm blew Hawke off-station, French ships might, in theory, make for their objective. As a place of resort, Quiberon Bay was an excellent stretch for retreating if you moved carefully in daylight. And thereabouts, farther from England than Brest and harder to watch, the military forces were concentrated. However, as a land-based French source, quoted in Hawke's correspondence,[6] had succinctly put it, 'All things are now disposing for embarkation, the troops arriving and joining. But how are they to get out? We see, within a league and a half of this, two large English ships with nine frigates of various sizes waiting for us . . . We see distinctly and without spectacles the English walking upon the decks of their ships . . .' How indeed were the French soldiers to get out? And how were their sailors to get in?

Deep into autumn, Conflans was proposing the perilous run which British superiority had denied him all summer. Assuredly an under-taking to win or lose it all, it disregarded Admiral Winter. Meanwhile, Captain Reynolds's watch had, through September and October, been intermittently augmented along the Breton coast and below. Summer had passed, autumn was slipping away and rational invasion weather with them. Meanwhile, on 15 September, Hawke briefed the Admiralty that he had 'sent the *Dorsetshire*; *Resolution*; & *Coventry* to cruise East & West from the entrance into the Petrius d'Antioche seven or eight leagues . . .' And after a call by Hawke on Hanway, commanding officer at Plymouth, they would now be reinforced by five ships.

Not that Conflans was such a fool as actually to seek a fight. It was straightforwardly a question of flight. His ships were excellent; if the crews were up to it, then the voyage out, pickup and flight north-west might be accomplished. The crews were not up to it. And, on 5 November, eternally auspicious day for Protestant England, Hawke received letters from the Admiralty Secretary, John Clevland, indi-cating 'positive orders sent to M. Conflans to put to sea directly and at all events to engage His Majesty's ships'.

When weather occurred hard enough to take Hawke off-station, Conflans must take it. He had been instructed to leave Brest and join the troops from whom no sensible strategist would ever have sepa-rated him. He had to dash for Quiberon Bay during a moment when Hawke was distracted. The idea of bringing enough soldiers to Brest by land seems not to have occurred.

From *Soleil Royal*, Conflans commanded twenty-one ships with a two hundred-mile lead over the English admiral soon to be butting out of Torbay. Meanwhile, Reynolds of *Firm* had taken five ships out of treatment in dry dock. Having done this with minimum essential repairs, he established mobile watch on the French coast southward, 'sending, as you run along backwards and forwards, a frigate to look as near as possible into Nantz [*sic*], Vannes and Port Louis, in order to discover what number of the enemy's frigates and transports that may be lying there'.

The transports were what mattered. Any private frolic pursuing prizes was slapped down. Reynolds was 'to make your principle [*sic*] object and from which you are, on no account to be diverted or drawn off by following the enemies' frigates'.[7] After assembling a dozen ships, he went to the coast near Nantes, and found the French soldiery there, snug and immobile. The folly of the grand design, the French command and a too-compliant Conflans, was to think that starting in the safe, wrong place, they could reach another safe place in the wrong weather. And, as observed, the crews were not up to it.

Typically of the Bourbon government's centralised ineptitude, the admiral had also been left with scratch crews, often Breton peasants, land-bred, conscripted and untrained. Even his better sailors had gone six months without exercise at sea. British gunnery had been obsessively stressed by their Lordships. French standards in this respect, as their best officers knew, were reliably inferior. All this would now be tested.

Conflans was able to escape Brest as Hawke was leaving Torbay and, with his two hundred miles' geographical lead and journey distance of 120 miles, might have expected to reach haven pleasantly ahead of his pursuers. His fleet had been spotted by a British provision ship, *Love and Unity*, pushing adverse winds sixty miles short of Belle Isle, round the corner from Quiberon Bay. But Conflans, needing a coast route as most direct line for the Bay, was being driven westward out to sea. Winds changing in different parts of the Atlantic deflected Conflans and carried Hawke where he wanted to go. Now, early on 20 November, Hawke, in the dark, had depth measured (seven fathoms), and, buffeted about by screaming winds, had sheets taken in. But at earliest light, 7.00 a.m., he directed *Magnanime* (Howe) to drive for land.

The unacknowledged objective of the French fleet was now to escape and use Quiberon Bay, an obstacle race of narrow passages and jagged rocks, as refuge. Reaching Scotland could only be accomplished by extending a given lead through swift, single-minded flight. Conflans could have had a naval battle in good weather, with the limited numbers of British ships patrolling Brest. With contrary winds dictating events, getting into Quiberon Bay and staying there, whatever King Louis' ministers said, was the solitary and shining option. For the duration of a November gale in the Channel, escape into Quiberon Bay was still the only game.

The French now spotted Vice-Admiral Duff, a terrible mistake. From the 50-gun *Rochester* he commanded five smaller ships, essentially for observation. Sensibly, when faced with the French fleet, they scattered north and south. Quite crazily, Conflans gave chase, wasting nearly three hours, and, at 9.45, he found Hawke's ships pursuing *him*. Wasting more time getting a fighting line together, Conflans had second thoughts and made for the Bay. If he went first, it was neither from cowardice nor necessarily panic. Leading his ships to safety was an essential duty recognised many hours too late. The French admiral seems overall to have fought a campaign underestimating time, distance and the enemy.

The French rear, under the admired Saint-André du Verger, which could and should have been largely through the entrance to the Bay, was out at sea when, between 2.30 and 2.45, British fire on it began. *Dorsetshire** and *Torbay*, then *Magnanime, Resolution, Swiftsure, Warspite, Montague* and *Defiance* fell upon the rear. This was the battle *outside* the Bay, which the French fleet's tail, four ships, could only lose. English ships, following the example of *Dorsetshire* and *Defiance*, could now fire upon the French as they passed, like Cromwell's soldiers planted behind a hedge at Naseby shooting down cavalry.

The battle was fought in whistling winds and walls of sea. It was an affair of several actions, a running affair which, as the wind drove the English forward to attack newly arrived French ships, became a dance – a kind of murderous excuse-me. The *Revenge* attacked

---

* The *Dorsetshire* 'bore away and engaged 5 of the enemy's ships at different times and continued chacing [sic] the van ships when our rear ships came up.' Quoted Geoffrey Marcus, *Quiberon Bay*, p. 152.

Formidable, new, 80 guns, command ship of the rear squadron, then *Magnifique*. The English *Magnanime* took over engagement with the French *Formidable*, and *Warspite* joined in. The mobbing of the rear flagship was concentrated work. She was surrounded but fighting on, her starboard side was shot into holes and, late in the afternoon, her foremast gone. Her captain, Saint-André, a model of nobility in a sailor, died in defeat a death anticipating Nelson's in victory. Wounded, he was taken to the quarterdeck, and from a chair attempted command and was killed. At which, his brother succeeded him and was shot, too, as was the second captain. Only after so much did the ship finally strike colours to *Resolution*.

To fire a broadside in a heavy sea, whatever happens at the other end, is a danger to the ship firing. Gun holes open to accommodate cannon, but the ship, immobilised, will admit water. So with *Thésée*, captain, Kersaint de Coëtnampren, a Breton count with distinguished East Indian service. Engaged by *Torbay*, *Thésée* moved less nimbly under the ferocious winds of that day than the English ship in the same dreadful swell. She went on her beam ends, took in the sea at her ports and, vertically and *instanter*, sank, drowning the captain and six hundred men, also Bretons. Some nineteen hours later, a handful of *Thésée*'s men, clinging to sections of a mast, were rescued by an English boat.

At 4.30 *Héros* was compelled by *Magnanime* to strike her colours, in seas too brutal for Howe, the victor, to put a prize crew on board. Conflans, returning from safety in the Bay, now came close to Hawke in *Royal George* and its immediate raking fire. *Intrepide*, heroically or ineptly, took part of Hawke's onslaught. The higher quality of British gunnery was winning the fight overall. Hawke directed *Royal George*'s cannon at *Superbe*. Her crew, 630 Bretons, went down without notice or due form at 4.14, all hands lost. Wellington's observation on land, that there was no spectacle save only a battle lost, more melancholy than a battle won, proved quite as true at sea.

'Night was now come', recorded Hawke, 'and being on a part of the coast, among islands and shoals, of which we were totally ignorant, as was the greatest part of the squadron, and blowing hard on a lee shore, I made the decision to anchor.'[8] The battle would shortly resume inside Quiberon Bay. Conflans, hopelessly cut off from the splintered remnant of his fleet, had withdrawn here as the least bad place to be. English ships joined him, in confusion rather than pursuit. Matthew Arnold's venue, 'Where ignorant Armies clash by night', catches well enough the dark bay confining French and English sailors on the night of 20–21 November 1759. *Héros*, earlier surrendering to the English *Magnanime* and then escaping, found itself anchored in the dark, close to its former captor. Such was the ferocity of wind and rain while ships travelled and knocked about like drunkards that, recorded *Resolution*'s log, some men, British sailors and rescued French, went near-mad, ignored all authority and, taking makeshift rafts, leapt into the sea to disappear forever.

The Bay was like a wine flask, with a wide space within and a neck running to the Atlantic, but a flask with islands and a mainland shore. Its most hopeful haven was the harbour of Croisic. As the light came up, two ships made for it, the flagship of Admiral Conflans, *Soleil Royal*, and *Héros*, so lucky so far, but no more. They ran ashore in the dark, wrecking both. Seven French ships of the line had been sunk, taken, wrecked or, like *Soleil Royal*, burnt, after wreck, by her own crew.

It had been a famous victory and a determining one. France had thereafter no naval squadron in the Mediterranean or Atlantic. The Seven Years War was not over, but whose victory it should be had been settled.

18

Deaths and Entrances:
George II and Lord Bute

An ironic consequence of Quiberon Bay coming on top of so many other victories was to restore goodwill among ministers. More precisely, Pitt stopped manipulating differences. He had played up the affair of Joseph Yorke having told Newcastle rather than Holdernesse about *La Dame inconnue* for all it was worth. He had flown it, along with the Garter question, as grounds for his own outraged resignation. Yorke must be excluded from the hopeful talks at The Hague, an Anglo-Prussian initiative which might (but didn't) lead to full peace negotiations. In the new, improved atmosphere, Newcastle was able to tell Yorke that Pitt was now treating the whole business as the 'slightest thing in the World'.[1] Hardwicke's son, fully briefed on the preliminary steps for The Hague, would be accredited to the proposed (non-materialising) congress at Augsburg. Pitt had used Holdernesse and his accidental slight as a ploy; and as a ploy, Holdernesse was being discarded.

Militarily, the year of victories was followed for Britain by the year of wrapping things up, supremely in Canada. As a soldier, Amherst lacked Wolfe's flair and inspiration. But he did, late and slowly, conquer Canada. There was very little French resistance left after Lévis's Parthian riposte. It was a matter of logistics – forcing the St Lawrence and map reading across half a continent. Against reduced resistance, Brigadier Murray, so recently humiliated by the enterprising Lévis, was to travel to Quebec along the St Lawrence, while Amherst, with the main force, would come in from the west from Oswego via Lake Ontario to cut off the French. It was a lot of ground to cover and Amherst was a careful driver. So not until September was he outside Montreal. When its defender, Vaudreuil, suggested a pause for news about peace negotiations in Europe, Amherst uttered flat but resonant words: 'I have come to take Canada and I will take nothing less.'² After which, Vaudreuil, having nothing in prospect but the grinding heroics of an unrelieveable siege, wisely surrendered.

Amherst, detained by an Indian fight, returned home after the champagne had been drunk. He would be disappointed of a triumphal entry, having taken a long time to win that half-continent by sound military administration, and had remained anticlimactically alive. Over later years, his reminiscent manner is said to have bored George III. That was a metropolitan view. Amherst had not got everything right, still less was he dashing. But succeeding Loudon, he had been the British commander successful in North America. Ministers provided what he needed, Pitt made preliminary, theoretical outlines. But decisions in the field were Amherst's, and, personally or through subordinates, through Ticonderoga and Niagara to Montreal over two years, he won. In America itself, he would be better appreciated. Contemptuous of the colonials, at least as soldiers, though good at motivating them, he would still be remembered in those four New England towns taking his name. When the limitations are recited, he had done the work of turning Wolfe's single brilliant stroke into the conquest of Canada.

Oddly, as the ministry began making steps toward a general peace, Pitt was at first quite cavalier about retaining Canada. The image of a procession from certain glory to certain glory with William Pitt at the high point of national exaltation omits a lot of calculation. Quebec, taken and died for in that high and splendid manner, had been looked at very coolly by Pitt days before the triumph was accomplished. A letter from Hardwicke to Newcastle of 31 October, six weeks after death and victory and a fortnight before the news, relays Pitt's moderate, sensible and starkly unsentimental thinking: 'He seemed really desirous of peace this winter and upon reasonable terms; saw the difficulties of carrying on the war in Germany for want of men; was desirous of keeping Senegal and Goree, seemed more indifferent about Guadeloupe, supposed we must have Minorca again, and by his manner of discourse, I should think keeping possession of Niagara, the Lakes, Crown Point and a proper security for our own colonies, the Bay of Fundy etc: was all that he had at present determined; that as to [the] rest, Quebec, Montreal, and even Louisburg [sic], they were points to be treated upon – not to be given up for nothing, but what might deserve consideration and be proper matter of negotiation . . .'[3] Even a year later, Pitt was willing, if Britain kept Guadeloupe and Goree, to retain in Canada, together with the fisheries, only the eastern provinces granted at Utrecht in 1713.

This is not to say that he was wrong. A number of historians and one notable contemporary, Bedford, would argue that the Thirteen Colonies and future United States might have been kept longer under the crown by the discouraging presence of thriving French colonies to the north. Pitt was, simply and rightly, weighing the odds, but such prudential caution with the rhetoric switched off is no part of the devotional image.

At this time, Pitt, like most people, wanted to get out of the war. The problem, as noted, was the fact of it being a conflict in parallels. Crudely, Austria was fighting Prussia for Silesia, Britain was fighting France for an expanding area of colonial and trade domination, primarily North American but now taking in the French Antilles and the West African slave coast. There was also, so remotely, and at such arm's length from ministers as not to have been dwelt on here, the Indian subcontinent, Robert Clive's near autonomous triumph. Beyond which, Britain and Hanover, plus sub-contractors like Hesse, were fighting France to keep her out of Hanover. These wars were not synchronised, and the appeal of an early peace was unequal over all. However between ministers, peace had arrived. Newcastle had saluted Pitt's indispensability as rallier of Parliament (and withholder of trouble). Meanwhile, British troops were now being sent, at Newcastle's call, but with Pitt's whole heart, at first four battalions, then six, for service under Ferdinand of Brunswick.

Pitt had become a strong supporter of the war in Germany and had lately gone public and been joined in this by Beckford. Yet despite transient enthusiasm, the Patriot and Tory constituency had disliked the whole business. A good deal of Pitt's life since the formation of this ministry had been spent looking over his shoulder at the people he had brought into a Commons majority. They needed Ferdinand's victories if they were to tolerate Ferdinand's subsidies and his British troops and commanders, subordinated, however gracefully, to this foreigner in his own foreign country.

Victories do not come because they would be terribly useful. The French effort in Germany could be concentrated. The latest commander,

Condé, was more capable than Richelieu or Clermont. Above all, comprehensive defeat at sea gave the Versailles court every motive to win on its other front and the numbers were good. Meanwhile, Frederick had been utterly preoccupied since Kunersdorf in August 1759. Enemy retreat from Berlin and the King's close-run victory at Torgau, 3 November 1760, would be the landmarks of a defensive war. The battle was drawn out, long and bitter, and, according to uncertain record, drew down on retreating soldiers Frederick's famous remark, in the German he tried to avoid, 'Hunden! Woult ihr ewig leben? [Dogs! Would you live forever?]' Ultimately, a long time later, the crucial triumph, Burkersdorf, 21 July 1762, would finally make Maria Theresia throw in her hand, giving Frederick the accomplished final defence of his expanded state.

However, in the autumn of 1760, the possibility of Prussian defeat raised concern that the defence of Hanover might not yet be fully secure. Requirements of great victories and a crossing of the Rhine were provincial. In such a climate, Ferdinand, by not being defeated and keeping the French occupied, was doing what he was asked and we needed. To do it, he needed money and more troops, British troops.

Hardwicke could see this, arguing that the Brunswicker was taking on the entire land forces of France, keeping them back from Hanover and from effective coalition with Austria against Prussia. 'I don't say with our friend, Mr Pitt that "without a battle I will not be for continuing the measures in Germany" another year; for I remember the great Duke of Alva's maxim that it is the business of a general always to get the better of his enemy but not always to fight; and if he can do his business without fighting, so much the better.'[4] Rationally, Pitt could see it, too, and would agree to the means, but he was watching his back. As Hardwicke noted in the same letter, 'Notwithstanding this, I agree that what Mr Pitt says will be the way of talking of nine parts in ten of the people of England.'[5] An unglamorous holding war went down very badly with a British public opinion for which victory was the recreational drug of choice.

Then again, things kept turning up. The death of the King of Spain, the refreshingly pacific Ferdinand VI, and the succession of Carlo IX of Naples as Carlos III of Spain, very able but not at this point very amenable, whispered 'Bourbon family pact'. King Ferdinand's moderate and English-descended premier, Ricardo Wall, was still on the scene, but the Spanish Ambassador in London, Fuentes, assumed a threatening line deemed to have Carlos's authority. He made claims to fishing grounds off Newfoundland and resurrected the dispute about Honduran logwood which troubled Anglo-Spanish relations much as marriage with a deceased wife's sister would haunt Victorian legislators.

Spain was a subject on which Pitt had, throughout the war, behaved with restraint. He had, as we have seen, back in 1757, proposed swapping the anachronism of Gibraltar for the war base of Minorca, something unacceptable to France. He had recognised the importance of keeping Bourbons apart, had avoided anything to embarrass the Spanish King or General Wall. He would, in the late summer of 1760, apologise for freelance naval excess in the *Guerrero* episode, a British attack on a Spanish ship for protecting a French one. But Spain was a conflict only postponed and the restraint strictly interim.

However, in the midst of debate, ministers were in death, that of King George II early in the morning of 25 October. Events suddenly appeared in a new light, as glaring as uncertain. With George, ministers knew where they were. He was a Hanoverian, as he might have said, *hin und rüch*. He was a soldier with a soldier's prejudices and a flammable temper, but could be talked round. The Old Corps Whigs suited him very well because they saw and understood the Hanoverian case back to the Act of Settlement as an undertaking against absolutism.

Notably more than his father, who, had the Tories shown a measure of sense, might have sought a broad-based ministry, George followed the Whig interpretation of history. Indeed, he was part of it. By contrast, his heir, the twenty-two-year-old George, Prince of Wales, reflected the fixed ideas of his mother the Dowager Princess, Augusta of Saxe-Coburg-Gotha. The personal hatred of George II and of Hanover itself ranked equally. Bubb Dodington six years earlier, 18 August 1754, had noted her 'very solicitous to push the war and wished Hanover at the bottom of the sea as the cause of all our misfortunes'. Her little court was the resort of politicians as out of things as the Princess, but often better placed than her for getting back in.

The new George was also the pupil of his tutor, John Stuart, 3rd Earl of Bute, also out, but steadfastly so. Logically, Bute should have been a sound Old Corps Whig. He was the maternal grandson of the Duke of Argyll who had risen against James II in 1685 and been executed for it. He had, like Pitt, enjoyed a Dutch education after Eton, and had pedantically taken his degree. He was married (happily) into the politically sound Wortley Montagu family. However, in 1747, in his mid-thirties, he struck up a genuine friendship with Prince Frederick, formally joining his court. He remained a man at the Opposition court after Frederick's cricketing death in 1751, winning (and deserving) the trust of his widow.

In the rough, ungentlemanly world of eighteenth-century journalism this could only mean that she must be his mistress. No serious historian has ever believed this, not least because John Stuart, 3rd Earl of Bute, was as uninterestingly chaste as William Pitt. Much more usefully, Augusta made her great friend tutor to her son, whose great (and deferred-to) friend he quickly became. That relationship was dear and intense in none of the ways glibly leapt at today. It rested upon gratitude in young George, awe at Bute's not negligible learning, also upon a shared elevation of principle beyond wisdom. Tutor and pupil were well suited. This was the relationship of an elder and a younger inept politician.

Bute was intellectually very competent, but dull, theoretical and pedantic. George, who did not learn to read until he was eleven, made up for his slowness by a mighty dedication. He was one of the very few people who would have been impressed by Bute for brilliance. However, unlike so many Princes of Wales, this young man was painfully, oppressively, steady. And, in fairness, Bute had worked hard assembling a political outlook, getting at much of Blackstone's Commentaries in manuscript. An impressive coup this; they were published in 1765! Bute's teaching, as seen in his letters, asserts a neutral/pacific foreign policy (ironically anticipating John Bright), an end to corruption and to party politics, beautiful and impossible things.

What got him into a private inferno stoked by Whig historians was an assertion, lifted from Bolingbroke, about a greater role over policy and patronage for the King. This was the cornerstone of the Whig theory of 'The Constitution in Peril' which has provided historians from Macaulay to Sir Lewis Namier to Jonathan Clark and Frank O'Gorman with fascinating dispute. In the present narrative of events and people, suffice to say that on paper, the Bute/George III domestic view was superficially in line with things which William Pitt (though bored by patronage) had often said, and in contradiction only of his view that the chief role in policy should be played by William Pitt.

For Pitt, the ascent of Bute, so close to the heir, had been a continuing anxiety which came and went across his main career and would always be waiting for him when the peppery old major general died. Bute was not a brilliant man but he was consistent. He had read his *Patriot King* and had taken Bolingbroke's high-toned rationalisation of his own exotic duplicity seriously. But Bute took most things seriously. During the negotiations setting up the brief Pitt–Devonshire Ministry, he had come with Temple on an expedition to Devonshire evidently to demonstrate Leicester House support for Pitt. Temple, writing to his brother-in-law, noted the ardour of his remarks to the duke, 'expressions so transparently obliging to us and so decisive of the determined purposes of Leicester House towards us in the present or any future day, that your lively imagination cannot suggest to a wish beyond them'.[6] An effusive declaration on behalf of something or somebody was natural in Bute. Perhaps the Leiden degree had left him better educated than most British politicians limited to Cicero. That had certainly been true of Carteret, upon whose career a wide and deep European culture conferred no help at all. Bute, despite effusions, was, in his innocent way, an idealist. His ideal would be embodied in a hero, and Pitt was a professional hero. It was a relationship doomed to enlightenment.

Pitt had dropped Prince Frederick in the best opportunistic manner when the future was a long way off and Henry Pelham lifting up a flap of the ministerial tent. But when Frederick died in 1751, Pitt, in Marie Peters's phrase, 'bewailed "the greatest Patriot Prince we ever had"'. Henry Fox observed, 'He is a better speaker than I am, but Thank God, I have better judgement.'[7] Alternatively, Pitt's judgement advised him to keep in with the people he had dropped in case he needed them again. He and Bute had stayed in occasional touch during Pitt's exile in office, Bute sending congratulations in May 1756 for heroics on the Militia Bill and addressing him as 'My worthy friend', which Rosebery thought patronising.[8] But that was simply Bute's way – stiff informality. Rosebery also thinks that 'the bond between Pitt and the young Court was now close'.[9] So it was – for the time being.

Pitt's communications to the confidant of the heir speak for themselves. On 10 October 1756 he tells Bute that 'Lady Hester is safely delivered of a boy [John, 2nd Earl and rather cack-handed general] who I think will live to be one day, an Englishman, and to bless, together with millions yet unborn, the happy influences of the princely virtues Ld Bute cultivates so successfully . . . the goodness that interests itself for the cottage of Hayes will pardon this gossip's note.'[10]

The correspondence ran through to 11 August 1758, Pitt's last non-routine letter September 1758, ninety-one letters in all, reliably florid and overblown, but also conveying information about Cabinet and the course of the war. They cooled sharply as Pitt adjusted to involvement in Germany. There was then a small but terminal tiff over the second St Malo raid and an insistent request by Bute for the promotion of Clerk, chief adviser on the coastal raids. Pitt snubbed it, provoking Prince George to write to Bute that 'He treats you and me with no more regard than he would do a parcel of Children', adding ominously, 'he seems to forget that the day will come, when he must expect to be treated according to his deserts.'[11]

However, on 25 October 1760, the Secretary of State perhaps experienced serious regret at the passing of the Elector of Hanover. George III in his first speech from the throne would soon interpolate into Hardwicke's draft of cool continuity an instant, living cliché: 'I glory in the name of Briton.' It came from the earnest heart, worked wonderfully as cheap publicity and should have worried every politician who heard it. Both Georges had grumbled about their squabbling native politicians and had been happiest with people like Walpole and Pelham who, with due, non-meddling regard for Hanoverian concerns, ran the British territory, fixed Parliament and held the front line. When Pelham died in 1754, George II had spoken of having 'no more peace'. George III would give Pitt, Newcastle, George Granville and an apostolic line of prime ministers very little of it. And Pitt had already attracted displeasure in the Prince of Wales.

At the end of April 1760, in George II's lifetime, Bute, working through another Scottish politician, Gilbert Elliot, had attempted to parley with the Secretary about his own future role. It was not something Pitt could be seen doing and a good example of what happened when an honest man tries to be shifty. Pitt rejected all thought of the scheme. To George this was 'the late instance in the transaction of Mr P perhaps the strongest that ever happened to a man of your strong sensations; he has shown himself the most ungrateful and in my mind most dishonourable of men, I can never bear to see him in any future ministry'.[12]

On 5 October, twenty days before his accession, the twenty-two-year-old Prince wrote to his tutor of the contemplated naval expedition to Belleisle, 'I myself imagine 'tis intended sooner or later for Germany if that should be the case I hope this nation will open her eyes and see who are her true friends and that her popular man is a true snake in the grass.'[13] The judgement of events here is on a par with the non-existent punctuation. However, it demonstrates that George was of his mother's mind, not just hating the German connection, but seeing it everywhere.

Ironically, the rhetoric with which Pitt had gathered together his political militia of Tories, Grenville Patriots and the British particularists of the City had come back to bite him. But George's maternal prejudices threatened the rationale on which Pitt and Newcastle were agreed. Even if the naval dominance, also a shared objective of ministers, had prevented a French army from invading Britain, the point made in Israel Maudit's widely circulating pamphlet, *Considerations on the Present German War*, resonated. Maudit argued that the French might still beat Ferdinand and take Hanover, in which case how many of Quebec, Madras, Bengal and the French Antilles would have to be exchanged for it, never mind the intended recovery of Minorca? And if the next, and self-willed, king did not give a rap for Hanover . . . ?

The isolationist part of Bolingbroke's and Bute's thinking was up and in business – ironically haunting the Pitt who had once talked this sort of thing. Pitt made great play of large notions of French ambition. That would recur and with more reason during the ministry of, ironically, the Younger Pitt, with the first revolutionary victories of 1792, when a British–Continental alliance, involving most German states, would preoccupy all the later ministers of King George III. But France had lost our part of her war. Our gains had been such as to get us and Hanover very good settlements. In broad terms it now made sense to make peace. But the terms were narrow and niggling so that making it became tediously difficult.

This was, though, the business of a reshuffled ministry. Bute did not spring instantly into formal first place; he hardly needed to. A privy counsellor since two days after the accession, he now dominated the Cabinet, though Newcastle remained at the Treasury. Over the next six months, his standing would be spelt out, his wife, like Pitt's, ennobled in her own right in the English list. Count Viry, who might well have been a minister himself so active had the Sardinian been, suggested that to bring Bute into office as the new King clearly wished, they might best remove Holdernesse from the Northern Secretaryship. This would regularise the King's and Bute's thirteenth-century double act of Monarch and Favourite. It made an honest Secretary of State of Bute. 'Favourite', however, was what everyone, led by the irrepressible John Wilkes, continued to call him. Holdernesse had had a bad time from almost everyone: bypassed by Newcastle, used by Pitt as a blunt instrument against Yorke, over *La Dame inconnue*, then abruptly dropped. He may have been relieved to be handsomely paid off and let go.

Bedford gave up Ireland to Halifax. But as the most pacific leading Whig, who had absented himself from Cabinet after a particular rant of Pitt's about the need to intensify the war, he was attractive to King and Bute. Attending ever more ministerial meetings, and in due short course Privy Seal, he was never meaningfully out. Legge, Pitt's man in the past and lingering as Chancellor despite those non-selling subscriptions, but no longer favoured, also went. He was replaced by a surprised Barrington, a professional public employee, holding office of some sort across thirty years. He was a good, conscientious administrator and honest with it. George III would value him, Newcastle rated him highly. However, Junius (probably Philip Francis, though scholarship rages), future author of some of the most ferocious vilipends in the language, would tell his printer 'Having nothing better to do, I propose to entertain myself and the public with torturing that bloody wretch, Barrington.'[14]

During much of this time, Pitt had been ill. The crippling and torturing gout had returned. Bute did not use the absence to make moves against him. Pitt's popularity, unlike his precise achievement, is not in dispute. He was backed by the City, certainly the outer, newer, rougher City, by the noisiest newspapers and the Street. Combative radicals like Potter and Wilkes, now at the threshold of his tumultuous day, were for him. The House of Commons, exposed to the intense penetrating personality and high-flying rhetoric, stood in awe. George, a very young King, and Bute, a theoretician within the Closet, were afraid of him. They wanted peace. Pitt, as we have seen, had talked peace, wide and reasonable concession, not sure that he would insist on all Canada. The trouble was that Pitt didn't do consistency.

The shape of a peace could be agreed round a table. The terms would be strong – we had won, if not the war then quite enough of it – but not overreaching. North American possession must revert to the terms of Utrecht, the strategic line as it had stood until Colonel Washington's unfortunate defeat. Minorca must, of course, come back, French troops be withdrawn from Germany. Quebec, Montreal and Louisbourg, antebellum French territories, were matters for discussion, 'not be given up for nothing', Pitt's words after Wolfe's victory, but not clutched too tightly. Pitt was still talking such give-and-take rationality with Hardwicke in mid-March 1761.[15]

One has to be clear that politics, and short-term politics at that, were the métier, the point and purpose of William Pitt. And, like all such people, he was hyper-alert to anything threatening his power. Very little that George III or Bute wanted was in itself unacceptable. But *they* wanted it and they, in getting it, would seem to usurp his position. Real politics, politician's politics, is nearly always about jealousy – both sorts, envy and fearful possession.

Devonshire records being told by Viry, as early as the day of the late King's funeral, 'that Pitt repented of having put himself too submissively into Lord Bute's hands, thinking there was not a proper return made, and probably jealous of the Duke of Newcastle'.[16] If this were so, his mood would have followed the acknowledgement of George and Bute that the duke should have the management of election signalled by the new reign. As Newcastle had been arranging elections at the right hand of Sir Robert Walpole, and was very good at it, as also Bute and the King had no coherent ideas of how to do it themselves, this should not have troubled Pitt in any way. But, as again, Viry related 'that they, meaning Lord Temple and family (always excluding Pitt), had been insinuating (and somebody had, even to the King), that by promising the Duke of Newcastle to choose the Parliament, they had thrown the king and this country absolutely into his [Newcastle's] hand'.[17]

This sort of thing was unimportant in itself, merely an illustration of ministerial squabbling, soon to play its part in ministerial discussions about conflict with Spain. Early in 1761, February and March, Pitt had been seriously ill, badly deprived of sleep, but negotiations were on foot. Hans Stanley, who had the goodwill of both Pitt and Newcastle, had been sent to Paris with powers at the end of April and had preliminary conversations with the Duc de Choiseul (dominant minister since December 1758), though the serious business would not start until November.

In the way of a quick and clear-cut settlement stood Spain. There existed side by side, in a too-desperate France and the activist views of King Carlos, a readiness to revive the family compact of Bourbon and Borbón, about which the British had been worrying since William III. There was also the ability of Pitt to see in this an exact image of the general threat seventy years earlier when Louis XIV had been so much the greatest monarch in Europe that two successive Popes had formed alliances with Calvinists and Anglicans to resist him. It wasn't like that in the 1760s.

Choiseul was indeed keen to revive the compact, but he did so in dark desperation after global losses. An able man, he nevertheless tended to reckless measures and had been behind plans for the amphibious landings so perfectly designed for annihilation. As for Pitt in French eyes, Choiseul saw him as 'a man who wished to push British conquest to the four quarters of the earth'. Choiseul was trying to mitigate defeat.

For Carlos reviving the pact was a response to having observed from Naples the long humiliation which English naval supremacy, contemptuously used, had inflicted upon Spanish trade and interests. Choiseul, conscious of the mistake made by France in overcommitment of arms and men to Austrian interests on the European continent, had, in March 1759, begun scaling this down. French numbers diverted to Bavaria, the Rhineland and Hanover were troops which might have been earlier quietly established in Canada, the Antilles or, indeed, India. Montcalm in Canada had led 3000 men to victory at Ticonderoga against 15,000 British and settlers. But as the contemporary English historian of eighteenth-century France, Colin Jones, says, it 'was asking too much to expect a string of victories'.[18] Pitt had been temperate in Cabinet about Spain and had seen no need to rush into anything, but his mood would change across 1761.

Anyway a shrewd idea that Spain might come in influenced the thinking of all ministers. The question was whether a revival of the compact might be averted and issues settled entirely by diplomacy. But

Pitt was now furiously for war, continuous, pre-emptive and yet further conquering war. Behind this shift lay other issues. Above all, domestically, there was Bute. He had come into government, was a fellow Secretary of State, exceptionally well placed with the King and very keen to achieve a peace. Then again, success of arms as it continued to take place touched Pitt in the most vulnerable place, his ambition.

However, the point at which Anglo-Spanish relations would break down was logwood*, bad cause but splendid pretext. The history of British logging on the coast of present-day Honduras and Nicaragua is buried in the remote illegalities of the seventeenth century. Logwood itself was wanted in the wool trade for dyeing. We had the wool and, rather than buy the dye-logs, we simply took them, something of a national habit. Richard Pares, defining historian of everything indicated in the title of his great study, *War and Trade in the West Indies*, sets matters out. 'The English seem to have come to the trade from buccaneering: first they plundered the logwood ships, then they seized upon the piles of it which lay ready near the creeks. Finally, they settled down to cut it for themselves, especially after the serious attempts of the English Government to suppress buccaneering forced them to change their career.'[19]

There was a long history of Spanish ejection and English return; and a sort of let was extracted from Spain in a treaty of 1670, reasserted at Utrecht in 1713. This was done at a time when the British claimed squatters' rights. Having been ejected from the main site, Campeachy, the authority of 'indulgence' which had applied there had been broached. Anyway, the intruders, now operating from another site a hundred miles away, outside even its province, Yucatan, were seen by Spain as breakers of its reasonable doctrine that no cutting and taking on its sovereign territory was legal without her express authority.[20]

Meanwhile, for reasons remote and near, Spain and the prospect of war with Spain grew. General Wall's moderation had, as it were, moderated, not at all out of a wish for war but because he did not trust Pitt. Spain had been monstrously bullied during the war, given the British navy's short way with anyone trading with the enemy. Pitt had long and vivid form as a voluble hater of Spain, who as counsel in Parliament for merchants cheating on the *Asiento* had demanded war and revenge against her. As Pares puts it, 'He had never been a

* Almost any wood may be cut into logs, but 'logwood' is specifically the product of *Haematoxylon campechianum*.

friend of Spain: from his first days in Parliament to his last, he was too easily fired by patriotic rant against the whole House of Bourbon. He kept this feeling in check, in order to avoid provoking what he called "a half-enlightened, irritable but too necessary Court".'[21] What Wall now saw, and Fuentes with him, was a separate peace struck with France to make way for a nation-to-nation war with Spain alone. In fact, says Pares, Pitt had seen what Newcastle had never believed, that Britain was strong enough to defeat both Spain *and* France. Not that Newcastle, with war finance to worry about and not anyway caring for such visions, wanted any such thing.

The Spanish ministers noted that, when privateering came up in general terms, Pitt could manage conciliatory language. But over logwood, in the isthmus, he refused any answer at all. So the issue had to be spelt out through the French at the conference. Wall would acknowledge 'in some shape or other' a British right to trade in logwood held by however dubious a title for over a century, but observed that the military backup, British forts and settlements acknowledged as illegal, had not been dismantled. They now should be. (The British, on the strength of Utrecht, 1713, had demanded, unsuccessfully, the demolition of forts *in France* – at Dunquerque.)

Pitt responded at the top of his loud-hailing form. It was all 'enormity and extreme offensiveness'. Put through France, it looked like 'a declaration of war in reversion . . . held out *in terrorem* on behalf of Spain'.[22] Hans Stanley, whose own patient diplomacy now stood in the balance, would tell Choiseul that such bullfrog talk was *fait pour la négociation*.[23] It is best seen as an attempt by Pitt to start another war. Unsurprisingly, it was the point at which the Bourbon family compact was formally re-established, coupled with a commitment that, failing a peace accomplished by 1 May 1762, Spain would declare war on Britain.

The alliance and war to which France and Spain would resort, out of Choiseul's desperation and Carlos's accumulated affront, was one to be fought over remote colonies which English naval supremacy must win. It was one Pitt wanted for reasons of aggrandisement. Later, when he had left office and the spoils of the war were bartered for, he would violently denounce the swapping of Havana for Florida. In his view that trade-off 'was no equivalent'. For, as he marvelled, 'from the moment the Havannah [*sic*] was taken, all the Spanish treasures and riches in America lay at our mercy . . .'[24]

This is a frightening speech. But one should allow alternative inter-
pretations. Was it essential evidence of Pitt's large purposes, making
the attitude of Spain and France in coming together entirely understandable? 'Treasures and riches . . . at our mercy' is certainly thinking
which, if suspected, makes for defence pacts between the parties threatened. Do his words lament an opportunity lost to wage aggressive
war and continue indefinitely a steady course of national conquest?
Is it a constant, if only intermittently displayed, thread in his discourse,
something like the jarring bell of a later century?

Or is it better to see this as Pitt trapped in his own habitual bombast?
Did he only want the Spanish war for cool purposes of gaining diplomatic edge at a delayed peace conference? He wasn't an insatiable
monster reliably and cool-headedly seeking open-ended domination.
But from time to time he talked like that, and he did so now. The
tendency to get a little drunk on thinking big and talking bigger was
certainly flashing bright when, in September 1761, Newcastle, relaying
Cabinet business to Hardwicke, described Pitt taking the opportunity
'to expatiate upon his great schemes and the almost certainty of the
success against the united force of the House of Bourbon', (and) 'how
there was not an hour to be lost'.[25]

It was not a cast of mind which this Cabinet shared. In December
1760, Bute had told Bedford, who had just accepted the Privy Seal,
that his own 'remaining at Court depended upon the behaviour of
two persons and two persons only. The Dukes of Bedford and
Devonshire. They had advised him to accept the Treasury under the
young King: If they would support him with spirit, he would remain
there, but not as a cipher in the closet.'[26] Bedford, 'his bright little
grace', as Chesterfield with easy condescension called him, could
almost be described as anti-war. He had seen very little merit in the
conflict and gave solid reasons as far back as 1759. That Year of Victories
had delivered. What really was the value of battling on expensively
for terms which would enrage France and bring her back to war?

Almost alone, Bedford had foreseen one essential risk. 'I don't know
whether the neighbourhood of the French to our North American
colonies was not the greatest security for their dependence on the
mother country, which will be slighted by them when their apprehension of the French is removed.'[27] He disliked Bute's role as promoted
favourite, but shared his instinct for conciliation and would thus, when

the time came, be happy to serve as principal negotiator. Devonshire, like his elder friend, Newcastle, had always thought the war necessary, but rejected open-ended yearning for more. Mansfield had wobbled in the face of Pitt's harangue, but would not be of his party.

The opposed ministers, Newcastle, the new Chancellor, George Grenville, Anson, Mansfield, Devonshire himself and, vitally, Bute, would now meet at Devonshire House 'to consider what was to be done to justify our dissent from Mr Pitt'.[28] They decided against drawing up a formal document, but agreed that they should call upon the young King and tell him. 'The King was much satisfied with them, pressed much to know whether I thought Lord Temple et cetera would go out. I told him they were much out of humour but it was impossible to say what they would do: that they had meant to force us into the measure but as we had continued firm, they must either yield or retire. Lord Temple had said to someone that Mr Pitt could not stay but that was no reason for him as he did not hold the pen.'[29]

For Pitt it was not quite the end. Rather, it was a choice: acceptance of a defeat within the Cabinet or making an end of his increasingly fraught dominion. He found ending things more acceptable. Not the King nor Bute nor the gathering ministers required Pitt to go, but he went.

19

Pitt Leaves: Victories Continue

The moderate men in government, like the King, wanted no further war. Members of the Cabinet had given him their reasons for resisting the pre-emptive action Pitt furiously advocated and they had been very welcome. In such circumstances, a baulked politician 'considers his position'. Most people were, in greater or less degree, afraid of the Southern Secretary. They were afraid, too, of his friends in Parliament, the City press and the Street.

However, as Marie Peters points out, public opinion was complex. Ironically, the arguments against continuing the German war and its subsidies, like those in Israel Maudit's influential pamphlet, cut both ways. For the war *as a whole* was costing too much money. Supplies voted by the Commons, standing at four million in 1754–5, had risen by 1761 to 19.5 million. Borrowing, at two million in 1756, was now £12 million. The National Debt had been doubled from £72 million in 1755 to £150 million in 1762.[1] A City address from Pitt's allies might talk of forcing France to 'a prescribed peace', or, as we might say, a dictated peace. But the serious financial world was prudently pacific, finding money tight and looking for a peace treaty to ease it.

Pitt would have been wise to stay in office; only Temple had backed him in the Cabinet Council dispute. The French and Spanish would have been as wise to keep talking. If they had pulled back from the threat floating above their ministers' memoranda, the peace could still be a relatively moderate one, with Florida never taken and so not swapped for a Havana, not taken either and perhaps less territory lost in North America. If those two countries were fool enough to fight on, they would lose. The French naval remnant, reinforced by Spanish ships, would see the British navy sink as many as it needed to add more succulent colonies to the collection. The case for Pitt swallowing his resentment over rejection of his call for war is subtler. The full glory was ready to fall into his hands, as he must have known. Accepting peace gave less but it would all be his to claim. If the peaceful faction in London were compelled to war, they would win without him.

Perhaps, as some argued, the Secretary was tired. He had a right to be: Pitt had done passionate intensity through two succeeding ministries and had been impressively strenuous. Again, he had been ill in the early months of 1761; perhaps that may have influenced his withdrawal. All this is possible cause, but Pitt was not accustomed to being voted down by colleagues. They had gone away, held a practical meeting, submitted their opinions and the reasons for them, delighted George III and nerved Bute to negate the proposal. It was a new and dismaying experience. Temple, who would leave at the same time, made off for his Buckinghamshire citadel. From there, in a sort of low dudgeon, he wrote on 29 December 1761 to his friend, John Wilkes: 'I can weep over this minion-minded country as well at Stowe as in Pall Mall.'² Wilkes himself, a pleasure to come for the new ministry, had made his first strong speech in Parliament on 13 November in defence of Pitt.

In Council the former Minister made a statement about having been 'called . . . by his Sovereign and he might say by the voice of the People to assist the State, when others had *abdicated* the service of it; . . . that it was called *his war*; that it had been a successful one, and more than hinted that the success was singly owing to him that the case was otherwise now; he saw what little credit he had in the Council from an union of opinion of some of the greatest persons in this Kingdom; . . . and that in his station and situation he was responsible and would not continue without having the direction; that this being his case, nobody could be surprised that he could go on no longer, and he would repeat it again that he would be responsible for nothing but what he directed.'³

For O.A. Sherrard, Pitt loyalist, writing in the early 1950s, 'It was a dignified and touching speech of farewell . . .'⁴ It was nothing of the sort. No one wishing to keep his dignity in retreat 'more than hints that the success was singly due to him'. No one with any judgement at all boasts that 'it was called his war'. There had been no 'abdication' at the start. Pitt had initially refused to work with Newcastle's people, and his chief power in the Commons was one of threatened disruption. For all the ardent despatches to commanders, it had *not* been his personal war. Nothing had been done without collective ministerial discussion and support. There was, too, the small matter of every commander in the field between five hundred and three thousand miles away taking the immediate and essential decisions. Ministers had felt uneasy about the French coastal raids, his one area of personal direction. Against their better judgement, they had acceded to his wishes – and had been proved right. This speech was Pitt very near his intermittent worst, resentful, grandstanding and graceless.

When the Secretary left office, he was offered first of all an earldom with the non-resident Governor Generalship of Canada at £5000 a year or the Chancellorship of the Duchy of Lancaster. Such largesse, remarked Bute, indicated that Canada would never be given up. When these were declined, Pitt, invited to make his own claim, suggested instead a barony (of Chatham) for his wife, Hester. The money he accepted in more modest form, a three-generation transferable pension of £3000 a year. Ironically for liberal posterity, it was to be drawn on the West Indian funds.

Now there is no dispute among even the coolest commentators that Pitt deserved a high-value reward, though Stanley Ayling's observation that he 'had earned his golden handshake ten times over' is going it. Samuel Johnson on £300 a year for the Dictionary thought his new income 'princely'. Certainly the parliamentary inspirer, rallier of the public and keen engager in war planning, as far as war could be planned, deserved reward. Which didn't make taking it anything but perfect folly. The offer came from Bute who did not intend Pitt any good. Pitt, in return for honour George having shown 'to those dearer than myself, comprehended in that monument of royal approbation and goodness which his majesty shall condescend to distinguish me',[5] gave thanks in terms of Chinese self-humiliation.

Accepting was, for the short term at least, a disastrous mistake. 'Politicians: they're all in it for themselves' is a sullen motif familiar to party workers on a million doorsteps. But all his life Pitt had been given to washing his clean linen in public. What Sir Robert might do with cheerfully impunity, Mr Pitt was denied in the too-white teeth of his own recurring utterance. Sensitive people, like Thomas Gray in Cambridge, a simple, scholarly fan in the past, were desolated. 'Oh that foolishness of a great man that sold his inestimable diamond for a paltry peerage and pension.' Gray's friend Horace Walpole wrote a disobliging little verse: 'Admire his eloquence – It mounted higher / Than Attic purity or Roman fire / Adore his services – our lions view ranging / where Roman eagles never flew; / Copy his soul supreme o'er Lucre's sphere / – But oh! beware Three Thousand Pounds a year.' Lord George Sackville, the epaulettes restored, was amazed at Temple's gallant solidarity in resigning too. He asked him why he should give up office, 'Mr Pitt's having made so great a bargain for himself and family'.[6]

Unpopularity flared up for Pitt in modest but embarrassing places beyond Horace's Strawberry Hill. The burgesses of 'our ancient and loyal corporation', wrote Lord Temple to Wilkes, when invited to drink Pitt's health, 'literally refused'.[7] This was worrying. Pitt was supposed to be the supremely popular war leader and his partisans wanted laudatory addresses from as many borough corporations as possible. The City, of course, went wonderfully over the top and set what should have been the key of celebration: 'If Virtue was a borough, Mr Pitt is re-chosen for it.'[8] Pitt published a letter of self-justification. It won a little response in the country, six congratulating boroughs – Exeter, Chester, York and Stirling by mid-November, then Cork and Norwich – with Leicester and King's Lynn refusing.[9] Six boroughs, three of them Tory, signing up was modest national rapture.

It wasn't fair but it was the price which Pitt, the great public personality of a government which had just acquired an empire, paid for twenty-six years' proclamation of his shining-bright difference from fallen men. Pitt the hero had been badly bruised, not by Pitt the pensioner but by Pitt the windbag. When the time came a few months later for Newcastle to be rewarded after a part-pushed, part-jumping departure, the duke discarded his customary indecision and flatly refused anything. Pitt was, indeed, as he kept saying, entirely clean. So was Newcastle, but the duke had never gone on about it. There may also have been a wish to enjoy his *Schadenfreude*. Though, ironically, Newcastle would leave in connection with the withdrawal of the Prussian subsidy over which he and Pitt were now at one. Pitt's popularity would be reasserted. There would be life after the peace treaty, and other people could be orated at, but taking money and matrimonial ermine was not just rotten politics but obvious rotten politics.

Meanwhile, Pitt going out was naturally part of Bute digging in. Essentially for a major minister, he now became one of the representative

Scottish peers able to sit in the Upper House. The ministry, amended after Pitt's departure on 5 October 1761, would feature the decisive personality of Pitt's alternative brother-in-law. The trouble with George Grenville was that he was no longer a Grenville.* The ablest of his aggrandising family, and quite as ruthless as the best of them, he was capable, numerate, hardworking. Though not, in his irritated, unsilken way, a major player in debate, he had been expecting more in the way of advancement than he had received.

He was tired of being Treasurer of the Navy for the third time, where during this naval war his administrator's gifts had been thoroughly useful.† What he wanted was the Exchequer for which, unusually at this date, he was actually qualified. It didn't come. Pitt, who had backed him during the 1757 negotiations, did not put himself out, and the omission was noted. Next, and oddly for a man agreed by everyone from George III to Henry Fox as talking too much, Grenville had coveted the Speakership when in 1760, after thirty-three years in the chair, the almost ancestral Arthur Onslow finally retired. Again Pitt fell short and still he lacked advancement.

Apart from naked (and shivering) ambition, Grenville had perfectly good policy objections to Pitt's conduct of affairs. Unlike his disobliging relation, he could count. The war was intolerably expensive and an extension of it, war against France and Spain, whatever the gambler's prospects, struck George, the chartered accountant, as too much. Though on the other hand, when Bedford went to Paris on Bute's business, too much would be let go for Grenville's hard-bargaining instincts. He had anyway been drawing closer to Leicester House. A good personal tie had already been made with Bute, the confidant, good to have ready with Bute, the First Minister.

That link was strong enough for Bute, when the great defiance of Pitt occurred, to have encouraged Grenville to decamp to Wootton, twenty miles from the family encampment at Stowe, to avoid the contagion of solidarity when jumping ship. Actually, the link was even

---

* Quite apart from his desertion from the family, he was caught between names. People who should have known better, including George III, insisted on calling him 'Greenville'.

† He had also brought in legislation to try to have seamen's wages paid regularly, a piece of conscious fairness in a hard-faced age.

stronger, nearer mild conspiracy. Grenville on 3 October had received from Bute an instruction 'to come to town as private as you can by yourself and . . . lose no time', also details of the Cabinet meeting of 2 October!'[10] He had been the second man within the family connection, a valued talent, not an incubus voting the right way. To Pitt and Temple, the whole thing was betrayal. To Grenville it was advancement. However, he delicately declined Pitt's own post as Southern Secretary. Instead, he nominated the new man, Egremont.

A war with Spain was still very likely. If Pitt's purpose had remained as level and realistic as his language in Cabinet, he could and would have treated the logwood question as one for discussion and graceful compromise. His dealings with the Spaniards at the end of 1760 had left Fuentes and Wall bitterly convinced that silence meant continued refusal. Pares is convinced of Wall's good faith, 'for a long time a real well-wisher of England [who] would have liked to make it the glory of his ministry that he had established a solid friendship with her'. 'This explains very well the warmth with which he resented the outrages of the English privateers and Pitt's flat silence about Honduras.'[11] Hardwicke, who so often seems the wisest mind in Westminster, had never believed in the reasonable Pitt. 'He sees that in order to obtain peace, so much of our acquisitions must be given up; and the populace, who have been blown to such an extravagant degree, and of whom he is unwilling to quit his hold, will be so much disappointed that he is ready to start* at the approaches to it.'[12]

Indeed, his insistent silence on a subject so bitterly touching Spanish self-respect looks like something done to raise the temperature in Madrid. A Pitt sincerely wanting the very good terms there to be taken, to meet a general wish for peace and make an end to ferocious expenditure, could have taken them and enjoyed general high credit. But at this point we are dealing with the overreaching Pitt, the man who would so soon be pronouncing in Parliament that 'from the moment the Havannah [sic] was taken, all the Spanish treasures and riches in America lay at our mercy . . .' (see supra, Chapter 18).[13] Pitt had played his cards extraordinarily badly: the yearning for open-ended conquest and eternal conflict with France – plus Spain – had put him out of office. He was self-condemned to watch his opponents conclude

---

* As a nervous horse starts.

the conflict on a scale which, under Pitt's seal, would have been saluted as a glory exclusively his.

The first irony now was that the peace party which had tried to avoid a war with Spain would have to fight it. The second irony was that they would win. Having 'the sole direction' which Pitt regularly demanded had very little relevance. Exactly like Pitt, the Bute Ministry listened to the relevant commanders. Where Spain was concerned, this meant Anson and the Admiralty who promptly advised 'a considerable reinforcement' of Saunders at Gibraltar.

With Egremont (like Grenville, inclined to seek hard terms) installed in the Southern Secretaryship, and the pacific Bedford on board, Bute had a mixed team for foreign affairs. He and the Cabinet were ready to treat on the logwood issue but they demanded prior assurances of pacific Spanish intentions. Closing on terms with Spain would have required a clearer commitment to finding agreement. A year earlier, as Pares deftly puts it, 'There was a race between the exhaustion of France and the rising anger of the Court of Spain.'[14] The Spanish had been largely driven to taking a high line by Pitt's silent British version of Hidalgo pride and cold hostility. Choiseul thought that, allied to Spain, France might win what she could not win alone. The Spanish were to understand that sitting out the war would likely mean no support against England later. This secured them to the suicidal purposes of Choiseul, for whom this latest throw ignored the last few years of naval evidence. The new King of Spain and his fired-up ministers missed the chance of not fighting Anson's navy. Which in its autonomous, highly competent way, went on winning naval encounters.

Meanwhile, Bute was afraid of seeming weak or unpatriotic. Pitt was now his enemy, and Pitt had the great resource of a name and a press. The irrational Street fury following Minorca was readily remembered. Newcastle, not generally associated with cutting irony, wrote coolly of his new colleagues, 'They breath [sic] war as much as Mr Pitt did: but from this principle, for fear of Mr Pitt's popularity, which *they* would endeavour to gain but will never obtain it.'[15] Amid such twin fogs in London and Madrid, a war at once against Spain, France's interests and the new British Cabinet's instincts, was stumbled into. Britain's Ambassador in Madrid, Lord Bristol, was told he might pack and leave.

Consequently, and as it turned out irrelevantly, an army must be prepared for Portugal, now threatened with invasion if it did not close its markets to Britain. This was the sort of thing a Minister had to watch for, Portugal being a British cadet, the business very good on both sides and Lisbon almost as much of a British base as Gibraltar. George Townshend, Wolfe's despised auxiliary, now worked directly with Ligonier as the designated commander, but they were scrambling for the numbers needed. Portugal was going to cost serious money and Newcastle, who had to raise it, had financial worries enough, hadn't been told in advance of the planning meeting. He was understandably irked and his own falling out advanced.

Bute had done nothing for ministerial cohesion when, at the Cabinet Council meeting, he mooted withdrawl of our troops from Germany. The proposal had much to do with the pressures of manning that additional expedition to Portugal, but there was also Leicester House prejudice, Dowager's thinking. It came at an unsuitable time. Ferdinand, now in partnership with the amiable and popular Granby, had been keeping the French busy enough with the defensive tactics dictated by chronically inferior numbers. But in July 1761 he had pulled off a sudden and brilliant victory over Broglie at Vellinghausen, near Dortmund.

It was all the more impressive for having been won when outnumbered two to one. Broglie's casualties against those of the Allies stood at 12 to 1.[16] Yet at the same time, Frederick was in the deepest trouble, Prussian armies having crumbled to a total of 69,000 men. Pitt, for all his politically directed hostility to the German connection, so recently and now seemingly so long ago, and despite the dust blown up by Maudit's pamphlet of November 1760, knew the value of both German theatres. And anyway, a *Kamaradschaft* existed between the Chevalier Pitt and Our Heroic Ally. Indeed, Pitt was blossoming into a positive zealot for the Prussian interest. But now, as Ferdinand had earlier noted to Frederick, of the new men in London, 'The British Ministry, are, with some exceptions, absolutely anti-continental.'[17]

Bute now talked of stopping the subsidy to Prussia. On top of which the appointment to Portugal of Schaumberg-Lippe was rather ominous for the Germans and a measure of Bute's extensive blind side. It was also a step too far for Newcastle, the unrelenting supporter of involvement in the German theatre. He stood by Old Corps doctrine. Britain had, to its immense constitutional benefit, a king from Hanover. His obligations there had to be respected and underwritten. Frederick, all humbug about a Protestant champion apart, was fighting this war as an essential ally. His defeat would release troops and have the psychological impact for which the age had no term but fully understood. The duke resigned as First Lord on 26 May 1762, replaced on the 27th by Bute, who also took the Garter.

Pre-emption against Spain importantly apart, no military priority divided Pitt from Newcastle. It was plain politics which mattered. With Bute as master, Pitt's judgement of continental war ceased to be military/strategic. The wish to drop Frederick, coming as it did from Bute, welded him deeper into the Prussian cause. By contrast, at this stage Newcastle had been thinking primarily as a Finance Minister, First Lord of the Treasury in working practice. Anxiety at the additional costs of a pre-emptive strike against Spain had influenced him against it. Leaving Frederick in the lurch was something else. It might be wonderfully opportune for Austria and, at one remove, sufficiently so for France and continuation of war. So ending the Prussian subsidy threatened a longer war more expensive yet. As it turned out, the succession of Frederick's crazed admirer, Grand Duke Peter, on the death of the devotedly anti-Frederickan Elizabeth, would save day and bacon for the King of Prussia. But this left Bute even more disposed to cut a subsidy he thought no longer needed.

Meanwhile, the war with Spain had been formally declared on 2 January 1762. A Cabinet Council of 6 January heard and was persuaded by Anson's proposal as to how we should invade Havana. It involved an initial expedition, four thousand troops, under Albermarle, sailing for Martinique. That was unfinished business from Pitt's time, and a hopefully successful Brigadier Monckton would join them there. The future naval hero, George Rodney, was told, if he hadn't already taken it, to stop besieging Martinique and prepare to join the main force to invest Havana. The French initiative at this time, which the French naval commander, Blénac, was told to take up, was an attack on Jamaica, the prize, a hundred years before, of Cromwell's navy.

What followed was a series of mutually cancelling mistakes by both sides. Blénac, sent to relieve Martinique, was delayed and found it taken, having fallen in February. The two French squadrons sent to Jamaica, having left separately from Brest and Rochefort, arrived well apart. The covering British force might thus have taken them on separately with every prospect of beating the pair. Its commander, Forrest, understood this but doing it was forbidden. So was his wish to join up with Rodney, bringing reinforcements, because the 'block-headed cowardice of Governor and council baulked him'.[18] (They wanted the squadron looking after them in Kingston Harbour.) Blénac, unchallenged, made it to St Domingue, settling down in the harbour at Cap François. But by now, Pocock, commander at the Leeward Islands, was besieging Havana.

However, urgent messages to Blénac and the Governor of St Domingue to mount a rescue seem to have received a response recalling Governor Fowke and Admiral Byng. So Havana fell to Pocock at the cost of a third of the Spanish navy, and Lord Albemarle at once imposed illegal duties upon the English merchants hurrying to flood the market with a new crop of slaves. Later, so late that peace had been settled at Paris, Colonel William Draper, having come from the East Indies and been picked up by nobody, would capture Manila. The inept invasion of Portugal having come to nothing, the Seven Years War was over, ready for quiet despatch of business, otherwise a peace conference.

The war being done, that would proceed with more despatch than the lingering eighteenth-century norm. The Peace of Paris (scripted at Fontainebleau) would be Bedford's Peace, and, famously, the Duke of Bedford detested war. But though dissent in the Cabinet over specifics would lead to a reshuffle, the avid City expectation that it would be a weak peace looking like a surrender didn't materialise. In October George Grenville, never happy with Bedford's concessions, would drag his feet over releasing Martinique, Cuba and St Lucia. Specifically, even before news of taking Havana reached London and Paris, he was demanding heavy compensation for its return.

Actual victory was announced in time to thoroughly embarrass Bute and underline his vulnerability. Grenville and Egremont, having thoughts of succeeding, stressed their credentials with the Opposition with a show of intransigence.[19] When Grenville demanded that the terms be laid before Parliament, he meant to expose Bute to hoped-for patriotic outrage, perhaps led by Pitt outside but with Grenville and Egremont active opponents of concession in their respective houses. The vanity of human wishes being exactly that, Egremont would soon be dead. Grenville, his dangerous impatience signalled to

George and Bute, could only be demoted. He would not be down long, but for the moment he was replaced by Halifax, shifted to a lesser post and kept quiet. Meanwhile, another move replaced him as Commons Leader with a brisk Henry Fox, who would push the preliminaries through with his usual amoral brio.

The preliminary terms, made without Germany, came up for signature in London on 3 November (full formal signing followed in Paris on 10 February 1763). They amounted to a rather sensible peace. The German conflict was nearly over, but the terms between Prussia and Austria would come a little later – in a hunting lodge at Hubertusburg in Saxony on 15 February 1763. Meanwhile, France evacuated every inch of territory held in and about Hanover. Bute had cut the Prussian subsidy, but he had come too late to slight Hanover.

Canada would now be British, down to and including Cape Breton Island and the forts and harbour settlements, so long besieged and defended. But the French retained some fishing access, and, deprived of those harbours, were allowed the little Newfoundland islands of St Pierre and Miquelon as bases and drying stations. Spanish Havana was swapped early in expectation of being taken, for French Florida, only fair since France had got Spain into all this. Guadeloupe (taken March 1759) and Martinique, the brand-new prize of February 1762, were returned. However, French and Spanish territory east of the Mississippi went to Britain, as did the huge Indian subcontinental gains of Robert Clive, plus Dominica, Tobago, Grenada and St Vincent, also Senegal, with only its neighbouring little slave island of Goree going back to France. Minorca, source of so much domestic grief and vital to the Mediterranean war which hadn't taken place, was always going to be replaced. It was duly swapped for Belle Île: all this and the internationally established right to cut logwood! The treaty was, of course, denounced.

For that matter, it was still being denounced by imperially minded historians nearly 150 years later. Sir Julian Corbett in the second volume of his *England in the Seven Years War* says: 'That we were in a position to exact still harder terms than we did is certain. Pitt would have done so and was minded, by crushing the French navy, body and soul, to put it out of her power ever to retaliate . . .' 'Sadly', he adds, 'many wise heads thought it impolitic; better, they thought, to be easy and rest content with a situation which would be endurable to a chivalrous enemy. To this end, we sacrificed much and to no purpose.'*

There were, too, foreigners denouncing the peace negotiations. Frederick, still short of terms not yet offered, had been left at Paris with his strategic places apparently open for Austrian options. Later defended as a paper muddle, it would in fact come to nothing. He wrote a volcanic letter to his Ambassador in London, Knyphausen. It told him to suborn the press with vivid copy about the evils done to England by the Butes of the Gothic and Renaissance centuries, the Gavestons and Buckinghams, and to call up parliamentary petitions from British cities against the Peace. The object should be to destroy Bute, so talk about his head being in danger for treason would not be out of order.[20]

It was not the first intervention by Frederick. In July, Knyphausen had been told 'to lose no opportunity that might occur in secretly inciting and embittering the nation against Bute and his administration, and to cast upon him the odium of any regrettable incidents . . . you will even incite as far as possible the authors of the current pamphlets to decry the conduct of this minister, so as to come constantly nearer to hurling him from his place'.[21]

As to the response of the British Parliament, Horace Walpole, usually, given his crotchets, a source to handle carefully, has given us a neat summary of the Lords debate of 9 December 1762 on the Peace preliminaries:

> Lord Shelburne and Lord Grosvenor rose to approve them. The Duke of Grafton, with great weight and greater warmth, attacked them severely, and looking full on Lord Bute, imputed to him corruption and worse arts. The Duke was answered by the Earl of Suffolk; and then Lord Temple spoke with less than usual warmth. The Favourite [Bute] rose next and defended himself with applause, having left aside much of his former pomp. He treated the Duke of Grafton as a juvenile member [he was twenty-seven], whose imputations he despised;

---

* The present writer's text for Sir Julian's work is the second edition of 1918, not very long before the future parties to the Treaty of Versailles assembled under, ironically, French leadership, to crush the body and soul of the German army and put it out of her power ever to retaliate.

and, for the Peace, he desired to have written on his tomb, 'Here lies the Earl of Bute, who in concert with the King's ministers, made the Peace'. A sentence often re-echoed with the ridicule it deserved and more likely to be engraven on his monument with ignominy than approbation . . . At ten at night the preliminaries were approved by the Lords without a division.[22]

In the Commons, Pitt spoke dramatically against the Preliminaries. He came there as he had before and would again, wrapped in flannel and distress. Pitt was ever and again a genuinely sick man tormented by a virulent affliction recurring through his life from the age of fourteen (see *supra*, Chapter 2). He was also a man of the theatre. This is rather confirmed by the innocent enthusiasm of Sir Julian Corbett: '. . . suffering agonies from the gout, unable to stand, at times hardly able to speak, he denounced it for three hours and a half'.[23]
Walpole again:

Mr Pitt, borne in the arms of his servants, who setting him down within the bar, he crawled by the help of a crutch and with the help of some friends to his seat; not without the sneers of some of Fox's party . . . the moment was so well-timed, the importance of the man and his services, the languor of his emaciated countenance, and the study bestowed on his dress, were circumstances that struck solemnity into a patriot mind, and did a little, furnish ridicule to the hardened and insensible. He was dressed in black velvet, his legs and thighs wrapped in flannel, his feet covered with buskins of black cloth and his hands with gloves . . . having the appearance of a man determined to die in that cause and that hour.[24]

Pitt never trusted subtlety; but the style of this oration demanded alexandrines, and the arguments made no sense. His preoccupation with stripping out the last vestiges of French fishing rights off North America was astonishingly off-key. An unimpressed Edmund Burke, who had praised Pitt highly in the *Annual Register* on his retirement, found it 'very tedious, unconvincing, heavy and immethodical' (*sic*). It jarred with an accumulation of very good things. Bedford's treasonable peace had, after all, left Britain the master of North America (with Havana now swapped for Florida), garlanded with sugar islands and slave stations, and France effectively finished in India. The speech was, in fact, the thinking of rage. One unacknowledged factor was that the war, now concluded, had gone on quite as brilliantly after Pitt's departure. The North American terms, which Pitt played down in order to be outraged about Martinique and Guadeloupe, were better than those he had been willing to accept and fitted his own historic position that North America was the chief object of the war.[25]

There was another dimension to high emotions in favour of a continuing war. Those parts of the City, also the Liverpool interest, engaged in the slave trade had been angry at Bedford's anticipated return of Guadeloupe. In October, Sir William Meredith presented a petition for retaining Guadeloupe in the candid interest of the slave trade. In the context of such manoeuvres, one ministerial supporter, Edward Richardson, referred to 'an incorporated set of city sharpers'.[26]

Yet the former Minister must also have realised the consequences had he followed his own pragmatic language to colleagues of a year earlier. A less sweepingly triumphant peace than Bedford's would have been concluded but it would still have been a triumph; and it would have been his! As it was, a mob stood near the doors of Parliament and a major campaign of Street hatred for Bute was well underway. This would find expression in a journal which became history in a better cause by way of being prosecuted. For into the course of events there suddenly leapt up, like a rather companionable Demon King, the extraordinary John Wilkes.

20

'That Devil Wilkes'

Wilkes is wonderfully different, another irregular peg whom history has had trouble fitting in. Liberals and Marxists have warmed to him as trouble for the authorities. Imperial and patriotic historians recognise an enemy of Pitt's enemies, the King and Bute, but 'An Essay on Woman' often shocks them the way it shocked Pitt. Above all, he is a kind of annexe to the Whig Theory of History. To the school which saw George and Bute as encroaching upon sacred liberties, Wilkes is a sort of off-White Knight directing his irregular weaponry against all the forces threatening upper-case Freedom. Macaulay was sensible about him 'as having until lately been known chiefly as one of the most profane, licentious, and agreeable rakes about town'.[1] Indeed, for historians retaining a sense of humour, Wilkes has been like Arnold Bennett's Denry Machin, The Card, devoted to the great cause of cheering us all up.

All of this has its charm, but what is not often stressed is the role of Wilkes as simple factionalist. His ties were all in Buckinghamshire, High Sheriff, Member for Aylesbury, improbable Colonel in the Bucks Militia. Much of that was owing to the genuine friendship of Richard Grenville, Earl Temple. Though to enter Parliament, at Aylesbury, the Grenville writ not running in the county town, Wilkes paid his own way, £7000 of it. Thomas Potter, son of the Archbishop of Canterbury,* was another Grenville connection and someone whom Pitt liked, despite a character altogether more sexually farouche than Wilkes's. Potter had urged a letter to Pitt in summer 1757 after the election. Wilkes was told, 'if you intend to make one of the friends of so inaccessible a minister, you will go further and by letter signify to him

* John Potter, Archbishop, 1737–47.

your election and disposition to enter into his connection'.[2] By writing at rather greater length he would make the government furious and his name very nigh immortal.

The *North Briton* is a unicorn among famous publications, but is at once legend and historical fact. Everyone has heard of it. Legal and constitutional historians descant on the legal and constitutional consequences of its suppression. These included arrest of author and printer through a general warrant given on the authority of the Treasury Solicitor, Philip Carteret Webb, and the subsequent declaration by Charles Pratt, Chief Justice of Common Pleas, that General Warrants were illegal. What seems hardly ever to appear is detailed quotation of what its authors* actually wrote and why the King, Lord Bute and P.C. Webb were so upset about it.

Beginning just before midsummer 1762, they aimed fusillades at the negotiations for ending the Peace of Paris and made steady war upon Bute and his Commons spokesman, George Grenville. Bute, conscious of a circle of enemies, had pre-emptively sought an advocate in the press. Tobias Smollett, author of *Roderick Random*, *Peregrine Pickle* and *Humphrey Clinker*, was a major and a very enjoyable novelist. He was also a Scot and something of a literary entrepreneur, employing writers on an industrial scale in producing everything from a translation of *Don Quixote* to the *Briton*, a flattish, unremarkable tribute to the broad wisdom of the Earl of Bute altogether lacking the mantrap bite of Smollett's own undisputed writing.

It was to be answered by Wilkes and Churchill in the *North Briton*.[3] The first issue, of 5 June 1762, attacks the Stuart enemies of 'the liberty of the press'. In the time of that dynasty, 'the Imprimatur of the Minister was scarcely ever given but to compositions equally disgraceful to letters and humanity. I do not however recollect that any of these hirelings ever ventured as the *Briton* of last Saturday has done, magnificently to display the <u>royal arms</u> at the head . . .'

Wilkes moves quickly on to royal usurpation, the Whig view, once widely accepted, of the Constitution in Danger, and, specifically, Bute as near treasonable subverter of that constitution. 'All opposition therefore to him [Smollett/the *Briton*] . . . is to be considered as an indignity

---

* Wilkes collaborated with Charles Churchill, another self-destructive libertine (and Anglican clergyman).

opposed to the administration and an affront to the higher powers who may be supposed to protect, perhaps to pay him. This is surely too stale a trick to pass . . .'

'[The *Briton*] affirms <u>the administration is conducted with such integrity as defies reproach . . . with such vigour and success, as one would think, might silence the most inveterate malice</u>. Name what <u>success</u>, the time when? The place where . . . ?' Actually the new ministry's successes, Martinique, Havana, Manilla, were coming down the line, but nothing deflects a determined press campaign.

In all this, the *North Briton* is playing Pitt's tune and comparing his record with that of his successor: '. . . as to vigour, the spirit of the war has for some months infamously languished, nor is it yet revived . . .' News of Martinique in March/April not having arrived, he is still able to contrast '. . . the glorious conquests of the late administration, to which no addition has been made'.

This is all knockabout, long familiar if less elegantly phrased, in the *Monitor*, which itself receives a friendly wave. And nobody in Bute's circle would take the trouble of reacting. But Bute is the target, getting him the purpose of the paper. Already the crime of Scottishness is floated. With the second issue, Wilkes is throwing oatmeal.

'I cannot conceal the joy I feel as a <u>North Briton</u>, and I heartily congratulate my dear countrymen on our having at length accomplished the great, long-fought and universal national object of all our wishes, the planting a Scotsman at the head of the <u>English</u> Treasury.' In praising two Scots, Gilbert Elliot and James Oswald, for their recent political advancement, the *North Briton* was not being unfair, Oswald, as mentioned, having entered Parliament in 1742 as a supporter of Walpole, only to change sides within days. Indeed, Oswald had been in office for all but four years since then.

We also get a view of the broadly improved, if wary, relations between Pitt and Newcastle, in agreement about the Prussian subsidy and eyeing their options for return. Politics in Opposition superseding policy, Newcastle even went through an exercise of Opposition to a peace treaty very close to his own long-term judgement. Elliot and Oswald are commiserated with for being 'obliged to serve under a noble Duke of a peculiar cast, whose views were most evidently neither to enrich himself nor to aggrandise us'. The *North Briton* is happiest proclaiming in the Scots a certain cash-careerism and salutes their undertaxation. He celebrates 'this wide-extended but glorious war', when 'nearly the sum of 20 millions will this year be raised on the subject though I thank heaven not a fortieth part of it will be paid by us'.

He rejoices cruelly at Bute's Garter and expects 'that now we have a <u>Scottish</u> nobleman at the Head of the Treasury, his Lordship will consider it the truest oeconomy to give some proper pensions to his countrymen, the Highland Chiefs which may save England the severe and expensive operation of quelling another insurrection . . .' If such pensions should be issued to the Clan Chiefs, 'I make no doubt they will as implicitly follow the Earl of Bute as they did the Earl of MAR'.*

The steady semi-genial Scotto-phobia continues in Number 3 of 19 June where the *North Briton* proclaims that he is 'like the *High & Mighty* GERMAN PRINCES ready to let out my pen and conscience to the best bidder. Some of my countrymen, with much bitterness, call me a *true scot.*' So, with a joshing stroke at his countrymen, 'sent out, like the Goths & the Vandals of old, to fill the civil and military posts in other nations . . .' it continues across eight months, until mid-March. It is freehanded, abusive, inviting the skean-dhu or broken bottle of Scottish displeasure, irking the Minister no doubt with an excess of long-since-lost English swagger, but not striking to the ministerial quick.

There were, though, eruptions and episodes in the paper's career. A courtier, Lord Talbot, Steward to the Royal Household, called Wilkes out, and Wilkes (who would later caress Samuel Johnson into a warm regard and friendly remarks about 'Jack Wilkes') charmed the pistols out of his hands. Political opinion looked on, Devonshire cheerfully defining the *North Briton* as 'the life and soul of the Opposition'.[4] Pitt, offended at the man and embarrassed by the ribaldry, was cold. When, in Number 25, Wilkes came out blazing for Pitt's war policy, Temple shifts from 'the daily abominations of the paper war' (*North Briton* included) to 'cannot sufficiently admire . . . unanswerable'.[5]

Wilkes was ceremonially polite to the King but obliquely kept up that legend of his mother's unlikely sexual thrall to Bute. It would all culminate when the preliminary articles of peace rolled smoothly over a Commons motion and Pitt's speech against them. Whatever

* Leader of the 1715 rising.

the noise on the street, in the *North Briton* or *Monitor*, Parliament was very easy about the Peace of Paris. Not only did Pitt's speech misfire but neither numbers nor indignation were there. Approval survived assault in the key division of 9–10 December with embarrassingly little opposition.

Varying his subject matter but not the essential target, in the spring of 1763, Wilkes chances his arm in Number 42 with charges of financial jobbery. 'The terms of the new subscription have been so injurious to the public, but so beneficent to the subscribers – that is the creatures of the Minister – that there was immediately an advance of seven per cent and in a very few days of eleven per cent. I shall however only state that at the even round sum of ten *per cent* I may not puzzle the Chancellor of the Exchequer. The whole loan amounted to 3,500,000l. Consequently in the period of a few days, the minister gave among his creatures and the tools of power 350,000l which was levied from the public.'

Excess feeds upon excess as he mouths at parasitic Scots benefitting 'under the *Scotsman*, a set of hungry voracious rapacious dependants have with the certainty of a peace and the sum of £3 1/2 million only to be raised, made above 11% from/the public funds'. And he addresses the King: 'Gracious and Best of princes, knowest thou this?'

Whatever the Gracious and Best of Princes knew was neither here nor there. The *North Briton* did obsequiousness to George to offset its constant image of the treasonable Scotsman and patron of thieving Scots who was George's 'Dearest Friend'. In March/April of 1763, abuse of Bute becomes pointless. The earl who, better than most politicians, has a claim to be considered a misunderstood man, has had enough. The *North Briton* has played its part. So has the *Monitor*. The Jackboot, punning corruption of his name and purported emblem of freeborn Englishmen supposedly writhing beneath it, exists in four hundred separate prints along with sketches of Princess Augusta's petticoat. In *North Briton* 5, Bute and the Princess have been compared to Roger Mortimer and Queen Isabella, celebrity royal adulterers of the 1320s.

This blaze of abuse, actionable today as libel, not to mention racial incitement, flourished in a rough-handed age. The *North Briton* was a campaign of political guerrilla war and attrition, and it had distinct

effects. At the High Sherriff's assize dinner in Guildford in the summer
of 1762, involving '120 of the first gentlemen', toasts were drunk
without problems to the sitting member, George Onslow* and to
Newcastle. Then the health of Bute was proposed, '. . . upon which
the whole company at once got up and would not drink it; there were
not two or three at most that drank it. This broke up the company.'[6]
By an almost theatrical irony, the toast had been proposed by the
Treasury Solicitor, Philip Carteret Webb, shortly to take centre stage.
There were physical manifestations, too. In November 1762 Bute had
been hissed and pelted on his way to the opening of Parliament. There
was even talk, to which Bute responded, of the Minister standing in
danger of assassination.

Against this, on 10 February 1763, the Peace of Paris had been
formally ratified and again, in the Lords, Bute had put up an effective
case for a piece of government business. He had won what mattered.
But the treaty taken care of, the urgent need for revenue produced
the Cider Tax or, rather and worse, Cider Excise. It was fiscal legislation perfectly designed for the talents of Wilkes, with all Opposition
men gathered behind him. The Chancellor at this time was Sir Francis
Dashwood, convenor some years before (in the company of Wilkes)
of the Monks of Medmenham, but in his brief political career, given
a harder time than such fun suggests. Dashwood was never in as much
trouble over girls and champagne as he would be over cider and perry
in the budget of 1763.

The tax was a delightful opportunity for Wilkes, coming as it did
just when his great issue, the Peace, had been lost. For the *North Briton*
Number 43, 'this odious & partial tax [which] is likewise to be enforced
in the most <u>odious</u> & <u>partial</u> manner possible by an extension of the
laws of <u>excise</u>. The very word is hateful to an <u>English</u> ear . . .' For all
the invective, on 10 April the budget passed as budgets do, and again
Bute had put up an effective case for a piece of government business
in the Lords. It may, however, have been unwise for the royal assent
to have been granted on 1 April. But Wilkes's assault was only the
most colourful objection to the Cider Tax. Opposition was general
and furious. Dashwood, at the receiving end, lacked the nerve for a
fight. Withdrawal would be a humiliation. Bute had intended to go

* Son of the former Speaker.

out at a high point and had alluded to Henri IV of France's great Minister, the Duc de Sully.[7] Dashwood's resignation and that of Henry Fox gave occasion and impetus, and eight days later he was gone.

In the view of Professor Schweizer he was 'physically ill, weary of politics and politicians, and unnerved by the savage attacks against him'.[8] Bute was a decent, intelligent man who had helped make a sensible statesmanlike peace. Unfortunately he was an outsider in politics and there is a tendency for the trade to gang up on outsiders and for them to lack the brazen durability of the professionals. For Lord Shelburne, chronicler within doors of this period, 'He was insolent and cowardly . . . he was rash and timid . . . he was ready to abandon his nearest friend if attacked.'[9] But Shelburne was one of those professionals. Bute would also for a long time be established in history/legend, in so far as they may be distinguished, as the Enemy of English Liberty. Wilkes, for all his endearing qualities, had established a long-running historical libel.

The appointment made public on 6 April 1763, of Bute's successor, George Grenville, gave the King no pleasure. Already, as Secretary of State, he had dragged his feet over the peace treaty which Bute and the King wanted. Grenville anticipated Gladstone rather than Disraeli in his treatment of the monarch: long, improving lectures. 'A dose so large and so nauseous often repeated was too much for anyone's stomach', said Henry Fox.[10] On top of all this, Grenville's competence, actually extensive, had been undermined by an encounter with Pitt a few weeks earlier in the Commons.

This took place in the March budget debate where the Cider Tax was introduced. An exasperated Grenville, facing a balance sheet that Pitt never deigned to read or understood, asked critics of the new impost where else he was supposed to raise the money. 'Where?' he said. 'Tell me where?' Pitt, famous for sarcasm but normally remote from humour, recalled a popular tune and began to sing lightly, perhaps to croon, 'Where, gentle Shepherd? Tell me where?' Nothing is so deadly in politics as an epithet which sticks. Grenville became risibly the 'Gentle Shepherd'. Pitt made his point more personal and venomous by leaving the House after making a deep bow to Grenville.

So, for the *North Briton* Number 43, of 26 March, Bute is replaced in the shy by George Grenville, whose ministry will shortly begin – on the wrong foot. It is Grenville whom, in the matter of the brand-new, affront-giving Cider Tax, Wilkes, without drawing breath, abuses even more virulently, though the budget went through. The rational case for it could be made and Grenville stubbornly made it. The war having been as expensive as feared, the Treasury had been compelled to look around for revenue. Walpole's sacred four shillings in the pound limit on the Land Tax was altogether too sacred to be raised, especially in a time of general want and hard rural times – the last fully acknowledged hunger riots (as opposed to those against prices) would take place three years later, in 1766.

The objection to Excise now, exactly as to Walpole's disastrous Tobacco Excise of 1733, went beyond simply being a tax which either mulcted producers or raised prices to consumers. What ignited the orators was the element of law being enforced outside the courts and in an un-English, peremptory style. For Wilkes it was hot-buttered toast and a choice of jam. When he had stopped orating and underlining about 'the birthright of an Englishman & the sacred palladium of liberty', he got to the very sharp point that the decision over an excise 'is not by a Jury . . . but of one or two justices or commissioners who may have private selfish views, and from whom there is generally no repeal . . .' The threat would soon enough materialise, he argued, that 'an insolent exciseman under the influence, perhaps by the order, of an insolent *minister* may force his way into the house of any private gentleman or freeholder who has been guilty of voting contrary to a municipal mandate'.

This wasn't hyperbole. Notoriously, excisemen in ports like Harwich* were signed up as pre-conditional voters for the ministry. Voting would remain public, open to landlord or employer retribution clean through the Reform Act when ballot proposals were dropped as dangerous, radical and unmanly until the Ballot Act of 1872. Men so much on call knew their duty, and the harassing of people voting the wrong way might fall within it. Excise, however helpful to a needy Treasury, was also a coercive political weapon. What Wilkes was saying found support on many hands and offered Pitt an excellent pretext for attacking the government in general and George Grenville, the renegade brother-in-law, in particular. As an issue, the Cider Tax pulled together Wilkes and the radicals, Pitt and his circle who overlapped

---

* See the author's *The Great Man*, pp. 326–8.

a little with them, and solid, well-informed rural opinion which found a coherent, expert voice in William Dowdeswell.

But the separate history of the *North Briton* and its provoking editor would in the next but one issue, Number 45 (23 April), finally explode. The paper, having made all its points several times over and given reverberant offence in exalted places, had done what it set out to do. Bute had left office. The *North Briton* had done as much as anyone to make his life unpleasant. It had been the focus of the campaign. But plans to wrap up had been postponed by the King's Speech of 19 April, eight days after Bute's resignation. The speech had congratulated ministers on the Peace about to be sealed; it also alluded comfortably to the Cider Excise. Wilkes was delightedly outraged. We had just seen 'the most abandoned instance of ministerial effrontery ever attempted to be imposed on mankind . . .' After a little more of this, he touched, as he supposed delicately, on George III.

He observed that 'every friend of his country must lament that a prince of so many great and amiable qualities whom England truly reveres, can be bought to give the sanction of his sacred name to the most odious measures & to the unjustifiable public declarations from a throne ever renowned for truth, honour, and an unsullied virtue'. As for Bute, there was a friendly reference to 'the foul dregs of his power, the tools of corruption & despotism . . .' Then he crossed the last line: 'a despotic minister will always endeavour to dazzle his prince with high-flown ideas of the prerogative power of the crown . . . I lament to see it sink even to prostitution. The King of England is only the chief magistrate of this country . . .' There followed a few sound precepts about the King's share in the executive power and the proper choice of his ministers.

It was by implication the full radical theory of royal and ministerial usurpation of ancient liberties. In the succinct judgement of George III's eminent biographer, Sir John Brooke, 'Grenville was accused of putting a lie into the King's speech and Bute of bribing the House of Commons to ratify the peace treaty.'[11] Ministers moved fast; Webb, as Treasury Solicitor, sought the best legal opinion, former Lord Chancellor Hardwicke. It favoured full action. The paper was seized; Wilkes, faster yet, turned up at six at the print shop, was admitted by officers, tore up the original text of 45 and spirited 46 away. He then went home, invited officers in and engaged in a friendly discussion of the question of General Warrants.

The immediate response of Grenville and his advisers had been to slap down the man who had plagued them and mocked the King. The stumbling majesty of the law would come thumping down on publication (seized) and author (arrested). A ministerial crisis and a newspaper scandal were taking place together and within hailing distance of a heavily contentious piece of revenue legislation. It was enough to cheer up any politician out of office. In due and distinctly elaborate course, Wilkes would be arrested, put gratifyingly in the Tower, be visited by leading Whigs and become a partner in the thriving slogan 'Wilkes and Liberty'.

However, the means which had been employed, a General Warrant, was something else. The arrest of the printer and invasion of the premises had involved this legally dubious device. On top of which, Wilkes was the duly elected Member for the Borough of Aylesbury. Privilege could be invoked and general warrants challenged. They were, with Pitt downstage, yet again wrapped in flannel, hobbling on crutches and in full throat. Making the case, he conceded that he had himself twice employed General Warrants. But that had been in wartime and so did not count. Newcastle observed mildly to Devonshire that 'Temple and Pratt are (I fancy) a little mistaken, when they call this warrant illegal and unprecedented. If I remember, I have signed many in the same form and words.'[12] This, of course, is the glory of Wilkes. The inspirational troublemaker had challenged something which, like Monsieur Jourdain speaking prose, ministers had been doing all their lives.

Nothing will be understood about the motivation of this immortal conflict over a good principle, to which Pitt usefully committed himself, without understanding that it was all about politics. It was right and good and it was useful. Pitt was positioning himself to come back. Relations with Newcastle were on a much easier base though Hardwicke disliked and distrusted him as much as ever. This was not only because his own advice had been involved and his son, Charles Yorke, had, as Attorney-General, made the distinction between parliamentary privilege in general terms and privilege over libel. Winning the good fight of barring General Warrants would fall to another political lawyer, Charles Pratt, Chief Justice of Common Pleas and Pitt's friend since school. On privilege, Pratt delivered a historic judgement: 'The person of a Member ought to be sacred; even if he should commit a misdemeanour, unless it is absolutely necessary to prevent further mischief. We are therefore of opinion that Mr Wilkes is entitled to the privilege of Parliament and therefore he must be discharged.'

Pitt and his faction and Newcastle and his were in the happy position of doing the legal, social and moral right thing and, in the process, doing down George Grenville. To make the party go properly, the Street and loyal (and menacing) addresses to Parliament all joined in. George Onslow, who had reported the rejected toast to Bute, described 'the many thousands' that escorted Wilkes home to his house, folk 'of a far higher rank than the common Mob'.[13]

Grenville, who had bored George III to distraction, would later, in February 1764, stand up in Parliament and defend it all against a histrionic Pitt. The case would take an elaborate and enjoyable course as the government had got hold of 'An Essay on Woman', Wilkes's (or Potter's) cheerfully abandoned sexual epistle of twenty years earlier – 'A few good fucks and then we die'. Rolled up with the charges of libelling the King, the ministry would have him re-expelled then outlawed, and provoke rather frightening riots. The Commons actually debated Number 45 and by 273 votes to 111, ordered it publicly burned by the hangman. At which ceremony, a mob of five hundred people pelted the presiding sheriffs, smashed their glass coach and rescued a text, clearly not for burning.[14] Pitt denounced General Warrants, but had turned upon Wilkes with a burst of high-flown sanctimony. To cite the Reverend Francis Thackeray, his most eulogistic biographer (1827), the former Minister thought that Wilkes 'did not deserve to be ranked among the human species – he was the blasphemer of his God and the libeller of his King'.[15] The judgement says more about Pitt than Wilkes. For he also twice denied the well-known friendly connection between the two men. Wilkes's biographer, Raymond Postgate, quotes a letter: 'Be assured that I shall always be extremely glad to promote your desires – (always meaning your virtuous ones) – and believe me with great truth and regard, dear Sir, your humble obedient servant.'[16]

The same morally affronted politician could find among his anathemas a shrewd handle against his renegade brother-in-law. Stanley Ayling, not normally a blind admirer of Pitt, says kindly that for him 'this issue became an issue of high principle'.[17] For Pitt, all principles were high, and all opportunities useful. By contrast, Temple, in his free and easy way, swung back and forth between a tutting sort of half-reproof and sheer admiration for Wilkes's cheek. Pitt was accused of manoeuvring to please Bute and make a deal with him. About motivation, Postgate is less complicated. 'Wilkes was clearly for the moment on the losing side, and inopportune loyalty to broken subordinates or allies was never one of Pitt's virtues. Wilkes was now an incumbrance and that was reason enough for rejecting him.'[18]

This was a period in which Pitt hovered. He was out, but not in full-time Opposition; the possibility of his return was canvassed. He could choose the issue on which to make the big speech, he could play for the younger and uncertain men of new connections like the followers of Lord Rockingham, but he would be no great prop to governments struggling for stability. The recurring ground of Pitt's rhetoric from his fall to his death was factionalism. He was against it. So was George III. It was an easy shot since no one dared proclaim the usefulness of factions. But the reality was that well-managed factions working together represented the best government the country was likely to get. Equally, George Grenville, however tedious at the Palace, was the most capable First Minister to hand. So, to a degree, Pitt would combine stands on specific issues which were creditable though rarely fully coherent, with a negative and destructive game.

However, the shift in the King's outlook was a force quite strong enough to make another Pitt Ministry serious politics. Given consistent health and better judgement, a *successful* Pitt Ministry might have come about. Immediately, in August 1763, the summons seemed to have come. Grenville had alienated the King not by policy or inadequacy. He had not just lectured George but, worse, because irrationally in a rational man, he saw the hand of Bute everywhere when that nobleman was securely shelved beyond realistic recall. This anxiety led to challenging the major royal say in ministerial appointments generally accepted at this time. Between First Lord and monarch there quickly developed a high-class demarcation dispute. George wanted to recall Pitt, provoking thoughts of Log and Stork.

However, when Egremont, who had taken Pitt's Secretaryship, suddenly died, a neat hole in the exact same place provided an opportunity. The prospectus offered by the former Minister was for a rejig of the 1757 coalition. Something not very clearly defined was to be done to offset the Peace of Paris and he would seek a Prussian alliance. The Pitt–Newcastle team *was* a faction, one about which George and Bute had written each other deprecating letters. The Peace had been negotiated, made, signed and ratified on all hands. The King of Prussia, taken up now, would have represented a dangerous adventure if the King of Prussia had wanted an alliance, which he did not.

It was worse than that. Pitt, though he could readily roll himself up into a ball of humility, had always had a taste for the absolute. On this occasion, 27 August 1763, he demanded as Secretaries of State Charles Townshend, endless trouble to come, and himself, Newcastle as Lord Privy Seal, young Lord Rockingham at the Admiralty and a number of other stipulated places. Meanwhile, there was for the King's consideration a list of 'Don'ts', notably, but not only, Mansfield, Bedford and Fox. It was a clean-out, a purge and a pre-emptive purge at that.

The support available was a measure of Pitt's standing in the eyes of Whigs. Devonshire, who had never liked him, had said that the party generally stood ready to accept him as head of government and to lighten his burden by excusing regular attendance in the Commons. Pitt's conduct demonstrated the extent to which the trading and accommodating politician he had often been was in retreat before the rigid triumphalist and factionalist. The War Cabinet had been as good as it generally was because of the accommodation and easiness which, despite occasional spats, it demonstrated. Pitt, who had been wanted as the adornment of something like the Bute/Grenville team, was laying down a full nomination at the threshold of the closet. He was behaving like Grenville but in a style more vivid and absolute. For George it was perhaps a case of 'Better keep a hold on nurse/For fear of finding something worse'. For, ironically, when a troubled George consulted Bute, the sinister Scottish conspirator of Grenville's imagination advised a return to George Grenville.

Pitt still cut a huge figure and he could find occasions to warrant the image. In fact, though not in general understanding, he was becoming unfit for ministerial office. He could not serve or share, and, as leader, demanded everything. His mind still lingered over the Peace, the reversal of which he had worked into his whole psyche. War retained its charm, and his mind strayed to new continental alliances, with Prussia and Russia to the fore. As he spoke with sonorous force on the liberal side in respect of constitutional issues at home, he dreamed adventure and new conflict abroad.

The proposal was at once wild and backward-looking, and this ministry dissolved in the royal closet before any faction could lay a glove on it. Grenville came back, continued to handle the finances well and the King badly. The Wilkes affair had created long, disturbing trouble, with the City, the Street and the courts all chipping in. Its major offshoot, General Warrants, would, in February, give Pitt another opportunity to expound at length. The action which mattered came, however, very properly in the courts on 6 December 1763, when a private prosecution of Wood, the under-secretary who had invoked them, was successful and Wood himself fined £1000.

The legality of General Warrants had been given its quietus by Pratt in the same action with some splendour. 'This warrant is uncon-stitutional, illegal and absolutely void: it is a general warrant, directed to four messengers to take up any persons without naming or describing them with any certainty and to bring them together with their papers . . . There is no authority in our law books but in express terms condemns them . . . If . . . higher jurisdictions should declare my opinion erroneous, I submit as it will become me, and kiss the rod; but I must say, I shall always consider it as a rod of iron for the chastisement of the people of Great Britain.'

In August 1763, however, with the King willing his return to office on mutually reassuring terms, Pitt had missed one chance by over-reaching himself. He would miss another in May 1765. Finally, in 1766, to the subsequent regret of his admirers, he would take the invita-tion up. Distrust of the King and a whole scenario about Bute would, in 1765, lead by an elaborate turn to Grenville's most self-injurious mistake, made in response to the King's worst error of this period. At this time, conspiracy nestled in every act of everybody else and Talleyrand's phrase 'Now what did he mean by that?' defined the mood in Parliament and Palace.

In the spring of 1765, after George had suffered a bout of (purely physical) illness which started a mistaken scare about consumption, it was thought prudent to make provision for a regency. George told Grenville that the Regency Bill to cover his death and a long minority should be left blank for him, the King, to fill in. Instantly, the hair trigger of Whig paranoia was touched. He was going to put in the

Dowager so that, if he died, royal prerogative and influence would devolve to Augusta/Isabella who would instantly impose Bute/Roger Mortimer to extinguish English Liberty. The reality, thinks Sir John Brooke, was that George, who intended to name the young Queen Charlotte, was busy *excluding* the Duke of York of whom, as of so many people, he disapproved.

Grenville, consulted after the King had made up his mind and unaware of the Duke of York element, saw a plot. Thus began what in the trade is called the Regency Crisis, a painful quarrel between monarch, ministers and Parliament. The Lords threw out the no-name bill 89 to 31. Ultimately a bill went through with the Queen as regent and Augusta as first reserve. But George had put himself in the wrong and deepened ministers' suspicions of a lingering Bute waiting his opportunity. Unrelated but frightening riots in mid-May, after the Lords rejected a bill penalising Italian silks, brought four thousand silk workers on to the streets.

Bad was made worse after a call from one of Grenville's ministers to put Lord Granby, that most soothing and English of soldiers, in charge to get a dispersal by good humour. George saw an affront to Cumberland and reappointed the duke as Captain-General, the post lost after Kloster Zeven. Grenville and his ministers saw the King working against them everywhere. But then, as George, before the riot broke out, had sent an intermediary (Northumberland) to the duke at Newmarket about possibly replacing the ministry, they had a point. In fact, the duke had gone into Kent to call upon Pitt and discuss reassembling in peacetime the Pitt–Newcastle Ministry which had done so well during the war. However, the visit failed completely. For five hours of being asked nicely, Pitt talked his health and made excuses. In the light of the collapse which would come *in* office, this looks like self-knowledge.

If it is possible to go out on a limb behind somebody's back, George had done it. The King had tried to get rid of a man who knew he had done this and with whom he was now stuck. Contrition was the only thing left. Cumberland, behaving throughout with great sense, explained as much to him, Grenville, knowing everything that mattered, called an emergency Cabinet meeting and conveyed its wishes to the Palace. After preliminary bluster, George submitted. Even so the submission exacted by Grenville would prop his dangerous resentment. He demanded and got a sweeping clear-out of Bute's connection. Bute himself must have no part in the King's business. Henry Fox, now Lord Holland, must forsake the money fountain of the Pay Office. Lord Granby must be Commander-in-Chief and the Cabinet name its Lieutenant for Ireland.

Most painful, however, was the removal of Scottish patronage from James Stuart Mackenzie, Bute's brother. This had to be complied with but it more than rankled. Mackenzie was someone made a promise personally by George, which George now had to break. Grenville had made the dispute with George personal. Given royal attachments to personal relations above solid administration, this meant a set determination to be rid of his ablest Minister and never let him return. It was a case of great folly on all sides.

21

Houses and Gardens: Cider and America

It is worth pausing the caravan of high policy and low intrigue to look at Pitt the man, husband, father, legatee, landowner, garden extender and house improver.

Undoubtedly Pitt loved his wife and needed her very much, especially as consolation on the many occasions of illness. At the time of their marriage in 1754, he spoke of 'an alliance the Duke of Bedford would ambition [*sic*], with every endearing and flattering circumstance of preference and joy'.[1] One might stress the element of advantage in consolidating the political clan which the Grenvilles undoubtedly were. However, it is probably fairest to agree with Wiggins, historian of the Grenvilles, that Pitt's relationship with those brothers and cousins also involved a kind of love. Marrying Hester followed logically on, with everything else secured for the marriage by Hester's own qualities.

Everything we know about Hester Pitt, or Lady Chatham, as George III had gladly made her, is to her credit. If she was political, it was the politics of loyalty. During his physical and mental illness, she was there, attentive, caring, picking up business chores where she could and giving an uninterrupted love to sweeten his turbulent condition. Thomas Hudson's compelling picture of 1750, before marriage, shows her in right-profile, dark hair pulled back and piled-up Grecian style. The face is essentially sad, but with a tentative mouth hinting at humour. She seems, amid the savage antipathies and score-settling of male politics, to have lived up to the dictum in a poem by Kingsley Amis (of all people), that 'Women are really much nicer than men'.

As with his wife, Pitt seems to have been entirely happy with his children. John, the eldest, his daughters, Hester and Harriot, William, the future Prime Minister, and James, seem to have been well loved.

Pitt's own letters here, though formal, are playful/grave. He writes in his unquestioned private character, paterfamilial, uxorious and preoccupied. Rosebery, quoting a letter to George Grenville concerning John's birth, in the summer of 1756, in ocean-going Victorian prose, said, 'Pitt had leisure to squander on his improvements and receive his son, John on John's entrance into the world. But his eye was vigilantly fixed on the distresses of the country.' Pitt, at this utterly personal, private moment, responds in Latin. 'Quae regio in terris nostri plena laboris',[2] and goes on to talk about the situation in the Mediterranean.

The boys and girls were the children of a man, forty-seven at marriage, involved up to the ears in politics, war and the rattling struggle of a furiously combative life. They were the children of pronounced middle age. William, coming when his father was fifty, is the object necessarily of surprised delight at his quickness, but enfolded in shared and projected ambition. Evident abilities spark his father's plans. With the earldom in 1766, John, the eldest, would acquire a courtesy title as 'Lord Pitt' and would be referred to in correspondence as 'Pitt'. It was doubtless the usage of a very formal century, but, like the playful office bestowed on William (b. 1759), 'Little Mr Secretary', it is slightly unnerving.

Pitt as man of property is interesting. First there had been Hayes, in Kent, then the great good fortune of Burton Pynsent. Anyone who has listened to Michael Heseltine talking about his Oxfordshire garden and the things he can do with his JCB to make it more beautiful will recognise Pitt's intense pleasure in his two gardens. Release, innocence of employment, that especial pleasure of creating everything Lancelot Brown vested in the word 'capabilities', are clear. Pitt, to his loss, was not a man for sitting under a tree with a book and a carafe. He had, however, found in his gardens something to assuage a lifetime of tearing urgency.

Hayes was not a Great House in the way of Castle Howard or Blenheim, but it was grand enough in all conscience. 'Twenty four bedrooms, brewhouse, laundry, dairy, stabling for sixteen horses, standing for four carriages, pinery, peachery, fenced park of sixty acres and one hundred and ten acres beyond' says Christie's sale catalogue in 1789.[3]

Burton Pynsent in Somerset, not far from Langport, passed to Pitt as reward for two of his causes. The supposed treason of the Peace and the locally damaging Cider Excise had enraged the testamentary and slow-dying owner, Sir William Pynsent, who had apparently been equally outraged in 1713 by the Treaty of Utrecht. The old gentleman had diverted the inheritance (originally his wife's) from a member of his wider family, a female cousin married to Lord North who had voted the wrong way over cider. The estate finally came to Pitt when Sir William died in January 1765, though he had knowledge of it before.

The estate would prove less therapeutic than Hayes. The preoccupation here was the house itself and an insistent engagement in pulling down and rebuilding. It would also involve him in a rolling litigation as the Pynsent family sought the property to which they felt entitled, claiming entail rights through the original bequest to Lady Pynsent. And only in 1771 did the courts finally decide in his favour. That apart, frantic change and rebuilding had large costs, but Pitt was constitutionally incapable of living at a steady rate. For a man who kept no mistress, was reliably sober, a stranger to cards, horse racing and gambling houses, and who did not, like the equally virtuous Newcastle, spend his own money on political ends, Lord Chatham, like William Pitt before him, was ever and again reliably broke.

Having in government during a devouring war regarded public money as the business of someone else, he treated private money as a charming encumbrance to be expansively lightened. Again, in harmony with his political style, Pitt liked show. George Grenville, attending the Palace as Prime Minister, learned of the abortive talks with the King in May 1765 by way of a generous scatter of blue and silver, livery of the Great Commoner's too many servants. Invariably there would be a private coach and a startlingly large retinue, noted by the unawed Edmund Burke. 'Before I close I ought to tell you', he wrote to Rockingham, 'that Lord Chatham passed before my door on Friday Morning, in a jimwhiskee drawn by two horses, one before the other; he drove himself. His train was two coaches and six, with twenty servants, male and female . . .'[4]

Lord Shelburne, who saw him close and, at different times, would admire and condemn him, was deadly. He 'acted the part so well that everybody was persuaded that he had a perfect contempt of both patronage and money, though those that lived to see him near . . . saw plainly the contrary'.[5] He was, of course, financially honest and had joined the minority tradition of Harley and Pelham in respect of interest at the Pay Office. However, the rewards of virtue, the Duchess of Marlborough's ten thousand in 1744, the £3000 a year pension of 1761 and Burton Pynsent, with its estate income from 1765 of between three and four thousand a year, never sufficed. All these, rolled together and conservatively invested, worth in current values just under a million a year *income*, still did not suffice.

One other non-political thing central to Pitt was his health. The gout and the mental condition it aggravated were not continuous in the mid-sixties, but the intermissions were fewer. They were accompanied by long, overlapping but not narrowly synchronous, blatant absences from Parliament. These might be tactical; they could also demonstrate the impossibilist pride which ran ever deeper through his character. Newcastle, who was looking to reconstitute the old coalition in peacetime, received this: 'I have no disposition to quit the free condition of a man standing single, and daring to appeal to the country upon the soundness of his principles and the rectitude of his conduct.' It is all very much *O Altitudo*.*

To reasonable people, to Lord Rockingham, William Dowdeswell, Lord Shelburne, even King George, this was all very hard to take. Government was fluid, the steady, jog-along, unaltitudinous government of Walpole and the Pelhams had been replaced by perpetual speculation about how long? and who next? Since the autumn of 1761, Bute had replaced Pitt/Newcastle, had been followed by Grenville, who had survived a Palace demission only because of Pitt's requiring 'the free condition of a man standing single' – in power.

Ayling, writing over thirty years ago but not starstruck, nevertheless compares Pitt's conduct with that of General de Gaulle, in the 1950s, 'waiting proud and aloof in his rural retreat to be summoned back to the helm, but insisting absolutely upon his own high terms for the service'.[6] It is an intriguing point, but the differences were more important. De Gaulle was in good physical and mental health. He knew what he was worth, and he was right. But he was more adored by self-abjecting followers like Michel Debré than deluded about himself. Unlike Pitt, he was a real, very able and original soldier. Like

---

* Sir Thomas Browne, *Religio Medici*: 'I love to lose myself in a mystery; to pursue my reason to an *O Altitudo*.'

all the best commanders, he understood military possibility and impossibility. His second great act, the first being refusal of surrender in 1940, was a retreat, the perfectly judged double-cross of the French Algerian conspirators who had called him up. Certainly, like Pitt, he talked in a contrived oracular third-person style, but he talked very much less. And he had at all times a healthy sense of humour and a great and saving cynicism. Everything about Pitt, early and late, but getting worse, was intense and self-preoccupied.

His behaviour got in the way of doing anything and of making a sound ministry. Witness an unimpressed Edmund Burke, writing to an Irish friend in spring 1765: 'Nothing but the intractable temper of your friend, Pitt, can prevent a most admirable and lasting system from being put together; and this crisis will show whether pride or patriotism be predominant in his character, for you may be assured that he has it in his power to come into the service of his country, upon any plan of politics he may choose to dictate, with great and honourable terms to himself ... A few days will show whether he will take this part or that of continuing on his back at Hayes, talking fustian, excluded from all ministerial, and incapable of all parliamentary service; for his gout is worse than ever, but his pride may disable him more than his gout.'[7]

This was written just before Pitt, as good as his word, tried to implement that stop list of major figures to be barred from the proposed coalition. One might argue that George III was in the wrong here. Though never the operator of a secret system as Whig legend (much encouraged by Burke) would have it, he carries some blame. Grenville was rough and rude and he went on, but he had a majority, he was making a decent job of restoring the finances. His mistakes on specifics did not stop him being a practitioner of good government. Following his earlier naval efforts, to actually pay sailors, Grenville was now trying seriously to have government salaries not just paid, but paid on time. He was interested, in a sensible nineteenth-century way, in the machinery of government.

He had secured Robert Clive's victories in India by the crisp expedient of sending Clive back to Bengal in 1764 and had used a minimum of naval presence off Central America to discourage understandable Spanish essays at offsetting their losses in Honduras. Even the American troubles, which would roll through many intervening hands to major calamity, had creditable origins. Stamp duty in the American colonies derived partly from trying to offset the general chaos of colonial financial administration. If George had not, in May 1765, gone behind his back to Pitt, he would have kept a capable First Minister. The comparison is with another immature monarch, Victoria, taking against Robert Peel, also a mistake.

When it finally came to replacing Grenville in July 1765, George would be beholden to Cumberland. William Augustus was only forty-four years old, but in a desperate condition with little time to live. But nephew, having restored uncle to full public standing, relied heavily upon his advice. Before the war, Cumberland, deploying Fox, had been a serious player. Had he lived on, he would have been guarantor, uncle (or godfather) to the next government. As it was, he promoted young Lord Rockingham into command, taken up on 13 July 1765. Then fifteen weeks later, at the end of October, he died.

Charles Wentworth-Watson, Marquess of Rockingham, was too young to be Prime Minister. His was a mind at once high and slow. He was yoked with Grafton, decent but more naive yet, and with the prosy evangelical, Perceval.* But he brought his own assets, mildy liberal aristocratic virtues, an instinct for leaning towards reform – and recognition that he was too young! For someone needing to learn, he was lucky in having as Chancellor the unsung, sensible man of mid-eighteenth-century politics.

William Dowdeswell became Chancellor, moved to fulfil his own crusade by abolishing the Cider Excise and gratifying the 103,000 households hit by it. He found the leeway to do this by shifting for revenue to non-excise retail duties at 6s. a hogshead. He was only third choice for the post after it had been turned down by Sir William Baker and Horace Walpole's favourite, the oversung Henry Conway. But Dowdeswell, country gentleman from Worcestershire, understood the economy, financial and commercial, and, as 'the Apple Chancellor', was quickly recognised as a leading figure. The appointment might, in footballing terms, be called a six-pointer, as the Exchequer had first been offered to Charles Townshend, clever, malicious, unstable, sparkling, and unfit for responsible office, who refused it.

Instructively, Townshend was a sought-after figure on the strength

---

* Father of the understandably assassinated Prime Minister Spencer Perceval.

of his rhetoric. The Irish politician, Henry Flood, commented in November of that year that 'there was no one person near Townshend. He is the orator, the rest are speakers.' It was a talent the age adored. He declined the dreary Exchequer for the Pay Office which brought him money and membership of a Cabinet he never bothered to attend. Dowdeswell, as Chancellor, did not officially sit there, but, in view of his usefulness, was pressed to come regularly and did.

The other prop, not in office but perhaps closest to Rockingham, was Burke. Rockingham might be young and not the most concentrated mind ever to work out of Downing Street. He had, though, the wit to recognise Burke's quality and to spark in the brilliant man from the Irish middle class and mixed marriage real affection and esteem, which were returned. The great disputant of British constitutional thinking and the territorial magnate not long out of adolescence made a handsome political marriage. Relations were reinforced by the complete failure of Pitt to show interest in, or respond to, Burke. Famously, Samuel Johnson, who rated him his intellectual equal, said that if you were caught in a shed with Burke during a shower, for half an hour, you would say, 'This is an extraordinary man.'*

This ministry was lost to Pitt. The Rockinghams were getting ready to move on the great dividing question of the Stamp Act, their leaders began as his admirers, but he seemed at this time able only to resent or snub them. Burke was employed by Rockingham as go-between with Pitt, and received with his full elevation of contempt. 'Mr Burke, I wonder that you should make that proposition when I have given it under my hand in a letter to Lord Rockingham that I will open myself upon that point to nobody but to the King himself.'[8] When Pitt came to form a government himself, Burke would not seek place. Horace Walpole, for all the volatility of his character judgements, put it very well. 'Edmund, though the idol of his party, had nothing of the pathetic and imposing dignity of Pitt, though possessed of far more knowledge and more reasoning abilities.'[9]

Yet the immediate purposes of the Rockinghams should have suited Pitt. They deplored Grenville's Stamp Act. From being so preoccupied with the outrageous settling of *his* war on moderate terms as to

---

* Johnson's taste in diminutives being what it was, Burke made up with the delightful playwright, Arthur Murphy, an Irish two-man act, Bur and Mur.

ignore that ill-advised piece of legislation, Pitt had grown eloquent
on the wrongs of the colonists, though never quite coherent. In one
of Horace Walpole's most famous quotations, he asked if 'we wanted
to sheathe our swords in the bowels of our brothers, the Americans',
an early outing for the 'Special Relationship'. But then nobody was
coherent. The Rockinghams spent 19–21 January 1766 debating the
issue. Rockingham himself, having moved from a prior wish to maintain and enforce it, settled upon straightforward abolition. Ministers
were, however, concerned about the precedent which sharp lawyers
among the difficult settlers might make from the void of no Stamp
Act and no statement of powers to make one.

The Cabinet's havering on this distinction mirrored the steady ambiguity of Pitt's pronouncements. On the one hand, he was stating the
most extreme position, that the Commons had no right to tax the
colonies at all! Yet he was emphatic about Parliament's high rights
and privileges over them in respect of trade and regulation of their
manufacturing economy. He was recorded saying, 'Give up taxing, but
control her absolutely in her manufactures and her commerce.' And
by suggesting that 'this should be done by outside tariffs' he pushed
incoherence a long way. He did more than that, the torrent of
eloquence flowing, as Temple remarked, like a spring tide.

Pitt identified with the Americans on English nationalist grounds
– they were ourselves put down somewhere else. But he had a deeper
streak of authoritarianism than many more conservative figures, never
mind the well-intentioned Rockinghams, and especially never mind
Edmund Burke, who would have the last word on all this. However,
his advocacy of repeal, whatever the codicils, was, strictly in the political short term, helpful. Rockingham himself, who had good lines to
merchants alarmed at an American embargo, was now, off his own
bat, for abolition. But people like Grafton took their cue from Pitt.

At the same time, the Cabinet promoted a Declaratory Act saying
that we were not taxing the Americans but that we had a right to do
so, a flapped hand, risking affront and demonstrating weakness.
Newcastle, holding, in this Cabinet, his last office, saw the latent
disaster and warned against it. The Declaratory Act, he said, 'would
prevent even the repeal from having its effect'.[10]

Any move on America was hampered by George III. The
Rockinghams, having opted for abolition, had to put it through

Parliament. George, back in touch with Bute, whom the Whigs saw under every bed, did something to put paranoia into credit. He told Bute and his friends in Parliament that they should feel free to follow their consciences against repeal in the lobby. His biographer's description, 'A very foolish thing', hardly says it. This was the monarch working against the measures of the government which has kissed his hands. You can't do that. Particularly is this so when he isn't expressing your views. Bute was straightforwardly against, Rockingham for. George favoured it as better than enforcing the act but, dithering like everybody else, wanted repeal with modifications. Not surprisingly, Rockingham innocently misrepresented this as full support and bad feeling spread like a stain.

What had happened to Pitt was that hubris had become central to his nature. Other governments, other politicians, existed only for his purposes. For some time, this state of mind coincided with the political climate. Pitt was the star, the crowd puller, the big name. For box-office triumph, substitute public and parliamentary authority: the producers wanted him in the film. On top of this, the Rockinghams were new, their leader was young, they felt like an accidental government. Accordingly, they yearned for Pitt and sent delegations to be gratified with an audience. By a particular irony, the most ardent seeker after the magic touch was the Duke of Grafton. All too soon, later in 1766, he would be granted his wish only to spend two years on the empty quarterdeck of a drifting ship.

Burke was no part of this yearning. Of all major political figures he had fewest illusions about, and least respect for, the Magus. He saw that the itch for power ran in Pitt with almost monarchical presumption and saw, too, the way his friends ran after the man. The trick was to stand up to him. Years later, Burke felt the need to give Rockingham advice. 'Lord Chatham shows a disposition to come near you, but with those reserves which he never fails to have as long as he thinks the [royal] closet door ajar to receive him. The least peep into that closet intoxicates him and will to the end of his life . . . This I am sure of, that as long as you make no approaches to him, but make yourself approachable *by* him, you stand in the fairest way to gain his esteem, and to assure yourself against his manoeuvres.'[11] This was said eight years after the first Rockingham Ministry fell, and still *needed* to be said.

In January 1766, with Grafton and earnest, tiring Conway threatening fatal resignation unless another beseeching approach were paid to Pitt, a further attempt *was* made. Sir John Brooke, who has a nice, short way with him, puts it perfectly: 'Pitt returned flattering professions and talked nonsense.'[12] If the Rockingham government was a disappointment, it was still a government. Its official head, however poor his debating skills, was still the head of a government. If it hesitated about how to handle the irksome people of the Thirteen Colonies, it got half the problem right. What followed would be more like the voyage of the Ancient Mariner.

The government, beset by Bute, having a poor line to the King, was fatally weak in putting its case, Rockingham the worst of a Cabinet of poor speakers, Dowdeswell, in his plain way, the best. But the Rockinghams, having lost the confidence of the King, were ready to go. They had done useful things beyond the two repeals – of the Cider Excise and the Stamp Act. They had followed the courts in getting rid of General Warrants and had liberalised trade with the Caribbean. But their ministry did resemble Wilde's Mr Bunbury. The doctors told Bunbury he couldn't live, so Bunbury died. George, in his dull, repetitive way, informed Bute that he looked to the man behind the resonant name to rescue him. 'I now hope God is giving me this line to extricate this country out of faction.' On 7 July 1766, the invitation was made. Pitt, after fluttering so long close to the royal commission, finally alighted.

22

Power Out of Mind

George had wanted a figure commanding support and providing stability. He shared Pitt's self-pleasing ingenuousness about 'rejecting faction for measures', a reliably meaningless slogan. What he got immediately was a burst of imperiousness. Pitt took only the Privy Seal, making Grafton nominal First Lord. Also, a grandiose impulse asserted itself. He wanted to buy off the offended Earl of Northumberland from a promise of the Mastership of the Horse now given to Lord Hertford, '. . . Lord Chatham then proffered honours to him. Lord Northumberland asked of what sort. Lord Chatham said the highest, a dukedom if he wished it; to which Lord Northumberland said the King would not do it. Lord Chatham . . . desired Lord Northumberland to go to the King from him to ask it, and to use his name saying he came from him . . .' When he had gone there and sent in a message, 'The King came out to him and Lord Northumberland laid his suit before him, saying he was come from Lord Chatham, the King coloured and looked embarrassed . . . He then went into his Closet, from which he returned in a short space, and told Lord Northumberland he would create him a Duke.'[1] At this point, Chatham had a straight writ to the King.

No former head of government would be tolerated in the Cabinet, so no Rockingham, despite keen loyalty and his useful following, and no Newcastle. Worse, told by Grafton that he would like to keep Dowdeswell at the Exchequer and that 'Lord Rockingham's being quiet would depend' on the new government's welcome, Pitt expressly barred him.[2] The most practical man of business, and the one person who knew what the real choices were in America, declined lesser and more profitable offices and went into expert and effective Opposition.

More immediately damaging evermore was the peerage. Pitt had played upon his plebeian status, delighting in the title 'The Great

Commoner'. Ennoblement would create a noble line. His clever son, William, was his second, coached in the Ciceronics necessary for the Commons. John, the unremarkable elder son, ultimately a well-liked, not very accomplished general, would carry the title. It was all vanity and vexation of spirit. The City supporters, and still more the London public, had been affronted in print and on the street. In parallel, Northington, Rockingham's Lord Chancellor, now did a deal, passing the office to Pitt's lawyer, Pratt, who became Lord Camden. Northington, meanwhile, took the Lord Presidency with a reversal to a sinecure and a cool £5000 a year. 'Had he', said Horace Walpole of Chatham, 'been as sordid as Lord Northington, he could not have sunk lower in the public esteem.'

From July to October, Pitt was well enough to essay Foreign Affairs: a dangerous alliance with Prussia and Russia. For what it was worth, an alliance against France was held out to us by Austria through Seilern, Austrian Minister in London, conditional upon *not* joining up with Frederick. Ironically, Pitt's old crotchet against continental entangle-ments made a sense in 1766 for a country replete with tropical spoil, not present in 1756. We had a big new garden to cultivate.

In fairness, talk of a triple alliance had been considered by Rockingham. However, Pitt, given to large notions, invested more than mistaken prudence in the project. It exemplified large and menacing military ideas about an uncompleted war. He was trapped in the uncompleted past, cut off by the rational terms of Paris 1763. He contemplated an assembly of power to do unimaginable and over-reaching things, and it was a dream. The preliminary steps involved a special envoy to St Petersburg for the Russian part of the imagined alliance. Hans Stanley, of the Paris negotiations, should now brush aside the ambassador, Macartney, who angrily resigned. And as the high mission faced, anyway, a thoroughly unresponsive Empress Catherine, it would be abandoned.

As for the Prussian link, Pitt and Frederick had said expansive things about one another. England, opined the King of Prussia, had found a man at last. It was a floral tribute but Pitt had projected in Frederick an ideal to put beside his ideal of himself, and had devoted much of a speech in the Commons, 6 December 1759, to eulogising our Heroic Ally. But Old Fritz was a realist who had bitten hard on defeat and knew its taste. At the very end of the war, 30 March 1763, with Silesia

secure, he had stopped at the field of Kunersdorf, scene of the great
defeat of 1759, which had killed off hopes of taking Saxony. He lingered
there in contemplation of the price of military glory, 'the distress and
hardship with which it had been acquired, in what physical depriva-
tions and struggle, in heat and cold, in hunger, filth and destitution
. . .' Then, he thought, 'you would have learnt to think quite differ-
ently about this glory.'[3] That sprang from an experience of the world
which Pitt had never come near.

The differences between Frederick and Chatham frequently marked
the distinction between substance and dream. The King of Prussia
fought in his wars and huddled with his officers for field decisions.
Pitt cited Demosthenes and proclaimed the triumph of his own
orations. In 1766, the English Minister was being played along by
Frederick as bogey to press Spain into the advantageous commercial
treaty he wanted. Chatham tried the imperious approach upon him.
A man knocked off his horse by a spent enemy bullet was not to be
jollied by verbiage. By November 1766 it was clear that Prussia would
not touch it. Disabused, and humiliated, Pitt flung out his staple rhetoric. Frederick was '. . . a mischievous rascal, a base friend, a bad ally,
a bad relation, and a bad neighbour; in fact the most dangerous and
evil-disposed prince in Europe'.[4]

Pitt was privately judged by another Prussian, the ambassador here,
who, according to von Ruville, dredging the Prussian archives,
reported: 'All the ministers in office came and paid their respects to
him and to each as he took leave the Earl handed a little note with
which the minister retired into a corner of the room, to read it and
to note down what Pitt had said to him.'[5]

That wasn't going to last. For a start, Chatham, however lofty, had
appointed a major talent, subordinate to nobody and not perfectly
sane. Charles Townshend, 'a man of splendid eloquence, of lax principles, and of boundless vanity and presumption . . .',[6] took the
Exchequer, a dangerous weapon in the wrong, clever hands. The major
cut in salary was offset by recent killings in East Indian stock bought
with his takings as Paymaster. Otherwise the Cabinet, mostly recycled
Rockinghams, was ardently loyal. Henry Conway and the young Duke
of Grafton had, under another command, yearned for Pitt. The
yearning would ease.

Foreign Affairs apart, Chatham had one large project. The East

India Company jangled ostentatious new wealth, much of it dubiously acquired, offensive to older, politer money and arousing the interest of a war-drained Treasury. With his own nabob connections balancing statist instincts, Chatham looked to control and annex. The government had been originator and authoriser of the trade. Robert Clive's remote and stupendously consequential Indian war had employed British resources. A letter from Clive in 1759 had told Pitt that so large a sovereignty 'as existed in Bengal' was 'too extensive for a mercantile company'. It 'required the nation's assistance'.[7]

The ministry, in Chatham's phrase, must have 'rights' in the proceeds. Clive was about to assume the office of the *Diwani*, second place with financial control, an obvious route to a diversion of revenue. What Chatham wanted was access by legislative assault to the growing Asian wealth now creating bubbles in the Amsterdam and Paris bourses. But while Chatham, in the Lords, proposed, Townshend, in undisputed command of the Commons, would dispose. And Charles Townshend had been doing nicely out of the unreformed Company.

Chatham saw 'a gift from heaven' to accomplish, in Pittese, 'the redemption of a nation'. The City of London, long loyal, demurred. Whatever was done to one chartered body, the East India Company, could be done to any chartered body – like the Corporation of the City of London. Chatham set up an enquiry into Company finances, but how far it got was another matter. Oddly, the proposal was introduced by the backbencher closest to Chatham, his mentor, Beckford. That commercial moralist, keen to sink the ships of foreign competitors, 'expiated justly', says Horace Walpole, 'on the devastation the company's servants had committed . . .' and 'who were practising all arts to convert into a selfish job a source of riches that ought to be conducted to national advantage'.[8]

Large schemes to annex Indian revenue were not going to happen. Negotiation passed to Shelburne, wildly unpopular, very intelligent and historical source. Things would be managed without supersession of a charter body or knocking down chartered rights. They were fixed by an old-fashioned cash deal: £400,000 a year to the Treasury and with the bubble-creating stock splits and further dividend increases forbidden without government permission. Meanwhile, Beckford's enquiry faded away. This was sophisticated dealing, remote from the mallet and jemmy approach of Beckford. As John Keay, historian of the Company, puts it, lesser measures 'established a highly significant precedent for parliamentary interference in the internal affairs of the Company'.⁹ It was finesse, and if Pitt ever did finesse in the past, Chatham didn't do it now.

The Chatham administration would soon cease to be his. He had been humiliated in foreign affairs, a subject he knew about. He was at sea in things financial and domestic. He had appointed a Chancellor of equal brilliance, insolence and bad judgement – and could not be rid of him. 'Chatham' was a great name, a dramatic presence, a mighty reputation – frozen in their shadows. His Cabinet, would, said Horace Walpole, become 'A Ministry of heterogeneous particles'. Townshend, according to Horace, well placed to know, was working upon Henry Conway, Secretary of State. The new Chancellor 'was incessant in inciting him to retire, by painting to him the pride and folly of Lord Chatham, the improbability of maintaining such shattered power, and alarming him with threats of resignation and leaving him alone in the House of Commons'.¹⁰

Even in tolerable mental health, Chatham had been a recurring absentee. For George he represented anxiety turning gradually into despair. Chatham had no taste for administration. Excepting Townshend, who, as another and sparkling orator, would dominate the Commons, neither had his Cabinet. Grafton, Conway and the rest were not stupid men and were very willing to work, but absolutely lacked the confidence to take things firmly forward. Conway was given to disastrous candour. George Grenville's diary gives us an idea: 'The most memorable event of the day was Mr Conway's speech who spoke doubtfully on the permanency of the Administration and twice affectedly called himself a passenger.'¹¹

With no loyal leader in the Commons, the ministry would always be vulnerable to ambush. It came from the snubbed Dowdeswell who, with Grenville and Bedford's heavy, Richard Rigby, actually amended the budget! Impossible now, it was sensational enough in January 1767 when Dowdeswell moved a reduction in the Land Tax of a shilling in the pound from four to three shillings – 25 per cent!

The Tories, irked by Chatham's indifference and, anyway, as agriculturists, delighted, joined in. Grenville, mocked two years back with Pitt's murmur of 'Where, gentle Shepherd?', offered a swingeing reaction. It was very much accountant against orator and surely touched obliquely on Chatham's improvidence as a frantic domestic builder. That brilliantly successful jest, he thought, was Chatham's style. 'He would spend money but left others to raise it. A fool could ruin an estate; a fool and a knave could ruin a nation.'[12] The tax reduction was pure Walpolean economics – and the county members flocked to it, as not safe *not* to vote for. Meanwhile, as Horace puts it, 'some of the Duke of Grafton's young friends, not suspecting a contest, had gone out of town that day'.[13] The division showed a majority for a three-shilling tax, of 206 to 188.

The Rockingham Ministry had, of course, done something useful in abolishing the stamp duty and another thing, not at all useful, in asserting the right to impose the duty. In this context, Townshend contemptuously dismissed Chatham's view, that, while it was wrong to impose stamp duty, we had an absolute right to regularise colonial commerce at will. In a speech of impressive arrogance in January 1767, he dismissed its central distinction between internal taxation and external duties as 'perfect nonsense'. Townshend had a good deal in common with Chatham, high abilities, especially as a speaker, bubbling assurance and an easy contempt for almost everyone else.

It all came out in the 'Champagne speech' of 8 March. Concerned with the East India Company imbroglio, it was highly alcoholic. 'He returned in the evening half-drunk with champagne', said Horace,[14] 'but more intoxicated with spirits.' The Chancellor continued, audaciously dismissive of supposed colleagues including Chatham, too low in the water on his last visit to London for sustained response. Townshend was newly rich, the East Indian coup having now been augmented with his wife's inheritance. He obtained Ireland for his brother and retrieved a family peerage for that rich wife. With most of the Cabinet afraid of him, Townshend could do anything and, as Chancellor, he would do something entirely disastrous. This followed in a budget adding the American colonists to the list of people for whom Charles Townshend didn't give a fig, imposing on those colonies an import tax on tea. A *lèse-majesté* to which Chatham, already on a downswing, could not summon an effective response.

The duties on tea (also glass, china and paper) would be charged at 3d. in the pound, aiming at £20,000 revenue. Townshend suggested forbidding the Colonial Assemblies further legislation until they paid costs for resident forces, punishment for defying the Mutiny Act. As

other options included coercive billeting and direct taxes, this passed
for moderate. Folly of the highest quality, it was the measure of
Chatham's absence from the Chatham Ministry. He would come up
to London in March 1767 and try to replace Townshend with North
who declined the place.

Frederick North, who, according to primitive history, 'lost us our
American colonies', was Townshend's antithesis, calm, good-
humoured, a first-rate financial technician, loyal (too loyal) to the
wrongheaded King. At the Exchequer in July 1766, he would have
produced sources of revenue saving everybody (especially North) from
the consequences of Charles Townshend. Alternatively, Chatham
might have retained Dowdeswell instead of suggesting the disreputable
Pay Office. Dowdeswell alone grasped the truth over America. There
was a simple, unpleasant choice. We could requisition taxes with
serious military strength. Alternatively, we could judge war against
Englishmen overseas not worth the flickering candles of authority and
revenue. The fact that Chatham, oblivious to this, accompanied eulogy
upon the Americans with a doctrine on trade assuring terminal
American affront, defined his continuing incomprehension.

He would now lurch clean out of tolerable mental health. Mr Keay
thinks he was 'slipping toward a dithering senility'.[15] Dithering certainly,
but 'senility' doesn't define his state. He would do crazy things and
would roll himself up in bed to escape all human intercourse. He had
vast megalomaniac building plans at the new Somerset estate. Then
followed an overwhelming need to go back to 'Dear Hayes'. It was
mad, sure enough, but you can come out of madness; senility has no
exits to the living. Horace Walpole is witness. 'His children he could
not bear under the same roof, nor communication from room to
room nor whatever he thought promoted noise ... His sickly and
uncertain appetite was never regular, and his temper could put up
with no defect. Thence a succession of chickens were boiling and
roasting at every hour to be ready whenever he should call.'[16]

From March 1767 he was absolutely unable to perform any public
business. In fact, going to Somerset at Christmas and only returning
in March after Townshend's open defiance was not, even by relaxed
eighteenth-century standards, compatible with heading a ministry. In
March, after he had failed to replace Townshend, Chatham seems just
to have subsided. He saw the King on 12 March for the last time as

Prime Minister. To remain as he did, *in absentia* and under care, ghostly head of government, followed from the inability of Grafton and Conway to make an end of things. They had, though, the excuse of George III's even greater lapse of duty.

George didn't like the conflicts and disorder created by the Minister's absence. The King, argues Brooke, thought Chatham would control the political conflict. If he thought that, he was living, like Chatham, in Chatham's past. Sympathetic revisionism plays down the selfishness and stupidity in George's character, and sympathy goes too far. He could have had sound and competent government from Grenville, but Grenville lacked respect. Grenville was quite sane; his ministers recognised his authority. But the King looked, if not quite to his ease, then certainly to his tranquillity. Swearing blind never again to employ a very capable minister without enquiry, then clinging to a man clean through the threshold of clinical insanity, is professional failure of some distinction.

Even as Chatham withdrew into 'the lowest dejection and debility that mind or body can be in',[17] the King now begged him by letter to stay and fight 'the factions'. He was writing to Chatham in Somerset, that 'Your duty, your own honour, require you to make an effort', when the replies to such letters came in Hester's hand pleading inability to leave his room. To selfishness and stupidity one might add stark insensibility. A moderately intelligent, moderately perceptive King would have recognised private calamity.

The madness of Chatham, like the madness of George III,* was intermittent. In the period from March (or rather earlier) to October 1767, it was absolute. He took it into his head that being away from Hayes, sold after the move to Burton Pynsent, was literally unbearable. He must have Hayes back, must return there. Hester, functioning like a loving mother, wrote sad, beseeching letters to Mr Thomas Walpole, the new owner, please to sell it back. He complied, as people tended to do for Pitt *and* Chatham. The cost and the trouble were enormous. Hayes, sold originally for £11,870, was repurchased for £17,400. In the interim, Chatham was let a house in Hampstead. He found the houses nearby an intrusion and wanted them removed or bought up.

---

* The King's porphyria, however exotic, was still madness.

Things were bad enough for Chatham to know it; power of attorney was made over to Hester. On the same principle, the effective leadership of the administration passed to Grafton. The Duke was a decent, well-purposed, only mildly indolent young man in his early thirties trying hard with limited aptitude and less authority. On 31 May and 4 June, he had meetings with the great man, finding 'his nerves and spirits . . . affected to a very great degree', the conversations 'truly painful: I had to run over the many difficulties of the Session; for his lordship I believe had not once attended the House since his last return from Bath . . . I was sorry to inform Lord Chatham that Mr Townshend's flippant boasting was received with strong marks of a blind and greedy approbation from the body of the House . . . It was with difficulty that I brought Lord Chatham to be sensible of the weakness of his Administration.'[18] They parted full of civilities, Grafton having told his leader that the Cabinet was desperate for a lead. Beyond that, he told Chatham that he did not think the administration could continue without allies. It had to be the Bedfords or the Rockinghams. Chatham expressed preference for the Bedfords, but that eventuality was some way ahead. At this moment, immobility was the way forward.

Conway, in his irksome, handwringing way, wanted to resign, setting a date, 22 July, and starting a further dispute. The Bedfords, now close to coming in, bringing their hard line on America, wanted Conway out. The Rockinghams, alternative partners after a reshuffle, and conciliatory toward America, wanted him to stay. An August compromise shifted him from the Secretaryship to be Lieutenant General of the Ordnance. Giving up those seals in January, he remained in the Cabinet to please George III. The story of Conway, a man discerning enough to make David Hume his secretary, also sensible and pacific – as so often with intelligent soldiers – but hapless between loyalties, symbolises the general disorder. The Duke of Richmond who, as became the left-wing direct descendant of Charles II, would later nonchalantly stand up to a raging Chatham, contemplated a motion of censure and moved towards the Rockinghams, also making friends with Burke. As Sir John Brooke interpolates amid doleful reports from limping ministers, 'If only Townshend could be induced to follow Conway, how simple it would all be.'[19]

Chatham was *hors de combat* at North End in Hampstead, looked after by the royal doctor, Wintringham, and Dr Anthony Addington.

Possessing beautiful manners and no disposition to the fashionable cruelties of the trade, preferring harmless 'good air', Addington may have been as good for the poor patient as any.*

Chatham was hapless. Grafton, assailed by some, deserted by others, wished to break free and invite in a new administration. In the way of such sense stood the motte and bailey of George III's understanding. Chatham had been his strongman. He now had the deranged Chatham, whom he entreated, '. . . I am thoroughly persuaded your own feelings will make you take an active part at this hour, which will not only give lustre and ease to the subsequent years of my reign, but will raise the reputation of your own political life . . .'[20] In other words, 'Buckle to and snap out of it.'

Chatham, replying, echoed and forwarded the sentiment, hoping that 'if the Duke of Grafton can be prevailed upon to remain at the head of the Treasury with a Chancellor of the Exchequer agreeable to his Grace, success to your Majesty's affairs in Parliament would be insured; . . .' He concluded by what he thought *the vital and indispensable part of an Administration, likely to procure ease and stability, to your Majesty's business namely the Duke of Grafton remaining where he is'.*[21] Across the summer, Chatham was planning an expansion of North End to thirty-four bedrooms and being fed through a hatch.

As Grafton's majorities fell – three in a division of 26 May 1767 – and as he struggled as a speaker, the duke, in July, brought in the Bedfords, split from the Grenvilles. Collective responsibility, caucus, the party's correct line, were, creditably, not what they have become. The longer it went on, the more the Pitt–Grafton Ministry reflected opposing views and unreconciled personalities. Camden, Shelburne and Conway belonged, in an exasperated way, to the Pitt Tendency. Hillsborough, an Ulster careerist of the grimmest sort, wanted to chastise the American colonies. (He would get his chance under North.) Grafton favoured moderation but, sadly, was the only member of his Cabinet who, defeated there, did collective loyalty.

This happened over tea and America. Ministers were clear enough about repealing Townshend's 1767 raft of duties on goods entering

---

* The doctor's period of attendance led to a friendship between young William Pitt and Addington's ten-year-old son, Henry, which would carry to the front bench and Downing Street for both youngsters.

Boston. But a faction following Pitt's doctrine of British supremacy over commodities – 'We won't hit you but we have an inalienable right to' – argued for a single impost. Hillsborough, a man naturally insensitive, holding the new, delicate Third Secretaryship (for America), proposed tea. A five to four majority supported the folly, Grafton unhappily accepting. It recalls the poll tax of the 1980s, something done against good judgement in a spirit of stumbling defiance, voluntary crucifixion.

Townshend flourished, taking malign delight in undermining colleagues, doing sober what the Champagne Speech had said half drunk. The Chatham administration was becoming ever less Chathamite. Then, in late summer, to a chorus of barely suppressed relief, Charles Townshend, in the pomp of his new wealth and Cabinet primacy, took ill – 'of a putrid fever' – and, on 4 September, died. Horace Walpole had liked him, but took the point. 'As a man of incomparable parts, and most entertaining to a spectator, I regret his death . . . ; but in a political light, I own I cannot look upon it as a misfortune.'[22]

However, good luck never stuck to Grafton; another irresistible cross beckoned. Townshend died, Wilkes came back. Returning from French exile and standing (after initial defeat in the City) for Middlesex, where, in March 1768, he was returned, Wilkes was short of money and spoke of needing 'to raise a dust' to improve his finances. Had the Grafton people and the King been respectively less pure and less vindictive, a swift high-yield sinecure would have saved them an infinity of bad notices. Grafton stood out against Cabinet voices raised to expel this lethal phenomenon from the Commons. For nearly a year that high wisdom, Ernest Bevin's 'complete ignoral', stuck. Then Wilkes, with an eye to more publicity, went in his favourite direction, too far.

London having become arguably a more violent city even than in the 1750s, there had been riots in St George's Fields, riots cleared by soldiers firing.* In December, he spoke of the event as a massacre. The takers of a hard line took it and demanded expulsion. Grafton, against his better judgement, went along with them. This sparked the sacrificial candidacy in Middlesex of a Colonel Henry Luttrell and

---

* They would fire again and cause deaths again in 1780 to stop the Gordon Riots – on the express orders of the Lord Mayor, John Wilkes.

the whole ministerial treadmill of re-election, re-expulsion, re-re-election and re-re-expulsion. This, after four full circuits, achieved the melancholy hilarity of an approved Commons motion that 'Colonel Luttrell *ought* to have been elected'.

The absurdity of the decision did not stop it from being upheld. Looking forward in swift parenthesis, the decision of Parliament was judged to be legal by Parliament beyond challenge, 221 to 152, on 8 May. Wilkes was also declared incapable of being elected to Parliament. The issue of voters and their rights would roll on for five years until, a brilliant Lord Mayor, entertainer of Canterbury and a clutch of bishops to dinner at the Mansion House, the recapacitated Wilkes was elected unopposed – no one daring to oppose him. Calling himself a Tory, not quite what it came to mean, with all the issues of press and voter freedom gradually resolved as he had argued them, John Wilkes, Prince of Troublemakers, lived happily ever after.

On top of everything else, Grafton's Ministry attracted the baroque prose of Junius. Sometimes it is merely sonorous: 'The liberty of the press is the palladium of all the civil, political and religious rights of an Englishman.' Sometimes – 'Is this the wisdom of a great minister? Or is it the ominous vibration of a pendulum?' – perfectly lethal. Francis (the likeliest Junius) had not been tutored by Edward Gibbon for nothing. How much the recovering Chatham knew of the Junius campaign is not clear. But he had a new lieutenant in John Calcraft, civil service clerk turned army contractor, whose protégé Francis was. Both were betting long term on Chatham and what he might do for them. 'The Palladium of English Liberty' proclaimed from such mouths was vapid heroics. Wilkes, however he might raise a dust and the wind, is still endearing, his campaign as candid as cynical, and, anyway, constitutionally therapeutic.

The Grafton Ministry existed because George III wanted it to. He had sought a clear, strong leadership to rescue him from 'Faction'. It had been; and Grafton himself had stayed on, clean-minded and honest. But the majority had wilted with reversals and ever-widening divisions until only faction could save it. With the Bedfords entering in November 1767, marshalled by Richard Rigby, the duke's lieutenant, man of business and factionalists' factionalist, taking a long lease of the Pay Office in June 1768, the irony was keen enough. Not altogether for nothing were the Bedfords known as 'the Bloomsbury Crew'.

Grafton had earlier confided to his autobiography words dismaying in a head of government: 'I must now turn again to the drudgery of Parliament.' By the turn of 1769–70, he had endured five vitriolic letters directly addressed to him by Junius. In July, he had been insulted by a recovering Chatham attending his first levee for two years. Grafton might be a modest talent, but he had carried coals and taken kicks. The behaviour was of a part with the man warm by requirement, swift to shift blame and drop unprofitable acquaintance. Chatham lacked the ordinary sense of obligation to, or consideration for, other people. When he wasn't insane, William Pitt was usually a little mad. Grafton, an easy, pleasant man who would later develop Unitarian/Quaker sympathies, quietly remembered the slighting ingratitude in the autobiography thirty years later.

Chatham, now, January 1770, set about persuading old lieutenants to resign. None too happily, Camden, then Lord Granby – like Mr Walpole selling Hayes – did as he wanted. Camden's departure may also have provoked tragedy. The Great Seal had to be taken up. A perfectly fit choice was Charles Yorke, second son of the late Lord Hardwicke. Connections apart, he was a gifted lawyer with an academic slant, perforce in politics. He had, though, in the Rockingham Ministry been chief advocate of the unhelpful Declaratory Act. Other people cajoled or bullied him into things he didn't want to do. Newcastle had talked him into resignation as Solicitor-General over General Warrants. Pitt had blocked his reversion to Attorney to make way for *his* man, Pratt. Now that Pratt as Camden had resigned (after Chatham's nagging), the great prize of English Law was open. On 12 January, Grafton offered it to Yorke. A nervous, anxious personality, Yorke was under pressure from the Rockinghams not to desert them by taking it. He refused it, dithered, accepted, quarrelled with his brother, finally accepted and, three days later, 20 January, was found dead.

'Suicide', said the ill-disposed, including Horace, who disliked him. 'A broken blood vessel', said the family. We don't know, but it was the sort of thing to kill a government not anyway keen on living. After a half-hearted attempt at replacement, Grafton, on 30 January, giving his successor, North, space to steel himself, finally went. It was victory, of a low sort, for Chatham, and opinion looked to his early return. Opinion was wrong.

23

America and Death: The Grand Finale

The Chatham of his last phase as he emerged from collapse was all contradiction. On the one hand, he was playing every kind of politics, with no scruple at all, to thrust aside Grafton who had carried the burden he had let fall. There was in the period of his recovery from July 1769 a consuming avidity for power. Dragging away Camden and Granby from Grafton was egocentric, destructive and in one case, a sort of blackmail. (Granby was in debt to Chatham's new, and former Foxite, middleman, Calcraft.) On the other hand, he would soon engage on issues – press freedom, (tentatively) parliamentary reform, above all, relations with America – where in some respects he was looking to the future. Pitt had always been a populist, playing initially on the middle-class discontents of the City. This had, by extension, brought the mob into play. The gap between the mob and what Chatham, in the style of Gladstone and the Soviet Union, liked to call 'The People' was wide. But both groups shaped what Pitt would say to them.

When mental and physical recovery were first apparent, 9 July 1769, Edmund Burke followed his call on the King: 'I heard . . . that he had certainly been in the Closet. He did not continue there above twenty minutes. It is not yet known if he was sent for, the shortness of the conference would seem to suggest that nothing at all has been settled. If he was not sent for it was only humbly to lay a reprimand at the feet of his most gracious master, and to talk some significant, pompous, creeping, explanatory, ambiguous matter in the true Chathamic style, and that's all.'[1]

Looking at the possibility of George III recalling the absentee Minister, Burke expressed the general Whig suspicion of the Palace: '. . . If indeed a change is thought on, I make no doubt but that they will aim at the choice of him as the puller down of the old, and the architect of the new fabric. If so, the building will not, I suspect, be executed in a very workmanlike manner and can hardly be such as your lordship will choose to be lodged in . . . [he passes on the report that] says that Pitt seemed to be in remarkable good humour on coming out of the closet.'[2]

Any good humour will have been mistaken. Pitt would never again be part of a ministry. It was not just the King who had been burned. The Whig leaders, Rockingham, Sir George Savile (a thoughtful man everywhere trusted), and Richmond were alerted to Pitt's impulses for lonely pre-eminence or spitting contempt. The King's immobility, once set against anyone, would keep office and Chatham apart. The mental illness was known, a good many enemies accumulated. He would scheme again, projecting himself as too highly destined for anything but 'absolute sole power'. This view he had let slip in a conversation recorded by Newcastle.[3]

Still, Chatham was back in the political world, able to speak, campaign and pursue questions. They would, on the whole, be relevant. He was no longer warming his hands before the embers of the last war. The proclamation across remoter Europe, for a Grand Alliance about fixing a 'cloud of glory', had come to nothing. The fustian would continue but he would concentrate on immediate issues.

That didn't stop some of Chatham's eloquence being humbug and snobbish humbug at that. Grandson of an India trader, he denounced the newer rich, men 'without connection, without any interest in the soil, importers of foreign gold'.[4] 'The riches of Asia', he declaimed, 'have been poured upon us and have brought with them not only Asiatic luxury, but I fear Asiatic principles of government.'[5] The lament at Asiatic luxury came from a man demanding at one of his two great houses not just the planting of cedars but their being planted immediately – at night – by torchlight! Such half-unhinged rubbish was, however, point of departure for a sober – if startling – call for electoral reform. Every major city already on the economic horizon – Manchester, Birmingham, Leeds – should have perhaps three Members. The speech illustrates the complexity of Chatham, a combination of serious foresight to practical ends combining with the paranoia.

The Great Reform Act was sixty-two years away and men would rise in the debates of 1831–2 to proclaim that if an atom of the most perfect constitution in the world were removed, civilisation would fall

in upon itself. Yet Pitt having made so sensible and advanced a suggestion, added, with a touch of Malvolio, that if it should not go forward,
then 'May discord prevail for ever'. However, discounting the baroque
moments, this was startling. Recognition in 1770 of the unrepresen-
tative nature of representation seemed, even to the quasi-liberal men
around Rockingham, folly, dangerous enthusiasm. Burke, taken aback,
thought it attractive but surely it wouldn't work. However, if
Rockingham and Grafton were complacent in their acres and boroughs,
Chatham's radical motives were unsteady, the detail more tentative
than the gesture. A nabob's grandson was snubbing nabobs.

Anyway, in attacking corruption, Chatham was providing a descant
to Dowdeswell who did a great deal of the detailed work for the
Rockinghams – hundreds of interventions across the spectrum of
issues – and who had most recently played the busiest part over
Wilkes and the successive Middlesex elections and expulsions. It was
Dowdeswell who turned corruption into a political issue with a speech
on the same day as Chatham's, 9 January 1770, following it up with a
motion of 25 January requiring the Commons in disputed elections
to follow only electoral law. It was this motion, coming within a
respectable forty-four votes of carrying, which persuaded Grafton that
his own race was run. His resignation came next day. But obligation
did not stop Chatham from resentfully asserting his position as part-
time but absolute Captain of the Opposition. He did this by blocking
another piece of Dowdeswell's work, a draft bill defining the powers
of juries in press libel cases, something that had been at the heart of
the legal dispute over the *North Briton*. Chatham then demonstrated
his leadership with a two-month sulk at an initiative unauthorised
by him. He managed some quotable rhetoric but Chatham would
never follow.

Yet his credit for a stand taken on the Thirty-Nine Articles and a
proposed right of Anglican clergy to pass on the most absurd of them
was derivative. He trod here on the heels, not of Dowdeswell, looking
over his shoulder at his three-cathedral home territory, but of Sir
George Savile. The Member for Yorkshire promoted a petition, then
a bill of 1773, seeking relief from submission to the Thirty-Nine Articles
as some of them were inconsistent with reason. Chatham very creditably spoke and voted the liberal way on all these issues, but credit for
liberal initiation, and for their own strong speeches, belongs to

Dowdeswell and Savile. Both men, neither well known today, beyond the company of professional historians, were the disinterested pioneers of a number of measures, liberal in the modern sense and foreshadowing the coming liberalisation of the New Whigs under Charles Fox. Chatham's legitimate credit is for recognising and joining.

His support would not, though, be universal at this time. But that shift to what we might almost call 'the Left' among the City men has its own significance. Chatham set enormous importance upon the City groupings. They were the front ten rows for his eloquence. If the City grew radical, it was natural for Chatham to respond. But in Pitt's new radicalism, there was an element of catering to the troops, except that there were limits. The City radicals now denounced impressment, and its gangs of coercive recruiters, natural cause for a late-flowering liberal. Instead, the Man of War was outraged, the Friend of Liberty mute.

He was, though, ready for greater involvement. His new and avidly active henchman, John Calcraft, was arranging a large celebratory social round, a grand dinner involving City and parliamentary following which should tie in the Rockinghams closer, followed by a remonstrance to the King. But the City would cease to be quite the same thing for Chatham after the death, 21 June 1770 (in the middle of his Lord Mayoralty), of William Beckford. This loss might not have involved, as Horace Walpole pertly announced, 'cutting off all his influence in the City', but certainly it diminished him there and took away a straightforward loyalist. The new radicals wanted serious electoral reform including triennial parliaments. This meant a reversal of the oligarchic shift of the Septennial Act, made under Stanhope so early in the Hanoverian era, away from the great arguing and idea-floating triennial parliaments of William and Mary and Queen Anne. William Dowdeswell, from whom there is no conscientious escaping, had attended the great dinner and was ready to launch a Triennial Bill.

North's government, however, was still the government. It had been easy enough to get rid of a tired and ready-to-jump Grafton. Frederick North, the King's choice, would be another matter. He had been Chancellor and Leader of the House under Grafton. He had an intelligent grasp of finance, a sense of humour and no enemies. To put it very Englishly, he was a thoroughly nice chap, and consequently a terrible opponent. He also, as Chatham had once done, enjoyed the King's support – cemented in with stanchions.

This strength deepened as the Opposition fell into a prolonged bout of kicking and scratching largely provoked by Chatham. In February 1770 he picked an extraordinary fight with Grafton. A debate about naval manpower led him into a private rant about 'secret influence', Old Whig paranoia against the King, and a slash at the Dowager Princess. Since George II's death, he said, there had been no 'original' (meaning independent) minister. Everything was governed by a secret influence which, he intimated, was the Princess's. Horace Walpole, relating this, quotes him as saying, 'he had been duped and deceived by it; and though it was a hard thing to say of himself, confessed he had been a fool and a changeling'. The King had 'great facility in granting everything in his closet, while in council or parliament, it was defeated by the faction of the secret intelligence'. (Grafton 'asked whether the King or himself had been pointed at by the Earl.')

Grafton, 'with dignity and grace', says Horace, 'declared that Chatham had pushed him into the Ministry', that he had the letters to prove it and 'that the happiest day of his life had been that of his resignation' . . . As for what Chatham had said, such words 'were the effects of a distempered mind brooding over its own discontents'. Chatham repeated the last words 'over and over' before making 'severe reflections on his grace's falsehood and deviations'.[6]

It resumed a month later. Dowdeswell (again) had been harrying North's Ministry with demands for accounts of the civil list to be made public, an aspect of the Whig preoccupation with Bute, to whom North used a friendly tone. In the Lords, when Rockingham followed this up, Chatham leapt in with a whirling assault all round. Firstly the King, who was slapped with a eulogy of George II, 'true, faithful and sincere' and expressing his dislikes candidly. This portrait was intended, says Walpole superfluously, 'as a satirical contrast to the reigning monarch'.[7]

As for Grafton, he was, said Chatham repeatedly, 'a novice'. He, Chatham, had never intended him for First Minister, something said in the teeth of his insistence to George that Grafton must stay in office. The duke, as Horace reports Chatham's words, 'had thrust himself into the function, removing Lord Camden and Lord Shelburne; but when the latter was dismissed, could he have crawled out, he himself should have gone to the King and insisted the Duke should be dismissed too'.[8] He added the grave charge that Camden had been removed for his vote in Parliament. The background to this had been Chatham's nagging alienation of his old friend from Grafton's Ministry. The duke held his ground and, after so much painful reticence, came out with a plain statement: 'Lord Chatham had wished him to hold his power only under himself, and had meant him for a cipher *regnante Caesare*.'[9]

The Opposition were generally behaving absurdly in parading their mutual resentments in a round dance of denunciation and counter-denunciation. But Grafton, at the end of three and a half years of tribulation, had found his occasions, and said bitter things calmly. However, the notion of Chatham's recovery looked like the narrowest of physical judgements. Meanwhile, as Burke would say of a later brawl in 1771, 'The Ministerial people looked on, as if they were in the boxes of the opera.'[10]

The domestic issue of late 1770/early 1771 was yet another proposal of serious reform from the hands of Dowdeswell. It flowed from the prosecution of Junius's printer, Henry Woodfall, pursued for criminal libel. The judge, Mansfield, executive and authoritarian, also Scottish, which mattered in 1770, but as a pure lawyer pre-eminent, had ruled that in a libel case criminality was a matter for judge not jury. Dowdeswell's legislation avoided a fight with the judiciary and kept parliamentary authority within its own writ. It was a bill to protect the rights of jurors in future. Pitt spat contempt privately before giving grudging support. The bill would not pass anyway; opposition was failing. The ideas of a grand coalition had dissolved in the acid of recrimination for which, though Grafton and the combative Richmond had played a part, prime responsibility lay with Chatham. Preoccupied with the figure he cut, the respect that was owed, the respect that had not been paid him, Chatham had strengthened North's strong hand by losing control and, in his allegations, coming uselessly and dangerously close to the throne for all the wrong reasons.

He would, though, in the latter part of 1770, enjoy an excursion on familiar, too-familiar territory. For the war which would have relieved Chatham from domestic issues and the trading of resentments seemed to be on its way. In midsummer 1770, Spain, or more precisely the Governor of Buenos Aires, retook the Falkland Islands, or even more

precisely the chief town, Port Egmont, and expelled the British authorities. Something like this had been expected. North's government
proceeded to use conventional diplomacy and probably quite
welcomed fulmination from Chatham. The Spanish, he said, were 'as
mean and crafty as they are proud and insolent' – our merchants plundered – no protection given – no redress obtained. The melodrama
rolled on, the orator orated. 'Ministers stood it at the hazard of their
heads.' Boringly, without exploding a pistol cap, North settled things;
he sent a diplomat. By the start of 1771, the diplomat's work was headline news, the Spanish to withdraw from Port Egmont and the legal
status of the Falkland Islands to remain in that relatively safe place –
the air – until some convenient, later, future time.

It was enough to make a retired colonel weep. This one ranted
on, invoking the Convention of Pardo, Sir Benjamin Keene's sensible
deal thirty or so years before over *Asiento* trade and grievance which
had nearly denied us the last war but one (and the messy draw it
produced). It was Dr Johnson who, four years later, in 1775, discussing
patriotism, said abruptly and for history, 'Patriotism is the last refuge
of a Scoundrel.' Whether his next reference is to Chatham is not
certain, but it seems very likely. The question was pursued, in his
insistent way, by James Boswell. 'I maintained that certainly not all
patriots were scoundrels . . . I mentioned an eminent person who we
all greatly admired.' JOHNSON: '"Sir, I do not say that he is *not*
honest; but we have no reason to conclude from his political conduct
that he *is* honest."'[11]

It was not now a question of honesty, rather of rational self-control.
Chatham's speeches of this period deteriorate. Formerly, he had done
irony and mockery as well as high-flown calls to the flag. He now
came close to screaming. A call for re-armament of the navy, apart
from being 45 per cent wrong on the number of fit ships available,
spread itself into an attack on the jury-rigged capitalism of the day:
'the miserable jobbers of Change Alley . . . the bloodsucker, that muckworm which calls itself the friend of government . . . the whole race
of commissaries, jobbers, contractors, or remitters . . .'[12] Otherwise
than from a very tired Marxist–Leninist on autopilot, such talk sounds
slightly mad.

United Opposition was not united, simple Opposition was not
effected. Lord North and George were free to get the most important

question, America, wrong, untroubled by intelligent Opposition putting them on the back foot and obliging them to think. Chatham and Dowdeswell both felt unwell and went away: Pitt to a bout of ill health and grand-scale sulking, Dowdeswell, who was consumptive, to die.

America would soon after become, for Chatham and everybody else, *the* issue. George III blamed everything upon faction, by which he meant the political parties then emerging as the form of government to replace kings. Sir John Brooke heartily agrees and in an extraordinary passage damns the Rockinghams as Munichites. 'From a military point of view it would have been better for Great Britain to have taken up arms in 1766 rather than in 1775,' over the Stamp Act rather than the Boston Tea Party. He adds a good deal of the usual dubious stuff about American love of liberty (or American love of American liberty). But the well-meaning politicians who withdrew the Stamp Act and passed the Declaratory Act here become The Guilty Men. 'The policy of appeasement – the refusal to make war until there is no alternative between war and national disgrace – so much applauded in 1938, so much condemned in 1940, has a long pedigree in British history.'[13]

For a generally respected historian, even one engaged in giving a Court view of George III, these passages are nonsense and rather shocking. A war fought in 1766 might have been successful, but superior American numbers, knowledge of the territory and recurring general resistance to all but the most murderous and blanket occupations suggest anachronistic nonsense. As Sir John was writing (publication 1972), the United States was seriously engaged – in the Defence of Liberty – in the fifth, sixth and seventh years of making war on Vietnam. Anyway, to have won in 1766 was to be certain of losing in 1780 or 1790, whenever British preoccupation elsewhere should give history its opportunity.

George had rid himself of faction. He had as his Minister not a creature but a clever, civilised man who had originally shared the King's error and, as he learnt better, would suspend judgement out of a loyalty perfectly ruinous. It was not that George III was stupid, though he was very stupid, rather that he had learnt too few things too well – and had learnt the need to be firm, ineradicably.

North had tried to make the intelligent move. His tea legislation brought cheaper tea to North America from the currently hard-pressed

East India Company. Unfortunately, this struck a blow at the most important force in American life, business. They, too, were respectable men
understandably irked by restraint of trade. North had been too rational.
He had, too, looked only at the high-flown reasons for defiance, the
Liberty script, missing the need for a pretext. The Boston Committee
of Correspondence saw the real horror of undercutting the market. 'The
tea was intended to destroy the Trade of the Colonies & increase the
revenue.' The British meant to make the colonies 'absolutely dependent
on the Crown, which will if a little while persisted in, end in absolute
Despotism.'[14] But that was only the talk. When the solid men of Beacon
Hill, dressed as Red Indians, got aboard a cargo ship and poured the
bargain tea into Boston harbour, not George nor his ministers would
trust any lodger in finesse. We would be firm, troops were sent in.

The Duke of Grafton would write sensibly about the conflict in
his autobiography: '. . . if a cordial reconciliation was not *speedily*
effected with the colonies, to lose America would be a lesser evil than
to hold her by a military force, as a conquered country . . . the consequences of holding that dominion by an army only, must inevitably
terminate in the downfall of the constitution and the liberties of
Britain'.[15] If the second passage sounds excessive to us, we must
remember that serious Whigs looked upon kings as bombs likely to
go off, decorative ornaments capable of springing to absolutist life.
They had not the advantage of reading Sir Lewis Namier, and confused
George's dull firmness with tyrannical potential. But it is the first part
of his statement which matters. If he had to, Grafton could live with
an independent America as George could not.

And as Chatham could not! The Chatham of the mid- to late seven-
ties impresses the sceptic as more honest and earnest than other Pitts
and Chathams. But he remained as contradictory and his doctrine as
unthought-out as at the start of the dispute. His doctrine was clear. We
had no right to tax the Americans. Money was a legislative thing and
taking it from people was the prerogative of the Parliament which some
of them had elected. The duty which the Americans owed was to the
King who couldn't tax. It was all good Pym and Hampden stuff. But in
its name, Chatham had previously insisted on our perfect right to regu-
late American trade; and to the very end, he proclaimed the language
of supremacy with much talk about loving fathers and beloved children.

When the business of the day was to pass the Bill for Sending

Troops to Boston, he spoke, 27 May 1774, of his '. . . unalterable opinion that this country has no right under heaven to tax America. We should rather pass an amnesty on all their youthful errors' (dumping tea and general defiance) but '. . . should this turbulence again exist after your proffered terms of forgiveness which I hope this House will accept, I will be among the foremost of those of your lordships to move for such measures as will effectually prevent a further relapse and to make them feel what it is to provoke a fond and forgiving parent.'

The parallel is too painful. 'I shall do such things, what they are yet I know not . . .' Yet at this time, Edmund Burke, famous as the man who was right about America, also underrated the full nature of colonial will. There must be conciliation, but the notion of giving up the colonies would not detain him. It was 'but a little sally of anger, like the forwardness of peevish children who, when they cannot get all they would have, are resolved to take nothing'.[16]

Burke detested Chatham, saw his flaws better than any contemporary, but, as the War of American Independence began, he asserted the full Chatham doctrine, what the right-thinking man was asserting in the spring of 1774: '. . . the only true friends [the Americans] have had or ever can have in England, have laid down, and will lay down, the proper subordination of America as a fundamental, incontrovertible maxim in the government of this Empire'.[17]

Chatham would make a poor start to the American war which, paralleling the real thing, would roll through British politics beyond the decade. North at his best set about not making enemies of the French Canadians by recognising with full official status the Roman Catholicism which happened to be the faith of almost all French Canadians. Historically, French Canada has been altogether more Catholic, commonly *dévot*, than France. Here sensibility was sense and the bill passed, setting a precedent for the realistic and enduring relationship with Canada, French and British, secured by Lord Durham in the 1830s. Chatham responded with a long and tiring rant about the 'Popery and arbitrary power'[18] which must flow from North's betrayal.

Quite how deep actual religious belief ran in Chatham is dubious. He was a political Protestant as an extension of being a political Englishman. He was not altogether engaged in what we now call conviction politics. Rather, he was an identity politician. In consequence, though rather less discreditably, he sounded like Lord

Randolph Churchill denouncing 'Rome Rule' in Paddington in 1886. As to the fighting, early belief had been that winning would be easy. So those arguing so early, 1774–5, against military action have historically a claim on very high ground. Grafton's claim that '. . . there never existed, at any time such another in purity of intention toward the public . . .',[19] though high-flown, is not absurd. Opposition to making this war was sense asserted against everything inherently wrong about 'firmness'.

There was quite a culture of firmness going right back to the Stamp Act itself. Hans Stanley, diplomat at the Paris negotiations, had told the reforming Rockinghams back in 1766 that if they repealed the Stamp Act, that 'will not content the Americans'; they would soon be back 'with the same decent and respectful opposition to your whole system of laws of American legislation'. The jurist, Blackstone, thought the colonies 'dependent on us, and if they attempt to shake off [their] dependence, we shall, I hope, have firmness enough to make them obey'. Charles Yorke, Hardwicke's soldier son, said, 'If the supremacy is not assured, no friend will trust you, no enemy will fear you.'[20]

Dowdeswell, now dying in Nice, had, in his 1768 memorandum to Rockingham, made the best judgement. Only two options existed: '. . . either to fight to the last, in which case this country will be undone, or to treat with the contending party, depart from your own dignity, weaken your authority, and giving up in time a part of your rights, preserve the rest'.[21] Once war began there was no rest to preserve. The option to fighting had changed from 'weakening our authority' to our giving it up entirely as, to the stricken lamentings of George III, we would.

Even so, the Opposition battled on, with Chatham promoting a motion 'To Withdraw Troops from Boston'. He attacked the use of soldiers as 'the prescription of a people condemned and not heard . . . America means to have safety in property and personal liberty. Those and those only were her object. Independency was falsely charged on her.'[22] His reading of American purposes was idealistic. He was being at once generous to the Americans and wholly unrealistic about what they wanted. Yet he had better sources than most people. He was holding over time a series of discussions with Benjamin Franklin, once ranked among the moderate men of the American interest, now coming to see independence as the only issue. Franklin spent four hours at Hayes with Chatham. He brought with him the address to the British people of the Continental Congress. For that motion to withdraw troops from Boston, Chatham brought the American spokesman with him to the Lords, intending to sit him below the throne where distinguished guests were admitted. But the bureaucratic rules denied them.

Franklin had been consulted in the framing of the bill Chatham presented. The provisions it offered for withdrawal made up an honest affair, some years too late. Revenue was to be raised by request. (As any British commander in America during the Seven Years War could have told him, getting contributions for what was their own defence had been poisonously difficult. Request was a dream.) The Quebec Act, with its wise deference to French Canadian Catholicism, would be abolished. The Continental Congress would be recognised and authorised to assess each state's revenue contribution. But Britain would maintain and assert a right, utterly unenforceable, to keep troops in any dominion, including America. Such thinking would get nowhere with George III's ministers and nowhere with the Congress.

The people who did rally round were the leading Whigs. Shelburne, the mysterious, very clever, obscurely unpopular major talent whose autobiography in respect of Chatham blends reverence and deadly analysis, gave support. As did Grafton, whom he had abused, Richmond, who could and did stand up to him and, of course, Camden. George III performed several miracles in his time: bringing the Whigs together was an outstanding example. Behind it lies the observation made by the Duke of Richmond, a down-the-line opponent of the whole confrontational policy and ready to repeal the Declaratory Act, one step which might have had some effect. The Duke, says William C. Lowe, 'like many of his fellow Whigs, . . . believed that curtailment of American liberty would herald repression at home'.[23] It wasn't true, but in the mid-1770s it wasn't an unreasonable belief. The willingness of the *Morning Post* to call the duke 'a traitor', as defeat in America loomed in 1780, catches the mood. Chatham was called even worse things by the King. 'Engine of sedition' catches the full style of royal unreason.

Things now happening were out of George's or Chatham's reach to put right. A letter from Camden to Grafton is succinct: 'America is lost and the war afoot. There is an end to advising preventive measures.'[24] The Battle of Lexington had taken place on 19 April, Bunker's Hill on 16 June. The same letter contains the postscript: 'Lord Chatham continues in the same melancholy way: and the house is so shut up that his sons are not permitted to entertain visitors.' The illness, all the illnesses, were back. From April 1775, two weeks before Lexington, until May 1777, when he briefly again emerged in the Lords, Chatham was intermittently ill. On the physical side he had deteriorated. A hernia, almost inoperable before chloroform and antisepsis, had added to the miseries of the gout or rheumatic fever which dogged him.

In parallel with all this, his private affairs were in a frightful state, which it was Hester's devoted and highly capable business to take care of. Chatham, as remarked, had every domestic virtue – chastity, sobriety and affection. But just as he could not trouble himself with the vulgar raising of funds for war by issues of government stock, so he had walked oblivious through the expense of house ownership, selling one, improving another, losing heavily on both. Burke, remember, had counted a retinue of twenty servants. The bills could not be met. Chatham regularly talked national ruin. In a speech of this time he announced that with the war he saw 'a cloud . . . ready to burst and overwhelm us in ruin'.[25] He was in a fair way to accomplishing his own.

Hester was juggling the two country houses, trying to get rid of Hayes for the second time, renting it out for a while, unable to sell it for the price he imagined. He borrowed £1000 from the friendly tenant on the strength of Hayes, which he couldn't sell, before edging the loan to £7000, then £10,000. He was offered consideration by North to seek a deal giving him his £3000 a year net (above all expenses and fees, a solid thousand more). This was blocked by George who, on his day, could outperform the meanest little Austrian clerk in Kafka. The fully made-up pension could pass to young William Pitt when Chatham should die or, as George put it, 'when decrepitude or death puts an end to him as a trumpet of sedition'.[26] Ironically, as the war which had been approached with bland confidence by our commander, Gage, got worse, the trumpet of sedition, back in approximate working order by late 1777, was suddenly wanted again.

Impossibly from what we know of Chatham's health, serious people right up to the Court now talked about another Chatham Ministry.

Defeat at Saratoga brought people to some of their senses. They knew they had lost and knew that they must get out. North, least ardent of warmakers, knew that *he* must get out. George, in his uninstructable firmness, did not. North, after Saratoga, was the prisoner of Downing Street. By March 1778 even George was responding part of the way. Pitt might come in, bringing Shelburne and other friends, with North still First Minister. It was perfect futility. Not only was Chatham dying, he still wanted, in the most affectionate, loving way, to assert British supremacy. He had broken with the Rockinghams on the grounds of their excessive reasonableness. 'I would as soon subscribe to transubstantiation as sovereignty, by right in the Colonies.'

He came to the Lords on 7 April, in the customary wrappings of flannel, large velvet boots and other comforts of his distress. He was supported by his son-in-law, Lord Moran, and, down from Cambridge, his startlingly clever son, William (to be Prime Minister in under six years), and made a speech of unrehearsed pathos. What could be made out through his low voice and incoherence was rage at the French, now understandably active, the 'ancient inveterate enemy'.[27] Few people could compete with Chatham at being inveterate. What could be made of it was a cry of 'No surrender' – to anyone. He fell down in a seizure and was taken to the Robing Rooms, then eventually back to Hayes. Briefly, he recovered, had William read him from the *Iliad* the account of the Death of Hector and, on 8 May, at Hayes, finally died. A state funeral at Westminster Abbey – on the vote of Commons not Lords, controversy flourishing happily yet – followed on 9 June and made way for historical argument.

Envoi

The points have been made through the story. Pitt as national hero, 'Towering figure' or 'Great Man' is more than suspect. His reputation flickered violently in his own time from acclamation, either as news of victory came through or as his noisy allies like the *Monitor* proclaimed him 'a darling minister'. The immediate reputation was very mixed, with Edmund Burke making a clear grasp of Chatham's pomposity and dismissing the oratory as fustian. He was, though, given full rapture by the Victorians, starting a little early, in 1827, with the Reverend Francis Thackeray who had the misfortune to be reviewed (seven years later and at opulent length) by Macaulay who split the Minister, like Henry IV, into parts one and two, William Pitt and the Earl of Chatham. Neither emerged happily. Little phrases attach themselves like burs: 'Pitt on his part, omitted nothing that might facilitate his admission to office.' Or, 'He clamoured for war with a vehemence which it is not easy to reconcile with reason or humanity, but which appear to Mr Thackeray worthy of the highest admiration.'

Those two quotations, picked almost at random from pages 380–81 of volume one of the *Critical and Historical Essays*, instantly point up two clear impressions about Chatham. He was, through the over-grown thicket of his asserted virtue, a man avid for power and he loved war indecently. In the case Macaulay is speaking about, the miserable affair of 1741–8, it was a war Walpole despised. Its chief British inspiration was the gouging greed of people like the slave plantation owner William Beckford, who wanted to destroy French trade, sink French ships and drown French sailors and said so in terms.

Overall, though, the exalted view of Chatham, if not so high-flying as the Reverend Thackeray's, survived for a long time, even affecting as good a historian as Basil Williams, writing in 1913. The reason is easy: approval was an imperial approval, reliably reasserted across imperial times. It is important not to present a matching response which blames an empire for being imperial. One must not be anachronistic. But Macaulay spent four years, 1834–8, a high servant of the Raj, laying down educational and penal practice in India: no anachronism in his views, then. Again, broadly, the Old Corps Whigs approved the struggle in Canada. Indeed, before the researches of Michael Durban and Ewen Fraser, the fact of Newcastle, Hardwicke and their allies *wanting a favourable result in* Canada was little noticed and not readily acknowledged.

There were, though, quantitative and qualitative differences. Newcastle and Hardwicke thought defensively, of limiting France. Pitt, as his emotions took over, expressed a clear wish to smash France for ever as some kind of eternal evil. There is nothing anachronistic in remarking which was the wiser, more civilised, indeed saner outlook. Chatham's misfortune is that his personality fits his views. He wanted a Great Nation to be the vehicle of the Great Man he knew himself to be. So far from anachronism, the unguarded heartfelt outbursts are fearfully contemporary. International law, as Macaulay also remarks, doesn't come into it.

We are talking power, greed for power, power as fulfilment. It does lead one to appreciate Walpole – and Newcastle and Hardwicke and the too-much-traduced Whigs. The appendix based upon David Owen's book *In Sickness and in Power*, coupled with Lord Owen's own recent conclusions on seeing the section here dealing with Chatham's breakdown, is highly instructive: not hubris syndrome but hubris, indeed psychosis.

If we look at events neutrally without legal or moral qualms, then, at the risk of sounding a touch Marxist/Determinist, it is reasonable to say that the Seven Years War was inevitable. There had been empires long enough post-Columbus, but the struggle for empty space in the American continent, expansion of trade in a mercantilist age certain that such trade was finite, was inevitable. Those factors made for a mighty accelerant. We stumbled into the war without Pitt. But with or without him, Britain was always overwhelmingly likely to win the naval part of it. The credit for that victory, as Richard Middleton argues in *The Bells of Victory*, lies with obscure people like John Clevland, long-term Secretary to the Board of Admiralty, with Sandwich, Bedford and, of course, Anson. They created, and their French equivalents, despite building some fine ships, did not, a navy to beat all-comers. Commanded by a roll call of senior officers, professional, aggressive and innovative, headed by Hawke, inspiration of Nelson, Britain did.

They won, Pitt did not. The only part of the war he initiated and for which he involved himself in detailed planning, was the running of Channel raids. All except the last were failures. They were taken against the advice of Hawke and other admirals – and Pitt never understood the stature of Hawke. The raids were political things, done to be seen being done, a keeping of press, Parliament and the Street at the stave's end, an idea tossed out by the great landsman Frederick of Prussia, for want of the direct help Pitt dared not then give him.

As to the European theatre, we see Pitt furiously assuring Leicester House and Bute that we must never engage there. We next see him approving lavish payment, then the sending of troops who, overall, performed very creditably. Ewen Fraser in his outstanding thesis argues that, had Cumberland's army been properly manned ahead of Hastenbeck, then defeat and all it implied might not have happened. He also reckons Pitt to have seen the German point all along, but to have opposed it at first and not only to quiet his faction. He also meant, says Fraser, partly to let colleagues run immediate risks while giving an impression of amenability and Cabinet pluralism. It might be so, but the theory gives Pitt credit for being a more complex Machiavel than he perhaps was. Countenancing scuttle against the King and Old Corps for *wanting* defeat at Rochefort was nearer Pitt's sort of politics, anger, frustration and irrational abuse – relayed at second hand.

At which point, the question is asked, how with such faults and limitations did Pitt become as successful and esteemed successful as he was? Pitt was an orator in an age which adored oratory. A self-conscious student of Cicero and Demosthenes, he knew the technique and art of rhetoric. He was also a dominant physical presence, 'the eye like a diamond' in Lord Shelburne's phrase. People will be led if someone, not clown or incompetent – and he was neither – offers to lead. Even more so will they follow a speaker utterly self-possessed, someone speaking perfect certainty. And what works with crowds can work with parliaments.

Comforted with apples at the Pay Office in 1746 by soothing, sensible Henry Pelham, Pitt was kept from his strengths, eloquence and uplift.

However, any major conflict, even without the fit of panic created by Minorca and 'Poor Byng', needs a presence, a trumpet, an enlarged personality. Pitt had such qualities in all four suits. He was an eidetic personality, a clear, sharply defined, unmissable public image. The point front of stage had to be filled. Henry Fox had bad nerves, William Murray knew his comfort lay in legal eminence. Pitt it had to be, and he was very good at it.

To parliamentary command he added a bustling, urgent manner, sometimes bullying, sometimes conciliatory. Newcastle's letters show a willingness to give Pitt grateful credit when he behaves and there must surely have been a manipulative aspect to his conduct. Machiavelli would certainly have recommended the force of uncertain temper. Again, so far as public reputation was concerned, Pitt was very good at taking the credit, and he had energetic cheerleaders in Beckford's *Monitor* and in the pamphleteering of Thomas Potter and the early John Wilkes. (The slightly older, very much wiser Wilkes, after being denounced as unfit for the human race on the strength of those risqué verses probably written by Potter, would return the scorn.) Then again, the defects of the man were strengths in a public figure. As somebody said about President Lyndon Johnson, 'He's not the kind of guy you hand your hat to.' Like many politicians, Pitt was an actor who concentrated upon the figure cut, the impression given, the deference obtained.

He did not win the Seven Years War, did not raise the money for it – Newcastle did that by recourse to Samson Gideon – did not have a system or scheme into which subordinate soldiers and sailors neatly placed themselves. He was the show business of war, useful certainly, perhaps at certain moments essential – but not a quality which on its own accomplishes victory.

We should see Pitt as a demagogue, highly intelligent but incapable of coping with detail, self-absorbed, fascinated by power, a man exalting the nation whose greatness should exalt him. Some people had called it his war, he said in his first speech after resignation.

There is deep divorce between Pitt's imaginings and the actual, fighting, killing, body-burying thing. Frederick the Great, whom we have seen knocked from his horse by a spent bullet and stopping to reflect at the field of Kunersdorf the price to other men of his final triumph, knew all about that. There is another chasm between the politician craving command and the long process of actual power, rationally conducted and contained. The British Empire proved by no means a bad thing. It had too many honest, unexalted people running it without much glory of their own for that.

It was not, despite the efforts of other trumpeters, much to do with glory but with government, steady, coherent, dull responsibility. With all of which William Pitt, Earl of Chatham, had so very little to do.

Appendix:
Chatham's Mental Condition

We know that on several occasions, notably for the greater part of his peacetime Prime Ministership, William Pitt descended into madness. That is not a word psychiatrists care to use, essentially because they know of too many causes and conditions behind any mental collapse. Wittgenstein's comment 'Whereof we do not know, thereof we should not speak' is sound doctrine. So, while readily chancing my hand all the time to speak and write about history and politics, I have just enough sense to do nothing of the kind about psychiatric conditions. However whereof we do not know, we may perfectly well ask someone who does.

In the case of Chatham and his mental condition, I have turned to Lord Owen (Dr David Owen) who has the experience and advantage of being both politician and psychiatrist. Politics being about power, it is important, vulnerable and dangerous. In an article written by David Owen with Dr Jonathan Davidson, for the learned journal *Brain*, memorable words are quoted from the social and medical historian, the late Roy Porter: 'The history of madness is the history of power. Because it imagines power, madness is both impotence and omnipotence. It requires power to control it. Threatening the normal structures of authority, insanity is engaged in an endless dialogue – a monomaniacal monologue sometimes – about power.'

The question of madness and power is faced in detail through specific twentieth-century and more recent great lives in Owen's earlier, full length study *In Sickness and in Power*, subtitled 'Illness in heads of government during the last 100 Years'.[1] It is a challenging and rather frightening work of medical enquiry reinforced with a politician's knowledge of politicians. United States Presidents and British Prime

Ministers are examined on the basis of known behaviour and of other
illness, then indicated, discharged or judged not proven. If that looks
a little ambitious, the calm, rational conduct of some heads of government needs such estimates when caught in the historic company of
quite enough national leaders clearly disturbed. Indeed, something
close to mental illnesss may even, when valiantly combated, forge
great strength. Owen cites 'The Suicide's Soliloquy', a poem of 1838
generally thought to be the work of the young and depressive
Abraham Lincoln.

The relevance of assessment in the present case is clear. To the
biographer of the febrile and sometimes distracted Chatham, what
most obviously arises from his very intelligent, highly lit, self-exalting
career is precisely the question of hubris – how much and how far?
In his introduction, Owen essays a definition of hubris. 'Hubris is
not yet a medical term. The most basic meaning developed in ancient
Greece, simply as a description of an act: a hubristic act was one in
which a powerful figure, puffed up with overweening pride and self-
confidence, treated others with insolence and contempt . . . Plato
saw this "rule of desire" as something irrational that drags men into
doing the wrong thing through acts of hubris.' Owen then goes on
to argue the notion, especially as to politicians, of 'hubris as a kind
of loss of capacity'.

'The pattern,' he says, 'is very familiar in the careers of political
leaders whose success makes them feel excessively self-confident and
contemptuous of advice that runs counter to what they believe, or
sometimes of any advice at all, and who start to act in ways that seem
to defy reality itself. Nemesis usually, though not always, follows.'[2]

'I want', he says, 'to find out whether hubristic behaviour of this
sort amongst political leaders can be linked to certain personality
types that predispose someone to act hubristically; and whether indeed
such personality types create a propensity in those who have them
to enter careers such as politics. Even more interesting is whether
some political leaders who do not have such personality types may,
nevertheless, start to behave hubristically simply as a consequence of
being in power.[3]

'In other words, can the experience of being in power itself bring
about changes in mental states which then manifest themselves in
hubristic behaviour? I believe it would be meaningful to speak of this

as a hubris syndrome that can affect those in power. A syndrome happens to someone, it is nature at work, a collection of features, be they signs or symptoms, which have a greater chance of appearing together than independently.'⁴

As Owen fears that the condition, if it exists in the first place, intensifies with a lengthening period in office, this is something of concern for those of us *not* in power, and his selection of symptoms becomes rather important. A head of government, he suggests, 'needs to present more than three or four symptoms from the following tentative list, before any such diagnosis should be contemplated:

- A narcissistic propensity to see the world primarily as an arena in which they exercise power and seek glory rather than a place with problems that need approaching in a pragmatic and non-self-referential manner;
- A predisposition to take actions which seem likely to cast them in a good light – i.e. in order to enhance their image;
- A disproportionate concern with image and presentation;
- A messianic manner of talking about what they are doing and a tendency to exaltation;
- An identification of themselves with the state to the extent that they regard the outlook and interests of the two as identical;
- A tendency to talk of themselves in the third person or using the royal 'we';
- Excessive confidence in their own judgement and contempt for the advice and criticism of others;
- Exaggerated self-belief, bordering on a sense of omnipotence, in what they personally can achieve;
- A belief that, rather than being accountable to the mundane court of colleagues or public opinion, the real court to which they answer is much greater: History or God;
- An unshakeable belief that in that court they will be vindicated;
- Restlessness, recklessness and impulsiveness;
- Loss of contact with reality; often associated with progressive isolation;
- A tendency to allow their 'broad vision', especially their conviction about the moral rectitude of a proposed course of action, to obviate the need to consider other aspects of it, such as its practicality, cost

and the possibility of unwanted outcomes; a wooden-headed refusal
to change course;

- A consequent type of impotence in carrying out a policy, which
could be called hubristic incompetence. This is where things go
wrong precisely because too much self-confidence has led the leader
not to bother worrying about the nuts and bolts of a policy. There
may be an inattention to detail which can be allied to an incurious
nature. It is to be distinguished from ordinary incompetence, where
the necessary detailed work on the complex issues involved is
engaged in but mistakes in decision-making are made nonetheless.'[5]

The present book has concerned itself with William Pitt the Elder,
a man who, as set out in Chapter 22, 'Power Out of Mind', collapsed
into complete incapacity. He had been a strong, dominant personality,
but long before the 1766–7 breakdown he had pushed self-assurance
to its limits, made speeches heavy with destiny and personal exaltation. Generations of schoolmasters have quoted to the Upper Fifth
the grand old cry of destiny: 'I know that I can save this country and
that nobody else can.' It was widely believed, partly because in the
full glow of empire it was part of national legend, but also because
such ringing self-belief commands submission.

It is not actually true. As argued above, England didn't need saving.
The worst she had to fear in the event of a disadvantageously drawn
war would be the same modest disappointments marking the
preceding war of 1739–46. And in the last year of that conflict, the
steadily improving Admiralty management and quality of seamanship, plus captains-at-sea fully realising themselves, had intimated
what would soon be achieved. Pitt would be an important contrib-
utor to the war effort as a keeper-up of morale, but he did not win
the war. His talent was for convincing people that he did. Seven years
after the Year of Victories (1759), facing the domestic politics of 1766,
he would make furious assertions of primacy, the little notes handed
out to Cabinet ministers for them to take into a corner and read!
Soon after which he retreated into mental collapse. So was Pitt
hubristic? Did he gather together the grand coalition of symptoms
which marks the full-blown condition of hubristic syndrome? Having
read David Owen on that topic, I sent him Chapter 22, which describes
the actual crisis, and asked *him*.

There follows, in full, his assessment of Lord Chatham in the light of his investigations, with a colleague and alone, of hubris syndrome. It stands below without interpolation:

There is little doubt that Pitt/Chatham had hubristic traits, but so do many politicians. But from what I have read of yours and a few others he had a much more psychotic history. Firstly, he appears to have had depression – I notice that William Hague on page 21 of his book on Pitt the Younger talks of the father's 'retreat into illness, possibly into what would later be called manic depression', and refers to the spring of 1777 when he became an invalid, refusing to see anyone other than a few chosen people. You in your draft Chapter 22 use strong descriptions of his changes in mood: 'From March 1767 he was absolutely unable to perform any public business' . . . 'under care, ghostly head of government' and later he withdrew into 'the lowest dejection and debility that mind or body can be in'. This sounds very like depression. You then say like George III's porphyria it was intermittent: incidentally some people think George III's mental symptoms were produced by lead poisoning or plumbism (Runyan W. McK, 'Progress in Psychobiography', *Journal of Personality* 56, 1988, 295–326).

Intermittent makes one think of Manic Depression or Bipolar I, as it is now called. You yourself refer to his 'megalomaniac building plans' and William Hague refers to his wish 'to continue in office only on the basis of an assured control of the government' (p. 12). That smacks of grandiosity or control freakery and at the very least considerable arrogance.

On balance, on very little real medical information, I would lean towards 'manic depression' as a diagnosis more likely than hubris syndrome. On my definition I exclude people with depression because they may well be also having manic depression. For example, LBJ had manic depression so I don't label him with hubris syndrome, but his hubris, like Nixon's, developed; it was progressive but Nixon had the complicating factor of being an alcoholic and suffering from depression.

Lloyd George, Chamberlain, Thatcher and Blair did not have depression and are therefore unlikely to be manic depressives either. Pitt/Chatham was odd in that as the 'Great Commoner' there is less sign of depression than when Lord Chatham. What effect gout has on all this is difficult to assess. Why, I started only 100 years ago with Theodore Roosevelt!

But you say he was an infrequent attender at the House of Commons and you mention anxiety. Anxiety often means depression. You also refer to him being 'low in the water', another hint of depression.

So we have an expert view. Pitt had profound mental problems, and some form of depression probably identifies him best. On the evidence, despite hubristic traits and a more psychotic history than most politicians, he falls short of the hubris syndrome.

I hope all this helps. But I would not think Pitt/Chatham is a candidate for hubris syndrome.

Notes

1. *The Interloper and the Diamond pp. 3–13*

• **1.** John Keay, *The Honourable Company*, p. 173. **2.** • *Ibid.* • **3.** *Hedges Diary 1681–89*, four vols, ed. Barlow and Yule, quoted in Sir Cornelius Dalton, *The Life of Thomas Pitt*, p. 32. • **4.** *Hedges Diary*, vol. I, quoted in Dalton, *op. cit.*, p. 31. • **5.** *Hedges Diary*, vol. II, quoted in Dalton, *op. cit.*, p. 31. • **6.** Quoted in Keay, *op. cit.*, p. 214. • **7.** *Ibid.* • **8.** Quoted in Dalton, *op. cit.*, p. 217. • **9.** *Ibid.*, p. 229. • **10.** *Hedges Diary*, vol. III, p. 165, quoted in Romney Sedgwick, *The House of Commons 1715–1754*, vol. II, p. 352. • **11.** *Ibid.*, pp. 352–3. • **12.** *Ibid.*, p. 351. • **13.** Dalton, *op. cit.*, p. 409. • **14.** *Hedges Diary*, vol. III, p. 69, quoted in Dalton, *op. cit.*, p. 390. • **15.** *Ibid.*, quoting *Hedges Diary*, p. 391. • **16.** Dropmore Archive, quoted in Dalton, *op. cit.*, p. 395. • **17.** Dropmore Archive, quoted in Dalton, *ibid.*, pp. 395–6. • **18.** Wentworth Papers, quoted in Dalton, *op. cit.*, p. 398. • **19.** *Hedges Diary*, vol. III, p. 93, in Dalton, *op. cit.*, p. 399. • **20.** Dalton main text, *op. cit.*, p. 399. • **21.** Dropmore Archive, vol. I, p. 23, quoted in Dalton, *op. cit.*, p. 400. • **22.** Dalton, *op. cit.*, *passim*. • **23.** Fortune Papers Boconnoc, vol. I, p. 86, quoted in Sedgwick, *op. cit.*, vol. II, p. 350. • **24.** Fortescue, quoted in Sedgwick, *ibid.*, p. 533. • **25.** Dropmore, quoted in Dalton, *op. cit.*, p. 402.

2 *Eton, Oxford and Northampton Barracks pp. 14–21*

• **1.** Lord Rosebery, *Chatham, His Early Life and Connections*, p. 30. • **2.** *Ibid.*, p. 28. • **3.** Quoted *ibid.*, p. 28, dated 4 February 1722. • **4.** Quoted Martin C. Battestin, *Henry Fielding: A Life*, p. 44. • **5.** *Ibid.*, p. 42. • **6.** *Ibid.*, p. 45. • **7.** Rosebery, *op. cit.*, referring to Lord Edmund Fitzmaurice, *Life of William, First Earl of Shelburne*, vol. I, p. 72. • **8.** Rosebery, *op. cit.*, p. 26. • **9.** Quoted Rosebery, *op. cit.*, pp. 34–5. • **10.** *Ibid.*, pp. 35–6. • **11.** *Ibid.*, p. 30. • **12.** *ODNB*, Marie Peters entry on Pitt. • **13.** Rosebery, *op. cit.*, pp. 43–4. • **14.** *Ibid.*, p. 46. • **15.** Quoted *ibid.*, p. 59. • **16.** *Ibid.*, p. 61. • **17.** Dropmore MSS, series 2, Add. MSS 69289, nos 17–18. Quoted *ibid.*

3 Meet the Grenvilles pp. 22–31

• **1.** Egmont Diary 2, p. 171. Quoted *ODNB*, Marie Peters entry on Pitt.
• **2.** Quoted in Maynard Mack, *Alexander Pope*, p. 596. • **3.** Quoted *ibid.*,
p. 596. • **4.** Lewis Wiggins, *The Faction of Cousins*, p. 293. • **5.** Quoted Romney
Sedgwick, ed., *Letters from George III to Lord Bute*, p. 230. • **6.** Historical
Manuscripts Commission (HMC) Carlisle, p. 104, 15 March 1733, quoted in
Paul Langford, *The Excise Crisis*, p. 65. • **7.** William Seward, *Anecdotes of
Distinguished Persons*, 4 vols (London, 1798). Quoted in Wiggins, *op. cit.*, p. 2.
• **8.** Battestin, *Henry Fielding*, p. 198. • **9.** John, Lord Hervey, *Some Materials
towards memoirs of the Reign of King George the Second*, ed. Sedgwick, 3 vols
(London, 1932). • **10.** Fitzmaurice, *Shelburne*, vol. I, pp. 56–7. Quoted Wiggins,
op. cit., p. 3. • **11.** Quoted Battestin, *op. cit.*, p. 198. • **12.** *Daily Gazetteer*, 9
September 1736. Quoted *ibid.*, p. 198.

4 The Peace of Sir Robert pp. 32–39

• **1.** Townshend to Newcastle, 12–24 August 1725, quoted in G. C. Gibbs,
'Britain and the Alliance of Hanover April 1725–February 1726', *EHJ* 87, January
1961, p. 271. • **2.** *Ibid.* • **3.** *Craftsman*, 16 January [OS] 1727. • **4.** Lord Rosebery,
Chatham, His Early Life and Connections, p. 149.

5 Poor Fred and the Patriots pp. 40–48

• **1.** • William Cobbett, *History of Parliament*, vol. 8, col. 1812, quoted *passim*
• **2.** William Coxe, *Life of Walpole*, vol. I, p. 524. • **3.** Lord Macaulay, 'The
Earl of Chatham', in *Critical and Historical Essays*, vol. 1, p. 377. • **4.** Cobbett,
op. cit., vol. 10 (1737–9), cols 1280–90. • **5.** Macaulay, *op. cit.*, pp. 378–80, *passim*
• **6.** Quoted Lord Rosebery, *Chatham, His Early Life and Connections*, p. 158.
• **7.** Cobbett, *op. cit.*, vol. 10, cols 464–7. • **8.** *Ibid.*, cols 464–7.

6 War with Spain: St Jingo's Eve pp. 49–68

• **1.** Lord Macaulay, 'The Earl of Chatham', in *Critical and Historical Essays*,
vol. I, p. 407. • **2.** Richard Pares, *War and Trade in the West Indies 1739–1763*.
• **3.** *The Present Ruinous Land – War proved to be a H——r War* (London, 1745),
pp. 21–31, quoted in Pares, *op. cit.*, p. 62. • **4.** *Ibid.*, p. 15. • **5.** *Cambridge Economic
History of Europe*, vol. IV (Cambridge University Press, 1967), p. 561. Quoted
M. S. Anderson, *The War of the Austrian Succession 1740–48*, p. 15.
• **6.** Pares, *op. cit.*, pp. 10–11. • **7.** *Ibid.*, pp. 10–11. • **8.** *Ibid.*, p. 11. • **9.** *Ibid.*, p. 20.

• **10.** *Ibid.*, p. 14. • **11.** State Papers 94.128. Quoted Pares, *ibid.*, p. 32.
• **12.** William Cobbett, *History of Parliament*, vol. 10, cols 1280–1290. • **13.** *Ibid.*, cols 1290–1298. • **14.** *Ibid.*, col. 772. Quoted Pares, *op. cit.*, p. 139. • **15.** *Ibid.*
• **16.** *Ibid.*, col. 848. Quoted Pares. • **17.** Frank McLynn, *France and the Jacobite Rising of 1745*. • **18.** Cobbett, *op. cit.*, vol. 10, col. 986. Quoted Pares.
• **19.** Anderson, *op. cit.*, p. 17. • **20.** Fitzmaurice, *Shelburne*, vol. I, pp. 34–6.
• **21.** Lewis Wiggins, *The Faction of Cousins*, p. 92. • **22.** Quoted in Edward Pearce, *The Great Man*, pp. 400–401. • **23.** Walpole to Trevor, Former HMC cataloguing, 14th Report. Quoted in Wiggins, *op. cit.*, p. 94. • **24.** R. Browning, *The Duke of Newcastle*, p. 95. • **25.** Philip Yorke, letter to Hardwicke, vol. 1, I, pp. 483–4, quoted Wiggins, *op. cit.*, p. 95. • **26.** Fitzmaurice, *op. cit.*, pp. 34–6.
• **27.** J. B. Owen, *The Rise of the Pelhams*, p. 7 and n. • **28.** Walpole to Sir Horace Mann, 16 December 1741. Quoted Sedgwick, *The House of Commons 1715–1754*, vol. II, p. 2. • **29.** Wiggins, *op. cit.*, p. 97. • **30.** Coxe, *Life of Walpole*, vol. I, p. 695. • **31.** *Ibid.*, p. 204. • **32.** O. A. Sherrard, *Lord Chatham*, vol. I, p. 81. • **33.** Coxe, *op. cit.*, p. 711. • **34.** *Ibid.* • **35.** Wiggins, *op. cit.*, p. 99.

7 Carteret, Pelham and Yellow Fever pp. 69–83

• **1.** Paul Langford, *A Polite and Commercial People*, p. 192. • **2.** William Cobbett, *History of Parliament*, vol. 13, col. 136. • **3.** *The British Champion or Admiral Vernon's Weekly Journal*. Quoted M. S. Anderson, *The War of the Austrian Succession 1740–48*, p. 1. • **4.** Anderson, *op. cit.*, p. 138. • **5.** *Ibid.*, p. 19. • **6.** Cobbett, *op. cit.*, vol. 12 (1741–3), col. 1035. • **7.** *Ibid.*, vol. 13 (1743–7), cols 136n, 465n. Quoted in *ODNB*, Marie Peters entry on Pitt. • **8.** Cobbett, *op. cit.*, vol. 16 (1765–71), col. 1092. • **9.** Langford, *op. cit.*, p. 191. • **10.** Seward, *Anecdotes*, vol. II, p. 280. Quoted Lord Rosebery, *Chatham, His Early Life and Connections*, p. 180. • **11.** Quoted *ibid.*, p. 182. • **12.** William Coxe, *Life of Pelham*, vol. I (1829), p. 258. • **13.** Quoted Rosebery, *op. cit.*, p. 217. • **14.** Coxe, *op. cit.*, vol. I, p. 258. Quoted in *ODNB*, P.J. Kulisheck entry on Henry Pelham. • **15.** J. B. Owen, *The Rise of the Pelhams*, p. 280. • **16.** Walpole letter to Pelham, August 1743. Walpole, *Letters*, ed. Mrs Paget Toynbee. • **17.** Cobbett, *op. cit.*, vol. 13, col. 1054n. • **18.** Marchmont Papers, pp. 170–87, quoted in Lewis Wiggins, *The Faction of Cousins*, p. 107. • **19.** Walpole, *Letters*, *op. cit.*, vol. 2, p. 8.

8 Drawing the War: Winning the Election pp. 84–94

• **1.** J. B. Owen, *The Rise of the Pelhams*, p. 227. • **2.** Frank McLynn, *France and the Jacobite Rising of 1745*, pp. 160–63. • **3.** M. S. Anderson, *The War of the Austrian Succession 1740–48*, pp. 191–2. • **4.** *The Royal Navy and North America*,

p. 254, quoted Anderson, *op. cit.*, p. 184. • **5.** William Coxe, *Life of Pelham*, vol. I, Henry Pelham to Newcastle, April 1747. • **6.** Pitt to Newcastle, 17 May 1747, Add. MS 32,711. • **7.** A. Hartshorne, *Memoirs of a Royal Chaplain, 1729–63*, quoted in O. A. Sherrard, *Lord Chatham*, vol. I, pp. 165–6. • **8.** Romney Sedgwick, *The House of Commons 1715–1754*, pp. 353–4. • **9.** Contemporary cartoon at British Museum/British Library, reproduced with letterpress in Sherrard, *op. cit.* • **10.** *Chesterfield Letters*, ed. Lord Mahon, vol. IV, Newcastle to Chesterfield, 1747. • **11.** Langford, *A Polite and Commercial People*, pp. 224–5. • **12.** *Ibid.* • **13.** Quoted in *ODNB*, Marie Peters entry on Pitt. • **14.** Letters, Pitt to Newcastle, 8 March 1754, Add. MS 32,711.

9 'What shall you think if he dies courageously?' pp. 95–112

• **1.** *The Political Journal of George Bubb Dodington*, ed. John Carswell and Lewis Arnold Dralle, 14, 15, 16 April 1754. • **2.** *Memoirs and Correspondence of George, Lord Lyttleton, 1743–77*, ed. R. J. Phillimore, 2 vols, 1845 quoted Wiggins, *op. cit.*, p. 165. • **3.** *Dodington Journal*, 10 June 1754. • **4.** *Chesterfield Letters*, ed. Lord Mahon 4 October 1755, to Dayrolles. • **5.** Walpole, *Letters*, vol. I, ed. Peter Cunningham, *passim*, p. 407, quoted Peters, *Pitt and Popularity*, p. 40. • **6.** *Chesterfield Letters*, April 1756, to Dayrolles. • **7.** Quoted Peters, *op. cit.*, p. 42. • **8.** *A New System of Patriot Policy Containing the Genuine Recantation of the British Cicero* (London, 1756), quoted Peters, *op cit.* • **9.** Walpole, *Letters*, 16 November 1755, Walpole to Mann. • **10.** *Dodington Journal*, August 1755. • **11.** *Ibid.* • **12.** Letters from William Pitt to Lord Bute (2 June 1755) in a chapter in the Festschrift *Essays Presented to Sir Lewis Namier*, ed. Richard Pares and A. J. Taylor, p. 109. • **13.** *Ibid.*, 5 August 1755, pp. 109–10. • **14.** Acton Lectures on Modern History, 1906. • **15.** Richard Pares, 'American versus Continental Warfare 1739–63', *EHR*, 1936. • **16.** *ODNB*, Daniel Baugh entry on Byng. • **17.** Rigby to Bedford, 1 June 1756, *Correspondence of John, Fourth Duke of Bedford*, vol. II, pp. 193–4. • **18.** Walpole, *Letters*, vol. III, ed. Cunningham, p. 17. • **19.** *ODNB*, Baugh on Byng, pp. 3–4. • **20.** *Ibid.*, p. 4. • **21.** *Grenville Papers*, vol. I, ed. W. J. Smith, p. 165. • **22.** *Ibid.*, Wilkes to Grenville, 16 October 1756. • **23.** *Ibid.*, Potter to Grenville, 16 October 1756. • **24.** *Chesterfield Letters*, London, 28 February 1757, to Dayrolles. • **25.** *Bedford Correspondence*, vol. II, Rigby to Bedford, 3 March 1757, pp. 238–9. • **26.** Quoted in Peters, *op. cit.*, p. 53. • **27.** *Ibid.*, p. 55.

10 Two Dukes, Fox and Pitt pp. 113–127

• **1.** *Dodington Journal*, 3 September 1755. • **2.** *Ibid.*, 9 May 1755. • **3.** J. C. D. Clark, *The Memoirs and Speeches of James, Second Earl of Waldegrave*, p. 157.

• **4.** *ODNB*, 2004–7, Peter Luff entry on Henry Fox, pp. 9–10. • **5.** *Chesterfield Letters*, vol. II, p. 197. • **6.** *Ibid.*, p. 203. • **7.** Walpole, *Letters*, vol. III, 29 August 1756. • **8.** *Chesterfield Letters*, late August 1756. • **9.** Quoted Lewis Wiggins, *The Faction of Cousins*, p. 179. • **10.** Marie Peters, *Pitt and Popularity*, p. 63. • **11.** *Chesterfield Letters*, 28 February 1757. • **12.** Horace Walpole, *Memoirs of the Reign of George the Second*, vol. II, ed. John Brooke, p. 145 • **13.** Ibid. • **14.** L. S. Sutherland, 'London and the Pitt–Devonshire Administration', essay published in her *Politics and Finance in the Eighteenth Century*, ed. Aubrey Newman, p. 83. • **15.** Bedford Memoirs and Speeches, p. 128, quoted *ODNB*, W. A. Speck entry on William Augustus, Duke of Cumberland. • **16.** *Grenville Papers*, vol. III, ed. W. J. Smith, early April 1757.

11 *Hastenbeck and Rochefort: Panic and Recrimination pp. 128–157*

• **1.** Christopher Duffy, *Frederick the Great*, pp. 128–9. • **2.** *Ibid.*, p. 130. • **3.** *Bedford Correspondence*, vol. II, p. 261. • **4.** Henckel von Donnersmarck, quoted Duffy, *op. cit.*, p. 132. • **5.** Newcastle to Hardwicke, 26 June 1757, Add. MSS 32871, quoted O. A. Sherrard, *Lord Chatham*, vol. II, p. 216. • **6.** Newcastle to Hardwicke, 3 August 1757, P. C. Yorke, *The Life and Correspondence of Philip Yorke, Earl of Hardwicke*, vol. III, pp. 16–61. • **7.** *Chatham Correspondence*, ed. W. S. Taylor, and W. H. Pringle, 6 August 1757, misdated 11 March 1757. • **8.** Sir R. Savory, *Her Britannic Majesty's Army in Germany*, pp. 28–9. • **9.** Quoted E. J. S. Fraser, *The Pitt–Newcastle Coalition and the Conduct of the Seven Years War: 1757–1760*, thesis Part II (unpublished and at the Bodleian Library, Oxford). • **10.** Add. MSS 32872, Newcastle to Hardwicke, f. 428. • **11.** *Ibid.* • **12.** *Ibid*, f. 358. • **13.** Yorke, *op. cit.*, vol. III, pp. 165–6, Newcastle to Hardwicke, 9 August 1757. • **14.** *Ibid.*, p. 166. • **15.** Horace Walpole, *Memoirs of George the Second*, vol. III, quoted R. Middleton, *The Bells of Victory*, p. 36. • **16.** Horace Walpole, *Letters*, vol. III, ed. Peter Cunningham, 29 September 1757, p. 105. • **17.** *Ibid.* • **18.** George to Cumberland, 15 September 1757, RA CP Box 56, quoted in Middleton, *op. cit.*, pp. 35–6. • **19.** Add. MSS 32872, Newcastle to Hardwicke, 27 July 1757. • **20.** Duffy, *op. cit.*, pp. 138–9. • **21.** Richelieu to Soubise, 3 October 1757, quoted Savory, *op. cit.*, p. 41. • **22.** Duffy, *op. cit.*, p. 135. • **23.** *Chesterfield Letters*, 15 August 1757. • **24.** Add. MSS 32872. • **25.** Add. MSS 32997, f. 248. • **26.** *Dodington Journal*, p. 328. • **27.** Clerk to Ligonier, printed in the official *Report into the causes of the Failure of the Late Expedition to the Coasts of France (1758)*, quoted Middleton, *op. cit.*, p. 26. • **28.** Chesterfield to Dayrolles, 4 July 1757, *Chesterfield Letters*, pp. 224–5. • **29.** As note 7, above. • **30.** Add. MSS 32872. • **31.** Devonshire to Cumberland, 8 August 1757, quoted in Middleton, *op. cit.*, p. 30. • **32.** *The Report of the General Officers*, pp. 77–80, quoted *ibid.*, p. 30. • **33.** Quoted unsourced R. F. Mackay, *Admiral Hauke*,

p. 166. • **34.** *Ibid.,* p. 166. • **35.** Cathcart papers, quoted Mackay, *op. cit.,* p. 172. • **36.** Quoted *ibid.,* p. 175. • **37.** Hawke's out letters, 14 December 1757, quoted in Mackay, *op. cit.,* p. 184. • **38.** Walpole, *Letters,* ed. Cunningham, vol. III, p.III. • **39.** Mitchell to Holdernesse, quoted in Bisset, *Life of Sir Andrew Mitchell,* quoted Middleton, *op. cit.,* p. 41. • **40.** *Chesterfield Letters* (Bradshaw edition), vol. III, pp. 187–8, quoted *ibid.,* p. 41. • **41.** Add. MSS 63079, f. 54, October 1757. • **42.** *London Chronicle 4/6 and 6/8 October 1757* and *Sir Fawkener to Cumberland,* RA CP Box 56, quoted *ibid.,* p. 41. • **43.** Ian Gilmour, *Riot, Rising and Revolution,* p. 290. • **44.** N-H N189 f. 471 (old cataloguing), Yorke, *op. cit.,* vol. III, 8 October 1757, p. 187. • **45.** Potter to Pitt, *Correspondence of Chatham,* vol. I, p. 277, quoted in Marie Peters, *Pitt and Popularity,* p. 94. • **46.** *Monitor* issues 117, 118, 120 and 121, quoted *ibid.,* p. 95. • **47.** *Chesterfield Letters,* p. 245. • **48.** Walpole, *Memoirs of the Last Ten Years of the Reign of George II,* 2 vols (London, 1822), end October 1757. • **49.** Newcastle to Hardwicke, 23 October 1757, Yorke, *op. cit.,* vol. III, p. 191. • **50.** All *ibid.,* pp. 186–7. • **51.** *Ibid.,* especially 23 October 1757, p. 192. • **52.** *Ibid.*

12 'It blew a perfect hurricane': Admiral Holburne's Voyage pp. 158–170

• **1.** R. Middleton, *The Bells of Victory,* p. 10. • **2.** Gertrude Selwyn Kimball, ed., *Correspondence of William Pitt,* vol. I, p. 53, *ibid. passim.* • **3.** Holburne to Pitt, HMS *Newark* off Louisbourg, 17 September 1757. *Correspondence of William Pitt,* vol. I, p. 106. • **4.** *Ibid.,* p. 108. • **5.** *Ibid.,* p. 109. • **6.** *Ibid.,* pp. 110–11, 4 September 1757. • **7.** *Ibid.,* Holburne to Pitt, *Newark* at sea, 29 September 1757. • **8.** Chatham MSS, quoted Stanley Ayling, *The Elder Pitt,* p. 196.

13 St Malo Stands, Louisbourg Falls pp. 171–191

• **1.** Ferdinand to George II Uelzen, 5 January 1758, Newcastle Papers cited [pre-cataloguing], quoted in Sir R. Savory, *Her Britannic Majesty's Army in Germany,* p. 57. • **2.** Savory, *op. cit.,* p. 57. • **3.** *Ibid.,* quoted p. 60, Lord Edmund Fitzmaurice, *Life of the Duke of Brunswick,* p. 10. • **4.** Anson to Hardwicke, 6 October 1757, P. C. Yorke, *The Life and Correspondence of Philip Yorke, Earl of Hardwicke,* vol. III, p. 186. • **5.** *ODNB,* Ruddock Mackay entry on Hawke. • **6.** Hawke out letters, 10 May 1758, quoted R. F. Mackay, *Admiral Hawke,* p. 195. • **7.** *Ibid.,* p. 197. • **8.** Fitzmaurice, *Shelburne,* vol. 37, quoted R. Middleton, *The Bells of Victory,* p. 69. • **9.** Walpole, *Letters,* ed. Cunningham, vol. III, p. 139, 11 June 1758. • **10.** *Ibid.* • **11.** Marlborough to Pitt, Hotham Papers (University of Hull Library), letters dated 6, 11 and 19 June 1758, sent from Cancalle Bay and 24 June at sea. • **12.** *Monitor,* 23 April 1758. • **13.** E. A. Fenn,

'Biological Warfare in Eighteenth Century America: Beyond Jeffery Amherst', *Journal of American History* 86 (2000), pp. 1552–80, quoted in *ODNB*, William C. Lowe entry on Amherst. • **14.** Gertrude Selwyn Kimball, ed., *Correspondence of William Pitt*, 11 June 1758. • **15.** *Ibid.*, 11 June 1758. • **16.** *Ibid.*, 23 June 1758. • **17.** *Ibid.* • **18.** *Ibid.*, 6 July. • **19.** *Ibid.* • **20.** *Ibid.*, 23 July. • **21.** *Ibid.*, 28 July. • **22.** Yorke, *op. cit.*, p. 198n. • **23.** *Ibid.* • **24.** Add. MSS 32884, quoted in Middleton, *op. cit.*, p. 80. • **25.** *Monitor*, 15 July. • **26.** *Ibid.* • **27.** *Ibid.*, 26 August.

14 Patriots Betrayed pp. 192–210

• **1.** *Monitor*, 29 June, quoted Marie Peters, *Pitt and Popularity*, p. 106. • **2.** *Ibid.* • **3.** *Walpole's Correspondence*, vol. xxi, ed. W. S. Lewis, Walpole to Sir Horace Mann, 29 June 1758. • **4.** J. F. H. Bonhomme, *Madame de Pompadour, Général d'Armée* (1880) p. 128. • **5.** Letters from Pitt to Bute, Richard Pares and A. J. Taylor, *Essays Presented to Sir Lewis Namier*, 23 June 1758. • **6.** *Letters from George III to Lord Bute*, ed. Romney Sedgwick, 2 July 1758. • **7.** *Correspondence of William Pitt*, ed. Gertrude Selwyn Kimball, pp. 266–7, Pitt to Amherst, 10 June 1758. • **8.** Christopher Duffy, *Frederick the Great*, pp. 155–6. • **9.** Peters, *op. cit.*, pp. 120–21. • **10.** *Chesterfield Letters*, p. 289. • **11.** *Ibid*, p. 290. • **12.** Add. MSS 32881, ff. 189–90. • **13.** P. C. Yorke, *Hardwicke*, vol. III, p. 88. • **14.** Quoted E. J. S. Fraser, *The Pitt–Newcastle Coalition*, p. 216. • **15.** Letters from Pitt to Bute, ed. Pares and Taylor, *op. cit.*, 23 June 1758. • **16.** Romney Sedgwick, 'William Pitt and Lord Bute, 1755–58', *History Today*, vol. VI (10.1956). • **17.** *Ibid.* • **18.** *Ibid.* • **19.** Fraser, *op. cit.*, p. 153. • **20.** Add. MSS 32883, Newcastle to Legge. • **21.** *Correspondence of Chatham*, vol. I, pp. 324–5, quoted Peters, *op. cit.*, p. 117. • **22.** *Monitor*, 11 March 1758, quoted Peters, *ibid.*, p. 107. • **23.** *Ibid.*, p. 106. • **24.** Quoted Fraser, *op. cit.*, Symmer to Mitchell, 20 July 1758. Add. MSS 32839, f. 100. • **25.** Quoted R. Middleton, *The Bells of Victory*, p. 77. Newcastle to Holdemesse, 27 July 1758. Add. MSS 32882, ff. 65–6. • **26.** *Ibid.*, f. 116. • **27.** *Ibid.*, f. 41. • **28.** *Walpole Correspondence*, vol. III, p. 165. • **29.** *Ibid.* • **30.** L. S. Sutherland, *Politics and Finance in the Eighteenth Century*, p. 394. • **31.** *Ibid.*, p. 394n. • **32.** Quoted *ibid.*, p. 395, Gideon to Newcastle, 26 September 1758. Add. MSS 32890, f. 295. • **33.** Quoted *ibid.*, p. 87. Add. MSS 17493, f. 49. • **34.** Quoted *ibid.*, pp. 87–8. • **35.** *Ibid.*, pp. 86–8. • **36.** *Ibid.*, Appendix A II.

15 Sturdy Yeomen and Slave Traders: the Militia and Goree pp. 211–219

• **1.** Stanley Ayling, *The Elder Pitt*, p. 176. • **2.** *Ibid.* • **3.** Sir R. Savory, *Her Britannic Majesty's Army in Germany*, pp. 133–6. • **4.** *Ibid.*, p. 138. • **5.** Christopher Duffy, *Frederick the Great*, pp. 130–32. • **6.** *Bedford Correspondence*, p. 374, Bedford to the Lord Primate of Ireland. • **7.** *Ibid.*, p. 375. • **8.** Quoted in Marie Peters, *Pitt and Popularity*, p. 145, *Monitor:* 2 June, 7 and 21 July, 25 August. *London Evening Post:* 9–12, 28–30 June, 12–14, 26–28 July. • **9.** Quoted *ibid.*, p. 146. • **10.** R. Middleton, *The Bells of Victory*, p. 85. • **11.** Nigel Tattersfield, *The Forgotten Trade*, pp. 13–14. • **12.** Richard Pares, *War and Trade in the West Indies*, p. 247. • **13.** Quoted Ayling, *op. cit.*, p. 239. • **14.** Add. MSS. 32892, ff. 55, Newcastle to Devonshire, 14 June 1759.

16 Hunt the Garter: Minden and Lord Temple pp. 220–243

• **1.** *ODNB*, Stuart Reid entry on James Wolfe. • **2.** H. B. Willson, *Wolfe, Life and Letters* (1908), Wolfe to Pitt, 22 November 1758. • **3.** *Ibid.*, Wolfe to Pitt, 24 December 1758, pp. 406–7. • **4.** Clevland to Holburne, 1 January 1759, quoted R. Middleton, *The Bells of Victory*, p. 105. • **5.** *Ibid.*, p. 138. • **6.** Richard Holmes, *Redcoat*, p. 17. • **7.** *Chatham Correspondence*, ed. W. S. Taylor and W. H. Pringle, pp. 425–30, quoted Ayling, *The Elder Pitt*, p. 261. • **8.** *Bedford Correspondence*, vol. II, pp. 374–6. • **9.** Frederick to Ferdinand, Reich Hennersdorf 1 July 1759 Westphalen III, quoted Sir R. Savory, *Her Britannic Majesty's Army in Germany*, p. 146. • **10.** Quoted Holmes, *op. cit.*, p. 81. • **11.** Sir John Fortescue, *Following the Drum* (London, 1931), pp. 32–3, quoted in Holmes, *op. cit.*, pp. 22–3. • **12.** Savory, *op. cit.*, p. 171. • **13.** Quoted Christopher Duffy, *Frederick the Great*, p. 209. • **14.** *Ibid.* • **15.** *Ibid.*, p. 189. • **16.** Add. MSS 32884, f. 181, quoted Lewis Wiggins, *The Faction of Cousins*, p. 218. • **17.** *Ibid.* • **18.** *Ibid.*, p. 220. • **19.** Add. MSS 32985, f. 288, 9 September 1759, quoted in *The Devonshire Diary 1759–62*, ed. Peter D. Brown and Karl Schweizer, p. 24. • **20.** *Devonshire Diary*, p. 36. • **21.** P. C. Yorke, *Hardwicke*, vol. III, p. 73, quoted Middleton, *op. cit.*, p. 142. • **22.** *Devonshire Diary*, p. 27. • **23.** *Ibid.*, pp. 29–30. • **24.** *Ibid.* • **25.** *Ibid.*, p. 36. • **26.** *Ibid.*, pp. 37–8. • **27.** O. A. Sherrard, *Lord Chatham*, vol. II, p. 303. • **28.** Yorke, *op. cit.*, vol. III, 15 October, p. 238, Add. MSS 32897. • **29.** *Ibid.*, pp. 238–9. • **30.** Middleton, *op. cit.*, p. 133.

17 'Where ignorant Armies clash by night': Quiberon Bay pp. 244–252

• **1.** Quoted R. F. Mackay, *Admiral Hawke*, p. 221. • **2.** *Ibid.*, p. 228. • **3.** *Ibid.*, p. 224. • **4.** Hawke's out letters, 13 October 1759, quoted Mackay, *op. cit.* • **5.** Hervey, *Naval History of Great Britain*, vol. V, p. 191, quoted Geoffrey Marcus, *Quiberon Bay*, p. 79. • **6.** Hawke's out letters, 10 October 1759, quoted Mackay, *op. cit.*, p. 230. • **7.** Admiralty Papers I/9222, 29 August 1759, quoted Marcus, *op. cit.*, p. 85. • **8.** Hawke's out letters, 24 November 1759, quoted Mackay, *op. cit.*, p. 253.

18 Deaths and Entrances: George II and Lord Bute pp. 253–268

• **1.** P. C. Yorke, *Hardwicke*, vol. III, pp. 97–100. • **2.** Quoted *ODNB*, William C. Lowe entry on Amherst, p. 2. J. C. Long, *Life of Amherst* (1933). • **3.** Yorke, *op. cit.*, pp. 241–2. • **4.** Hardwicke to Newcastle, 14 September 1760, Add. MSS 32911, ff. 285–7. • **5.** *Ibid.* • **6.** Quoted *ibid.*, pp. 484–5. • **7.** Quoted Marie Peters, *ODNB* entry on Pitt. • **8.** Lord Rosebery, *Chatham, His Early Life and Connections*, p. 454. • **9.** *Ibid.*, p. 254. • **10.** Letters from Pitt to Bute, included in Richard Pares and A. J. Taylor, *Essays Presented to Sir Lewis Namier*, p. 115. • **11.** Quoted *ibid.*, p. 166, letters Prince George to Bute, no. 24. • **12.** *Ibid.*, letters George III to Bute, no. 57, pp. 45–6. • **13.** *Ibid.*, no. 60, p. 47. • **14.** Quoted Dylan E. Jones, *ODNB* entry on Philip Francis (Junius), *Junius Letters* 386. • **15.** Hardwicke to Newcastle, 17 March 1761, Add. MSS 32920, ff. 270–71. • **16.** *The Devonshire Diary 1759–62*, ed. Peter D. Brown and Karl Schweizer, p. 48. • **17.** *Ibid.*, p. 53. • **18.** Colin Jones, *The Great Nation: France from Louis XV to Napoleon*, p. 243. • **19.** Richard Pares, *War and Trade in the West Indies*, p. 41. • **20.** *Ibid.*, pp. 42–3. • **21.** *Ibid.*, p. 584. • **22.** Quoted Stanley Ayling, *The Elder Pitt*, p. 287. • **23.** *Ibid.*, p. 288. • **24.** Cobbett, *History of Parliament*, vol. 15, cols 1263–7. • **25.** Newcastle to Hardwicke, 21 September 1761, quoted Yorke, *Hardwicke*, p. 325. • **26.** *Bedford Correspondence*, vol. II, p. 425. • **27.** Sir Julian Corbett, *England in the Seven Years War*, p. 173n. • **28.** *Devonshire Diary*, p. 136. • **29.** *Ibid.*

19 Pitt Leaves: Victories Continue pp. 269–282

• **1.** Figures from Cobbett, *History of Parliament*, vol. 15, cols 513 and 1006, quoted Marie Peters, *Pitt and Popularity*, p. 197. • **2.** Guildhall MSS 214/1, quoted George Rudé, *Wilkes and Liberty*, p. 21. • **3.** P. C. Yorke, *Hardwicke*, vol. III, pp. 279–80. • **4.** O.A. Sherrard, *Lord Chatham*, vol. III. • **5.** *Chatham Correspondence*, ed. W. S. Taylor and W. H. Pringle, 4 vols (1838), pp. 146–53, quoted Stanley Ayling, *The Elder Pitt*, p. 292. • **6.** *Grenville Papers*, vol. I, ed. W. J. Smith, letter from Sackville to Temple, October 1761. • **7.** *Ibid.*, p. 406, letter from Temple to Wilkes, 22 October 1761, quoted Lewis Wiggins, *The Faction of Cousins*, p. 247. • **8.** *Ibid.* • **9.** Peters, *op. cit.*, p. 213. • **10.** Add. MSS 32796, ff. 393–9, quoted Wiggins, *op. cit.*, p. 249. • **11.** Richard Pares, *War and Trade in the West Indies*, p. 558. • **12.** Yorke, *op. cit.*, p. 245. • **13.** Cobbett, vol. 15, *op. cit.*, col. 1264. • **14.** Pares, *op. cit.*, p. 572. • **15.** Add. MSS 32928, f. 260, letter Newcastle to Hardwicke, 23 October 1761. • **16.** Sir R. Savory, *Her Britannic Majesty's Army in Germany*, pp. 318–26. • **17.** Quoted *ibid*, Hildesheim, 30 April 1761. • **18.** Pares, *op. cit.*, p. 591. • **19.** Cf. Pares, *ibid.*, pp. 604–6. • **20.** Letter Frederick to Knyphausen, 10 September 1761, quoted Sir Julian Corbett, *England in the Seven Years War*, 2nd edn, p. 360. • **21.** *Grenville Papers*, vol. I,

p. 467, quoted *ibid.*, p. 353. • **22.** Add. MSS 51380, f. 181, Walpole to George III, pp. 175–6. • **23.** Corbett, *op. cit.*, p. 363. • **24.** Add. MSS 51380, f. 181, Walpole to George III, pp. 176–8. • **25.** Pares, *op. cit.*, p. 610n. • **26.** Add. MSS 38200, f. 311, Richardson to Charles Jenkinson, 17 April 1763, quoted Rudé, *op. cit.*, p. 20.

20 'That Devil Wilkes' pp. 283–298

• **1.** Lord Macaulay, 'The Earl of Chatham', in *Critical and Historical Essays*, vol. 1, p. 441. • **2.** Add. MSS 30867, Potter to Wilkes, 28 June/1 July 1757. • **3.** *North Briton/Briton*, the sniping war between the *North Briton* and the *Briton* over eight months from Issue I (*NB*), 5 June 1762, through to March 1763. • **4.** John Bleakley, *Life of Wilkes* (1917), quoted Rudé, *Wilkes and Liberty*, p. 21. • **5.** *Ibid.*, p. 22. • **6.** P. C. Yorke, *Hardwicke*, vol. III, Newcastle to Hardwicke, 11 August, p. 407. • **7.** Cf. Lord Edmund Fitzmaurice, *Shelburne*, vol. I, pp. 140–41. • **8.** *ODNB*, K. W. Schweizer entry on Bute, p. 6. • **9.** Fitzmaurice, *Shelburne*, pp. 140–41. • **10.** John Brooke, *King George III*, 1974 edn, p. 185. • **11.** *Ibid.*, p. 242. • **12.** Add. MSS 32948, f. 189, Newcastle to Devonshire, 2 May 1763, quoted Rudé, *op. cit.*, p. 29. • **13.** Quoted *ibid.*, p. 27, Onslow to Newcastle, 6 May 1763. Add. MSS 32948, f. 238. • **14.** *Ibid.*, pp. 35–6. • **15.** Francis Thackeray, *Wilkes*, vol. II (1827), p. 44. • **16.** Raymond Postgate, *That Devil Wilkes* (Constable, 1930), pp. 80–81. • **17.** Thackeray, *op. cit.*, p. 44, quoted Stanley Ayling, *The Elder Pitt*, p. 317. • **18.** Postgate, *op. cit.*, p. 81.

21 Houses and Gardens: Cider and America pp. 299–308

• **1.** Wyndham, *Eighteenth-Century Chronicles*, vol. II, p. 191, quoted Lewis Wiggins, *The Faction of Cousins*, p. 161. • **2.** All at Lord Rosebery, *Chatham, His Early Life and Connections*, p. 455. • **3.** Quoted Stanley Ayling, *The Elder Pitt*, p. 325. • **4.** *Letters of Edmund Burke*, ed. Harold Laski, Burke to Rockingham, 30 July 1769. • **5.** Fitzmaurice, *Shelburne*, vol. I, p. 59. • **6.** Ayling, *op. cit.*, p. 322. • **7.** *Letters of Edmund Burke*, ed. Laski, Burke to Henry Flood, 18 May 1765. • **8.** *Ibid.*, Pitt to Burke about Rockingham. • **9.** Horace Walpole, *Memoirs of the Reign of George III*, vol. III, *op. cit.*, p. 15 • **10.** P. D. G. Thomas, *British Politics and the Stamp Act Crisis* (1975), pp. 35–6, quoted *ODNB*, John Cannon entry on Charles Yorke, p. 3. • **11.** *Letters of Edmund Burke*, ed. Laski, 5 December 1774. • **12.** John Brooke, *King George III*, p. 215.

22 *Power Out of Mind pp. 309–321*

• **1.** *Grenville Papers*, vol. III, pp. 384–5. • **2.** *Correspondence of George III*, vol. I, p. 380, quoted *ODNB*, Patrick Woodland entry on Dowdeswell. • **3.** Quoted Christopher Duffy, *Frederick the Great*, p. 243. • **4.** W. von Ruville, *William Pitt, Earl of Chatham*, vol. III, p. 184. • **5.** Ibid. • **6.** Lord Macaulay, 'The Earl of Chatham', in *Critical and Historical Essays*, vol. 1, p. 469. • **7.** Quoted John Keay, *The Honourable Company*, p. 362. • **8.** *Ibid.*, p. 88. • **9.** *Ibid.*, pp. 379–80. • **10.** Walpole, *Memoirs of the Reign of George III*, vol. III (Yale UP 2000), p. 86. • **11.** *Grenville Papers*, vol. III, p. 396. • **12.** Walpole, *George III op. cit.*, p. 99. • **13.** *Ibid.* • **14.** *Ibid.* • **15.** Keay, *op. cit.*, p. 379. • **16.** Walpole, *George III op. cit.*, p. 140 *passim*. • **17.** *Lyttleton Papers* 6.620, quoted *ODNB*, Marie Peters entry on Pitt, p. 27. • **18.** Augustus Henry, Duke of Grafton, ed., *Anson Autobiography and Political Correspondence*, pp. 136–9. • **19.** John Brooke, *The Chatham Administration*, p. 158. • **20.** *Chatham Correspondence*, ed. W. S. Taylor and W. H. Pringle, vol. III, p. 275, quoted Brooke, *op. cit.*, p. 160. • **21.** *Ibid.* • **22.** Walpole, *Letters*, ed. Mrs Paget Toynbee, vol. VII, p. 129.

23 *America and Death: The Grand Finale pp. 322–335*

• **1.** *Letters of Edmund Burke*, ed. Harold Laski, Burke letter to Rockingham, 9 July 1769. • **2.** *Ibid.* • **3.** Add. MSS 32977, f. 42. • **4.** William Cobbett, *History of Parliament*, vol. XVI. • **5.** *Ibid.* • **6.** All at Walpole, *George III*, vol. iv, p. 150. • **7.** *Ibid.*, p. 153. • **8.** *Ibid.* • **9.** *Ibid.* • **10.** Burke to O'Hara, 2 April 1771, quoted Stanley Ayling, *Edmund Burke: His Life and Opinions*, p. 393. • **11.** James Boswell, *Life of Johnson* (Everyman edn), pp. 547–8. • **12.** Quoted Ayling, *op. cit.*, p. 395. • **13.** All at John Brooke, *The Chatham Administration*, pp. 282–3. • **14.** All quoted Theodore Draper, *A Struggle for Power* (Little, Brown, 1996), p. 393. • **15.** Augustus Henry, Duke of Grafton, ed., *Anson Autobiography and Political Correspondence*, p. 277. • **16.** Speech on Conciliation with America, Burke, *Works* 450–509, quoted Ayling, *op. cit.*, p. 79. • **17.** Letter to New York Assembly 1774, quoted Ayling, *ibid.*, p. 79. • **18.** Cobbett, *op. cit.*, vol. 17, col. 1403. • **19.** Grafton, *op. cit.*, p. 278. • **20.** All quoted Draper, *op. cit.*, p. 281. • **21.** Quoted *ONDB*, Woodland entry on Dowdeswell, p. 6. • **22.** Cobbett, *op. cit.*, vol. 18, col. 319. • **23.** *ODNB*, William C. Lowe entry on Richmond, p. 4. • **24.** Grafton, *op. cit.*, p. 279. • **25.** Cobbett, *op. cit.*, vol. 19, col. 317, quoted *ODNB*, Marie Peters entry on Pitt, p. 32. • **26.** Fortescue, *Letters of George III*, quoted Ayling, *op. cit.*, p. 407. • **27.** Cobbett, *op. cit.*, vol. 19, col. 1023.

Appendix: Chatham's Mental Condition pp. 341–346

• **1.** David Owen, *In Sickness and in Power: Illness in Heads of Government during the Last 100 Years* (Methuen, 2008), p. xxv. • **2.** *Ibid.* • **3.** *Ibid.*, p. xxvi. • **4.** *Ibid.* • **5.** *Ibid.*, pp. xxvi–xxvii.

Bibliography

PRIMARY SOURCES

MANUSCRIPT

British Library: Newcastle papers Add. MSS 32858–947 33035

PRINTED

Parliamentary Records
London Library and Hull University Library
The Parliamentary History of England from the earliest period to the year 1803 (ed.
William Cobbett), 36 vols (London, 1806–20)

VOLUMES USED

Periodical Publications (all British Library):

Briton
Champion
Con-Test
London Chronicle
London Gazette
Monitor
North Briton
Patriot
Test

Unpublished D.Phil theses (The Bodleian Library):

Durban, Michael, *The Prince of the Whigs: the Life and Career of William Cavendish,
Fourth Duke of Devonshire* (Oxford University, 2003)
Fraser, E.J.S., *The Pitt-Newcastle Coalition and the Conduct of the Sever Years
War 1757–1760* (Oxford University, 1976)

Oxford Dictionary of National Biography (ONDB):

Amherst, Jeffrey
Anson, George

Augustus, William (Duke of Cumberland)
Barrington, William Widman
Beckford, William
Boscawen, Edward
Byng, John
Calcraft, John, the Elder
Cavendish, Lord John
Cavendish, William (4th Duke of Devonshire)
Conway, Henry Seymour
Dowdeswell, William
Fox, Henry
Francis, Sir Philip
Grenville, George
Grenville (Grenville-Temple), Richard (2nd Earl Temple)
Hawke, Edward
Henley, Robert
Hervey, Augustus John
Hill, Wills
Holles, Thomas Pelham, (Duke of Newcastle)
Howe, Richard
Hyde, Henry
Keppel, Augustus
Keppel, George
Lennox, Charles
Ligonier, John
Montagu, John
Oswald, James
Pelham, Henry
Perceval, John
Petty (formerly Fitzmaurice), William
Pitt (née Grenville), Hester, Countess of Chatham
Pitt, William
Pratt, Charles
Rigby, Richard
Savile, Sir George
Stuart, John
Temple, Richard (1st Viscount Cobham)
Townshend, Charles
Wentworth, Charles Watson
Wolfe, James
Yorke, Charles
Yorke, Philip

PRINTED AND PUBLISHED BOOKS

Anderson, M. S., *The War of the Austrian Succession 1740–48* (Longman, 1995)

Ayling, Stanley, *The Elder Pitt* (Collins, 1976)

—*Edmund Burke: His Life and Opinions* (Cassell, 1998)

Barlow and Yule, ed., *Hedges Diary 1681–89* (1887)

Battestin, Martin, C., *Henry Fielding: A Life* (Routledge, 1989)

Bedford, John, *Correspondence of John, Fourth Duke of Bedford*, vol. II (Longman, Brown, Green & Co., 1843)

Black, Jeremy, *Natural and Necessary Enemies: Anglo-French Relations in the Eighteenth Century* (Duckworth, 1986)

Blaming, T. C. W., 'That Horrid Electorate', *Historical Journal* 20, 1977

Bonhomme, J. F. H., *Madame de Pompadour, Général d'Armée* (1880)

Brewer, J., *Party Ideology and Popular Politics* (Cambridge University Press, 1976)

Brooke, John, *The Chatham Administration 1766–68* (London, Macmillan, 1956)

—*King George III* (Constable, 1972: Panther Books, 1974)

—ed., *Horace Walpole, Memoirs of the Reign of George II*, vol. II (Yale University Press, 1985)

Brown, Peter, *The Chathamites* (Macmillan, 1967)

Brown, Peter D., and Schweizer, K. W., eds, *The Devonshire Diary 1759–1762* (Camden 4th Series vol. 27, London, Offices of the Royal Historical Society, 1982)

Browning, R., *The Duke of Newcastle* (Yale University Press, 1975)

Carswell, John, and Dralle, Lewis Arnold, eds, *The Political Journal of George Bubb Dodington* (Clarendon Press, 1965)

Christie, I. R., *The End of North's Ministry* (St Martin's Press, 1958)

—*Myth and Reality in Late Eighteenth-Century British Politics* (Macmillan, 1970)

Clark, J. C. D., *The Memoirs and Speeches of James, Second Earl of Waldegrave*

—*The Dynamics of Change: The Crisis of the mid-1750s* (1982)

Cobbett, William, *History of Parliament*, vols 8, 10, 12, 13, 15, 16, 17, 18, 19

Colley, Linda, 'The Apotheosis of George III', *Past and Present* 102, 1984

Corbett, Julian, Sir, *England in the Seven Years War*, vol. II (Longman, Green & Co., 1907, 2nd edn, 1918)

Coxe, William, *Life of Walpole*, vols I and III (London, 1798)

—*Life of Pelham*, vol. I (London, 1829)

Craig, W. H., *The Life of Lord Chesterfield* (John Lane, 1907)

Cunningham, Peter, ed., *Horace Walpole: The Letters*, vol. III (Richard Bentley, 1857)

Dalton, Cornelius, Sir, *The Life of Thomas Pitt* (Cambridge University Press, 1915)

Dodington, ed. Wyndham, *The Journal of the Late George Bubb Dodington: March 8th 1749–February 6th 1761* (E. Easton, 1784)

Draper, Theodore, *A Struggle for Power* (Little, Brown, 1996)

Duffy, Christopher, *Frederick the Great: A Military Life* (Routledge & Kegan Paul, 1985)

Fenn, E. A., 'Biological Warfare in Eighteenth-Century America: Beyond Jeffrey Amherst', *Journal of American History* 86, 2000

Fitzmaurice, Edmund, Lord, *Life of the Duke of Brunswick* (1901)

—*Life of William, First Earl of Shelburne*, vol. I (Macmillan, 1912)

Gibbs, G. C., 'Britain and the Alliance of Hanover April 1725–February 1726', *EHJ*, 87, January 1961

Gilmour, Ian, *Riot, Rising and Revolution* (Hutchinson, 1992)

Henry, Augustus, Duke of Grafton, ed., *Anson Autobiography and Political Correspondence* (John Murray, 1898)

Hervey, A., *Augustus Hervey's Journal*, ed. Erskine William Kimber (1953)

Hervey, John, Lord, *Some materials towards memoirs of the Reign of King George II*, ed. Romney Sedgwick, 3 vols (London, 1932)

Holmes, Richard, *Redcoat* (HarperCollins, 2001)

Jarrett, Derek, ed., *Horace Walpole, Memoirs of the Reign of George the Second* (Yale University Press, 2000)

Jones, Colin, *The Great Nation: France from Louis XV to Napoleon* (Penguin Books, 2002)

Keay, John, *The Honourable Company* (HarperCollins, 1993)

Kimball, Gertrude Selwyn, ed., *Correspondence of William Pitt when Secretary of State*, 2 vols (Macmillan, 1906)

Langford, Paul, *The First Rockingham Administration 1765–1766* (Oxford University Press, 1973)

—*The Excise Crisis* (Oxford University Press, 1975)

—*A Polite and Commercial People. England, 1727–83* (Guild/Oxford University Press, 1989)

Laski, Harold, ed., *Letters of Edmund Burke: A Selection* (Oxford University Press, 1922)

Lawson, P., *George Grenville: A Political Life* (Oxford Clarendon Press, 1984)

Lewis, W. S., ed., *Walpole's Correspondence*, vol. xxi (Yale University Press, 1937–74)

Lindsay, Jack, *1764* (Frederick Muller, 1959)

Macaulay, Lord, *Critical and Historical Essays*, vol. I (Everyman edn, 1907)

Mack, Maynard, *Alexander Pope* (Yale University Press/W. W. Norton, 1985)

Mackay, R. F., *Admiral Hawke* (Clarendon Press, 1965)

Mackesy, Piers, *The Coward of Minden: The Affair of Lord George Sackville* (Allen Lane, 1989)

McLynn, Frank, *France and the Jacobite Rising of 1745* (Edinburgh University Press, 1981)

—*1759: The Year Britain Became Master of the World* (Pimlico, 2004)

Mahon, ed., *Lord Chesterfield: Letters to his Son* (J. B. Lippincott, 1892)

Marcus, Geoffrey, *Quiberon Bay* (Hollis and Carter, 1960)

Middleton, R., *The Bells of Victory: The Pitt–Newcastle Ministry and the Conduct of the Seven Years War* (Cambridge University Press, 1985)

Namier, Lewis S., *England in the Age of the American Revolution* (Macmillan, 1963)

—and Brooke, J., *The History of Parliament Commons 1754–1790*, 3 vols (1964)

O'Gorman, F., *The Rise of Party in England: The Rockingham Whigs 1760–82* (George Allen & Unwin, 1975)

—*The Emergence of the British Two-Party System* (Edward Arnold, 1982)

Owen, J. B., *The Rise of the Pelhams* (Methuen, 1957)

Pares, Richard, *War and Trade in the West Indies 1739–1763* (Clarendon Press, 1936)

—'American and Continental Warfare 1739–63', *EHR*, 1936

Pares, Richard and A.J. Taylor, eds, *Essays Presented to Sir Lewis Namier* (Macmillan, 1956)

Pearce, Edward, *The Great Man: Sir Robert Walpole* (Jonathan Cape, 2007)

Peters, Marie, *Pitt and Popularity: The Patriot Minister and London Opinion during the Seven Years War* (Clarendon Press, 1980)

Plumb, J. H., *Sir Robert Walpole*, 2 vols (The Cresset Press, 1956 and 1960)

Roberts, M., *Splendid Isolation 1763–80* (University of Reading, 1970)

Rodgers, N. A. M., *The Command of the Ocean* (Penguin Books, 2004)

Rosebery, Lord, *Chatham, His Early Life and Connections* (Arthur L. Humphreys, 1910)

Rudé, George, *Wilkes and Liberty: A Social Study of 1763–1774* (Clarendon Press, 1962)

Ruville, W. von, *William Pitt, Earl of Chatham*, 3 vols (1907)

Savory, Reginald, Sir, *Her Britannic Majesty's Army in Germany* (Oxford, 1966)

Schweizer, K. R., ed., *Lord Bute: Essays in Re-interpretation* (Leicester University Press, 1988)

Sedgwick, Romney, ed., *Letters from George III to Lord Bute* (Macmillan, 1939)

—*The House of Commons, 1715–1754*, 2 vols (HMSO, 1970)

Seward, William, *Anecdotes of Distinguished Persons*, 4 vols (London, 1798)

Sherrard, O. A., *Lord Chatham*, 3 vols (Bodley Head, 1952, 1955, 1958)

Smith, W.J., ed., *The Grenville Papers being correspondence of Richard and George Grenville*, 4 vols (John Murray, 1853)

Sutherland, Lucy S., in *Politics and Finance in the Eighteenth Century*, ed. Newman, Aubrey (The Hambledon Press, 1984)

Tattersfield, Nigel, *The Forgotten Trade . . . Accounts of the Slave Trade from the Minor Ports of England 1698–1725* (Pimlico, 1998)

Taylor, W. S. and Pringle, W. H., eds, *The Correspondence of Chatham*, (John Murray, 1838–40)

Thomas, D. G., *John Wilkes: A Friend to Liberty* (Clarendon/Oxford, 1996)

Waldegrave, James, Earl, *Memoirs from 1754–58* (London, 1821)

Walpole, Horace, *Memoirs*, 2 vols, ed. Eliot Warburton Henry Colburn (1851)

—*The Letters*, ed. Mrs Paget Toynbee, 16 vols (London 1903–5)

Wiggins, Lewis, *The Faction of Cousins: A Political Account of the Grenvilles* (Yale University Press, 1958)

Wilkes, J., *A Whig in Power (H. Pelham)* (Evanston, North Western University Press, 1964)

Williams, Basil, *Life*, 2 vols (1913)

Willson, Beckles, ed. Wolfe, *Life and Letters* (Heinemann, 1909)

Yorke, P. C., *The Life and Correspondence of Philip Yorke, Earl of Hardwicke*, 3 vols (Cambridge University Press, 1913)

Ziegler, Philip, *Addington: A Life of Henry Addington, First Viscount Sidmouth* (Collins, 1965)

Index

Abercromby, General James, waiting for artillery, 188, 211, 221

D'Abreu, French minister in London, 106

Acton, Lord, English historian, and 'The Third Silesian War', 102

Addington, Dr Anthony, Chatham's physician, 317–318

Addington, Henry, later Viscount Sidmouth, as boyhood friend of younger William Pitt, 318

D'Aiguillon, Duc de, French commander to invade Glasgow, 214, 246

Albemarle, Lord, at Havana, 278

Amherst, Jeffrey, General, to Canada chosen by Ligonier, hates Indians, 182; bound for Canada, 182–183, 186 passim; overruled by Boscawen; 187, 199, 211–212, 221; steps open after Quebec, 226–227, 253–254

Amis, Kingsley, novelist, on women, 299

Anne, Queen of England, 1702–14: 24, 40, 49, 197

Anson, George, Lord, Admiral, First Lord, major victory at Finisterre, 78, 84; thinks Channel the priority, 105; sentiment against, 109; admiralty works, 115; saved for the Admiralty by Hardwick 125; against Rochefort plans, 140, 147, 149, 152; wants ships brought back, 170, 173; takes on St Malo raid, 175–177, 214–215, 223; wisdom over Halifax reserve, 227, 242, 257, 261, 268, 275, 287, 297, 326, 337

Argyll, Duke, favours bullying Spain, 58, 67

Arnall, William, Walpole's polemicist, 45

Arnold, Matthew, poet, quoted, 252

Ashburnham, Lord, 144; large preparations detail, 158

Atterbury, Francis, Bishop of Rochester, plotter 25, 32, 58

Attlee, Clement, British statesman, 70

Auden, W.H., poet 'History must say Alas', 225

August, King of Poland, Elector of Saxony, 37

Augusta (Dowager) Princess of Wales, 99, 116, 190–191

Ayling, Pitt biographer, 214, 271, 293, 302

Bacon family, Walpole allies in Norfolk, 30

Baker, Sir William, 304

Barnard, Sir John, monied man, 207

Barrington, General Sir John, takes Guadeloupe, 219

Barrington, William Wildman, Viscount, War minister, spells out the absence of any change in policy with advent of WP, 121–122, 262

Bastide, Colonel, French soldier in Canada, plans overheard, 184

Battestin, Martin, American biographer of Fielding, 29

Bauffremont, Chevalier de, naval captain, makes for Canada, 159

Beauharnois, Marquis de, avoids fight with Barrington, 218

Beaupreau, French general, commands 6 battalions at Minden, 233

Beckford, William, sugarplanter, owner of 30,000 slaves, prime ally of Pitt, 38, 50, 59, 111; wants Byng reprieved, 122, 129; demands Rochefort inquisition, 152–154; 'spurns hirelings'... 'dastard souls', 181–182; inquiry comments in Daily Beast mode, conscience 203, 207, 255, 312; death, 325, 331, 339

Bedford, John Russell, Duke of, enters Broadbottom Ministry, 78; Pitt's antithesis on war, 82; considered for Govt, 125, 130; sees monopoly in West Indian conquests, 219; rallies Irish gentry, 227, 243, 259, 262; almost alone saw American threat to the mother country when free of the French threat, 267; Bedford's peace, 278, 295, 299

Belloc, Hilaire, British/French writer, quoted, 236

Bengal, Dahwood, Nawab of, 5; lays siege to Madras, 7–8

Bennett, Arnold, modern novelist, 283

Bertie, Lord Robert, role at Gibraltar, 105–106

Bevin, Ernest, C20 statesman, 'complete ignoral', 319

Bigot de Moroques, French admiral, 1

Blackstone, Sir William, jurist, 258, 332

Blair, Tony, British politician, 'not depressive', 345

Blakeney, General William, withstands siege of Fort St Philip Minorca, but exhausted, honourably surrenders, 108–109

Bland, Dr, Headmaster of Eton College, 14

Blenac-Courbon, Rear-Admiral Charles, at Guadaloupe, 219

Bligh, Major-General for Caen, cut dead by George II after failure, 191, 206

Blount, Martha, friend of Alexander Pope, 31

Bolingbroke, Henry St John, politician/adventurer, 28–29, 36, 40, 45, 51; Bute takes seriously, 259–260

Bompart, Admiral, Maximine, 244, 246

Bond Denis, MP, churchwarden, fraudulent converter, 27–28

Bosgowen, Admiral Edward, attacks French ships, starts Seven Years War, 104, 183, 185; briefs Pitt on Louisbourg 186–187; vetoes assault on Louisbourg, 215

Boswell, James, biographer, quoted, 328

Bouquet, Colonel, recommends smallpox-infected blankets for Red Indians, 182

Braddock, General, fails and dies at Forks of the Ohio, 103

Bragg, Grenadier Captain, does well at Louisbourg, 186

Bristol, Lord, Ambassador to Madrid, 244, 275

Britiffe, Sir Robert, Walpole ally in Norwich, 30

Brodrick, Admiral Thomas, at Rochefort, 148–149, 156

Broglie, Victor-François, Duc de, march to Cologne, 193, 230–231, 276

Brooke, Sir John, historian, 291, 329

Brown, Lancelot ('Capability'), gardener, 27

Brown, P.D., historian – and Devonshire's Memorandum, 239

'Bunbury, Mr', Wilde's character compared with the Rockingham ministry, 308

Burchett, William Pitt's Eton tutor sends his father encouraging letter, 13–14, 16

Bute, John Stuart, Earl, Prime Minister, Scot, 29, 284–287, 289, 295, 297, 307, 338

Byng, John, ill-advised admiral, 26; sweeps Scottish east coast during '45 rising, 79, 91; elected at Rochester in 1754, sent to Minorca waters, 104; misinformed by Fowke – loiters, 105; engages Galissonière, 106–108; events at Minorca, 109–*passim*; friends rally to him, 122; sympathy grows, 123, 126, 151, 154; in men's minds at Rochefort trials – example, saving Mordaunt, 157

Calas, Jean, French Protestant falsely accused, broken on the wheel, 144(n), 145

Calcraft, John, Admiralty agent, adviser to Pitt, 136, 209, 246, 320, 322–325

Camelford, Lord, Pitt's nephew, 44

Carlisle, Earl of, death provokes Garter Crisis, 236

Carlo IX of Naples, becomes Carlos III of Spain, 256–257, 264, 268

Caroline of Ansbach, Queen to George II, 19, 32, 139

Carteret, John, Lord, later Earl Granville, enters government 65–66, 70–71; drifts into war, 73; speaks fluent German, 75; preferred as Minister by George II, too far away from Westminster politics near war theatre, 77; light view of the '45 risk 79, 83, 85, 259

Chamberlain, Neville, British statesman, 345

Charles I, King of England, 36, 152

Charles II, King of England 53, 67

Charles V, Holy Roman Emperor (16C), 35

Charles Edward Stuart, Young Pretender, and a contemplated '59 rising, 80; possibilities, 115, 123, 245

Chatham, John Pitt, second Earl, 260, general 260

Chesterfield, Philip Dormer Stanhope, Earl of, 20; dismissed for wrong vote, 37, 37, 61, 67–68; oppose and admires Carteret, 75, 78, 81, 91; on Pelham, 97; on Byng's chances, 110; mild despair, 116–117; foresees bloodshed, 117; foresees Cumberland's failure, 121, 134, 141–142; on 'Pitt–Newcastle marriage' and the need to keep it together, 144, 151–152; half-believes Pitt's slanders of the King and Newcastle, 154, 167, 201, 213, 262

Child, Sir Josiah, leading figure in the East India Company, 4

Choiseul, Etienne-François Stainville, Duc de, 264, 265

Cholmondeley, Lord, Walpole's son-in-law, inherits Cobham's command, 25

Churchill, Winston, British statesman, 70; mistakenly compared with Pitt, 115

Churchill, Lord Randolph, deranged C19 politician, 332

Chute, John, Catholic friend and correspondent of Horace Walpole, 106

Cicero, Marcus Tullus, orator, 338

Clerk, Colonel Robert, proposer of Rochefort expedition, 144, 149, 151, 260

Clermont, Louis, Comte and Abbé de, French general, 172, 193; lectured by La Pompadour, 194–196, 256

Clevland, John, Secretary to the Admiralty, achievement there, 115, 214, 217, 223, 248, 337

Clive Robert, 255, 279, 303, 312

La Clue, French admiral, waits for Boscawen, 244

Cobbett, William, 146

Cobham, Richard Temple, Lord, soldier and political rebel, 22, 24; stripped of offices by Walpole, 26, 28, 38, 60–61, 67; sticks to his quarrel, 81; anxious that the family should profit, 91

Colville, Admiral, with frigates for Canada, 227

Condé, Prince de, French general, 256

Conflans, Marshal de, French naval commander, 1; endangers his fleet by chasing observation ships before Quiberon Bay, 2, 166; to invade Essex, 214, 244, 247–249

Contades, Louis-Georges, Marquis de, French general, 205; commanding from Versailles, 230

Conway, Henry Seymour, friend of Horace Walpole, soldier and ineffective politician, 144, 150, 177, 192, 304; threatens resignation, 308; years for Pitt 311, 313, 316–318

Corbett, Sir Julian, military historian, 278, 278–80, 281

Cornwallis, Earl, military commander, at Gibraltar Council of War, 106, 150

Cotton, Sir Hynde, leading Tory, enters government, 78

Coxe, Reverend William, Archdeacon of Wiltshire, biographer of Walpole, 65, 66

Cromwell, Oliver, 'No man goes so far . . .' 128; Naseby comparison at Quiberon Bay, 250

Cumberland, William Augustus, Duke of, Captain General 79, 83, 96, 98; favours reprieve for Byng, 123; commands in Hanover theatre, 127; good administrator, 131; Hastenbeck disaster, 131–135; compounded by calamitous convention of Kloster Zeven, 138–139, 141, 144–146, 155, 170–171, 202, 220–221, 228, 241, 297; dies, 304, 338

Cumming, Slave trader and Quaker, lobbies for attack on Senegal and Goree 217–218

Dalton, Sir Cornelius, biographer of Diamond Pitt, 8; 'attempts sympathy for the old brute', 9

Dashwood, Sir Francis, libertine and Chancellor of the Exchequer, 288–289

Daun, Leopold, Graf von, Austrian Field-Marshal, Frederick the Great's most capable opponent, 215

Dayrolles, Solomon, Chesterfield's correspondent, 97, 113, 142

Debré, Michel, French statesman, Premier from 1958, 302

Demosthenes, Greek orator, 338

Denis, Vice Admiral, Sir Peter, assaults five French ships in succession, 2, 148

Devonshire, William Cavendish, 4th Duke of, 106; briefly takes Treasury, 118; quality, 119, 147, 207, 209, 219; Garter crisis, 238–241, 259, 267, 268 292, 295

Dickinson, Emily, major American poet, '. . . on whose forbidden ear . . .', 226

Dickinson, Marshe, City politician, 111

Dinwiddie, Robert, Governor of Virginia, 100

Dodington, George Bubb, diarist, itinerant politician, 40, 45, 63; elected for own pocket borough (Melcombe Regis in 1754), 95; defines Pitt, 96, 99; records Pitt's opinions, 113, 124, 193

Dorrell (Mr), captain of merchant ship in the Hughli River, 4

Dowdeswell, William, MP, 'the Apple Chancellor', takes on the Cider Excise, 291, 302, 304; best speaker in first Rockingham Cabinet, 308; blocked for Exchequer by Pitt, 309; with Rigby and Grenville defeats budget, 313; alone grasps the truth over America, 315, 324; proposes Triennial Bill, 325; seek publication of Civil List, 326; bill to protect Jurors, 327; ill with TB leaves England, 328; dies at Nice, 332

Drake, Sir Francis, Elizabethan privateer and national hero 84, 146

Draper, Colonel William, captures Manila, 278

Dreves, officer serving Ferdinand at Minden, 230

Drury, Major-General at St Malo, 177

Dubois, Cardinal, French First Minister during Regency, 33

Dubois de la Motte, French Admiral, 150, passes up taking dis-masted ship, crew suffer calamitous typhus epidemic, 170

Ducour, French Governor of Louisbourg, 185

Duff, Captain, pursued by French before Quiberon Bay, 2, 250, 257

Duffy, Christopher, biographer of Frederick the Great, after Kolin, 130; on Ferdinand, 235

Dundonald, Lord, killed at Louisbourg, 185–186

Dupleix, Joseph, French governor of Pondichéry, sees no point in an Indian war theatre, 88

Durban, Michael, Oxford scholar, 337

Durham, John Lambton, Earl of, C19 statesman, 331

Earle, Gyles, Chairman of Privileges Committee, 64

Eden, Sir Anthony, C20 British statesman, 70

Edgcumbe, naval captain, brings Boscawen's Louisbourg despatch to Pitt, 186

Edward, Prince, brother of George Prince of Wales, sent on Caen raid as public relations, 190, 297

Edwards, Richard, heads the East India Company factory at Balasore, 4

Effingham, Lord, at Gibraltar council of war, 106

Egmont, John Perceval, Lord, ambitious diarist, 2, 32; play down Krefeld, 200, 304

Egremont, Earl of, George Grenville's brother-in-law, replaces Pitt as Southern Secretary, 274–275; aspires then dies, 278, 294

Eliot, Gilbert, intermediary between Bute and Pitt, 260; slashed at in the North Briton, 285

Elizabeth, Czarina of Russia, 101; enters war, 120, 277

Elliot, Admiral, 148

Elliott, British officer, pushes into St Servant 'with the light dragoons', 179

Emerson, Ralph Waldo, American essayist, famous quotation given at full length, 198

Estrées, Duc D', crossing the Weser, 131, 132–133; wins Hastenbeck, 134, 140

Etherege, Sir George, Restoration playwright, 91

Eugene, Prince of Savoy, Imperial soldier, 36

Evans, Sir Richard, Court jeweller, given Jane Pitt's power of attorney by Diamond Pitt, 11

Eyles, Sir John, white-collar criminal, 27–28

Farnese, Elizabeth, wife of Philip V, Queen of Spain, 34–35, 37; folly of, 69

Ferdinand VI, King of Spain, new reign of sensible king, 87

Ferdinand of Brunswick, to Halle, 140, 144; outstanding commander, 171–173, 193–4; on St Toenis Tower, 195; wins Krefeld, 196; established man, 197, 199; 'near genius for independent command', 200, 203–204; no illusions, 205, 215; response to fall of Minden, 228–229, 230, 234–236, 256; defeats Broglie at Vellinghausen, 276

Fielding, Henry, novelist, playwright, Eton contemporary of Pitt, loathing for Eton, 15, 29; satirises Robert Walpole in Pasquin, 31; rallies the press, 92

Fisher, J.C., French general, snatches Minden Town back, 228

Fleury, Cardinal Guillaume, Chief Minister of France, 38

Forrest, Captain, in Jamaica, 278

Fowke, General, at Gibraltar, misinforms Byng, 'inexcusable', 103, 278

Fowke, Lieutenant RN, senior officer under Holburne at Halifax, 168

Fox, Charles, Whig leader late 18C, 43, 325

Fox, Henry, leading Whig, father of Charles, 64, 77, 82–84, 96–98, 106; warns and attacks Newcastle, 111; bitter encounter with Pitt, 114; afraid of political heights, 114; fears the blame, ambition and nerves, 119; backer of Test, 122–125; Paymaster, 126, 153, 187, 202, 214, 259, 273; leads Commons, 279, 289, 295; made Lord Holland, 298

Francis, Philip (the Elder), hand in Test, 122

Franklin, Benjamin, American polymath, 332–333

Franz of Lorraine, husband of Maria Theresia, 37

Fraser, Charles, of Inverallochie, Jacobite officer allegedly protected by Wolfe, 221

Fraser, E.M.S., Oxford scholar, 133; on Pitt's moves, 146, 153; 'flurry of notes', 203, 337–338

Frederick II (The Great), King of Prussia, inherits and plans to replace Austria, 69–70; deist and homosexual, 70; takes Silesia, 86; seeks British alliance, 101; seeks English supplies, 121, 128; defeat at Kolin, 129; shattered, 130–131, 133; sees flaw in Kloster Zeven, 139; to Magdeburg, 140; wins Rossbach, 141; wins Leuthen, 142–143, 171, 181, 200; dreadful Zornberg, 205, 215; ignored by Ferdinand, 229, 233; Kunersdorf, 235, 242, 256, 277, 280, 295; wooed by Chatham, 310; reflects on price, 311, 339

Frederick Lewis, Prince of Wales, 39, 40–45 passim, 61–63, 67, 80; getting call to war from Pitt, 81; dies 1751, 94, 99–100, 119, 237, 258–259

Frederick William I, King of Prussia, 69

Fuentes, Carlos, Spanish ambassador in London, 254, 274

Gaitskell, Hugh, British statesman, 71

Galissonière, French admiral, engagement with Byng, 106–107

Gardiner, Arthur, Byng's flag-officer on the Ramillies, subject of cover, 107

Gaulle, President Charles de, French soldier and statesman, 202, 302–303

Geary, Admiral Sir Francis, 247

George I, King of England, 24, 32, 39, 229

George II, King of England, 24, 32, 37–39; attacked by Pitt, 41–43, 49, 66–68, 70; opposition anti-George, 74; abroad and '45 sceptical, 79, 83–85; debt to Pelham, 86; loathes Pitt, 95; anger at Byng, 108–109; insulted by Temple, 110–111; smouldering displeasure, 120, 129; thinks Byng a coward, 123, 131; overwhelmed by Hastenbeck, 132–135, 137; devastated by Kloster Zeven, 138; military privileges of appointment, 148, 150; abused by Pitt after Rochefort failure, swears and rages about Rochefort, 156, 162, 165, 165, 171, 172; understands Hawke's feelings 175, 176; snubs Bligh, 191; thanks Ferdinand, 193, 205–206, 229; rage at Sackville, 234–235; Garter crisis, 236–41, 251; sudden death, 257; funeral, 263, 338

George III, King of England, 40; as Prince of Wales, 176, 198–199; distrusts Pitt, 198–199, 205–206, 237, 259–68 passim, 270, 271, 273, 279, 287, 291, 293–294, 296, 299, 302–304, 306–307, 309; seen by Chatham last time as PM, 315–318, 323, 325–329, 332–335, 346

George V, King of England, hates abroad, 129

Gibbon, Edward, historian, captain in Hampshire militia, 217, 319

Gideon, Samson, pre-eminent financier, close to Pelham, 89, 93; advises Newcastle in War finance crisis and delivers subscription, 208–210, 339

Gideon, Sir Sampson, son of above, receives baronetcy

on advice of Newcastle, in recognition of father's
  services, 210
Gilbert, W.S., playwright quoted, 59
Gilsa, Major-General von, reinforced at Luebbecke by
  British troops, 230
Gladstone, William, C19 statesman, 322
Godfrey, Peter, Company colleague of Diamond, 10
Gore, Sir John, MP, follows Gideon's advice, 209
Gosling, Sir Francis, banker advised by Gideon, 210
Gotha, Duke of, 136
Gower, Earl, enters ministry, 78
Grafton, Augustus Henry Fitzroy, Duke of, 280, 307–309,
  311
Granby, John Manners, Marquis, General serving in
  Germany, 206; adored by his men, 234; 'bumbling
  brave and kind', 235, 275, 297–298, 321–322
Grau Mollwitz, Frederick's favourite horse, foils French
  attempt to steal him 235
Gray, Thomas, poet, 19; Wolfe love of the Elegy, 220;
  desolated at Pitt's conduct, 271
Gregory XIII, the Calendar Pope, 89
Grenville, George, brother of Temple, later Prime
  Minister, 26, 81,99; Treasurer of the Navy, 126, 260,
  268, 273, 275, 278, 284, 289–291, 293–296, 298–299;
  letter quoted, 300, 302–303; Stamp Act, 304, 313, 316
Grenville, Henry, a lonely Grenville, made Governor of
  Barbados, 82
Grosvenor, Lord, 280
Grosvenor, Robert, MP, 136
Gustavus Adolfus, King of Sweden, 128

Halifax, Lord, to Ireland, 262
Hamilton, Governor of Jamaica, 52
Hampden, John, radical statesman, 330
Hardwicke, Philip Yorke, Earl of, the Company, 16, 95;
  kills Militia Bill, 98; his marriage act offends Fox, 114;
  retires, 126, 127, 131–132, 144–146, 155–156, 175–176, 187,
  212, 237, 242, 253–254, 256, 260; on Pitt, 274, 291–292,
  332, 337
Hardy, Admiral Sir Charles, blown out to sea, 184–185
Hardy, Thomas, poet, novelist, 'We are the People of
  England', 92
Harley, Robert (Earl of Orford), First Minister to Queen
  Anne, 49–50, 67, 83, 302
Harvey, Colonel, leads Inniskillings under Ferdinand,
  229–230
Harvey, Frederick, naval historian, 247
Hawke, Admiral Sir Edward, leading English admiral,
  talks about beer, 1; pursues French ships, 2, 84, 87,
  106; replaces Byng, 109; burst of success, 147–48;
  against Rochefort raid, 140, 147–49; misses plague
  ships, 150–151; sees futility of raids, 153, 156;
  unnecessary quarrel, 174–175; bombards Le Havre,
  202, 207, 228, 243; Chapter 17 passim
Hay, William, MP for Seaford 90, 127
Healey, Denis, British statesman, 70
Hedges, William, of the East India Company, 3, 5
Henley, Robert, lawyer made Lord Keeper, 126
Henriques, adviser to Legge at Treasury, 208
Henry IV, King of France, 289
Henry, Prince of Prussia, handles retreat, 130
Hervey, Augustus, Admiral Byng's friend, memoirist,
  106
Hervey, John, Lord, courtier and memoirist, 129
Heseltine, Michael, 300
Hesse-Cassel, Landgrave, 136, 137
Hillsborough, Wills Hill, Earl of, 96, 99, 113, 318, 319
Holburne, Francis, admiral to take troops to Canada,

1757, 159; 'contrary winds and bad weather these
  fifteen days past', 162; Pitt, 7 July, instructs to pursue
  French fleet if it turns for home, 162; Pitt, 18 July,
  tells him to stay where he is, 164; Pitt informs him of
  already departed and unreachable relief ships and in
  same despatch of their being reached after all,
  164–165; Holburne sends account of his voyage to
  Holdernesse, 167–168; sends six ships to protect
  Anapolis . . . 'we saw sixteen sail, six of them
  dis-masted', 169, 191
Holdernesse, Robert Darcy, Earl of, Northern Secretary,
  124, 126, 132–133, 135, 142, 144–145, 152, 205, 216–217,
  226, 236, 253, 261, 226
Holmes, Officer under Holburne at Halifax, 168
Holmes, Richard, contemporary historian, describes
  Quebec fight, 226
Holstein-Gottorp, Duke of, German general, admired but
  on loan, 172, 194, 196–197, 223, 233
Hopson, General Thomas, dies off Guadaloupe, 219
Hosier, Francis, admiral in preceding war, 35; dies with
  eight captains and 3,000 men of yellow fever, 72
Howard, Colonel Charles, Walpole supporter in Excise
  crisis, 27
Howe, Captain, later Admiral and Earl, 148; bombards
  Aix fort, 149; problems, 174, 177, 179–180, 249
Howe, Viscount, killed at Ticonderoga, 188, 206
Hume Campbell, Alexander, MP for Berwick, widely
  admired as speaker, modest career, 'talks Billingsgate
  rhetoric' says Chesterfield, 97
Hume, David, philosopher, secretary to Conway, 317

Isabella, Queen, 287

James II, King of England, 257, 286
Jenkins, Robert, merchant captain, his ear, 59
Johnson, Lyndon, US President, 81; handing hat, 339
Johnson, Dr Samuel, praises Christopher Pitt, 3, 122;
  scapegoating of Byng, 123, 134, 213, 271, 305; on
  'Patriotism', 328
Jones, Colin, contemporary English historian of France,
  264
Joseph, son of Maria-Theresia, misses King of the
  Romans, 87, 101; as Emperor, 102
Jourdain, M. (Molière's character), 292
Junius aka (probably Philip Francis the Younger), 262,
  320–321, 327

Kafka, Czech novelist, 334
Karl-Wilhelm-Ferdinand, The Erb-Prinz (of Brunswick),
  141, 172, 194–196; Minden, 230
Kaunitz, Wenzel, Graf, key Austrian Minister, wants
  French alliance, 102
Kearns, John, historian of the Company, 3, 6
Keay, John, historian of East India Company, 312, 315
Keene, Sir Benjamin, Ambassador to Spain, abused by
  merchants as 'Don Benjamin', 53, 328
Kennedy, Robert, US senator, 81
Keppel, Captain Augustus, ordered to slave coast, 218
Kersaint de Coetnampren, French Breton admiral, 1;
  leaves Africa for Canada in 1757, 159; drowning of the
  Thésée's entire crew, 251
Khynhausen, a Prussian ambassador in London, 280
Kidd, Captain William, pirate, 7
Kingsley, William, officer sent to Germany, 206
Kipling, Rudyard, quoted, 16; lacks Pitt's contempt for
  common soldiers, 46
Knowles, Admiral Sir Charles, thinks Louisbourg
  'ruinous', 87; dislikes Rochefort plan, 140, 147–148

Lacour-Gayet, French military historian, 246

Laforey, reconnaissance officer under Holburne, 168

Lancaster, Osbert, C20 cartoonist and artist, 231

Langford, Paul, Oxford historian, 71; on Carteret's rational purpose, 75; on response to Jewish Bill, 92

Lawrence, Charles, Governor of Halifax Nova Scotia, vitally opens despatches for Amherst, 227

Layer, Christopher, unsuccessful plotter, executed, 25, 32

Lee, George, Chairman of Privileges Committee, destroys Walpole, 64–65, 100

Legge, Henry, unwise choice for Chancellor, 125; pushed for First Lord, 126, 136; thought he knew something and was wrong, 207–208; disastrous lottery, 209, 262

Lehndorff, van, Prussian nobleman, 235

Leopold I, Holy Roman Emperor, 34

Leopold of Anhalt Dessau, Frederick's ally, beats Saxons at Kesseldorf, 85

Lestock, Vice Admiral Richard, lets down Admiral Matthews, absolved, 72–73, 107

Leszczynski, Stanislow, French candidate for Polish throne, 37

Levis, General, French commander in Montreal, defeats Murray outside Quebec, lays siege, 227; ships destroyed by English, 228, 253

Ligonier, Sir John (Jean-Louis) British C-in-C, 144–147, 152, 174; chooses Amherst, 182, 213, 215, 219, 220–222

Lincoln, Abraham, American President and statesman, 342

Linwood, Richard, monied man, 207

Lloyd-George, David, British statesman, 345

Locker, Lieutenant William, Hawke's aide, Nelson's guide, 174

Loudon, General, Lord, Commander in North America, 153; supposed underperformance, 158; deploys to Halifax, 159; reports Baufremont's move, 163; told by Pitt of 1000 extra men, 164; blamed, 170

Louis XIV, King of France, 34–36, 115, 264

Louis XV, King of France, his ministers' plans, 1, 6, 37; tied to the family pact, 70, 86; not Louis XIV, 115, 140–141, 250

Lowe, William C, American commentator, 333

Lowther, Catherine, engaged to Wolfe, 220, 223

Lowther, James, future first Earl of Lonsdale, brother of Catherine, 220

Luttrell, Colonel Henry, parliamentary candidate, 319–320

Lyttleton, Christian, sister-in-law to WP, 22

Lyttleton, George, friend of Pitt from Eton, 22, 31; bad verse, 44; forces vote, 61–62, 67, 81; back at Okehampton, reverts to the Pelhams, 90, 95

Lyttleton, Sir Richard, 118

Macartney, Minister to Paris, resigns, 310

Macaulay, Thomas Babbington, Lord, major English historian, 21, 43; on return of the Tories, 49, 336–337

MacBean, English artillery captain at Minden, 231

McDonald, Captain, French speaker, bluffing his way on Heights of Abraham, 226

McKellar, Captain Amherst's officer, 184

MacKellar, Major Patrick, survey of Quebec approaches, 223, 258

Mackenzie, James Stuart, brother to Bute, forced out by Grenville, 298

McLynn, Frank, contemporary historian, on Jacobite strength, 58, 86

Macmillan, Harold, British statesman, 76; events dear boy, 136

Mann, Sir Horace, minister in Florence, 138–139, 151, 192, 206

Mansfield, William Murray, Earl, Lord Chancellor, as letter writer, 20; fears politics, 96; option to lead Commons, 111–112; ablest man not available, 119; legal view rolled over, 139, 152, 268, 295, 327, 338

Mantell, reconnaissance officer under Holburne, 168

Mar, Earl of, '15 Jacobite leader, 286

Maria Theresia, 'Queen of Hungary', 35–37; loses imperial election, 70; loses Silesia, 77, 80, 86, 101; pregnancy, 117; celebrated Kolin, 130; woman wronged and vengeful, 135, 201; throws in her hand, 256

Marlborough, Charles Spencer, 3rd Duke, commands at St Malo, 176; detailed reports, 177–181; passim, comes well out of it, 190, 197–206

Marlborough, John Churchill, 1st duke, 29, 36, 70, 75, 77, 85, 86, 102, 144, 235

Marlborough, Sarah, Duchesss, drawn haunting Pitt, 91

Martin, Samuel, Treasury official, untrustworthy, 207

Matthews, Admiral Thomas, is let down by Vice Admiral Lestock, cashiered, 72–73, 107

Maudit, Israel, controversialist, pamphleteer, 261, 269, 276

Maxwell, Sir John, Grenadiers at Minden, 229

Meredith, Sir William, petitions for slave traders to keep Guadeloupe, 282

Messervy, valued ship builder, dies, 184

Middleton, Richard, historian quoted, 127, 337

Mitchell, Dr Adrian, Minister in Berlin, urges Frederick to try harder, 133–134, 142, 151; city men think German subsidies better last year, 204

Monkton, Brigadier Robert, at Halifax N.S., 183, 224, 227; at Martinique, 227

Monroe, Colonel, Loudon's deputy, 159

Montcalm, Marquis de, outstanding French soldier commanding North America advances, 159; takes Fort William Henry, 159; at Ticonderoga, 187, 211, 224; dies, 226, 264

Montgomery, F.M., C20 British soldier's long life compared with Wolfe's death, 227

Montgomery, Lieutenant, 12th Foot, recorder of Minden, 232

Moran, Lord, Chatham's son-in-law, 335

Mordaunt, Sir John, General to Rochefort, 144, 147; writes off Rochefort, 148–149, 154; not to be shot, 157, 171, 197, 221, 228

Mostyn, Major-General Jack, at St Malo, 177, 222

Mountbatten, Admiral Lord, excused disaster at Dieppe, 108

Munchhausen, Hanoverian Chief Minster meeting D'Estrées, 132

Murphy, Arthur, Irish playwright, hand in Test, 122, 305

Murray, Lord George, Pretender's General, retreats from Derby, 80

Murray, Major, Amherst officer at Louisbourg, 185; defeated by Lévis at Quebec, 227, 253

Namier, Sir Lewis, dominant English historian, 258, 260–261

Newcastle, Thomas Pelham Holles, Duke, His Intelligence Service, 1, 16; deplores George Grenville's rapacity, 6, 26, 35, 39; analytic speech on Spanish trade, 57–59; 'hostilities by sea', 62, 76, 78; raising men and ships 'against', 45, 79–81, 83, 85; too keen on Dutch episode, 86, 88–89; finds Pitt a seat, 90; disgusted at Jemmy's job, 91; supports Archduke Joseph, 101; Fox mutters out, 111; poor fighter/poor hater, 112, 114; facing hysteria, 115; standing down, 116; out, 119; his policies continued, 121, 124; returns, takes the Treasury, 126–127; Pitt govt think seriously, 131–132; odd to cavil at a troop of horse, 131–132; wanting 9000 men for Germany, 133–136; in Sussex, and Pitt being sensible, 137; spots flaw in Kloster Zeven convention, 139–140; heads off Hanoverian neutrality, 139–140, 142, 144, 155; smells motives, 155; (ironically) 'All equally guilty, all should be punished', 156; never believed in coastal raids, 201–202; 'the Claremont peaches are not yet ripe enough', 203, 205; '. . . consider the whole Globe', 205; seeks help of Samson Gideon to meet huge costs of the war, 208–209; 'The heart (Channel) must be secured in the first place', 214, 219; keeping ministry together, 237–241, 253–255, 262–264, 268, 272, 275–277; praised in *North Briton*, 285, 288, 292–293, 295, 302, 321, 323, 337

Nicolai, General, commands French right at Minden, 231, 233

Noailles, Duc de, better class of French general, 70

Norris, Alderman, wants troops in Flanders, 73–74, 84

North, Frederick, Lord, described, 315, 318, 325, 327–331, 334–335

Northumberland, Hugh Smithson, Earl of, becomes Duke, 309

O'Gorman, Frank, contemporary English historian, 258

O'Hara, Lieutenant, reports on Minorca, 105–106

Oberg, Lieutenant General, seizes crossings, 195–197

Ogle, Admiral Sir Challoner, quarrels v. General Wentworth, 72

Onslow, Arthur (later Earl), Speaker of Commons, 64; finally retires, 273

Onslow, George, son of Arthur, 280, 293

Orleans, Philippe, Duc de, French Chief Minister/Regent, 33

Ormande, James Butler, Duke, Jacobite soldier, Robert Pitt admires, 10

Oswald, James, MP, 63, 124, 285

Owen, Dr David, contemporary politician and psychiatrist, 337, 341–344

Pares, Richard, historian of C18 trade wars, 50–51; 'inferior negroes', 52; describes English plunder in Central America, 265, 275

Patten, Captain, reports from Cadiz 'eight large ships', 162

Paxton, Nicholas, Walpole's Treasury Solicitor, refuses to give evidence, 67, 69

Peel, Sir Robert, C19 Prime Minister, 128, 304

Pelham, Lady Catherine, widow of Henry Pelham, 109

Pelham, Henry, Prime Minister, 45; riposte to Pitt, 47, 60, 66; Robert Walpole's horse for later succession, 68; moves into leadership, 76–77; alert to '45, wants minimum retribution, resigns, bounces back, 80–81, 83; wants peace in 1746, 86, high-quality statesman-ship, 87–88; tolerance and decency, 92; dies (1754), 94, 109, 127, 208–209, 259, 266, 302, 338

Peter III, Russian Czar, on accession brings Russia into alliance with Frederick, 277

Peterborough, Earl of, general in Spain in early 1700s, 174

Peters, Marie, historian, biographer of Pitt, 93

Philip V, intermittently mad, King of Spain, 34–35, 51, 53–54, 60–61; withholds payment, 62

Philipps, John, Welsh Tory, enters Ministry, 78

Phillips, English artillery captain, important role at Minden 231

Pitt, Ann, sister of WP, vivacious letters to WP, 20

Pitt, Christopher, poet, clergyman, 3–4

Pitt, Harriot, daughter, 299

Pitt, Hester, née Grenville, wife, character, 93; especially needed in 1751–54 during his first illness (1751–54), 94; indispensable after mental collapse – taking power of attorney, 316–17 320

Pitt, Hester, daughter, 299

Pitt, James, son, 299

Pitt, Jane (Innes), wife of Diamond Pitt, berated by him,

10; denounced, 12; goes to Bath, 11; letter from WP, 19

Pitt, John, 'The good-for-nothing Colonel', 9–10; seat in Parliament, cut out of will, 12

Pitt, John, 2nd Earl of Chatham, 299, 310

Pitt, Lucy, daughter of Diamond Pitt, marries General Stanhope, 9

Pitt, Robert, son of Diamond Pitt, father of William, smuggles diamond in his shoe, 6, 9–14

Pitt, Thomas, grandfather of William, detested by the East India Company, 3–5; identified with the great diamond as 'Diamond Pitt', 6; withstands siege of Madras, 7–8; buys several properties, 9; quarrels with the family, 10–12 *passim*, 13, 16, 21, 50

Pitt, Thomas (the younger), son of Diamond, helps in smuggling the jewel, 8–9; more or less sane, 12–13, 21; allegations against him, 44

Pitt, William, the Elder, later Earl of Chatham, 8, 10, 13; at Eton, 14–16; at Oxford, 16–18; humble letter to father (Robert Pitt) 16–17; at university in Utrecht, 18; Cornetcy of horse – paid for by Walpole's Secret Service?, 18; Northampton barracks then continental tour, 18–20, 21, 22, 23, 24, 25, 29, 30, 31; as new member, 32, 33, 37, 38, 40; speech on Frederick Lewis's allowance, 41, 42, 43; sharp new talent in opposition, 44, 45; denounces 'standing army', 46, 51; threatens Spain in tirade, 54–5, 60; stays silent, 61; squeaks onto Committee of Accusation, 66; calls for Walpole to be sent to the Tower, 67; talks up war, 70, 73; violently insults Carteret 1742, proud of Carteret's friendship, 1770, 74; considered for office post-Walpole, but talks too much, 78; spoiling speeches, 79; Paymaster to the Forces, 82; £4,000 a year, 84, 88; his credit slips with Opposition, 89; under fire, 91; seriously ill, 94; has claim on promotion, 1754, 95–96; serenades the Americans, 97; Militia Bill, 98; pursues Bute, 100, 103; 'apt man in debate', 112; rages at Hanoverian subsidies to Dodington, 113; they are his aversion, 114; portentous assaults, 115; 'Oh my dying country', 116; refuses to work with Newcastle and Hardwicke, 118; portrayed as Perseus, 119, 120; eats his words over Prussia, resigns after Temple is dismissed by King, 123; after the *Interministerium* is made Southern Secretary, 126, 127; sees America as open space, 128, 131, 132; needing new doctrine, 133; his negative is 'decent and friendly' says Newcastle, but large sum of money agreed for Prussia, 135; total reversal of policy – friendly, 136; money to Landgrave, talk of 'southern options', 136, 142; attracted to coastal raids, 143, 144; soothes allies, 145, 150, 152; hysteria after Rochefort, 153–5; 'Outrageous' says Newcastle, 156; Canada chief priority, 158; tells Admiral Holburne about Dubois's squadron sailing from Europe, tells Loudon of reinforcements, 164; tells Holburne of ships designated to him, missed, then caught up with, 164; Invites Holburne to chase returning French fleet, 163; reverses this order, 165, 166, 167; 'May a degenerate people profit in the school of misfortune', 168; Loudon's 'Treachery', 170, 174, 182–183, 188; rising assurance, 189; abject letters to Bute, 190–91; great shift in policy, 193; another naval raid, 194; recognises Ferdinand as a winner, 197–198; bucking up Amherst, 199–200; glaring inconsistencies, 201; unreserved champion of settler interests, 202; 'knows the steps of the dance', 203–204; knows nothing about finance, 207, 208; begins to follow Newcastle in concern at risk of French invasion, 215–16; pushes for a militia, 217; urgent for a

Slave Coast operation, 218, 222; after Quebec Victory, gives thanks to God, 228; Garter crisis, 237–41; having got his way, stops splitting the Cabinet 253, 255; Hardwicke's dry comment, 256; furious to make war on Spain, 265; Treasure and riches . . . at our mercy', 267; defeated in Cabinet – resigns, 268; should have stayed, 269; possibly tired – boasts wildly, 270; accepts pension – loses credit, 271–272, 274–275; knows the value of the German war theatre, 276–277, 282, 287; 'Gentle Shepherd' episode, 289; accused of trying to please Bute, 294, 295, 296; has ministry talks with Cumberland, 297; undoubtedly loves his wife, 299; as man of property, 300; always reliably broke, 301, 308; ennobled as Earl of Chatham, 309–10; violently abuses Frederick for declining an alliance, 311; East India issues, 312; mocked by George Grenville in Parliament, 313–14; mental illness apparent, 315–16; power of attorney made over to Hester, 317, 318–319, 321–325; blames Grafton abusively in the Lords, 326, 327; abuses business 'the bloodsucker, the muckworm . . .', 328, 329; calmer – more constructive now, 330; rages at Catholic emancipation in Catholic French Canada, 331; brings Benjamin Franklin to the Lords, 333; physical deterioration, 334; collapses in the Lords, taken to Hayes, dies, 335, 336, 337, 338, 340, 344

Pitt, William, the Younger, 'Little Mr Secretary', 298–299 310; asked by dying father to read the death of Hector from the *Iliad*, 335

Pocock, Rear-Admiral George at Havanna, 278

Pompadour, Jeanne Poisson, dit Madame de, mistress of Louis XV with large political authority, instructs General Clermont, 194

Pope, Alexander, poet, friend of Cobham, *Epistle to Cobham*, 25

Postgate, Raymond, Wilkes's biographer, 293–294

Potter, Thomas, friend of Wilkes, disappointed Patriot, attacks Pitt, 90; on mob, 109; active for Pitt, 119, 153, 262, 283, 339

Pownall, Thomas, Governor of New York, General Loudon's envoy to London, reports August 1757, 166; on 'the peculiar temper of the people' and the blowing up of Fort William Henry, 166–167

Poyanne, French Lieutenant General, commands Carabiniers at Minden, 232

Pratt, Charles, lawyer, later Earl Camden Lord Chancellor, friend of Pitt from Eton, 16, 284, 292; General Warrants, 296; ennobled, 310, 318, 321–322, 326

Pulteney, William, leader of Country Whig opposition to Robert Walpole, 33, 44; Tories ally with, 49, 63–64; enters government, 64; ministerial lassitude, 76

Pym, John, C17 radical statesman, 330

Pynsent, Lady, 304

Reynolds, Captain David, on coastal watch, 248–249

Richelieu, Duc de, at Calais, 86; mediocre soldier, 140; offers to withdraw troops across the Weser, 141, 172, 156

Richmond, Charles Lennox, Duke of, 220, 317, 323, 327

Rigby, Richard, Bedford's lieutenant reports Minorca failure, 105–6; Temple's 'insolence', 122–123, 313, 320

Ripperda, Jan Willem, freelance Dutch diplomat, 34

Rockingham, Charles Wentworth Woodhouse, Marquis of, Prime Minister, 294–295, 301–302; forms ministry, 304; as PM, 305–307; worst speaker in Cabinet, 310, 322, 324, 326, 333

Rodgers, Nicholas, leading naval historian, makes limited case for raid, 153

Rodney, Vice-Admiral, 148, 276, 278

Rolt, Edward Bayntun, fatal petitioner at Chippenham, 65

Rondet, French court jeweller, bribed by the Pitts, 8

Rosebery, Archibald Philip Primrose, Earl of, Prime Minister and biographer of Pitt, rhapsodises on Pitt, 14, 16, 20; deplores Grenville influence, 22, 38–39, 259, 299

Rushout, Sir John, Country Whig MP, 33

Russell, Lord John, future Prime Minister, 21

von Ruville, Wilhelm, (German) biographer of Pitt, 311

De Ruyter, Admiral Michael, C17, destroyed British base in Goree, 218

Sacheverell, Dr Henry, Anglican fanatic, 23, 32

Sackville, General Lord George, unpopular, 97; 'several reputations, all bad,' 17–177, 180, 199; to Germany 206, 229–230; his disgrace, 233–235, 272

Saint-André du Verger, French admiral, heroic death, 251

Saint-Germain, Comte de, French general, 173, 193, 215

Saint-James, Duc de, fatal charge at Minden, 232

Sandwich, John Montague, Earl of, enters government, 78; overplays hand with Dutch but negotiates well, 86; valuable work at Admiralty, 115, 214, 217

Sandys, Samuel, Country Whig, later Chancellor, 33

Saunders, Admiral Sir Charles, 264, 310, 332

Savile, Sir George, 323–325

Savory, Sir Reginald, historian of British army in Germany at this time, 232; on Sackville, 234

Saxe, Maurice de, Marshal, outstanding French soldier of 1740s war, 78; his victories, 87, 140

Scarborough, Earl of, 38

Schaumberg-Lippe, General Graf von 173, 276

Scheele, Hanoverian general, at Minden, 233

Schlieffen, officer of Ferdinand at Minden, 230

Schweizer, K.W., British historian, with P.D. Brown, finds Duke of Devonshire's Memorandum, 239

Sedgwick, Romney, historian of parliament, 63

Seilern, Christian August, Graf von, Austrian minister in London, 310

Shebbeare, Dr John, Tory pamphleteer, blazes at treatment of Byng, 123

Shelburne, William, Earl of, later Prime Minister, 30, 59, 83, 280, 289, 302 312, 318, 326, 333, 335, 358

Sherlock, Thomas, Bishop of Salisbury, suggests opportune election, after victory promoted Bishop of London, 89

Sherrard, O.A., Pitt biographer (1952–58), 'Pitt's heavy heart', 92; 'like another Achilles, stalked to his tent', 241

Shippen, William (Will), humorous Jacobite Tory MP, 33, 36

Shirley, William, Governor of Massachusetts, role in Canadian conflict, 87

Smith, Captain John, junior officer proclaiming 'His Majesty's domains in France', 199

Smollett, Tobias, novelist, editor of the Briton, 284

Soubise, Charles de Rohan, Prince de, and general, 140–141, 195, 205

Speke, Henry, naval captain (of *Resolution*)

Spoeken, Freiherr von, general commanding British troops, 229, 231, 233

Stair, Earl of, 38

Stanhope, James, Earl, general in Spain then First Minister, 33

Stanhope, Philip, Chesterfield's natural son and correspondent, 154

Stanley, Hans, English diplomat/politician, 264 310, 332

Suffolk, Earl of, 280, 301

Sully, Duc de, C16 French statesman, 289

Sutherland, Dame Lucy, Oxford historian, on 'Con-Test', 122; 'most expensive war', 208

Sutton, Sir Robert, MP, dishonest diplomat/politician, 27

Talbot, Lord, calls Wilkes out, 286

Talleyrand, Charles Maurice de, great French statesman, quoted, 296

Tattersfield, Nigel, historian of the slave trade, 219

Temple, Richard Grenville, Earl Temple, lifetime ally of WP, 16,22, 26, 30, 67; complex character, 91, 92; brave stand over Byng, 122; dismissed, 123–124, 202; Garter Crisis, 268–270, 272, 274, 280

Thierry, French pilot – Protestant refugee – adviser on Rochefort, knowing the coast inadvertently taken away by Howe on Aix Fort mission, 145, 148–149, 155

Thomas, Edmund, one of the Chippenham petitioners of 1742 undermining Walpole's majority, 65

Thurot, François, French privateer, to menace Irish coast, 227–228

Titley, diplomat working with Joseph Yorke, 143

Torrington, Viscount, father of John Byng, 108

Touchett, merchant, attempts to warn Pitt about dangers of Senegal climate – ignored, 218

Townshend, Charles 1674–1738, Viscount Townshend, Robert Walpole's ally before split, 34, 36

Townshend, Charles 1725–1767 (grandson of the above), 97, 152, 295, 304; 'boundless vanity', 311, 312; Champagne speech 314, 315–317, 318, 319; dies, 323

Townshend, George, soldier summed up by Horace Walpole, replaces Wolfe's choice, the expert, Ralph Burton – railed at by Wolfe, 222, 224, 225, 227; designed for Portugal, 276

Turner family, Walpole allies in Norfolk, 30

Vanbrugh, Sir John, restoration playwright, 91

Vanneck, Sir Joshua, 'monied man', 207; with Gore, he meets Gideon's advice, 209

Vaudreuil, Pierre de Rigaut, Marquis de, commands at Montreal, 253–254

Vernon, Admiral Sir Edward, survives, 72; rhetoric of, 73, 84

Vincent, Sir Matthias, East India Company Chief in Bengal, 4–5, 21

Viry, Count, Sardinian Minister in London, 137; 'postman to Quality Street', 237, 262–263

Voltaire, F-M. Arouet de, relates Byng's death in Candide, 110–111, 128, 145

Wager, Sir Charles, Admiral, admits fear of the sea, 39

Waldegrave, Earl, infantry commander, at Paramé, 179, 231, 235

Waldegrave, Lord, Ambassador at Paris, 61; defines Fox, 114

Wall, Ricardo, Spanish Premier, 256–257; doesn't trust Pitt, 265–266, 274

Walmoden, Marianne von, Lady Yarmouth, 20, 139; Pitt calls, 118

Walpole, Sir Edward, Robert Walpole's ancestor had held Order of Bath, 32

Walpole, Horace, diarist, political commentator, as letter writer, 19–20; Cobhamites 'selling' themselves for profit, 82; relates Minorca news to Mann, 106–109; sums up G. Townshend, 119; notes Pitt's Prussian turnabout, 121; Cumberland talk, 138–139, 144, 151, 155; satirises St Malo raid, 177; mocks coastal raids, 192, 206; derides Militia, 217, 272, 280; on Chatham's condition, 304; compares Pitt with Burke, 305–306, 310, 312–315, 319, 321, 325–326, 339

Walpole, Horatio, younger brother of Robert Walpole, 35, 65

Walpole, Sir Robert, former Prime Minister, 18–19, 22–24, 27–33, 35–47, 49–51; measured reply to Pitt's pro-war oration, 56–60; dismissal demanded, 62; fall, 63–64; becomes Earl of Orford, 67, 69; war proves his point, 73, 75; suggests Pitt, 77; top-dog views, 78, 80, 98, 119, 125, 127; Pardo, 138, 260, 263, 271 290, 302, 336

Walpole, Thomas, purchaser of Hayes, 316; sells Hayes back, 321

Wangenheim, Georg August, Hanoverian general, 231, 233

Warren, Commander, share in Louisbourg capture, 87

Washington, Colonel George, defeated at Forks of the Ohio, 100; then successful retreat, 103, 263

Wayne, 'Mad Anthony', lethal US general, 182

Webb, Philip Carteret, Treasury Solicitor, 288, 291

Wentworth, General, quarrel with Admiral Ogle, 72

West, Gilbert, connection of the Grenvilles, 31

West, Admiral Temple, 107, 159

Westphalen, Christian von, guides Ferdinand before Minden, 228

Whiteford, James, officer to Germany, 206

Wiggins, Lewis, American scholar, chronicler of the Grenvilles, 22, 28, 237, 299

Wilkes, John, disturber of the peace, 26, 90; 'poor Byng', 109, 262, 269, 272; Demon King, 282; First Denry Machin, 283; chapter 20 (283–298) passim, the North Briton, returns, 319–320, 324, 339

William, King (William III), Thomas Pitt supports, 5, 264

Williams, Basil, historian, 33

Williamson, Captain Amherst's officer, 184

Wilmington, Sir Spencer Compton, nominal successor to Robert Walpole, 65; dies, 76–77

Winchelsea, Lord, prospect of the Admiralty, 124

Wittgenstein, Ludwig, Austrian philosopher, 341

Wolfe, James, first American engagement, 151; at Louisbourg, 183–186, 187; improved bayonet drill, 211–212; Quebec plans and fight, 220–226; last message, 227–228, 238, 242–243, 245, 253–254

Wolfenbuttel, Duke, 136

Wood, William, industrialist, metal-founder, 29

Woodfall, Henry, Junius's printer, prosecuted, 327

Worge, Colonel Richard, marine commander takes Goree, 219

Wyndham, Sir William, Tory leader in Commons, 32; walks out, 60; dies, 61–62

Yonge, Sir William, Walpole lieutenant, 64

Yorke, Charles, son of Hardwicke, 292; appointment and death, 321

Yorke, Colonel Joseph, at Berlin Court, 143; damns Abercromby, 187, 238–239, 332

Zastrov, Hanoverian soldier, Cumberland's deputy, 172